Experiencing Social Research

A Reader

Kerry J. Strand
Hood College

Gregory L. Weiss
Roanoke College

PEARSON

A and *B*

Boston • New York • San Francisco
Mexico City • Montreal • Toronto • London • Madrid • Munich • Paris
Hong Kong • Singapore • Tokyo • Cape Town • Sydney

Senior Series Editor: Jeff Lasser
Editorial Assistant: Heather McNally
Senior Marketing Manager: Kelly May
Composition and Prepress Buyer: Linda Cox
Manufacturing Buyer: JoAnne Sweeney
Cover Administrator: Joel Gendron
Editorial–Production Service: Omegatype Typography, Inc.
Electronic Composition: Omegatype Typography, Inc.

For related titles and support materials, visit our online catalog at www.ablongman.com.

Between the time Website information is gathered and then published, it is not unusual for some sites to have closed. Also, the transcription of URLs can result in unintended typographical errors. The publisher would appreciate notification where these errors occur so that they may be corrected in subsequent editions.

Library of Congress Cataloging-in-Publication Data

Experiencing social research : a reader / [editors] Kerry J. Strand, Gregory L. Weiss.
    p. cm.
  Includes bibliographical references.
  ISBN 0-205-40448-0
    1. Social sciences—Research—Methodology. I. Strand, Kerry. II. Weiss, Gregory L.

H61.E96 2005
300'.72—dc22

2004058711

Printed in the United States of America

10 9 8 7 6 5 4 3   09 08 07 06 05

Contents

Preface   vii

About the Authors   xi

Overview of Social Research

chapter **1**   **Experiencing Social Research: Choices, Challenges, Constraints, and Compromises**   **1**

Getting Started: Choosing a Topic   2

Choosing a Research Design: Method, Measures, Samples   3

Ethical Issues and Considerations   7

Collecting, Organizing, and Analyzing the Data   8

The Rewards of Social Research   10

chapter **2**   **Why Do Social Research?**   **13**

The Relative Influence of Youth and Adult Experiences on Personal Spirituality and Church Involvement   _15_
Thomas P. O'Connor, Dean R. Hoge, and Estrelda Alexander

An interview with . . . Thomas P. O'Connor   27

Young Dads: The Effects of a Parenting Program on Urban African-American Adolescent Fathers   _33_
Carl Mazza

An interview with . . . Carl Mazza   42

chapter **3**   **Research Design, Sampling, and Measurement**   **47**

Cigarette Smoking and the Disenfranchisement of Adolescent Girls: A Discourse of Resistance?   _51_
Marjorie MacDonald and Nancy E. Wright

An interview with . . . Marjorie MacDonald   69

Rebellion, Modernity, and Romance: Smoking as a Gendered Practice in Popular Young Women's Magazines, Britain 1918–1939   73
Penny Tinkler

    An interview with . . . Penny Tinkler   86

Quantitative and Qualitative Approaches

chapter **4** **Experimental Research**   **93**

The Impact of Social Structure on Mate Selection: An Empirical Evaluation of an Active-Learning Exercise   *95*
John F. Zipp

    An interview with . . . John F. Zipp   106

The Effect of Enforcement on Merchant Compliance with the Minimum Legal Drinking Age Law   *111*
Richard Scribner and Deborah Cohen

    An interview with . . . Richard Scribner   118

chapter **5** **Survey Research**   **123**

Spankers and Nonspankers: Where They Get Information on Spanking   *127*
Wendy Walsh

    An interview with . . . Wendy Walsh   141

Predictors of Fear of Criminal Victimization at School among Adolescents   *145*
David C. May and R. Gregory Dunaway

    An interview with . . . David C. May   157

chapter **6** **Nonreactive Research: Content Analysis, Accretion Measures, and Using Existing Statistics**   **161**

Race, Gender, and Status: A Content Analysis of Print Advertisements in Four Popular Magazines   *165*
Melvin E. Thomas and Linda A. Treiber

    An interview with . . . Linda A. Treiber   175

*Graffiti on the Great Plains: A Social Reaction
to the Red River Valley Flood of 1997* 181
Carol A. Hagen, Morten G. Ender, Kathleen A. Tiemann, and Clifford O. Hagen, Jr.

_____ *An interview with . . . Carol A. Hagen* 191

*Capital Punishment and Deterrence: Examining
the Effect of Executions on Murder in Texas* 197
Jon Sorensen, Robert Wrinkle, Victoria Brewer, and James Marquart

_____ *An interview with . . . Jon Sorensen* 207

chapter **7** **Field Research** **213**

*Neither <u>Real</u> Americans nor <u>Real</u> Asians? Multigeneration
Asian Ethnics Navigating the Terrain of Authenticity* 215
Mia Tuan

_____ *An interview with . . . Mia Tuan* 232

*Exceptions to the Rule: Upwardly Mobile White
and Mexican American High School Girls* 237
Julie Bettie

_____ *An interview with . . . Julie Bettie* 251

*The Glass Phallus: Pub(lic) Masculinity
and Drinking in Rural New Zealand* 259
Hugh Campbell

_____ *An interview with . . . Hugh Campbell* 272

chapter **8** **Historical and Comparative Research** **279**

*"Button-Down Terror": The Metamorphosis
of the Hate Movement* 281
Barbara Perry

_____ *An interview with . . . Barbara Perry* 297

*Ties That Bind: Correlates of Adolescents'
Civic Commitments in Seven Countries* 303
Constance A. Flanagan, Jennifer M. Bowes, Britta Jonsson, Beno Csapo, and Elena Sheblanova

_____ *An interview with . . . Constance A. Flanagan* 318

Preface

In the late 1970s, M. Patricia Golden compiled an anthology of research articles aimed at undergraduate students studying social research methods. The book had wide appeal to professors and students alike, not only because it provided diverse examples of solid sociological research, but also because of its distinctive approach. Social research was *not* presented as an orderly, abstract, and predictable process bound by rigid rules and standardized procedures, but rather as a fundamentally human activity, with all the messiness and unpredictability, joys and frustrations, and uncertainties and challenges that such activity entails.

Golden's book, *The Research Experience*[1], revealed the human dimensions of sociological research by means of short personal essays written by each researcher in which they told about the experiences of doing the research. Some wrote about how their choice of topic was inspired by a piece of personal history, an unexpected opportunity, or some profound social changes taking place in the 1960s and early 1970s—urban race riots, campus antiwar activity, the emergence of the hippie subculture, and changing roles of women. They wrote about the difficulties, and difficult decisions, they faced at different stages of their research. They reflected on what went well and what they wished they had done differently, what was most aggravating and what was especially gratifying, what they learned and what they thought their research contributed. All those things are part and parcel of the whole business of doing social research, but are seldom discussed in the pristine accounts in textbooks and academic journals.

We have compiled this anthology very much in the spirit of Golden's earlier work, and with a similar approach. Our most basic goal is to help students learn about social research by giving them easy access to engaging, full-length research reports that clearly illustrate the range of concepts, approaches, and techniques that they read about in their textbooks. We have taken care to include examples of works that assume the range of different methodological approaches—qualitative as well as quantitative, applied and theory-driven, critical, interpretive, and positivistic—illustrating nearly every mode of data collection and analysis from historical analysis to participant observation to analysis of large databases using multivariate statistical models. We have also made a special effort to choose articles that students will *like*—that is, articles on topics that are relevant to their own lives and experiences, that deal with issues that they are likely to consider important, and that are otherwise accessible and appealing. The articles we have chosen come from a range of quality academic journals in sociology as well as journals whose contributors are not all sociologists, but who use the methods of social science research. Because some of the best current social science research relies on elaborate statistical models and other analytical strategies that are beyond the scope and comprehension of the average undergraduate student, we provide Method of Analysis sections with clear explanations of these more advanced analytical strategies.

We think a social research methods course should do more than just train students in the approaches and techniques of social research. It should also enable them to look critically at the research they read and to understand and appreciate the contribution of social research to the development of knowledge about the social world. To these ends, we cast a wide net across the discipline and include articles from many different *subfields* of sociology and related disciplines—criminology, family studies, gender, disaster research, mass media, health care, religion, rural sociology, race and ethnicity, social movements, comparative studies, evaluation research, historical analysis, and the scholarship of teaching and learning. We also recognize and include the diverse purposes served by social research—not only to advance knowledge in sociology, but also to evaluate programs or policies, uncover forms and mechanisms of social injustice, assess community needs, and identify fruitful directions for social change. Students will read about research that draws on concepts and theories from different courses and topics in which they have some background and that, by example, demonstrate the relevance of social research to their own intellectual interests and career plans.

Finally, we follow Golden's lead and make every effort to show students that social research is a thoroughly human enterprise. As such, it is seldom as orderly and abstract as it seems, but instead is influenced by a variety of constraints: personal preferences and circumstances, limited resources, unexpected glitches, and serendipitous findings. Experienced researchers know that the seemingly rigid research rules and protocols in textbooks that tell us just what to do and how to do it are really better seen as *guidelines* for making decisions throughout the research process. To help students understand how these decisions are made—that is, how researchers *really* carry out their work—we follow each research article with a short interview in which we ask each researcher about different aspects of her or his research experience. Some questions we asked of every person we interviewed, such as: What led you to choose this topic? What are the advantages and disadvantages of this particular approach? What does your research contribute? What, if anything, would you do differently if you were to take on this project again? We also asked specific questions tailored to individual projects, for example, how a researcher gained access to a particular field site, earned the trust of young respondents, located obscure primary sources, learned to take field notes, worked collaboratively, organized reams of data, came to terms with unexpected results, assured respondents' anonymity, and struggled with the challenges and miseries of writing. Their responses are thoughtful, engaging, and illuminating.

One more commitment underlies this book. We believe that introducing students to the experiential aspects of social research does more than help them learn about social research. We think it also helps students to begin to think of themselves as social researchers. If education is to be empowering, as we think it should be, then we share an obligation to help students become not only informed and critical *consumers* of social science research, but also *discoverers* and *producers* of knowledge about the social world. Doing research is largely about making informed choices that are nonetheless continually subject to constraints and limitations that are both within and outside of the control of the researcher. Seeing science as an imperfect human construction and research as a worthwhile but nonetheless flawed human activity is not only good sociology, it is also the basis for coming to see oneself as having agency in the realm of sociological work and the world at large.

This book is intended as a supplement to textbooks in social research methods. As such, we avoid lengthy explanations of research strategies, techniques, approaches, and methods, but instead point out where and how the research articles and interviews *illustrate* and *illuminate* material from the students' textbooks. Following a brief introduction in Chapter 1, Chapter 2 features two articles whose authors were motivated by strikingly different purposes—one a decidedly applied project aimed at evaluating a program for teenage fathers, the other a test of different theoretical approaches to explaining adult religious involvement. Chapter 3 highlights the critical choices researchers must make about the design of their research. Here we include two articles that illustrate dramatically different approaches to the same basic research question—one a historical, qualitative content analysis of popular magazines, the other a large-scale analysis of secondary survey data, both of which ask what influences young women to smoke cigarettes. Taken together, these articles introduce the range of rich possibilities from which researchers choose as they go about making decisions about the topic and purpose of the research, research design, sampling, data collection, measurement, and ethical issues. Here, as throughout the book, interviews with the researchers bring them and their work to life as they shed light on how and why the researchers made the decisions they did. The remainder of the book is organized around the major methodological approaches in sociological research. Chapters 4, 5, and 6 look at mainly quantitative approaches (experimental, survey, and nonreactive research). Chapters 7 and 8 focus on approaches that are largely (but not exclusively) qualitative: field research in Chapter 7 and historical and comparative research in Chapter 8. In every case our approach is the same: to provide engaging examples of social research accompanied by introductory and interview material that connects the research examples to course material and explores the experiential aspects of doing social research.

Acknowledgments

This project is informed and inspired to a great extent by our many years of teaching social research methods to undergraduate students, both in and outside of the classroom. We are grateful to them for keeping us on our toes and always on the lookout for ways to help them discover what an exciting venture social research can be. Thanks to Marit Berntson of Roanoke College for her very helpful suggestions regarding the statistical inserts. Thanks also to the helpful folks at Allyn & Bacon: Sara Owen, Andrea Christie, Krista Groshong, Heather McNally, and especially Jeff Lasser, whose unwavering enthusiasm for our project has been so appreciated. Last, to the ones who give us inspiration in our private lives, we give love and thanks: to Janet and Lacy from Greg, and to Kirkley and Nathan from their favorite mom.

NOTE

1. M. Patricia Golden (editor), *The Research Experience.* Itasca, IL: F. E. Peacock, 1976.

About the Authors

Kerry J. Strand is the Andrew G. Truxal Professor of Sociology at Hood College in Frederick, Maryland, where she has taught basic and advanced research methods and supervised students' independent research projects for over 20 years. Her own areas of research have included the medicalization of pregnancy and birth, gendered labor markets, women's education, and, most recently, the effects of reform-based mathematics teaching on college women's math-related attitudes and persistence. She has also published papers and presented workshops on service learning, community-based research, and other topics related to undergraduate teaching and learning. She is the lead author of *Community-Based Research and Higher Education: Principles and Practices* (Jossey-Bass, 2003).

Gregory L. Weiss is Professor of Sociology at Roanoke College in Salem, Virginia, where he has taught research methods and supervised students' independent research projects for over 25 years. He founded and served as Director of the College's Center for Community Research for eight years. His own areas of research have included end-of-life decision making, the process of writing do-not-resuscitate orders, the availablilty of palliative care for general medical hospitalized patients, and the influence of gender on health-related behaviors. He has also published papers and presented workshops on assessment of sociology programs, external reviews of sociology departments, community research centers, and other topics related to undergraduate teaching and learning. He is the lead author of *The Sociology of Health, Healing, and Illness,* Fourth Edition (Prentice Hall, 2003).

chapter 1

Experiencing Social Research
Choices, Challenges, Constraints, and Compromises

People do social science research for many different reasons: to meet the requirements of a graduate degree, to determine the effectiveness of a social program, to contribute to sociological understanding about some social phenomenon, to inform public or corporate policies or practices, to test an existing theory, to increase one's chances of earning tenure at a college or university, and sometimes just to satisfy one's curiosity about something. No matter what the pragmatic circumstances or intellectual interests that motivate researchers, they use social science research to help them achieve the same basic goal: to answer questions about the social world. And they all agree that the methods of sociological research provide the best and most effective ways to find those answers.

Social science researchers share something else: formal research training that gives them familiarity with the rules, procedures, and protocols that govern the research process and that allows them to have confidence in the knowledge that research produces. What is not always clear to beginning students of research methods is that these rules, procedures, and protocols do not tell us *how* to do research. Rather, they serve as *guidelines* for the choices that researchers must make at each stage of a research project—choices that come down to questions of what to study, how to study it, and how to analyze, interpret, and present results. These choices themselves are influenced and constrained by all kinds of factors, many of which are out of the researcher's control. Some have to do with the researcher's own training, experiences, interests, preferences, goals, and personal circumstances. Others include things such as resources (time, money, facilities, equipment, transportation, and so on); special interests of sponsors, colleagues, or faculty mentors; access to sites or people; as well as some amount of chance—unexpected events that force researchers to change course and make new decisions throughout the life of the project. Put another way, research seldom proceeds according to the rather abstract, linear, and predictable steps outlined in textbooks. What might seem like immutable rules are in fact more like guidelines that help us make the choices that must be made at each stage of the research.

In the pages that follow, you will experience social research from two different angles: published journal articles describing and reporting the results of research projects and interviews with the authors of those articles about the actual experience of doing research. There is much to be learned from both. In this chapter we want to introduce you to what it is like to carry out a social research project and to some of the ways that various factors shape and influence decisions that researchers make throughout the research process, from choosing a topic of study to writing the report and submitting it for publication.

Getting Started: Choosing a Topic

The first decision—what to study—can be overwhelming, especially to a beginning researcher who may be under pressure to find a topic for a class assignment, a thesis, or a dissertation. Many researchers whose articles are reprinted here came to their projects almost purely by chance, and not by means of a deliberate decision-making process. Indeed, more than one researcher that we talked with advised students looking for a research topic to "take advantage of what's there" or, put another way, "look for data where you live." For example, Carol Hagen and her colleagues excitedly gathered data in the form of graffiti that popped up all over Grand Forks in the aftermath of a flood in 1997, even as they themselves lost homes and possessions to the rising waters and despite the fact that Hagen was at the time completing a thesis on an entirely different topic. Carl Mazza needed a dissertation topic and found a research project in an evaluation of a program in which he was working, while John Zipp started with a wish to ascertain the effectiveness of a teaching strategy that he had used for some time in his classes. Perhaps the easiest way to find a topic is to join a project that is already in progress, which is frequently possible for graduate students. This was the case for Linda Treiber, who as a master's student was invited by Professor Melvin Thomas to assist in an ongoing content analysis of magazine advertisements; and for Thomas O'Connor, who was happy to assist Dean Hoge in a follow-up to an earlier study of religious involvement of people from adolescence to adulthood, a topic that had long interested him.

Of course, the particular intellectual interests of researchers virtually always figure into the choice of a research topic; after all, no one wants to be involved in a project on a topic that she or he finds irrelevant or boring. But sometimes those interests themselves are a result of chance. Penny Tinkler became intrigued by the history of women and smoking after being offered (and turning down) funding from the tobacco industry to pursue that topic. Barbara Perry describes her growing fascination with hate crimes and hate movements as purely serendipitous—a result of reading along with her husband, who did a research project for a class on that topic. Of course, researchers' theoretical interests often come not from chance, but from their own life experiences and political commitments. This was certainly the case for Mia Tuan, whose own status as a "one-point-fiver" (read her interview to learn what that means) sparked her curiosity about third and fourth generation Asian ethnics and their experiences with prejudice and discrimination. This is also true, to one extent or another, of virtually all the researchers with whom we spoke, perhaps most clearly those whose work is expressly aimed at exposing, explaining, and reducing or eliminating the inequalities by gender, ethnicity, race, age, and class that permeate social institutions and social life. You will "hear" their commitment as they talk about not only their choice of research topic, but also their hopes regarding the potential contributions of their work—improving antismoking programs for Canadian girls (MacDonald), eliminating features of curricula that undermine achievement of working-class high school Latinas (Bettie), raising awareness of the racism and classism that continue to pervade print media (Treiber), undermining ill-informed support for the death penalty (Sorensen) and spanking (Walsh), going public with what had been an invisible gender struggle in a small town in New Zealand (Campbell), challenging stereotypes of young African American fathers (Mazza), and so on. The value freedom and objectivity that we demand of social science research drive the research process, as they should. However, most sociologists would argue that the choice of a research topic is one aspect of research that is, and *should be,* a largely subjective one, shaped by the experiences, intellectual interests, and commitments of researchers.

Choosing a Research Design: Method, Measures, Samples

When it comes to the details of research design, the possibilities seem endless. Indeed, it is the case that any given research topic can be approached in myriad ways or, put another way, that any number of different approaches to studying some social phenomenon might yield equally valuable—though perhaps very different—insights and understandings. There is no one correct way to study anything. However, making good choices about what method or methods to use, how to measure variables and which variables to measure, and what to study and how to select a sample, requires that we understand the options available and the strengths and drawbacks of each. To do that, we need formal training and a good textbook in social research methods. Making decisions about the design of research also requires that we take into account the many kinds of constraints—for example, the availability of time and money, or the wishes of sponsors—that impact our choices. The researchers we interviewed provide some valuable insights into the process of deciding on the research design.

Choosing a Method

Often the choice of research approach is not really a choice at all, but a matter of opportunity or expediency. A number of researchers with whom we talked signed on to a project that was already underway, had access to an appealing data set that had already been collected, or had limited time and money and hence chose a method that was expedient and inexpensive (such as survey). When researchers have some choice in the research design, two factors seem most influential: the methodological skills of the researcher and the aims of the research.

The choice of research approach is often influenced by researchers' own personalities, training, department, or discipline. Hugh Campbell is a social anthropologist in a department that particularly values close-to-home ethnographic research. When he looked for a site in which to conduct an ethnographic study, he settled on a drinking establishment in rural New Zealand. Mia Tuan explains that she gravitated toward qualitative interviews with multigeneration Asian ethnics because of her own preference for a research approach that allowed her to have what she calls "guided conversations." Carl Mazza felt right at home with a before-and-after experimental design to evaluate his program for teen fathers because, for him, it resembled the "continuum of growth" that informs all of his work as a social worker and an educator. Many social scientists simply prefer the precision and predictability that come with quantitative approaches such as survey. Others choose historical and comparative approaches because they particularly like history, which usually means they are also firmly convinced that the best way to understand any social phenomenon is as it emerges in particular historical circumstances.

Perhaps the most important consideration when researchers make their decisions about research design is the purpose of the research. Social scientists often choose quantitative approaches because, for good or bad, numbers talk and quantitative designs allow them to attribute causality in ways that qualitative approaches do not. This was the case for Carl Mazza, who notes that having solid numerical data to back up his claims of success for the program for young dads was critical in convincing foundations to fund the program. For Jon Sorensen, using existing data to test the deterrence hypothesis was the method of choice in the highly politicized area of death penalty research. Whereas survey researchers often choose that approach for pragmatic reasons—efficiency and cost—those that we interviewed also cite other strengths of that approach, including the benefits of connecting with large numbers of people and being able to ask a wide range of questions.

Researchers who choose qualitative approaches do so with particular research aims in mind as well. Mia Tuan says that only in-depth interviews allow people to tell their own tales and enabled her to delve into themes, probe and follow different leads, and tell the richer, more personal stories that helped her understand the Asian ethnic experience. Similarly, Julie Bettie sought an understanding of race and class in the worlds of working-class Latina high school students from their own perspectives, experiences, and voices. The qualitative content analyses conducted by Penny Tinkler and Carol Hagen and colleagues were dictated at least in part by the exploratory nature of their research. And, finally, it is easy to see that Hugh Campbell would not likely have uncovered the rich and subtle insights about men's behavior in pubs by means of questionnaires or interviews.

The Sample

Decisions about sampling—what or who will be studied—should be guided first and foremost by the aims of the research. If generalizing to a population from which a sample was drawn is of importance to a researcher, then a sampling procedure designed to produce a representative sample will likely be selected. If a researcher intends to conduct in-depth interviews with a small number of subjects, then a random sampling procedure may not be feasible. Nonetheless, as with other aspects of social science research design, the selection of a sample is in reality shaped by a variety of constraints and considerations, many of them outside the control of the researcher. A first and basic decision is what the unit of analysis will be. Sometimes this is obvious—individual people comprise the elements of most survey analyses, for example—but in some studies, such as content analyses and many kinds of qualitative research, it is not. Rather, the units of analysis might be businesses (Scribner and Cohen's alcohol merchants), representations in magazine such as ads, stories, or pictures (the Thomas and Treiber article), or hate groups with websites (the Perry article).

Sometimes sampling is simply not an issue because the sample is predetermined. This is true when researchers join a research team in the second phase of a longitudinal study (such as the study of adult church involvement by O'Connor and his colleagues), in evaluation studies where the participants in a program are likely to be selected by the agency and not the researcher, and when archival or secondary data are used. In the latter case, the cost- and time-saving benefits of using existing data sets may be offset by limitations and potential bias in their samples. MacDonald and Wright note with some regret that their large secondary sample of high school students in British Columbia excludes Vancouver, the largest city in the region and one where smoking and drug rates are known to be lower. Wendy Walsh notes that her findings about parents' spanking have somewhat limited generalizability because the large database that she uses consists solely of white, Midwestern mothers. In some cases, the sampling plan was subject to change during the research because of factors outside the researcher's control. The organization that funded the study of adult church involvement insisted that the researchers include three denominations despite their proposal to cut it to two because of limited resources. Richard Scribner notes that what started out as a plan to take a stratified sample of all alcohol outlets in New Orleans had to be modified to meet the demands of the local Alcohol Beverage Control Board; the result was a less-than-ideal, much smaller convenience sample.

Even when researchers do have some options regarding the selection of their sample or field site, their decisions may be subject to any number of practical considerations and unexpected circumstances. When Julie Bettie needed a field site where she could examine the intersection of race, class, and gender in people's life experiences, she got help from an acquaintance who had a friend who was a respected teacher in a local high school, which gave her access to a site that provided rich data and in which she could explore and examine some of her theoretical interests. Once there, she used snowball sampling to find students willing to speak with her. The sample of post-flood graffiti analyzed by Hagen and her colleagues consisted of as many examples as they were able to find and record given the constraints of time (the graffiti was eventually removed) and access (roads were often blocked). A convenience sample was also used by Barbara Perry, who was limited to studying hate groups with web sites. Hugh Campbell illustrates nicely how a field researcher might choose a site quite purposively and systematically: He began by surveying the general characteristics of thirty-two pubs in a rural region of New Zealand but ended up choosing a pub that was in fact somewhat atypical because of its location in what was reputed to be one of the toughest drinking towns in New Zealand. As Campbell's interview reveals, he had some regrets about this choice over time.

Choosing and Measuring Variables

Once a sample is decided on, researchers must choose which variables to include and decide how to measure them. In explanatory quantitative research, we usually start with something that we wish to explain, which then becomes our dependent or outcome variable: adult religiosity, merchants' violation of drinking laws, adolescent smoking, homicide rates, parents' views of spanking, young people's civic commitment, students' understanding of a concept, and so on. Then the challenge is to identify one or more independent, or predictor, variables—those that we think might be accounting for, influencing, or producing the outcome or dependent variables. How do researchers go about deciding which independent variables to include in a study? One important way is to look at previous studies: What variables have others found to be important? Are there some potentially important factors that haven't been considered? David May and R. Gregory Dunaway examined the existing research and then set out to see if the factors that predict adults' fear of crime—such as previous victimization, gender, and what they call "perceived neighborhood incivility"—are also good predictors of fear of crime among young people. Similarly, Constance Flanagan learned from previous work that how democratic and inclusive the school climate is has an impact on adolescents' civic commitment, regardless of country. Jon Sorensen's research examines the deterrence hypothesis—the idea that homicide rates are influenced by the number of executions in a given time period. For him, a major challenge was to identify *other* factors that might influence homicide rates, so as to control for them by building them into his model. In experimental design, the challenge of which variables to include is typically a little different. In two studies included in this book— John Zipp's test of the impact of a teaching strategy and Carl Mazza's evaluation of the impact of a special program for teenage fathers—the independent (or treatment) variable is obvious. What is not always obvious with this sort of study is just what outcomes one expects. What specific learning goal should the teaching strategy be achieving? What are the expected results of a particular intervention, policy, or program? Here identifying the dependent variable(s) is most problematic and likely to present the greater challenge to the researcher.

Descriptive and exploratory research, including qualitative approaches, present the social scientist with a slightly different challenge. Instead of translating concepts into distinct variables, researchers go into the field with a list of questions, ideas, or sometimes little more than a general sense of what they will begin looking at and for. Eventually they organize and code data into themes, motifs, or generalizations that may emerge during and after data collection, rather than being identified before the research begins. This is the case for a number of studies in this book, and some researchers mention in their interviews how hard it was to organize data and make decisions about how to categorize or classify the ads, stories, comments, graffiti, behaviors, representations, or experiences that they observed or heard from respondents. What categories best capture the different kinds of post-disaster graffiti, representations of women smoking, or the "product promises" illustrated in magazines advertisements? What are the patterns in men's drinking and conversation in rural pubs and what do they tell us about hegemonic masculinity in this setting? Which of the many family circumstances and life experiences mentioned by Mexican American girls have an impact on patterns of mobility that differentiate them?

Choosing which variables or concepts to include can be a bit daunting; deciding how to measure them can be even more of a challenge. Decisions about how to measure variables are critical, because invalid or unreliable measures can introduce substantial bias into a study. Also, some variables are, for different reasons, simply hard to measure. This is true of a number of rather complex constructs that researchers measured and report on here, such as school climate, fear of crime, civic commitment, and religious involvement. To measure variables such as these, quantitative researchers typically use composite measures, or indexes, that they develop themselves or adapt from previous research. A good example is the research on adult religious involvement by Thomas O'Connor and his colleagues, for which they needed measures of complex behavioral and attitudinal variables. They created the Youth Program Participation Scale and the Traditional Sexual Beliefs Scale to measure two of their independent variables; for a third, respondents' adherence to traditional Christian creeds, they adapted work of previous researchers—a common and accepted practice—to create the Youth Creedal Assent Scale. In every case, they explain how they developed their measures and something about their level of confidence in the validity and reliability of each.

Another measurement challenge faces researchers using secondary or existing data. Because the data were usually collected for another purpose, researchers must use what is there regardless of whether it perfectly meets their research needs. Marjorie MacDonald notes that the "school bonding" measure available to her and Nancy Wright for their adolescent smoking study was not as complete as they would have liked. Jon Sorensen and his colleagues had to turn to a number of different archival data sources for control variables to include in their model predicting homicide rates in Texas. This meant they sometimes had to use "proxy" or substitute measures—for example, the number of physicians per 100,000 residents became a proxy for the availability of emergency services, a factor that is known to affect homicide rates. Constance Flanagan and her associates had a slightly different challenge: to develop measures of civic commitment, school climate, and other factors that would be valid across different cultures. In her interview, Flanagan notes that she and her colleagues from five different countries spent many hours on email developing and reworking measures that would be equally valid for students in seven different countries: Australia, Sweden, Hungary, Russia, the Czech Republic, Bulgaria, and the United States.

Measurement presents many different challenges to qualitative researchers as well. In quantitative research, measurement bias is largely intrinsic to the measure that is used. In qualitative research, the data are a result of the researcher's observations and interpretations and are subject to more diffuse sources of bias. Barbara Perry points out that she had to be vigilant about maintaining distance and objectivity as she described and interpreted the rhetoric of hate groups on the Web. Similarly, Mia Tuan took care not to let her own experiences and assumptions color her interpretation of the stories her Asian ethnic respondents told. In perhaps the most dramatic example, Carol Hagen and her colleagues, as victims of the flood *and* researchers studying the impact of that victimization, had to work to control bias as they vacillated between the roles of researchers and subjects in the course of their research. Other qualitative researchers relate how they minimized bias by consulting regularly with colleagues about how to categorize observations to ensure reliability and by taking care to speak and even to dress in a "neutral" way to avoid influencing responses.

Ethical Issues and Considerations

Contemporary social scientists must be very sensitive to issues of ethics as they design and carry out their research. The most immediate and obvious challenge is how to protect the privacy, dignity, and physical and emotional (and sometimes legal) well-being of the people who are to be studied. Researchers build such protections into their research in a variety of ways. When adolescents are the participants, researchers such as David May are required to secure permission from parents. Interestingly, even though Marjorie MacDonald and Nancy Wright used secondary data collected from young people in their study of adolescent smoking, they were nonetheless concerned because they were analyzing data for a slightly different purpose than was understood when permission was originally secured and the data first collected. Designing research that protects privacy often requires taking pains to ensure that no identifying information appears anywhere in the data that are saved or in the research reports. To this end, Hagen and her colleagues were careful not to capture any identifying information in photos or descriptions of graffiti that they collected, and the field researchers whose work we include here clearly disguise or hide any information that would allow the reader to identify the site where they collected their data or the people with whom they spoke. Thomas O'Connor describes the special care he and his colleagues took to avoid making people feel "invaded" as the researchers re-entered their lives in the second phase of a longitudinal study about adult religious involvemenet.

The ethical issues that researchers face are more than just about protecting the privacy of participants, however. Carl Mazza confronted an ethical dilemma that is often found in medical research: that participants who are not part of the treatment group are denied the benefits that came with the special intervention program that he was evaluating (though in this case, the teen fathers eventually were given access to those benefits). Julie Bettie was sensitive to the problem of "othering" certain categories of people in her field site and to betraying the trust of the young high school women in her study. Finally, the implications of one's research can raise rather profound ethical concerns. Barbara Perry feared that her research on hate groups would serve their ends by providing them an additional platform for their hateful rhetoric. Linda Treiber worried that the evidence of persistent racism in advertisements would create a sense of defeat and resignation rather than inspire people to work for change. When Hugh Campbell published his research describing problematic drinking behavior among a sizable group of men in a small town, some people were very upset, which forced him to deal directly with sensitive issues related to honesty and "research positioning." Jon Sorensen states that he is acutely conscious of the fact that his findings about the impact of the death penalty could be used to justify executions or, in the opposite vein, to prevent executing offenders who might then go on to murder innocent citizens. He echoes the sentiments of others when he suggests that one important aspect of being ethical is *doing good research*—being as objective and honest as possible and taking the utmost care in the design of the research, the collection of data, and the presentation and interpretation of data, material, and findings.

Collecting, Organizing, and Analyzing the Data

For most researchers, the implementation of research design is the most exciting stage of a research project. Because most of the decisions about how to do the research have already been made, one might also assume that this stage is the easiest. However, that is not always the case. In fact, the challenges of collecting, organizing, and analyzing data (which, we should note, are often done somewhat simultaneously, especially during qualitative research) may mean that researchers have to draw on considerable creativity and flexibility to deal with dilemmas and crises, large and small, that may arise.

The process of collecting data seldom goes as smoothly as planned. Thomas O'Connor and his colleagues found out after they were well into data collection that their respondents were very enthusiastic to talk—and talk and talk and talk—about their church involvement and spiritual lives. The interviews were taking so long that the researchers had to stop and retrain interviewers to help them keep the interview on track and prevent respondents from talking for hours. Barbara Perry had to take a break from data collection midway through her research as well, but for a very different reason: She began to have terrifying nightmares about the hate group members whose rhetoric she was reading for hours each day. Penny Tinkler describes many of the headaches involved in archival research with old magazines, including delays and errors in processing her library requests and the difficulty of recording endless details about the magazines in the library when she wasn't able to photocopy all that she desired. Richard Scribner describes having to change data collecting plans because some liquor stores were in neighborhoods that couldn't be safely navigated at night, and because others simply closed during the course of the research. Hagen and her colleagues found that data disappeared as well, because officials cleared away some graffiti before they were able to observe and record it. In fact, most of the researchers we interviewed had at least one story to tell about an unexpected glitch or problem in data collection that forced them to abandon or revise at least some aspect of their original data collection plan.

Organizing and analyzing data after they have been collected can present a challenge as well. Qualitative researchers typically deal with reams of field notes from which they must tease out themes, motifs, concepts, and relationships. Some researchers whom we interviewed admit to doing this with low-tech aids such as Post-it notes and highlighters, and some use more sophisticated techniques, such as computer software designed to organize qualitative data. Content analyses may produce reams of a different sort: piles of magazines, photos, or other data sources that simply take up a lot of room. Those researchers, too, may find it equally tedious and difficult (but eventually rewarding) to comb through data looking for patterns that help them to make sense of it all. For all researchers, basic logistics alone can be a major hassle. Mia Tuan learned this when she lost some valuable data when a package sent by a research assistant got lost in the mail.

Quantitative researchers may face slightly different challenges as they organize and analyze their data. For David May, one was the realization that many students were not taking the questionnaire seriously and were marking responses randomly. That required instituting reliability checks—methods of determining which questionnaires were bogus by looking at patterns of students' responses. Sometimes researchers recognize late in the project that a particular measure lacks reliability or validity. This was true for Wendy Walsh, who realized that the mothers interviewed were unclear about what was meant by a "neutral message" about spanking, leading her to question the validity of that question. Quantitative researchers may also face challenges in analyzing their data when such analysis requires familiarity with statistical software packages and, sometimes, sophisticated and specialized multivariate statistical techniques. Carl Mazza had to relearn how to use SPSS (Statistical Package for the Social Sciences) to compile and analyze his data because he had largely forgotten what he learned about it some years earlier. Jon Sorensen's data on homicides in Texas required time series analysis, something with which he had no experience at the time he undertook his study.

The Rewards of Social Research

Social science research is hard work. Moreover, it requires time and money, expertise acquired through specialized training, and personal qualities such as persistence, flexibility, creativity, resourcefulness, humility, intelligence, and the ability to accept criticism and even outright rejection of one's work. But as you will see as you read the words of researchers whose work is included here, the satisfaction that comes from doing research can be enormous. Some of that satisfaction comes just from having taken on a meaningful project and seeing it to completion. Seeing one's words in print is particularly gratifying for many. The researchers we interviewed also cite many other reasons for feeling good about their work. They offer many suggestions to beginning researchers about how to get the most from the research experience.

A major source of satisfaction to researchers has to do with the implications or uses of their research. In a few cases, researchers we talked to could point to concrete positive outcomes of their efforts. Richard Scribner and Deborah Cohen's research led to more routine compliance checks of liquor merchants in New Orleans. Carl Mazza's evaluation project was a critical factor in securing subsequent funding for the program that he evaluated, as well as providing him national forums in which to share his findings and a model for other teen parenting programs. Others, such as Constance Flanagan, Carol Hagen, Linda Treiber, and John Zipp, took satisfaction from others' expressed interest in knowing, and perhaps using, their results. More commonly, researchers' satisfaction comes from what they see as *potential* contributions of their research—the understanding of some phenomenon, or of policies or practices that will somehow make society or people's lives better. Examples of this appear throughout our interviews. We were surprised at how many social scientists we talked with have thought long and carefully about the implications of their work—not just its meaning in theoretical terms but, more often, how it might shape and inform policies, programs, or public perceptions in areas as diverse as school curricula, law enforcement, disaster response, teaching techniques, parent education, criminal law, anti-smoking campaigns, and hate crimes.

Finally, our interviews make clear that social scientists derive enormous satisfaction from the *process* of doing research. Some cite the pleasures of working closely with colleagues, professors, assistants, and students. Others find gratification in getting to know and giving voice to those whom they study, such as the "amazing" working-class high school women whose strengths so impressed Julie Bettie. Some researchers find great satisfaction in what they have learned from doing the research, such as how to do a particular form of statistical analysis, having a new experience with content analysis, or simply getting a first chance to "get our hands dirty . . . and actually do" research (in David May's words). John Zipp found gratification in doing classroom-based evaluation because he was able to combine the two parts of his academic self—teacher and scholar. For many social scientists, an important kind of satisfaction that the research process brings is what we might call the "joy of discovery." Barbara Perry refers to the pleasure of watching themes emerge and how, like a giant jigsaw puzzle, everything started to make sense as she gathered more data. Penny Tinkler similarly describes her excitement at finding evidence of women's smoking in early magazines and her satisfaction at "teasing out the subtleties of the representations" in the magazines. Others, such as Carol Hagen and Mia Tuan, note the gratification that comes with making a contribution to sociological understanding by filling in a gap in the literature. In fact, despite the time and effort required to produce quality social science research, and the frustrations that come with dealing with all the constraints within which they must work, you will seldom hear social scientists talk about their research without a sense of excitement, commitment, and joy. Clearly social research is not only important to society and to the discipline of sociology and related areas of study, but it is also deeply rewarding to researchers. We are delighted to welcome you to the world of social research, and we encourage you to think about becoming not only a *consumer* of the knowledge such research produces, but also a *discoverer* and *producer* of your own knowledge about the social world. As John Zipp puts it, "The world is waiting for us to study it."

chapter 2

Why Do Social Research?

Why is social science research a better way to discover or create knowledge than other techniques? After all, on a daily basis we all rely on many sources of information about the social world: our own experiences, the wisdom of others whom we respect, messages that we hear from a range of media sources, simple common sense, understandings that have been handed down to us, and our own insights and interpretations. What makes systematic, scientific approaches to gathering information superior? The two articles in this chapter were selected to help you begin to answer that question, along with some others: What purposes do research findings serve? What relevance can social science research have for real people in the real world? Who does social science research? How is it that different research approaches answer different questions or answer questions differently?

One common way of categorizing social research is as either basic or applied. The first article here is an example of basic research. Thomas O'Connor and his colleagues set out to identify factors that contribute to adult church involvement and personal spirituality and, in the process, to test the usefulness of three theoretical approaches that have most often guided previous research on this topic. Although they point out that Christian church leaders wanted to know what accounts for adult church involvement, that is not the primary motivation for their research. Rather, they are driven by the desire for understanding and for testing existing theories about church involvement and spirituality. Like the research by O'Connor and his colleagues, Carl Mazza's study is quantitative, explanatory, and uses a longitudinal design. In contrast, however, it is a clear example of applied research—specifically, an evaluation of a therapeutic social work intervention in a program for teenage fathers. Although Mazza uses a different research design from that used by O'Connor (experimental design versus survey), the more important difference is that Mazza's research is not about understanding for its own sake or examining theories, but instead has an immediate and practical application: determining whether a particular kind of intervention is effective.

The articles and interviews in this chapter also provide some insight into why and how social research is a superior way of knowing about the social world. For example, common sense would lead us to believe that young people who attend church and Sunday school regularly, pray frequently, and have parents who are churchgoers are more likely than others to remain active in church as adults. However, O'Connor and his colleagues find that none of those variables impact adult church involvement. Carl Mazza, in his interview, is quite persuasive regarding the importance of research for social work practitioners. Because he was able to demonstrate the program's effectiveness with numerical data that came from a rigorous research design, his agency implemented it, foundations funded it, and he received national attention (including an article in *People* magazine), which resulted in requests from agencies across the country who wished to replicate his success. Would he have achieved all this by sharing only his impressions or anecdotal evidence? Probably not.

These articles and interviews also provide some insight into other aspects of social science research, many of which we will illustrate throughout the book. One is that social science research is not done just by sociologists. Carl Mazza is a social work professor. Thomas O'Connor is an experienced social science researcher, as well as a former monk, who holds degrees in law, philosophy, theology, and counseling. In contrast, his second author, Dean Hoge, is a sociologist who is well-known for his extensive research in the area of sociology of religion. Another aspect of social science research is that researchers have a wide variety of venues in which to publish and present their work including many different topic-oriented, interdisciplinary journals. *Adolescence,* for example, encourages submissions from fields as diverse as physiology, psychology, psychiatry, education, and sociology that are addressed to some aspect of the second decade of human life. *The Journal for the Scientific Study of Religion* publishes research from sociology, political science, and psychology about religion in the modern world.

Finally, the articles in this chapter also help to show the limitations of thinking about social research in either/or terms—that each project is either applied or basic, sociology or something else, quantitative or qualitative. Mazza's evaluation study includes an extensive review of the research on African American adolescent males and teen fathers, and despite his express aim of evaluating the effectiveness of one particular form of intervention, his research also challenges us to rethink some of the sexist, ageist, and even racist assumptions underlying popular and scientific thinking about teenage fathers. O'Connor and his colleagues set out to examine some theories but also hoped to provide concrete, useful guidelines to church leaders who wished to develop programs to encourage adult involvement in their churches. Mazza, O'Connor, and almost all the researchers whom we interviewed and whose work we reprint here talk about the potential relevance of their research for the world outside their own offices and computer laboratories. Most of all, they share a commitment to the view that social science research is the best way to learn about the social world and that understanding that world is a worthy goal in and of itself, as well as a necessary first step toward bringing about some positive change.

The Relative Influence of Youth and Adult Experiences on Personal Spirituality and Church Involvement

Thomas P. O'Connor, Dean R. Hoge, and Estrelda Alexander

We surveyed 206 young adults who had grown up in middle-class churches in three denominations—Baptist, Catholic, and Methodist—who were first studied at age 16 in 1976. The goal was to assess the relative strength of youth and adult influences on their personal religious and institutional church involvement at age 38. The determinants of these two outcomes at 38 varied widely. For personal spirituality such as private prayer, attending Bible classes, and reading religious material, we found strong youth and adult determinants such as the denomination of one's youth, church youth group participation, having an experience since high school that changed their feelings about the church, and attending church with one's spouse. For church involvement, however, all but one of the determinants occurred after age 16, mainly the experiences of being inactive in church after high school, switching denominations, having children, and going to church with one's spouse. Social learning theory was the best theory for explaining these findings.

Church leaders of all Christian denominations want to know what factors produce Christian adults who have an active spirituality and are engaged in their churches. How important are childhood experiences for determining adult church involvement and personal religiosity? What kind of adult experiences have the most long-lasting spiritual effect? What causes some young adults to remain involved in church and others to depart? Do adult experiences supersede or build on youthful influences in determining adult spirituality and

church behavior? Do structural influences such as denomination or gender interact with individual factors to produce greater or lesser involvement in religious practice?

Questions such as these have stimulated much research, including the present article. We report results of a longitudinal study of youth in Baptist, Methodist, and Catholic denominations who were studied at age 16 and 22 years later at age 38. To explain the importance of our study and situate it theoretically we need to review prevailing ideas of religious change and commitment during youth and early adulthood. These are basically nascent theories based on past findings about the importance of different influences on adult religious practice, especially church involvement. They can be categorized into three types: family life cycle theory, social learning theory, and cultural broadening theory.

Family life cycle theory states that the needs and tasks an individual must address during different parts of the family life cycle determine his or her church involvement. Research has found that church disaffiliation occurs most often in the teenage years and the early 20s, with less disengagement after the early 20s and often a reentry into church life later when the young adult is building a family (Roozen 1980). Adult church involvement is stronger for married persons than single persons and stronger for persons with children than for those without (Mueller and Cooper 1986; Stolzenberg, Blair-Loy, and Waite 1995). Stolzenberg, Blair-Loy, and Waite (1995) suggest that religious disaffiliation and reaffiliation are influenced by the strength of family ties, marital history, and attitudes to family life. Other researchers point out that the influence of family life may be gender specific. Since men's religious roles are less institutionalized or socially defined than women's, men's involvement in church may depend more on nonreligious factors such as changes in family status (Wilson and Sherkat 1994).

Social learning theory views religious behavior as a learned behavior arising out of a particular life context. As life contexts change, people change, primarily by observing role models and practicing new behaviors (Bandura 1977). Thus, early socialization into a religious tradition is a result of the model provided to children by parents and other adults (Hunsberger 1983; Hoge, Johnson, and Luidens 1993). In the teenage years when peer influences tend to outweigh parental influences, teenagers will become less church involved as they learn new behaviors from their peers that help to relate them to their changing situations. Similarly, as an adult, a person's own set of attitudes, beliefs, and values and those of his or her adult friends will influence that person's religious and church involvement. Social learning theory would suggest that religious learning will vary from one denomination or religious group to another depending on the kind of religious modeling and practices that are most prevalent in each group.

Cultural broadening theory (also called "localism theory") considers church involvement in terms of "plausibility structures" (Cornwall 1989). This perspective contends that in a highly differentiated and pluralistic modern society, the maintenance of a particular religious worldview requires that a community of people support one another's belief in it in daily interaction. A "local orientation" characterized by involvement with local institutions and networks of friends and family (as opposed to a "cosmopolitan" orientation), should predict higher rates of church involvement (Roof 1978). Cognitive broadening that occurs during high school and college can produce "liberalized social attitudes, greater cosmopolitanism, religious skepticism, and a sense of moral and religious relativity" (Hoge, Johnson, and Luidens 1993). College experience,

regional or geographic relocation, interfaith marriage, or other shifts in one's life may disrupt one's interactions with earlier religious practices and church networks and so lead to lesser involvement in the church (Roozen 1980; Hoge and Petrillo 1978a).

Past research into determinants of adult religious involvement has had limitations. Many of the studies asked adult respondents to recall aspects of their childhood and youth rather than gather independent data about those early years. Only a few, such as Myers's study of the inheritance of religiosity, Dudley's study of Seventh Day Adventist youth from age 16 to 26, Dillon's study of religious involvement from adolescence through adulthood, and the present study, utilize information gathered at widely different points of time (Myers 1996; Dudley 1995,1999; Dillon 2000). In addition, few studies were able to study denominational variations, and many studies focused only on church involvement as an outcome to the neglect of personal religious involvement. The present study overcomes these limitations because its design permits a longitudinal study of both personal religious and church involvement across three denominations.

We tested three general hypotheses that were based in the theories of religious development discussed above. (1) Family-related experiences during adulthood, such as marriage and having children, will produce both greater church and personal religious involvement. (2) Due to social learning, greater religious involvement as a child and greater religiosity of the family of origin will foster adult church involvement and personal spiritual practice. (3) Adult experiences producing cognitive broadening, such as college education and interfaith marriage, will reduce religious commitment. We were also interested in exploring the relationship between personal religious practice and institutional church involvement and the influence of childhood denomination on adult religious practices. If attendance at church declines, does personal religious practice also decline, or are personal religiosity and church attendance two independent religious constructs?

Do different denominations influence the adult religious behaviors of their young members in different ways?

Method

The study is a follow-up to a 1976 study by Dean Hoge and Gregory Petrillo. They gathered extensive data on 451 Baptist, Catholic, and Methodist 10th graders regarding their faith development, church involvement, and religious attitudes (Hoge and Petrillo 1978a, 1978b; Hoge, Petrillo, and Smith 1982). The subjects in the original study, most of whom were aged 16, belonged to 35 churches in the Maryland suburbs of Washington, DC. Most were in white middle- or upper-middle-class churches. Most also attended church regularly and participated in church youth programs. Hoge and Petrillo set out to study all the 10th graders who were on the churches' roles; 68 percent of the 10th graders responded. The original sample contained some bias, since youth who participated in church programs were disproportionately cooperative in data collection.

We set out to interview all the subjects who had participated in the earlier study. The earlier data and records had been preserved and we searched for the 451 target persons in a variety of ways. We visited the churches again, and in all but one of them we were able to hire an informant who had a long history of involvement with the congregation to help find the target persons. In addition, we used Internet and phone book searches, and asked the subjects we located for information about the other subjects in their church. Using these methods we found some current information on 285 (63 percent) of the original subjects and conducted a phone interview with 206 of them in 1998 (a few interviews took place toward the end of 1997). Thirteen people declined our interview offer, three were out of the country, two were deceased, and we were unable to make contact with the remaining 61. Not counting the two deceased people, we interviewed 46 percent of the target population. The present article is based on

these 206 cases (61 original Baptists, 68 original Catholics, and 77 original Methodists).

We checked on possible biases by comparing the youth data for the 206 adult subjects with the 245 cases from the original sample whom we did not interview on gender, mother's church attendance, father's church attendance, respondent's church attendance as a youth, participation in church youth programs, and belief in the importance of church teachings. We found that the two groups did not differ significantly on these variables except that the 206 persons in the follow-up study had reported slightly higher church participation by their mothers ($p < 0.05$). We conclude that our data has a small bias in that the follow-up persons were reared in homes that were a little more church involved than the original sample.

Description of the Sample

In both the original and the follow-up samples 55 percent of the respondents were female and 45 percent were male. The denominational breakdown across studies was also similar; in 1976 it was 33 percent Baptist, 34 percent Catholic, and 33 percent Methodist, and in 1998 it was 30 percent originally Baptist, 33 percent originally Catholic, and 37 percent originally Methodist. Approximately half (55 percent) of the follow-up sample were female—original Baptist 56 percent, Catholic 50 percent, and Methodist 58 percent. The post-high-school experiences of the adults in the three denominations were also surprisingly similar. We found no significant differences ($p < 0.05$) among original Baptists, Catholics, and Methodists on gender, race, age, education level, having attended a Christian college as opposed to a different college, employment status, marital status, number of marriages, having children, and number of children. Thus the three denominational groups had many demographic and life cycle variables in common and this reduced the possible confounding effects of the demographic and life cycle variables on our outcome variables.

Most of the subjects were 38 years old and nearly all (97 percent) were white. A majority of the respondents (74 percent) were currently married, while 18 percent were never married, 8 percent were divorced or separated, and 1 percent were living with a partner. A surprisingly high percent (88 percent) of those who were ever married were still in their first marriage, 12 percent were in their second, and 1 percent were in their third. Seventy percent of the subjects had children, an average of 2.2. The subjects were well educated; 15 percent had a high school diploma, 17 percent had some college, and the rest had a bachelor degree (39 percent), a master degree (21 percent), or a professional/doctoral degree (9 percent). Of those who went to college, 26 percent attended a Christian college. However, only 14 percent were ever active in a Christian campus ministry or group. Baptists were much more likely to have been active in campus ministries or groups (27 percent of Baptists; 5 percent of Catholics; 7 percent of Methodists). Most (87 percent) were employed (12 percent were homemakers, 2 percent were unemployed) and the occupations of the subjects place them in the middle- or upper-middle class; the majority were college professors or administrators, teachers, physicians, engineers, managers, business owners, accountants, lawyers, sales workers, and government employees.

Table 1 presents some of the findings about the history and current religious involvement of our subjects. The first four rows of Table 1 show that for all three denominations the frequency of church attendance drops from age 16 to age 38 but the frequency of private prayer actually increases during this time. This is a very interesting finding because it gives us our first clue that personal religious and church practice are different aspects of adult religiosity. Overall, 79 percent of the sample said they had at some time been inactive in church, i.e., had attended church less than 12 times a year. Men and women were equally likely to become inactive. However, the percentage that became inactive after high school was almost significantly different (p = 0.053) across the three denominations: for Baptists it was 69 per-

cent, for Catholics 81 percent, and for Methodists 86 percent. The age of becoming inactive varied, with most (68 percent) becoming inactive by age 21; the average age for becoming inactive was also 21. Almost half (48 percent) of those who became inactive said they did so for personal or motivational reasons such as "being too busy," "busy with family obligations," "lack of interest,"and "feeling bored or lazy;" about 20 percent named reasons that pertained to some conflict with faith or the church, such as "disagreed with church," "doubted the faith," and "disliked worship style;" about 16 percent named geographical or family reasons like "left home," "moved away from family," and "no more parental pressure;" 6 percent gave interpersonal reasons such as "disliked the pastor," "spousal influence," and "influence of friends;" 6 percent were unsure; and 4 percent gave other reasons.

Over half (58 percent) of the respondents who had been inactive said they became active again later, and by age 38 a majority of our sample (67 percent) were currently active: 72 percent of the original Baptists, 69 percent of the Catholics, and 60 percent of the Methodists (not significant at p < 0.05). However, not all returned to the same denominations; 62 percent of the original Baptists were actively Baptist, 81 percent of the Catholics stayed Catholic, and 62 percent of the Methodists remained Methodist (significant at p < 0.05). Most (62 percent) became active again between the ages of 23 and 30; the average age was 28. The age pattern for becoming inactive and active again is similar to that found by Hoge, Johnson, and Luidens (1993) and by Hoge et al. (2001). The main reasons the respondents gave for becoming active again were related to marriage and children or to spiritual needs. About 25 percent said "children," 22 percent said "spiritual need" or "marital problems," 15 percent said "influence of spouse," 6 percent said "influence of others," 6 percent said "conversion," and the rest gave other responses.

We asked, "Since you completed high school, has there been any particular event, experience, or relationship which has changed your feelings about the church?" Over half said yes (Table 1).

TABLE 1 *History of and Current Spiritual and Church Involvement by Original Denomination*

	Baptist (N = 61) %	Catholic (N = 68) %	Methodist (N = 77) %
*Percent attending church (weekly or more) as a youth	82	83	58
*Percent attending church (weekly or more) as an adult	51	38	30
Percent praying privately (very or somewhat frequently) as a youth	20	18	13
Percent praying privately (weekly or more) as an adult	62	43	38
*Ever become inactive in church? Yes	69	81	86
Mean age for becoming inactive	21	22	20
Mean age for becoming active again	29	28	27
Currently active in church? Yes	72	69	60
Currently a member of a church? Yes	79	76	68
*Mean hours per month spent on church affairs of any kind, including worship (as an adult)	11.7	7.2	8.9
Ever have an event since high school that changed your feeling about church? Yes	52	63	57
Result of event? (N = 119)			
Church was more important	63	50	70
Church was less important	31	43	21
No difference	6	7	9
Personal religious practice as an adult (weekly or more) in last year			
*Attended a prayer meeting	18	4	5
*Attended a Bible study class	30	3	8
*Read the Bible	53	16	26
*Listened to Christian programming on radio or TV	46	10	17
Read a religious book other than the Bible	21	13	13

Note: *Significant at 0.05 by F-test or chi-square.

Baptists, Catholics, and Methodists were equally likely to have had such experiences. What were the experiences? About 24 percent said it was marriage and/or having children. About 22 percent told of a conflict with the church or a minister or priest, usually about sexual issues, marriage, remarriage, or being gay. About 21 percent said it was the death of a family member or loved one, illness of a loved one, or their own illness. About 14 percent spoke of learning that had enlarged their horizons, of exposure to other religions, or of their investigations about religion. About 10 percent told of positive experiences with pastors or religious friends. The effect of these experiences varied depending on what happened. Respondents who told of marriage, children, deaths, or illnesses tended to say the experience made the church *more* important to them. Respondents who told of conflict with church leaders or disgust at church irregularities said the experiences made the church *less* important. On balance, the events made the church *more* important. Table 1 also shows that original Baptists compared to Catholics and Methodists spent the highest number of hours per month on church affairs and were also significantly more likely to engage in adult personal religious practices such as attending prayer meetings, Bible study classes, reading the Bible, and listening to Christian programming on radio or TV.

Dependent and Independent Variables

Dependent Variables

We identified three outcome or dependent variables: (1) ever became inactive in church life; (2) personal religious involvement; and (3) church involvement. Our first outcome variable—becoming inactive in church—could be defined as an interim outcome variable because it took place prior to the time of our adult survey but after our youth survey. Our second and third outcome variables were the level of personal religious involvement or spirituality and the level of church involvement at the time of our adult survey at approximately age 38. We constructed our two final outcome measures by factor-analyzing a wide range of available outcome measures at age 38 into three different dimensions. Using the variables that fell into the first two dimensions, we constructed two outcome scales or measures, with higher scores indicating: (1) greater personal religious involvement; and (2) greater church involvement. These two outcome measures—personal religious involvement and church involvement—intercorrelated at 0.63.

The *Personal Religious Involvement Scale* was made from seven items (Cronbach's alpha = 0.86). Six were self-reports of religious activities within the last year: attended a prayer meeting; attended a Bible study class; read the Bible; listened to Christian programming on radio or TV; had a personal time of devotion or prayer; and read a religious book other than the Bible. They were scored: weekly or more = 3; occasionally = 2; and never = 1. The seventh question asked about how many times the person has prayed privately in the last seven days. The responses were scored; more than once a day = 3; about once a day = 2.5; several times = 2; about once = 1.5; and never = 1.

The *Church Involvement Scale* was composed of four items (Cronbach's alpha = 0.81): church attendance in the last year, scored in three levels; number of hours spent in an average month on church affairs including time for meetings, committee work, travel, study, and worship, scored from 0 hours to 23 hours; "How often in the last year have you given money to your church?" and "How often in the last year have you volunteered for a religious activity?" scored: weekly or more = 3; occasionally = 2; and never = 1. All responses were to range from 1 to 3.

Independent or Predictor Scales

In our analysis to predict our three outcomes we used a wide range of individual items from the youth and the adult surveys such as gender, denomination, education level, and marital status. In addition we created four scales that were theoretically appropriate to our analyses. From the youth data we created a seven-item *Youth Creedal Assent Scale* (from King and Hunt 1975) that measures general adherence to traditional Christian creeds (Cronbach's alpha = 0.84). For example, two items state, "I believe in eternal life," and "I believe that God revealed Himself to man in Jesus Christ." This scale correlated –0.46 with the *Youth Religious Relativism Scale*, which was constructed from five items, such as "All the great religions of the world are equally good and true," and "not all the churches have God's truth; many are in serious error" (Cronbach's alpha = 0.83).

We also created a two-item *Youth Traditional Sexual Beliefs Scale* composed of two strongly agree to strongly disagree items scored from 5 to 1: "Publications that dwell on and illustrate sex acts should be banned from newsstands" and "It is morally right for a couple committed to each other to have premarital sexual intercourse." After the scoring for the latter question was reversed, the two items correlated at 0.37. The Youth Traditional Sexual Beliefs Scale score correlated 0.48 with the Youth Creedal Assent Scale and –0.39 with the Youth Religious Relativism Scale. This measure of sexual beliefs as a 16 year old proved to be important in predicting whether individuals dropped out of church life. Finally, the youth data contained seven different measures for youth group participation (Bible study groups, retreats, trips, service projects, choirs, lectures/courses, and youth worship services) and from these we created a *Youth Program Participation Scale* composed of the mean of the seven measures coded: very much involved = 3, quite involved = 2, slightly = 1, not at all = 0, and not offered = 0 (Cronbach's alpha = 0.85). The Youth Program Participation Scale correlated 0.39 with the Youth Creedal Assent Scale, –0.32 with the Youth Traditional Sexual Beliefs Scale, and 0.19 with the Youth Traditional Sexual Beliefs Scale.

Predictors of Becoming Inactive in Church

We have already described how a large majority of the sample (79 percent) said they had, at some time, become inactive in church, i.e., had attended church less than 12 times a year. To see what youthful variables would predict this intermediate outcome (dropping out from church) between age 16 and 38 we used logistic regression to analyze the influence of our individual and scale youth variables identified above. We entered each of the youth variables into a forward step (likelihood ratio) logistic regression to see if they would predict which respondents had never become inactive versus those who had. Surprisingly, only three of the youth variables remained in the equation at the 0.05 significance level: a yes/no question that read "Has there ever been a period in your life when you reacted either partially or wholly against the beliefs taught you?"; frequency of church attendance; and the Youth Traditional Sexual Belief Scale. On the question regarding reacting against beliefs, the odds on those who had never rebelled staying active after adolescence were 2.9 times

higher than for those who had rebelled. On church attendance, the odds on those who attended weekly or more staying active were three times higher than for those who had attended less than weekly. On traditional sexual beliefs, the odds on those who held more traditional sexual beliefs staying active increased in a linear fashion as subjects scored higher on this five-point scale.

This unexpected finding about the influence of sexual beliefs alerts us to the importance of sexual issues for high school youth. Possibly, sexual morals and sexual problems may be more important than parental religious practices and theological issues in determining the future church involvement of teenagers.

Predictors of Personal Religion and Church Involvement at Age 38

In a first test of the importance of the youth factors on the two main adult outcomes—personal religious and institutional church involvement at age 38—we constructed numerous correlations. Of the two outcome scales, experiences and attitudes during youth tended to be more often and more strongly correlated with personal religious behavior at age 38 than church involvement. Gender, frequency of church attendance, and frequency of private prayer were significantly correlated with personal religious practice but not with church involvement. Denomination, Bible knowledge, church youth program participation, youth creedal assent, youth religious relativism, and youth traditional sexual beliefs were significantly correlated with both personal religiosity and church engagement.

Having examined the relationships between the variables of interest at a bivariate level, we turned our attention to a multivariate analysis of the impact of the youthful and adult independent variables on the two main dependent variables—the 1998 measures of personal religious involvement and church involvement. First we selected the five most powerful youth predictors and the six most powerful adult predictors in our data from the results of preliminary regression analyses involving a wide selection of youth and adult variables that could have potentially predicted the outcome variables. In this fashion we eliminated several of the youth variables, including: years of Catholic school and of CCD (for Catholics), years of Sunday school (for Protestants), parental church attendance, respondent's church attendance as a youth, Bible knowledge, and the Youthful Relativism Scale. We also eliminated several of the adult variables, including interfaith marriage and current marital status. Having selected the 11 most powerful youth and adult predictors we again used regression analysis to regress the predictor variables on our two outcome variables. Table 2 depicts the regression solutions.

Table 2 shows two models for each of the outcome variables, first a test of the predictive power of the youth variables at age 16, then a test of all variables gathered at age 16 and at age 38. From the adjusted R^2 figures we see that the youth variables predict personal religious involvement at age 38 (adjusted $R^2 = 0.297$) much better than they predict church involvement (adjusted $R^2 = 0.094$). It is striking that no measures of parental religious involvement remained in either of the models and that denomination and gender (two structural variables) remained in the model predicting personal religious involvement from the youth variables. This finding reinforces a finding from the original baseline study. The study in 1976 gathered questionnaire data from the parents of the youth and tested various models of value transmission from parents to youth but found weak parent-youth correlations on a whole series of variables. The strongest determinant of the young people's religious beliefs and behavior was the

TABLE 2   *Regression Coefficients for Predictors of Three Adult Outcomes (Betas)*

	Personal Involvement Youth	Religious All	Church Youth	Involvement All
Youth Variables				
Gender (female = 1, male = 0)	0.14*	0.06	0.12	0.02
Original Baptist vs. other (Baptist = 1, others = 0)	0.31*	0.31*	0.11	0.06
Frequency of private prayer	0.14*	0.07	0.02	0.04
Church Youth Program Participation Scale	0.27*	0.32*	0.22*	0.24*
Creedal Assent Scale	0.07	0.05	0.06	−0.04
Adult Variables				
Ever inactive in church life? (yes = 1, no = 0)		−0.19*		−0.26*
Particular even or experience that changed your feelings about the church? (yes = 1, no = 0)		0.16*		0.02
Years of education		0.00		0.00
Joined a different denomination (yes = 1, no = 0)		0.26*		0.30*
Have children (yes = 1, no = 0)		−0.03*		0.13*
Respondent and spouse attend church together (yes = 1, no = 0)		0.08		0.27*
Adjusted R^2	0.297	0.494	0.094	0.395

Note: *Significant at 0.05.

Method of Analysis

Multiple Regression

Multiple regression is a statistical test to help researchers measure the simultaneous influence of two or more independent variables on a dependent variable. For example, research may show that both gender and age individually influence the likelihood of individuals getting an adequate amount of exercise. Multiple regression will help us understand the influence of gender and age (taken together) on exercise level. Because all forms of social life, including human attitudes and behaviors, are shaped by many factors, multiple regression helps us to determine the total influence of two or more factors. Multiple regression uses variables that are measured at the ratio level, that is, on a numerical scale with zero meaning none. For example, if we ask someone how many hours of television he or she watches in an average week, we would receive a number, and if someone said zero, that would mean he or she does not watch any television.

Three dependent variables are examined in this article: (1) having ever become inactive in church life, (2) personal religious involvement, and (3) church involvement. The authors examined the influence of several potential influences (independent variables) on these three dependent variables. These influences include gender, denomination, education level, marital status, and four scales (variables that are a composite of several pieces of information): (1) Youth Creedal Assent (seven items on adherence to traditional Christian creeds), (2) Religious Relativism (five items regarding respect for religious faiths other than one's own), (3) Traditional Sexual Beliefs (two items on beliefs regarding sexually explicit publications and premarital sex), and (4) Program Participation (on participation in seven different types of religious programs). The data set is especially interesting because respondents were asked questions at age 16 (in 1976) and again at age 38 (in 1998).

Table 2 summarizes key parts of the multiple regression analysis for two of the independent variables: personal religious involvement and church involvement. Column A identifies the most influential of the variables that were obtained in the earlier study when respondents were age 16 (referred to as "youth variables") and the most influential of the variables obtained when respondents were age 38 (referred to as "adult variables").

Columns B and C focus on personal religious involvement. Column B shows the influence of only the youth variables, and column C shows the influence of both the youth and adult variables. Columns D and E focus on church involvement. Column D shows the influence of only the youth variables, and column E shows the influence of both the youth and adult variables. The values reported are betas. Beta values tell us how much influence each of the variables *individually* has on the dependent variable. A minus sign means the variables are inversely related (that is, as one goes up, the other goes down). The highest absolute number (that is, ignoring the +/− sign) in this column identifies the independent variable that has the largest influence on the dependent variable. When only the influence of the youth variables on personal religious involvement is examined, being a Baptist (as opposed to being a member of one of the other religious groups) has the largest influence (.31). This can be interpreted that being a Baptist increases personal religious involvement by .31 units. When the youth and adult variables are considered simultaneously, the Youth Program Participation Scale (.32) and being a Baptist (.31) have the largest influence on personal religious involvement.

Some of the betas have an asterisk next to them. The bottom of the table tells us this means the relationship between this independent variable and personal religious involvement is "significant at .05." This refers to the likelihood that a relationship really does exist between these two variables. This can be interpreted that there is at least a 95 percent chance that the two variables are actually related (that is, that we would have found this same relationship if we collected information from everyone in the population).

The R^2 (reported at the bottom of the table), roughly speaking, tells us how much influence all of these variables together have on personal religious involvement. Its possible range is 0 to 1.0. For the youth variables only, the value is .297, which means that these variables explain about 30 percent of personal religious involvement. When the youth and adult variables are both considered, the R^2 value increases to .494—almost 50 percent of personal religious involvement is explained. The third and fourth columns should be interpreted in the same manner. When only the youth variables are considered, which independent variable

(continued)

Method of Analysis (continued)

has the largest influence on church involvement? When the youth and adult variables are considered simultaneously, which variable has the largest influence on church involvement? What percent of church involvement is explained only by the youth variables? By the youth variables and the adult variables considered simultaneously? Do these independent variables do a better job of explaining personal religious involvement or church involvement?

---

denomination they belonged to, not the specific beliefs or behaviors of their parents (Hoge, Petrillo, and Smith 1982).

The adjusted R^2 for the youth variables on personal religion was 0.297, and the adult variables added another 0.197, for a total of 0.494 compared to a total R^2 of 0.395 (0.094 for the youth variables plus 0.201 for the adult) for church involvement. The predictors of adult personal religious behavior were original denomination, participation in church programs as a youth, never becoming inactive, changing denomination as an adult, and having spiritually important experiences as an adult. The predictors of adult church involvement were participation in church youth programs, never becoming inactive, joining a different denomination, having children, and attending church with one's spouse. Thus, the strongest predictors of church involvement occurred *after* age 16 but the predictors of personal religious involvement occurred *before* and *after* age 16.

We were surprised how weak the youth variables were as determinants of church involvement at age 38. The only aspect of youth that proved to be a significant predictor was the amount of involvement in church youth programs. Parents' church attendance (as reported by youth), years of Catholic school, years of Sunday school, private prayer, and church attendance as a youth turned out to be nonsignificant. The *type* of youth group involvement was not very crucial; involvement in choir or folk groups and participation in trips and Bible studies were as predictive of age 38 church involvement as were lectures, courses, and youth worship services. Table 2 shows that events after age 16 were by far the most important determinants of church involvement at age 38: never being inactive, joining a different denomination, having children, and attending church with one's spouse.

Are there differences between men and women in the determinants of personal religious and church involvement at age 38? We calculated regressions for each gender separately and found that the predictive power of the combined variables was consistently stronger for the men. In particular, two adult variables had stronger betas for the personal religious involvement of men than for women. The first variable was whether the men were ever inactive in church life. Having been inactive in church life seemed to have had a more lasting impact on reducing men's personal religious involvement and church involvement. Second was whether the men had joined a different denomination (and this move was no doubt due partly to the influence of their spouses). The men who had switched were relatively stronger in personal religious involvement and church involvement at age 38. While the exact interpretation of these findings is unclear, we were able to predict men's personal religious involvement at age 38 somewhat better than women's, and the difference was in the adult variables. This finding agrees with Stolzenberg, Blair-Loy, and Waite (1995) and Wilson and Sherkat (1994).

Conclusion

Our longitudinal study of youth in the suburbs of Washington, DC provides new insights into questions and theories about what factors produce Christian adults who have an active spiritual life and are involved in church. First, how pervasive is the pattern of dropping out and returning? It is clearly the norm. Overall, 79 percent dropped out at some time, and of them, 56 percent returned by the time we re-interviewed them. Second, youth and adult variables differentially condition personal spirituality and institutional church practice. Adult influences have a greater impact on a person's church involvement in their late 30s than on their spiritual practices. However, both youth and adult experiences influence personal religious involvement and the combined impact of the youth and adult variables means that personal religious involvement is more predictable than church involvement. Church involvement is mostly determined by adult experiences, not earlier religious upbringing, practices, or beliefs.

Third, the finding that almost none of the youth variables gathered at age 16 predicted church going at age 38 was unanticipated, especially because we had a wide variety of variables to test on these persons from when they were 16 years old. But with one exception—youth group participation—none of the youth variables could predict the person's church involvement when they were 38 years old.

Fourth, do denominational differences at age 16 continue until the persons are in their late 30s? Yes. Compared with subjects who were originally Methodist or Catholic, original Baptists were more personally religious in their adulthood. However, original denomination was not predictive of the level of church involvement as an adult.

What religious aspects of childhood and youth have the most long-lasting effects on the personal adult religious involvement of middle-class youth? To our surprise it was not parents' church attendance, the amount that parents talked to their children about religion, frequency of church attendance as a youth, years of Catholic school, years of Catholic CCD, or years of Protestant Sunday school. It was: (1) the culture of the denomination in which the person was raised, including its teachings and habits; and (2) the amount of involvement in church youth programs. Baptist youth were more involved in personal religious practices as adults than either Methodist or Catholic youth.

Something in their Baptist upbringing that we could not specifically measure had a global effect on them. Youth of all denominations who were more involved in church youth groups of any kind were also more involved in personal religious practice.

The youth in our sample were from middle-class families, and many had achieved a high level of education. We had suitable information to assess any impact of higher education and cultural broadening on them after age 16, and our measures of these factors all proved weak. The cultural broadening theory does not appear to have explanatory power for middle-class youth. Rather, factors such as the overall religious culture of the family and denomination, church youth involvement, and later experiences of becoming inactive or joining a different denomination proved more important. Therefore, two theories—social learning theory and family life cycle theory—were somewhat supported by our study and each one proved most useful for a particular outcome. Social learning theory was very pertinent for explaining both personal religious and church involvement, as most of the important factors, e.g., participation in church youth groups, becoming inactive in church, joining a different denomination, can be understood as occasions within which religious modeling and learning takes place. Family life cycle theory was not really pertinent for explaining personal religious involvement and was only somewhat related to church involvement because of the importance of having children. Future researchers need to include denomination as a variable of interest and distinguish between personal and public adult religious outcomes when assessing which factors in childhood and young adulthood predict adult religiosity.

REFERENCES

Bandura, A. 1977. *Social learning theory*. Englewood Cliffs, NJ: Prentice-Hall.

Cornwall, M. 1989. The determinants of religious behavior: A theoretical model and empirical test. *Social Forces* 68(2):572–92.

Dillon, M. 2000. Tracking religious involvement over the life course: Evidence from a 70-year longitudinal study. Paper read at American Sociological Association. Washington, DC.

Dudley, R. L. 1995. Grace, relevancy, and confidence in the future: Why Adventist young adults commit to the church. *Journal of Psychology and Christianity* 14(3):215–27.

———. 1999. Youth religious commitment over time: A longitudinal study of retention. *Review of Religious Research* 14(3):218–27.

Hoge, D. R., W. Dinges, B. Johnson, and J. Gonzales. 2001. *Young adult Catholics: Religion in a culture of choice*. Notre Dame, IN: University of Notre Dame Press.

Hoge, D. R., B. Johnson, and D. A. Luidens. 1993. Determinants of church involvement of young adults who grew up in a Presbyterian churches. *Journal for the Scientific Study of Religion* 32(3):242–55.

Hoge, D. R. and G. H. Petrillo. 1978a. Determinants of church and participation and attitudes among high school youth. *Journal for the Scientific Study of Religion* 17(4):359–79.

———. 1978b. Development of religious thinking in adolescence: A test of Goldman's theories. *Journal for the Scientific Study of Religion* 17(2):139–54.

Hoge, D. R., G. H. Petrillo, and E. I. Smith. 1982. Transmission of religious and social values from par-

ents to teenage children. *Journal of Marriage and the Family* 44(3):569–80.

Hunsberger, B. 1983. Apostasy: A social learning perspective. *Review of Religious Research* 25(1):21–38.

King, M. B. and R. A. Hunt. 1975. Measuring the religious variable: National replication. *Journal for the Scientific Study of Religion* 13:13–22.

Mueller, D. P. and P. W. Cooper. 1986. Religious interest and involvement of young adults: A research note. *Review of Religious Research* 27(3):325–45.

Myers, S. M. 1996. An interactive model of religiosity in inheritance: The importance of family context. *American Sociological Review* 6:858–66.

Roof, W. C. 1978. *Commitment and community*. New York: Elsevier Press.

Roozen, D. A. 1980. Church dropouts: Changing patterns of disengagement and re-entry. *Review of Religious Research* 21(4):427–50.

Stolzenberg, R. M., M. Blair-Loy, and L. J. Waite. 1995. Religious participation in early adulthood: Age and family life cycle effects on church membership. *American Sociological Review* 60:84–103.

Wilson, J. and D. E. Sherkat. 1994. Returning to the fold. *Journal for the Scientific Study of Religion* 33(2):148–61.

Thomas P. O'Connor is the Administrator of Religious Services for the Oregon Department of Corrections. He is an attorney from Ireland who has worked on religious, treatment, and evaluation issues in U.S. social services and criminal justice for the past twelve years. O'Connor was a Carmelite friar (monk) for nine years, working in Ireland, France, and Washington, DC. He has degrees in law, philosophy, theology, and counseling. He has published on the integration of religion and treatment in corrections, and has a Ph.D. from the Catholic University of America. In 2003, Haworth Press published his edited book *Religion, the Community, and the Rehabilitation of Criminal Offenders*.

Dean R. Hoge is professor of sociology at the Catholic University of America in Washington, DC. His main area of specialization is the sociology of religion and values, and he has carried out numerous studies of clergy, church trends, finances of religious bodies, and attitudes of members of different religious denominations. He has published about 100 journal articles and book chapters. Recent books include *Evolving Visions of the Priesthood: Changes from Vatican II to the Turn of the New Century* (with Jacqueline E. Wenger) and *The First Five Years of Priesthood: A Study of Newly Ordained Catholic Priests*.

Estrelda Alexander is a political theologian who is currently an associate professor of pastoral theology at Regent University in Virginia Beach. At the time she participated in this study, she was serving as Associate Dean for Community Life at Wesley Theological Seminary in Washington, DC. Her expertise includes the intersection of spirituality and openness to social justice, ecumenism, multiculturalism, and urban church growth. Her work has centered mainly on involvement and leadership of women and minorities in Pentecostal and Charismatic renewal movements. She is currently working on a definitive theological history of African American Pentecostalism as well as a comprehensive work on the lives and later ministries of the women who were involved in the Azusa Street Revival.

An interview with . . .

Thomas P. O'Connor

How did you become interested in the topic of young people's spirituality and church involvement?

The topic itself was suggested to me by Dean Hoge, the lead author of the study that was done twenty-two years before our study. He always wanted to do a follow-up of the original study and came to me and asked me if I would be interested in taking that on. (I was a part-time graduate student at the time, as I also was involved with a research organization that worked with social organizations helping them evaluate their work.) I had some interest in the area (I'd been working a lot with spiritual development and stages of faith in my own studies) and a chance to do a follow-up to the original study was very interesting to me. I suppose my own journey, too, in and out of church—having been reared pretty religiously, then dropping out for a number of years, then coming back pretty strongly into religion—had given me an interest in that whole area of development.

Why did you pick this methodological approach, survey research? Are there particular strengths of this approach for studying this research question?

I think that with this kind of study, dealing with religiosity or faith development, survey research gives people a chance to explore and to give some context to the work, in addition to giving us concrete, quantifiable data. I think that combination makes survey research very attractive for this subject matter. Dean Hoge is a noted survey researcher. That was another practical reason for using this approach: You go to your strengths on the team, and Dean had particular methodological strength in that area. Also, practically speaking, it really wasn't possible to do it any differently. We didn't have the subjects close at hand, and there was no other way to do this research. But I also think you have to connect with people in the field, and survey research is very good for that.

Were there any particular challenges of doing this research—in particular, doing a longitudinal panel study, which required that you track down all the respondents from the study many years earlier?

That was a major task, maybe 60 or 70 percent of the whole research effort. Dean did the original study, and from the beginning he always knew he wanted to follow up on it. He was very careful in archiving the data and collecting as much information as he could to allow him to do the follow-up study when he could get to it. He wanted to do it a lot sooner than 22 years after the original project and approached several different people to take it on, but he never got it going. So it was difficult for him to get back to the data, even though he had a great data set for a longitudinal study and it was pretty unique in the field. But he finally found me and I was willing to do it. Then we had to look for funding sources. The Louisville Institute gave us a grant to do it, but even then there was a question mark around whether the grant would be big enough to allow us to do it. Originally, for reasons of cost, we were only going to do two of the denominations, but the funders were not happy with that. They wanted three denominations, so they sort of made us stretch to that. Even though we had good records, it was a huge amount of work: retracing the steps, understanding the original data set, coding it property, and finding the people. Estrelda Alexander was the person who managed that whole part of the work. It was a long journey to get in touch with people, but I think we did pretty well with the response rate that we had. The paper mentions the different ways that we used to reach people. Initially, we went to the churches and found people in the church who would look over the church records with us and try to find people that they knew. So that was a good strategy initially, but it didn't yield a huge amount of results. The internet searches, the phone searches, and asking people we found to identify other people really helped us to increase the N. So that process really did take a long time—to get the addresses, to contact people and ask if they were interested in doing a follow up—and as a result, a huge amount of work went into just getting the data.

How did you come to collaborate on the project? What do you see as the disadvantages and advantages in collaborating?

I think collaborating is crucial. The more I am involved in doing research, I find that a team approach is really essential to being able to completing projects. In this project, there was a three-person team, but there were also people that we used as researchers. Dean brought great strength to the project: He wasn't very involved in the actual carrying out of it, but his experience and methodological knowledge were crucial . Without him, I don't think we would have gotten our two articles published (this one, and another one coming out in *Sociology of Religion*). He kept us going by being dogged: "OK, here's this part, now to the next part." That was his role. My role was getting the funding, conceptualizing it, and working and working and working the data. There were so many data that we had from the original study and it was a huge task to consolidate the data and make it manageable and make it fit in with the theoretical models that we were using. Estrelda's Herculean effort was the mechanics of doing the searches, building the data file, contacting the people, getting everything together. None of us could have done it all, so the team approach was crucial. And also, it's a lot more fun to do it with others.

Were there any unexpected events or developments that you faced in doing your research, and how did you deal with those?

We didn't expect that, in the interviews, it was hard to get people to stop talking. We had some open-ended questions, and people just wanted to talk. People were fascinated by the study and very keen to talk, because a lot of them had remembered the original study. We could see that there was this interest and curiosity about what had happened to other people and they had a lot of stories to tell. So we had to train the interviewers how to cut it off to keep the interview moving; that was unexpected. Also, we did the study and were moving along well, and got to the stage where we had papers to present at the religious research association meetings—but then something happened and we dropped off the face of the earth for a long time before we took it from that stage to the publication stage. I'm not even sure what happened, but we certainly ran out of steam. Again, Dean rescued the project by sort of bringing us back together. It was unexpected, too, how tasks and roles fell to people. We didn't have any clear idea of that in the beginning, but it fell to people's strengths. To me, that was unexpected.

What are the implications of your findings? That is, what do they suggest about the usefulness of the different theories that you examined to explain church involvement in adult life?

Earlier I said that we were going to go with only two denominations, but the funders asked us to do the three. That was a crucial decision, because that role of denomination emerged as being a very important factor So, the influence of denomination on personal religiosity, but not so much on church involvement, was an important finding. The theories were essential for helping us to gather and to work with the data, again, going back to that point that there were so many data that we had to work with, and the theories were very helpful in helping us organize the data. In the end, we were surprised at the findings because the whole thrust of the field to that point was on the importance of the family life cycle, and we just didn't find much support for that explanation. Having longitudinal data and splitting the outcome variables into the three categories of personal, religious involvement, and church involvement really helped contribute to those theoretical models. Then, that social learning theory seemed to make so much sense to us and all of the data seemed to fit into that, where only parts of the other data seemed to fit into the other theories, and some of them not at all.

What were the ethical challenges or issues involved in the research and how did you deal with them?

I guess the biggest issue is going back into people's lives when they don't expect you are coming back into them. You have to be very careful there. What we did was to go back to the leadership of the churches of each of their denominations—the bishops, the pastors, and so on—and ask them if they thought it would be appropriate to follow up with people. So we had a letter from each of those leaders endorsing the project and, again, that was because they were interested from the practical side of things in what is happening with people. Once we got that endorsement, we wrote a letter to people, explaining what we were doing, offering to fill them in on the results, and encouraging their participation. We tried to make clear that we were being careful in what we were doing, that we had their churches' interest and backing to do this, and that they were really going to be contributing to something worthwhile. We stressed that their churches supported the research. I think that was the biggest ethical challenge we faced. I don't even know if we would pass a human subjects review board now, because we didn't have consent at the beginning to follow-up with people, which raises some ethical questions.

The finding that later church involvement is so little influenced by all of the youth data was discouraging to church members and bodies. When you find discouraging findings like that, you still need to get them out there and stand behind the methodology—that this is what was found, and not try and look at ways to smooth it. That was an issue for us, as well.

What were the most difficult or frustrating aspects of doing the research?

The most frustrating part was the complexity of gathering the data, going out in the field, finding the names, keeping track of all that, and following up with people. That took an awful lot of attention and was the most technically difficult part of the study. For me, personally, the most difficult—and it represents only about 5 percent of work on the whole project—was writing the article, articulating the concepts, and getting it all to publishable standards. That is, to me, the most difficult part. The amount of time that goes into that is so little compared to the whole project, but it is so hard.

What was the most satisfying about the whole experience?

The relationship between Dean, myself, and Estrelda. I'm surprised, even to this day, how strong the connection came to be among us; that has been very satisfying. Then obviously, getting the articles published—getting past that part of it was very satisfying for me, personally: the sense of completion.

If you were to do the research again, what might you do differently?

There were many people who came in and out of the project at different stages, including many different people who helped with the interviews. What I would do differently is to have a better plan for the interviewers. We were not prepared for the actual mechanics of doing the interviews over the phone. We made it work finally, but that's because we tried a number of things that didn't work, and it took us a lot longer than it should have.

What important lesson would you share with students that you drew from the research experience?

When you are working with a team, you need a leader to follow it through—someone who takes the overall responsibility, which was a role that I took. There has to be somebody who is committed to taking it all the way and who can see the different parts. Also, a theory-based paper takes a lot of up-front work—the literature search, writing the whole introductory section/literature review, reading and understanding the research, and then making the intellectual connection between what you have read and the data you are working with. Although it is difficult technically to collect data, it is almost easier than the intellectual work up front and at the end. Both of those are key tasks—maybe they don't take up the largest amount of time in the project, but they are what hold it together, and that work pays off tremendously in the end. Another lesson is that it doesn't have to be fancy. You might start off with it being very fancy—you know the famous quote from Churchill or someone, "I didn't have time to be short"—I think you have to have time to work with the concepts to make them very simple. That takes time. What you need is not a fancy theory, but a clean one, and that just takes work.

Questions to Think About

1. Why do O'Connor and his colleagues use a longitudinal, panel design? What are some particular strengths of this approach and what, according to O'Connor, were some of the main drawbacks?

2. According to O'Connor, what are some of the benefits of collaboration? What do you expect would also be some drawbacks to working on a research team? If you were planning to do collaborative research, what would you consider as you choose your potential collaborators?

3. What do you learn about the role of theory in social research—and the relationship between theory and data—from reading this article and the accompanying interview?

4. O'Connor and his colleagues received financial support for their research from an outside funder. Does that make this applied research? Why or why not? How did the wishes of the funding agency affect their research?

5. List all the variables that O'Connor and his colleagues included in their model. Which are dependent and which are independent? Which ones did they have some choice about, and which ones were predetermined? Are there other variables that you would have included? What are they?

The Effects of a Parenting Program on Urban African-American Adolescent Fathers

Carl Mazza

Sixty urban African-American adolescent first-time fathers were randomly assigned to two groups to study intervention strategies that would help them develop better and more consistent relationships with their young children. The fathers were administered a pretest interview schedule to determine their present quality of life as well as their relationships with their children. In addition to biweekly parenting classes, each member of the experimental group was assigned a social worker with whom he met weekly to assist him with his life needs. The control group was offered weekly parenting classes that focused on learning how to meet the infants' needs. At the end of six months, both groups were interviewed again. Findings indicated that the experimental group made significant gains in employment, vocational planning, feeling positive about their current relationships with their children, using birth control, being able to plan for the future, and increasing the number of close friends.

During the last two decades, the child welfare field has focused increased attention on the needs of adolescent parents. The term "adolescent parents," however, has frequently been a euphemism for "teenage mothers." As a result of the Adolescent Health, Services and Pregnancy Act of 1978, adolescent maternity and mother-baby programs grew throughout the U.S. Yet despite the number of programs available, few of them concern themselves with adolescent fathers. Adolescent males were to be offered only one service: information regarding pregnancy prevention. This highlights the fact that adolescent fathers are frequently neglected both as potential resources to their children as well as clients with their own unmet needs.

The purpose of this study was to measure the impact of individualized social work intervention with African American adolescent fathers. The study also focused on whether adolescent fathers responded differently to interventions focused on "adolescent issues" rather than only on being a "father."

Review of the Literature

Adolescent Fathers

Prior to 1960, little was written about single parenthood, let alone on unwed adolescent paternity. Vincent (1961) found that for every 25 studies on unwed mothers, only one was on unwed fathers. Yet the 1950s saw a dramatic increase in the number of adolescent pregnancies. A few studies were completed on unwed paternity in the 1960s (Caughlan, 1960; Perkins & Grayson, 1968; Pannor, 1968).

The early literature states that unwed paternity, in itself, should not be thought of as proof of "pathology," rather it should be seen as a point of stress (Caughlan, 1960). Perkins and Grayson's (1968) study of adolescent males in a juvenile detention center found that three quarters lived in single-parent female-headed households; felt deserted by their own fathers; expressed some obligation to marry the girls, not out of love, but to keep their children from growing up "hating" them; and felt "self-hatred" for their status as unwed fathers. Pannor (1968) studied 94 unwed fathers who ranged in age from 15 to 52 years, and findings reflected both judgmental and objective assessments of the fathers. Among the findings were: refusing to use contraceptives was "indicative of the fathers' immaturity"; "unmarried fathers lacked a strong masculine identity"; "unmarried mothers knew the names of the fathers"; "unmarried fathers were able to function adequately in a controlled society"; "younger fathers did not necessarily display delinquent behavior"; and "when unmarried fathers continued to be involved with the mothers, both the fathers and mothers were more able to realistically plan for the baby's future" (Pannor, 1968, pp. 48–49).

Other studies have found that most adolescent and young adult unwed couples have had an ongoing relationship prior to the female becoming pregnant; the young unwed fathers provide emotional support to the children even if they cannot provide financial support; paternal extended families become a viable resource for support to young mothers and children; and there are continual, ongoing relationships between young fathers and their children (Allen & Doherty, 1996; Hendricks, 1981; Miller, 1994; Resnick, 1994; Wade, 1994).

African-American Adolescent Fathers

Hendricks (1981) categorized 8 sets of problems that unwed adolescent African-American fathers encountered throughout their adolescent years: providing financial support for the children; relationships with the children's mothers; relationships with the mothers' families as well as their own; being restricted in their freedom resulting from the needs of the children; attending and completing school; employment; coping with the physical and emotional demands of being fathers; and responsibilities inherent in setting a good example for the children. As a result of fatherhood, adolescent males, including African-American males, enter the workplace earlier than their peers (Hendricks, 1981; Pirot-Good, 1995). However, they are more likely not to complete high school and thus earn less than their peers, when they reach their mid-twenties (Pirot-Good, 1996). Despite these problems, most unwed adolescent fathers view their parenthood as a positive opportunity for growth and development (Allen

& Doherty, 1996; Hendricks, 1981; Miller, 1997; Wade, 1994).

Urban African-American adolescent fathers, by definition, are hindered by historical limitations. They live in a society that considers them "lesser" as a result of racism; experience the prejudice that holds that fathers are the less important parents; and, often, lack adequate financial resources. Ockerman (1979) states that when certain groups are held at a lower level of esteem, the individual members who have internalized this value system will judge themselves accordingly. The resulting anger can be channeled either into "acceptable" forms of action such as sports or the arts, or directed inward, resulting in drug addiction, alcoholism, depression, and excessive gambling—all in an attempt to shut out the outside world.

This chronic sense of low self-esteem, depression, and apathy leads to hopelessness and the inability to believe that there can be a positive future. Such alienation can be transmitted from one generation to the next, creating an intergenerational depression (Perrucci & Pilisuk, 1973).

Clark (1989) divides the African-American adolescent residents of the inner cities into three main groups: the achievers, the overt delinquents, and the in-between. The achievers are those who insist on going to school and then to college. They receive support and encouragement from their families, friends, and teachers and map out a plan for their future which they are determined to fulfill. The overt delinquents concentrate their efforts on aggressive, rebellious, defiant, and ultimately self-destructive behaviors. They feel the rejection of the larger society intensely, so they reject (or appear to reject) the larger society and its values and customs. They feel that because of the limitations placed upon them by the ghetto, "success," largely defined as economic achievement, if it comes, will be through a "street life" of crime, violence, and aggression. Incarceration and early death are seen as inevitable and perhaps also as badges of honor.

The largest group in the ghetto is the "in-between." These young men are aware of the larger society's values and aspirations and have not rejected them, but feel inadequately equipped to live up to them. Without successful intervention, they grow up to be marginalized adults who accept the imbalance of power and opportunity.

This group represents the largest number of participants in social service programs. They are the ones who accept the societal value of paternal responsibility—of being able to provide financially and emotionally for their children—but at the same time, they question their ability to succeed. They want to enroll in educational and vocational programs, but are uncertain of their ability to complete them; they want to obtain employment, but question their employability; they want to love and care for their children, but are unsure that they have the patience and understanding to do so. They fear that they may not have anything of value to offer their children. These doubts can block their ability to learn and incorporate appropriate parenting skills such as consistency and nurturing (Allen & Doherty, 1996; Hendricks, 1981; Miller, 1997).

Thus, in order for them to become consistent, nurturing parents, they need to feel more confident about themselves. This requires individualized social work interventions.

Present Study

This study explored the needs of urban African-American adolescent fathers and how to best meet these needs so they can experience personal success and become consistent and nurturing fathers. Since these fathers frequently have unmet emotional needs of their own, the study hypothesized that those who become involved in a therapeutic relationship with a professional social worker, augmented by available services and programs, will evidence significant positive change. This would be reflected by increased success in establishing and meeting individual goals, developing stronger support systems, and developing more consistent and positive feelings about their relationships with their children now and in the future. Further, it was presumed that male social workers would be better able to establish an effective therapeutic relationship and provide a positive role model for parenting.

Method

Sample

The study sample was composed of 60 urban African-American adolescent fathers, living in lower income neighborhoods of New York City, randomly divided into an experimental and a control group. All were first-time fathers between the ages of 16 and 18 years. Their children's mothers were all receiving services either through a teen mothers' support program at a local hospital or in a mother-baby group residence. The mean age of the children was 9.0 months at Time 1. On average, the couples had known each other for close to a year before the young women became pregnant. The fathers were initially contacted through the adolescent mothers' programs. The mothers were asked if they thought that the fathers would be interested in participating in a fathers' program. The social work researcher then asked the fathers if they wanted to participate in a program designed exclusively for young fathers. Issues regarding confidentiality were discussed with the fathers, and each was randomly assigned to either the experimental or control group.

Procedure

An interview schedule was administered to both groups at two separate times. In order to control for cultural differences, the study was limited to African American men between the ages of 16 and 18 from one geographical area. Thirty fathers were randomly assigned to each group. The interview schedule at Time 1 measured their current perceptions of themselves, of their children, of their children's mothers, their support systems, their ideas of fatherhood, and their goals for the future. Subsequently, the experimental group received weekly individual counseling, biweekly group counseling, educational/vocational referrals and placements, medical care and referrals, housing and legal advocacy, cultural and recreational activities, and parenting skills training. The specific interventions for the young men in the experimental group were established after asking each one to verbally list those areas in his life where he thought he would need assistance. The control group received only the weekly group parenting skills training; however, they were invited to participate in the hospital's or child welfare agency's case planning for their children. In six months (Time 2), after the subjects once again were administered the interview schedule, their responses were compared to their initial answers. Data were analyzed through the use of SPSS and chi-square analysis.

Initially, a nonprofit child welfare agency provided release time for a social worker to develop this experimental program. Once the program was designed, foundation grants were obtained for the expansion of the experimental program to include a second social worker, a parenting instructor, and an educational-vocational counselor. The staff included both black and white professionals. The experimental program eventually became permanent within the agency.

Findings

Results of this study indicate that programs for young fathers that focus only on teaching parenting skills are ineffective. Statistically significant changes noted between the control and experimental groups related to employment rates, vocational plans, current relationship with child, predicting the quality of the future relationship with child, ability to develop a ten-year plan, frequency of practicing family planning, number of close friends, and person with whom a problem can be discussed.

Rates of Employment and Vocational Plans

Employment and the ability to support a family is a basic expectation of fatherhood in our society. Likewise, the existence of vocational plans and possession of marketable skills speak to the ability to financially plan for the future. At Time 1, the majority of the young fathers in both the experimental and control groups were unemployed (see Table 1). By Time 2, 29 of the 30 participants in the experimental group (97%) were employed,

while only 8 of the 26 participants in the control group (31%) were employed, a highly significant finding ($p < .01$).

Another statistically significant finding was in regard to the existence of vocational plans. At Time 2, 87% of the experimental group respondents had specific vocational plans, compared to 50% at Time 1. In contrast, the control group experienced a slight decrease in the existence of vocational planning.

Current Relationship with Child

When asked to rate the quality of their current relationship with their children at Time 2, 77% of the experimental group reported that it was "excellent" or "good." This is significantly higher than the 50% of the control group who selected "excellent" or "good" for this variable.

Expectation of Future Relationship with the Child

The fathers were asked to predict the closeness, quality, and consistency of their relationships with their children in the future. This variable addresses the fact that many urban adolescents do not see any positive future for themselves. By Time 2, 63% of the experimental group projected that their future relationship with their children will be "excellent," compared to only 27% of the control group.

Development of a Ten-Year Plan

The ability to develop long-range plans speaks to the ability of the young fathers to organize themselves to do so. Persons can plan for the future only if they believe there will be one. When asked about a ten-year plan (Table 1), there was a statistically significant change in the experimental group's ability to develop such a plan.

Use of Contraceptives

Those in the experimental group greatly increased their use of contraceptives. At Time 2, 90% of the respondents in the experimental group said that they "always" or "often" used

TABLE 1 *Statistically Significant Variables*

	TIME I (PREPROGRAM)		TIME 2		
	Experimental (*n* = 30)	Control (*n* = 30)	Experimental (*n* = 30)	Control (*n* = 26)	*p*
Employment					
Yes	47%	33%	97%	31%	.01
No	53%	67%	3%	69%	
Vocational Plans					
Yes	50%	47%	87%	42%	.01
No/Don't Know	50%	54%	13%	58%	
Current Relationship with Child					
Excellent/Good	53%	47%	77%	50%	.02
Fair/Poor	46%	53%	23%	50%	
Future Relations with Child					
Excellent/Good	94%	83%	96%	73%	.02
Fair/Poor	6%	17%	4%	27%	
10-Year Plan					
Graduate from School	2%	0%	7%	0%	.01
Employment	68%	66%	90%	49%	
Don't Know	30%	33%	3%	50%	
Use Birth Control					
Always/Often	10%	7%	90%	73%	.01
Sometimes	90%	93%	10%	27%	
Define Being a Man					
Strong/Protector	26%	36%	3%	43%	.01
Provider	10%	13%	7%	19%	
Responsible	43%	37%	90%	38%	
Other	20%	13%	0%	0%	
Number of Close Friends					
0	30%	40%	10%	35%	.03
1–2	63%	50%	74%	61%	
3–4	6%	10%	16%	4%	
Discuss a Problem with . . .					
Relative	3%	20%	3%	23%	.01
Friend	33%	33%	13%	27%	
Child's Mother	10%	10%	10%	15%	
Social Worker	9%	13%	73%	8%	
Don't Know/No One	45%	24%	0%	27%	

Method of Analysis

Chi-Square

Chi-square (χ^2) is a popular statistic for determining the relationship between two categorical variables. In this article, Mazza uses chi-square to determine the effects of participation in a special parenting program (the independent variable) for adolescent, African American fathers on a series of dependent variables, including employment, vocational plans, current relationship with child, and use of birth control methods. Mazza wants to learn if there are any benefits in adding weekly meetings with a social worker, to help with life needs, to the traditional biweekly parenting skills class.

The relationships between categorical variables are often presented in table format. In Table 1, percentages are reported for the experimental and control groups for easier reading and to facilitate comparisons. The chi-square statistic, the results of which are reported in the second half of the table, is calculated using raw numbers that are often not reported. A full analysis considers these percentages and the χ^2 results. With regard to the employment variable, 47 percent of the experimental group (which received the added meetings with a social worker) and 33 percent of the control group (which received only the biweekly parenting skills class) were employed at the beginning of the study. By the end of the study, the percent employed had more than doubled in the experimental group (to 97 percent) but had remained about the same (31 percent) in the control group. As you compare the before and after data for each group, you will detect consistent advantages for the members who received the weekly meeting with the social worker in addition to the parenting skills class.

However, are these differences significantly large enough that we can be confident that they are an effect of the program and not simply due to chance? Calculation of the chi-square statistic answers this question. Although the exact chi-square values are not reported in this article, the level of probability that a relationship really exists (that is, that the program had an effect) are reported. By convention, researchers want the level of probability that the relationship is due to chance to be less than 5 percent. (In other words, we wish to be at least 95 percent confident that the relationship really exists.) The *p* value represents the level of probability that the relationship is due to chance. Because the value of *p* is less than .05 for all nine dependent variables, we can conclude with more than 95 percent confidence that the additional parenting program added to the biweekly meetings really did help participants on all of these measures.

birth control, an increase from 10% at Time 1. At Time 2, 73% of the control group stated that they "always" or "often" used contraceptives, compared with 7% at Time 1.

Description of Being a Man

The subjects were asked to provide a description of what it means to be a man, since it was felt that as the young men's sense of self and vision of the world increased, their descriptions of what it means to be a man would become more complex and emotionally laden (Table 1). At Time 1 both groups gave similar responses. The most frequent response was "responsible," with 37% of the control group and 43% of the experimental group selecting this response. At Time 2 there was a statistically significant change for the experimental group, with 90% of the respondents choosing that term. The control group, on the other hand, remained relatively stable at 38%.

Number of Close Friends

The number of close friends speaks to the issue of isolation, and its opposite, support systems. Growth in the number of close friends can obviously result in an increase in a person's support network (see Table 1). At Time 2 there was a statistically significant change in the experimental group, but not in the control group. The modal response at Time 2 in the experimental group remained "two close friends," as indicated by 57% of the respondents, compared to 40% at Time 1. The most frequent response in the control group was "zero close friends," with 40% at Time 1 giving this answer and 35% at Time 2.

With Whom Would the Young Fathers Discuss a Problem?

Discovering with whom, if anyone, the young fathers would discuss a problem speaks to the existence of support systems and its antithesis, a sense of isolation. By Time 2, 73% of the experimental group selected "social worker" as the answer. The control group's most popular response was "friend," which was selected by only 27%. By Time 2 no one in the experimental group selected "don't know" or "no one," compared with 19% and 8%, respectively, for the control group (Table 1).

Discussion

Of all the variables measured in the study, none was more dramatic than the change in employment status within the experimental group. By Time 2, 29 of the 30 respondents had obtained employment. There are several reasons for this success rate. First, the social work relationship was instrumental in helping the young men recognize their strengths and talents. In so doing, the young men began to face the world of work with more confidence, determination, and, ultimately, success. Second, one of the social workers was responsible for networking for jobs, and he convinced several small business owners to employ a few of the young men. He also contacted some local city politicians for possible employment leads. Third, several of the young men also received job leads through people at the schools they now attended. The program stressed and supported education and was instrumental in helping many of the young men return to high school. This often meant helping them enroll in small alternative schools where they would receive a good deal of individualized attention. Thus, their involvement in school and finding employment were often related.

The casework intervention also allowed the young men to become more goal oriented, self-directed, and self-confident, as reflected in their ability to develop a 10-year plan. The number of career choices in the experimental group increased from four at Time 1 to eight at Time 2. As the young fathers began to recognize and believe in more of their own strengths, the number of perceived options that were available to them increased. Likewise, as they began to feel more successful, their expectations of potential career choices increased.

Most of the young men in the experimental group recognized the importance of their role in raising and caring for a child; consequently, they took precautions to prevent another pregnancy. Further, the experimental program placed strong emphasis on family planning. After six months, many of the young men seemed to have incorporated this idea as reflected in their increased requests for free condoms from the social workers.

Moreover, the experimental group significantly decreased what appears to be their sense of isolation by increasing the number of close friends. With the experimental component including both group sessions and recreational activities, many of the new friendships seemed to have resulted from their interactions within the program. Also, a rise in positive sense of self and self-confidence and involvement in other social institutions, such as school and the world of work, facilitated the establishment of new friendships.

Another aspect of decreasing the sense of social isolation is reflected in the answers to the question concerning whom the young fathers would select to discuss a problem. At Time 2, nearly three quarters of all respondents in the experimental group stated that they would talk to their social workers. Certainly this speaks to the importance of the therapeutic social work relationships. The social workers were not only seen as supportive and nurturing, but also seen as important role models.

The control group did not experience any significant change in any of the variables measured. The services offered in the control group were based on the assumption that the adolescent fathers could become better parents simply by acquiring parenting information. However, it appears that since the young fathers did not recognize their own strengths and potential, the parenting information could not be incorporated into their lives.

Limitations of the Study

Since all of the subjects were African-American adolescent males residing in one urban community, the generalizability of the findings are limited. Further, since all of the young fathers voluntarily participated in the study, it is possible that they were more motivated to seek and accept help than other adolescent fathers. Moreover, both social workers in the study were males, further limiting the generalizability of the outcomes.

Future Research

More research is needed on all aspects of adolescent fatherhood. Cultural and societal factors should be examined as to how they define young men's roles as fathers. Social and governmental institutions such as schools, pediatric clinics, child welfare agencies, and after-school programs need to be studied to determine how they encourage the participation of young fathers within their programs.

Practice Implications

The study has demonstrated that young African-American men can certainly be engaged in social work relationships, and make significant changes in their lives. Indeed, the social workers did not have much difficulty in developing therapeutic relationships with them. When these young men feel respected, liked, and wanted, they are very willing to enter into social work relationships.

What made the experimental group so successful were these close therapeutic relationships with the social work staff. The relationships not only individualized the services offered, but much more importantly, they helped the young men feel good about both themselves and the services available to them. The social work relationship provided them with a supportive environment and the opportunity to learn about themselves, to discover their strengths, to realize their importance, and to confront their weaknesses. It broke down their feelings of isolation and loneliness and gave them someone to connect with. It also gave them role models, not just as fathers or men, but as people worthy of respect.

The social workers in the experimental group were enthusiastic and had a sense of commitment. They had consistently high, but realistic, expectations for the young fathers, and never had any doubt that the young fathers could learn skills, find and maintain employment, and maintain loving relationships with their children. This enthusiasm seemed to be transmitted to the young fathers, increasing their sense of self-worth.

Since the two social workers in the experimental group were of different races, the findings indicate that race was not a factor in the success rate.

Policy Implications

When adolescent parenting is discussed in American society, a frequently asked question is, "Can teenage boys become good fathers?" The mere asking of the question implies that young men neither want to be nor are responsible fathers. The question is sexist and ageist, and certainly can also be racist since the typical mass media portrait of out-of-wedlock adolescent parents is of young people of color. Social policies both on the governmental and social service levels have often ignored these young fathers. While local governments on occasion now make some small provision for services to adolescent fathers, the money and resources allotted is minute when compared to the amount allocated to young mothers.

Child welfare agencies that provide services to children need to examine their policies concerning fathers. Fathers continue to receive fewer services than mothers, who are still viewed as the primary parents. Yet there is a great difference between "primary" and "only" parent. In order to serve the best needs of infants and children in child welfare placements, agencies need to rethink their commitment to young fathers, and develop opportunities for them to become involved with and act in the best interests of their children.

Although the provision of comprehensive individualized services to young African-American fathers may be expensive and may require specialized funding, the benefits far outweigh the costs. The benefits are to both individuals and society in terms of adding to community participation, increasing the pool of competent potential employees, lessening the societal burden of caring for indigent children, lowering crime rates, and improving quality of life. Most importantly, it builds families and holds them together.

Conclusions

This study points out that developing programs for young fathers that focus only on teaching parenting skills is not enough. Such skills training becomes effective only when parents believe they have something to offer to their children. Young African-American fathers have many unmet needs of their own. They need therapeutic social work relationships where they can discover their strengths, explore their feelings, and face their fears. They need to use the social work relationship as a tool for modeling not just appropriate parental behavior, but also social behavior. Further, they need other services such as educational/vocational referral, group counseling, legal and housing advocacy, medical care, and recreational and cultural activities.

The therapeutic relationship "allowed" the young fathers to accept these other services and use them successfully. Thus, the importance of the social work relationship must be acknowledged.

REFERENCES

Allen, W., & Doherty, W. (1996). The responsibilities of fatherhood as perceived by African-American teenage fathers. *Families in Society, 77*(2), 142–155.

Caughlan, J. (1960). Psychic hazards of unwed paternity. *Social Work, 5*(1), 24–38.

Clark, K. (1989). *Dark ghetto: Dilemmas of social power* (2nd ed). Hanover, NH: Wesleyan University Press.

Hendricks, L. E. (1981). *An analysis of two select populations of black unmarried adolescent fathers.* Washington, DC: Howard University Institute for Urban Affairs and Research.

Miller, D. B. (1997). Influences on parental involvement of African-American adolescent fathers. *Child and Adolescent Social Work Journal, 7*(3), 363–378.

Ockerman, J. D. (1979). *Self-esteem, and social anchorage of adolescent white, black and Mexican-American students.* Palo Alto, CA: R and E Research Associates.

Pannor, R. (1968). The unmarried father. Demonstration and evaluation of an assertive casework approach. In National Council on Illegitimacy (Ed.), *Illegitimacy: Data and findings for prevention treatment and policy implications.* New York: National Council on Illegitimacy.

Perkins, R. F., & Grayson, E. S. (1968). The juvenile unwed father. In National Council on Illegitimacy (Ed.), *Effective services for unmarried parents and their children: Innovative community approaches.* New York: National Council on Illegitimacy.

Perrucci, R., & Pilisuk, M. (1973). Racism, poverty; and inequality. In H. A. Faberman & E. Goode (Eds.), *Social reality.* Englewood Cliffs, NJ: Prentice-Hall.

Pirot-Good, M. A. (1995). The family background and attitudes of teen fathers. *Youth and Society, 26* 351–356.

Pirot-Good, M. (1996). The education and labor market outcomes of adolescent fathers. *Youth and Society, 28,* 236–262.

Resnick, M. D., Wattenberg, E., & Breuer, R. (1994). The fate of the nonmarital child: A challenge to the health system. *Journal of Community Health, 19,* 285–401.

Vincent, C. E. (1961). *Unmarried mothers.* New York: Free Press.

Wade, J. C. (1994). African-American fathers and sons: Social, historical and psychological considerations. *Families in Society, 75,* 561–570.

Carl Mazza is an assistant professor of social work at Lehman College of the City University of New York. He sits on the board of directors of Exodus Transitional Services, a nonprofit organization located in East Harlem, New York, working with people transitioning from prison. He is also a consultant to In Arms Reach Children's Services, the Women's Prison Association, and the Osborne Association. In addition, he is affiliated with Northshore Children and Family Guidance Services in Westbury, New York. He has worked in the fields of criminal and juvenile justice and child welfare for over twenty-five years, and has published on incarcerated parents, children of incarcerated parents, adolescent fathers, men in groups, and practicing social work in prisons. Mazza is presently working on a book concerning contemporary issues regarding fatherhood in the United States.

An   interview   with . . .

Carl Mazza

How did you become interested in the topic of adolescent parenting?

Prior to starting the research, I had worked for about ten years with juvenile delinquent boys. Whenever one of the boys' girlfriends got pregnant, he became very concerned about it. So, from my own experience, I realized that the stereotype of the uncaring, selfish teenage boy was not true. When I began working as director of a group home, there were two homes: one was for teen mothers and their babies, the other was for pregnant teens. Although the programs were very well run, they offered very few services to the fathers-to-be. I knew from my experience that the guys I worked with in the past couldn't have been unique, so that's how I became interested in this. Also, at the time I was finishing my doctoral classes and I needed to get a dissertation topic, so that was a big motivation as well. Something I really appreciated that I heard in graduate school was "Do research on what is available." Unless you get a big grant or something and can go off and do research in an area or a place that you don't know anything about, you have to start where you are in your life experience, and that's what I did.

So you chose this program because it is the one that you were already working with?

Yes, that was the starting point. I had done some consulting work teaching parenting skills to men and I knew that I wanted to put together a parenting program for the boys—certainly not the same intensity as for the girls (since it was a residential program for the girls), but something for the young fathers. I had an idea that what I did for thirty-year-old middle class men, in terms of parenting, probably would not be appropriate with these young guys. But all I found were traditional parenting programs, so I decided to create my own and then to evaluate it as I went along.

What led you to this particular research design?

As a social worker and as a teacher, I always got most excited about the process—that is, starting with the client or the student at point A and looking back six months later and seeing where there has or hasn't been growth. This is something that I get satisfaction from, both as an educator and as a social worker. So when I was thinking of research designs, a Time One and Time Two seemed perfect to meet my needs by showing if there is any continuum of growth, and also as a way to judge if this program was going to be effective or not.

What do you see as some of the particular challenges that face social scientists who are doing applied research/evaluation research?

The big thing, I think, is time. In the regular course of a day there is never enough time, and then to do this research on top of that can be very difficult. You can do research without a whole lot of money, but part of the problem within the social work profession is this idea that you are *either* a researcher *or* a practitioner. If you do research, you need time to do it, and lots of people don't want to give you that time. So while I was doing this research—and even though people knew I was doing this in large part because of my doctorate—I often got the sense that it is "them or us," which I don't think is helpful either to our profession or our clients. That makes it difficult to get the support I needed, especially in terms of time. That was a challenge sometimes.

Were there any unexpected events, developments, or challenges that you faced?

Part of the difficulty in this sort of research design is that a lot of time has to pass between Time One and Time Two and I couldn't expedite the process; I just had to wait until Time Two. So I couldn't say, "I'm going to clear my calendar this week and concentrate on this" because I had to wait for the calendar date, and that became a bit frustrating when I wanted to move the research forward. Another problem was that Time One and Time Two didn't occur all at the same time, as boys continued to enter the program.

What about findings? Which were most surprising and least surprising?

What was least surprising, but in some ways most rewarding, was that as the young men in the experimental group really began to feel more cared about and cared for, they developed more support mechanisms. They felt better about themselves, so they found the strength to develop more support on their own. And as the supports developed, they got more success and felt even better about themselves, and it became a real positive cycle. What I learned about the importance of the relationship with the social worker was gratifying, but also probably the least surprising. That's because I'd been lucky in my experiences as a social worker and have worked with people who believed I'd been helpful in my relationship with them. I think what was most surprising was not really a finding, but what we learned about many of the young men. On the surface they looked like pretty "together" guys—they were healthy, they looked relatively happy, they were in good shape, they dressed pretty well. But when the social workers got to know them, the number of them who were one step away from being homeless was amazing. They would spend a couple nights at an aunt's house, then they'd go to a friend's house and fall asleep in front of the television with the hopes that they wouldn't be woken up. Here was an amazing number of relatively healthy sixteen-year-olds who had never gone to a dentist in their lives, who hadn't had a wellness physical in seven years. Those things surprised me the most. Intellectually you know that exists, but putting a face on those statistics (for example, of young people who have never visited a dentist) I found pretty powerful. And I think the closeness to homelessness was a very surprising finding.

What are the contributions and implications of your findings?

I was extremely fortunate because I worked for an agency that was very supportive of my research in many ways. Once I finished the research, I reported the results in grant proposals and managed to get funding for a separate program that still exists to this day, though I am no longer with the program. The agency used everything that was in the experimental program—individualized relationships with social workers, and so on—and that was incredibly satisfying because I could see the impact of my finding about what works. Some of this is having a wider effect, too. When I was in the program, some foundations that funded us put money aside for public relations, so during the first couple of years of the new program, some of the boys and I were on several television shows, in documentaries—there was even a story in *People* magazine about the program. We were contacted by people from across the country, especially because of the *People* article, and some asked permission to replicate our program. Whether it was ever actually replicated I don't know, but I think we did a very positive thing in challenging the stereotype of uncaring, immature, selfish teenage fathers. I like to think that this has had an impact on wider views of adolescent fathers. Certainly the fact that young men who have been in our program have led wonderful lives—good men, good fathers—bodes very well for the program and how we operated it.

Were there any particular ethical challenges or issues in your research?

The main ethical dilemma had to do with who got the benefits of the research. In order to limit the number of variables that I had to consider, I only included African American adolescent fathers in the research, mostly because at the beginning there were more African American kids than any other group. But I was conscious of the fact that the kids in the study shouldn't get more than the other kids and tried to make sure that the other young men in the program weren't being ignored or neglected. Another ethical challenge is one that we always face in this sort of research; that is, early on I could see positive changes in the boys in the experimental group that I didn't see to the same degree in the control group. I was tempted to say "Let's stop the study and give these kids [the control group] the same services." But of course we couldn't do that because if we didn't have the control group, we'd have nothing to compare the experimental group with. Once the research was done, we incorporated those guys in so they ultimately got the same services as the experimental group, but it was an ethical dilemma, to see something working that you don't make available to everybody.

Any other frustrations?

One I talked about already: the length of time between Time One and Time Two. Also, managing my time was hard. I was never a full-time researcher, and had to do this on top of other things, so time management was an issue. And statistics have never been my strong point, so once I got my data I needed to get someone to help me use SPSS [Statistical Package for the Social Sciences] to analyze it. That was a bit frustrating because I wished I were better at that myself. I had studied it in graduate school, but always thought "I'm never going to use this."

If you were to do the research again, is there anything you would do differently?

If I were to repeat this study, I would not limit it to one ethnic or racial group. Actually, it would be interesting to repeat it without limiting it to one racial or ethnic group and see if the results would be the same. My gut feeling is that they would be exactly the same. I think that is the only thing I would do differently. I am also more experienced with IRBs [Institutional Review Boards] than I was then. That project was done about two months before IRB approval became mandatory. Since then I've gone before the IRB a number of times and that was a new experience initially. Like anything, I've learned how to do that and how to work with them.

Are there any lessons that you learned that would be useful to share with students?

One is that you can't enter research with the idea that you are either a researcher or a practitioner; social workers need to be both. Also, research is more than just the accumulation of knowledge; I think my study is a good example of this. Because of this research, this became a funded program. Finally, don't underestimate the value of numerical data. The reality is that the program would not have been funded unless I came into the foundations with some results. It is never easy to get money from foundations, but it was probably ten times easier getting into the door with numbers rather than saying "This is what I think we should do, this is what feels right." I had data to back me up. Many social workers think they are not great with numbers, but that is probably the most important lesson.

Questions to Think About

1. How do Mazza's own values and beliefs (and perhaps those of the social work profession) come into play in his research—his choice of topic, critique of previous research, conclusions, and implications?

2. What is Mazza's main ethical concern? In your view, how serious an issue is it? Is there a way that a researcher can avoid this issue in this sort of research (that is, experimental design that is assessing the benefits of some intervention or treatment)? How?

3. What are some ways that time figures into Mazza's research, both in the basic research design and in some of the frustrations and challenges he faced in carrying out his evaluation project?

4. What are Mazza's outcome (or dependent) variables? Where do they come from? What do the outcome variables in any program evaluation represent?

5. What might be another, different approach to evaluating the effectiveness of the intervention that Mazza studies? What might be some benefits or limitations of your alternative approach?

6. How important is social science research training for practitioners (social workers, counselors, educators, and so on)? What are some of the tensions between practice and research? Why do you think they exist?

chapter 3

Research Design, Sampling, and Measurement

Some of the most important decisions that a researcher must make, apart from deciding *what* to study, have to do with *how* to study—the basic design of the study, what variables to include and how to measure them, and what or whom to include in one's sample. The articles in this book were chosen to illustrate a wide range of research designs and approaches and, in response to our questions, all the researchers tell us something about why they made the choices they did about the design of their research. What led them to choose a qualitative or quantitative approach? How did they decide what variables to include and how to conceptualize and operationalize each? What are the factors that they considered in choosing a sample? Their answers, and the articles themselves, give much information about the many different factors that influence decisions about research design—things like people's own proclivities and training, the particular needs of a sponsoring agency, the pattern of previous research in the area, and the availability of a site or data set.

In this chapter we include two articles that deal with the same general topic— smoking as a gendered practice—but they do so using dramatically different research approaches, one quantitative and the other qualitative. Marjorie MacDonald and Nancy Wright employ secondary analysis of survey data to explore gender differences and other factors that correlate with smoking among Canadian high school students. Penny Tinkler prefers a qualitative and historical approach; she explores representations of smoking in magazines aimed at young women in Great Britain from 1918–1939. Although their research designs could hardly be more different, each faced decisions that all social science researchers must make regarding what to study (the sample) and how to study it.

MacDonald and Wright chose secondary analysis to explore gender differences in smoking, with particular attention to how girls' decisions to smoke might be influenced by certain conditions of their lives, particularly their school climate and their relationships with school administrators and parents. The research focus came from

MacDonald's observations during an earlier evaluation project about teen smoking. As she explains it, the large survey database had a number of advantages, mainly that she was familiar with it, it was available and easy to access, and it contained the variables that she was interested in exploring. The large size and representativeness of the sample also make their conclusion—that girls and boys smoke for very different reasons—all the more compelling, particularly as it implies the need for radically new approaches to smoking cessation programs in high schools.

Penny Tinkler was also quite familiar with her data sources as a result of previous research: qualitative and historical content analysis that explored how popular young women's magazines represented gender and gender relations in Britain in the mid-twentieth century. When her focus turned to smoking, the same approach using some of those same magazines made practical sense. But as she explains in her interview, the choice of this research design was a good one for a number of other reasons as well: The magazines contained many different kinds of images of women smoking, their 1920s emancipation theme suggested a connection with women and smoking, and they were targeted across social class and age groups, two additional variables that were important to Tinkler's study. As a social historian working in a sociology department, Tinkler's training undoubtedly helped shape her choice of method as well.

Choosing a sample is usually quite different for quantitative and qualitative researchers, yet some of the same principles and considerations shape this decision-making process for both. For quantitative researchers, representativeness is critical. MacDonald and Wright describe in some detail the different stages of the process by which their sample was selected and in what ways the resulting sample is (and is not) representative and thus does (and does not) allow them to generalize their findings. Tinkler, on the other hand, describes a sample that was chosen with quite different criteria in mind—not generalizability, but rather analytical usefulness by virtue of the kinds of images and audiences that are most important to her study.

Finally, each study illustrates different dimensions and challenges of measurement, another key feature of research design that poses somewhat different challenges to quantitative and qualitative researchers. MacDonald and Wright chose their variables ahead of time and describe in great detail how each is operationalized in the original study from which their data are drawn. In contrast, and like most qualitative researchers, Tinkler develops her concepts and measures largely in the course of her data collection, rather than as part of a research plan that is in place before the research begins. Her measures are not entirely emergent—she has a fairly clear idea of what she is looking for when she begins her data collection—but the narrative of her article suggests the greater fluidity of measurement as well as other kinds of decisions made by qualitative researchers.

These two articles illustrate other important aspects of social research apart from the features of research design. Both assume a feminist research perspective. Whereas Tinkler explores how smoking became gendered with the help of representations in popular magazines, MacDonald and Wright examine the ways that the structural powerlessness and alienation of young women help to explain their alarming rate of smoking. Both claim to offer only description rather than any sort of causal explanation of the phenomena they study. In addition, the implications of their research are quite different. Tinkler's analysis is engaging and informative, but it suggests no action agenda. In contrast, MacDonald and Wright's findings suggest that to be effective, anti-smoking campaigns for adolescent girls ought to focus not on individual behaviors, but rather on changing the structure and organization of the oppressive settings within which young women live their lives.

Cigarette Smoking and the Disenfranchisement of Adolescent Girls: A Discourse of Resistance?

Marjorie MacDonald and Nancy E. Wright

The consequences of smoking for women are of particular concern in light of recent observations that more adolescent females than males are taking up smoking. To date, few studies have explored gender differences in depth, but we do know that males and females smoke for different reasons and that current smoking prevention programs may be differentially effective depending on gender. Recent evidence suggests that the school environment may have an important influence on smoking. The purpose of this study, therefore, was to explore gender differences in the relationships between cigarette smoking and adolescents' experiences of school climate and their relationships with the school and significant adults in their lives.

A secondary data analysis was done using a data set derived from a student survey conducted in 20 secondary schools in British Columbia (BC), Canada, which included 8,179 students in grades 8 to 12. Analyses were primarily descriptive. The results demonstrated that adolescent girls who smoke are more likely than either males or non-smoking females to experience powerlessness in their school environment and to feel considerably less attachment to the school. Female smokers are more likely than males or female nonsmokers to be engaged in oppositional, distanced, and unsatisfactory relationships with important adults in their lives, particularly those who are in positions of relative power and authority. These findings are discussed in relation to critical and feminist perspectives that suggest smoking is part of a larger discourse of resistance within schools. The implications for health practitioners are discussed.

Background

In Canada, smoking causes more than 20% of all deaths (Makomaski Illing & Kaiserman, 1999; McCreary Centre Society, 2001). Tobacco use is the leading cause of preventable disease, chronic disability, and premature death throughout the Western world (Health Canada, 1999; Johnston, O'Malley, & Bachman, 2000). Regular tobacco use is clearly linked with diseases such as lung cancer, chronic bronchitis, coronary heart disease, and emphysema (Health Canada, 1999). Approximately half of all long-term smokers will die prematurely as a result of smoking, and one quarter will die in middle age (McCreary Centre Society, 2001).

Most people who are going to smoke have begun by the time they are 20 years old (United States Department of Health and Human Services [USDHHS], 1994). Smoking rates among adolescents have been on the rise since 1990 in Canada (Health Canada, 1999) and 1992 in the United States (Johnston, O'Malley, & Bachman, 1993, 2000). By grade 10 (ages 15 to 16), nearly two-thirds of Canadian students have tried smoking, and 17% to 23% smoke daily (Health Canada, 1999). In the United States, at least 3.1 million adolescents and 25% of 17- and 18-year-olds are current smokers (USDHHS, 1994). These statistics closely mirror those of other Western countries.

Smoking as a Women's Health Issue

The health effects of smoking do not appear to affect young men and women equally. Pope, Ashley, and Ferrence (1999) have identified a number of health consequences of smoking unique to women. The growth of young women's lung function is more severely affected by smoking than that of young men. Life expectancy is lower for

51

women than men when they have similar patterns of tobacco consumption, inhalation, and age of initiation. Female smokers experience sex-specific risks related to menstrual irregularities, impaired fertility, and earlier natural menopause (Hobbs et al., 1997). Finally, the leading cause of cancer death in North American women is lung cancer, which has exceeded breast cancer since 1993 (Pope et al., 1999).

These health risks for women are of particular concern in the context of recent evidence that adolescent girls are taking up smoking in greater numbers than boys. In BC, the population rate of current smoking by adolescent females is 17% compared with 13% for males (McCreary Centre Society, 2001). Across Canada, 23% of grade 10 females are current smokers, compared with 17% of males (Health Canada, 1999). In 1998, the rate of smoking among American adolescents was higher for females at 29.1% than for males at 26.2% (Johnson et al., 2000). Other Western countries show a similar trend toward higher smoking rates by 13- and 15-year-old females as compared with males (Health Canada, 1999; King, Wold, Tudor-Smith, & Harrel, 1996; Laugesen & Scragg, 2000). Not only do more adolescent females than males smoke tobacco, but women are more likely than men to smoke for a longer duration over their lifetimes. Pierce and Gilpin (1996) estimate that for adolescents who begin smoking now, females will smoke for at least 20 years while males will smoke only for 16 years. Collectively, these data reflect an alarming international trend.

Explanations of Smoking Initiation and Maintenance

There has been extensive research on the determinants of smoking onset and progression among adolescents (for reviews see Best, Thomson, Santi, Smith, & Brown, 1988; Conrad, Flay, & Hill, 1992; Flay, d'Avernas, Best, Kersell, & Ryan, 1983; Health Canada, 1995, 1999). It is difficult, however, to synthesize and compare the results of the many studies because they differ considerably in terms of the age, ethnicity, and socioeconomic

status of the participants as well as location, culture, setting, and measurement. Nonetheless, common influences on and reasons for smoking initiation and maintenance have been identified, including parental (Flay et al., 1994; Griffin, Botvin, Doyle, Diaz, & Epstein, 1999; Stanton & Silva, 1991), peer (Aloise-Young, Graham, & Hansen, 1994; Flay et al., 1994; Skinner & Krohn, 1992; Sussman, Dent, Flay, Hansen, & Johnson, 1987; Urberg, 1992) and sibling smoking (Murray, Kiryluk, & Swan, 1985; Stanton & Silva, 1991), access to and availability of cigarettes (Altman et al., 1992; Jason, Ji, Anes, & Birkhead, 1991), socioeconomic status (Blane, Hart, Davey-Smith, Gillis, Hole, & Hawthorne, 1996; Graham & Der, 1999), personal characteristics such as rebelliousness (Best, Brown, Cameron, Manske, & Santi, 1995; Santi, Cargo, Brown, Best, & Cameron, 1996), low expectations for academic success (Chassin, Presson, Sherman, Corty, & Olshavsky, 1984), social bonding and relief from social anxiety (Crisp, Sedgwick, Halek, Joughlin, & Humphrey, 1999), weight management (Crisp et al., 1998) and socioeconomic factors (Amos, 1996; Graham & Der, 1999).

Gender Differences in the Influences on Smoking Onset and Progression

Gender differences in the influences on smoking have not been well explored. Many studies on the determinants of smoking onset and maintenance have not involved an analysis of the data separately by sex, and when they have, often no differences have been found (e.g., Aloise-Young et al., 1994; Ary & Biglan, 1988; Bertrand & Abernathy, 1993; Doherty & Allen, 1994; McGee & Stanton, 1993). Even when sex differences are identified, a gender analysis of these differences is uncommon. For the most part, differences between the sexes have been reduced to differences in specific variables, and researchers have implicitly assumed that there are no differences in the socialization, life experiences, roles, and social expectations between males and females (Cohen et al., 1996). This assumption is evidenced by what is not included in the survey instruments.

Few smoking researchers have approached their studies from a theoretical perspective that would lead them to develop the type of measurement in which important and meaningful gender differences could be identified and explained. If the questions are not framed through a gender lens, then there is little chance that such differences and explanations will be discovered.

There have been, however, a few studies to identify gender differences in the reasons for smoking initiation and maintenance. For boys, smoking onset has been associated with having a best friend who smokes (Amos, 1996), having symptoms of depression (Sarigiani, Ryan, & Petersen, 1999), and being either shy or aggressive (Cohen et al., 1996). Adolescent boys' smoking has been also associated with an increased acceptance of "deviant" behaviour, rebelliousness (Best et al., 1995; Santi et al., 1996) peer pressure, authoritative parenting, and having friends who engage in "problem behavior" (Simons-Morton, Crump, Haynie, Saylor, et al., 1999).

Girls, on the other hand, appear to smoke for quite different reasons. Adolescent girls who have low self-esteem are more likely to begin smoking (Amos, 1996), although more recent evidence suggests that a subset of smoking adolescent girls demonstrate high levels of self-esteem and may be more socially skilled than their nonsmoking peers (Michell & Amos, 1997). Adolescent girls smoke because they are trying to fit in and develop a "cool" image (Cohen et al., 1996; Health Canada, 1995), or to construct a personal identity characterized by toughness, independence, and fun-loving and nonconformist behavior (Lloyd, Lucas, & Fernbach, 1997; Lucas & Lloyd, 1999; Michell & Amos, 1997; McCracken, 1992). Peer and family influences also have been identified as being more important for girls than boys (Griffin et al., 1999; Seguire & Chalmers, 2000). Getting into trouble at school (Simons-Morton, Crump, Haynie, Saylor, et al., 1999), having a rebellious nature, rejecting adult authority, needing peer approval, and personal dissatisfaction (Best et al., 1995) also have been associated more strongly with smoking by adolescent girls than boys. Young women often

continue to smoke as a method of weight control and to relieve stress (Amos, 1996; Cohen et al., 1996; Crisp et al., 1998; Crisp, Sedgwick, et al., 1999; French, Perry, Leon, & Fulkerson, 1994; Fried, 1994; Sarigiani et al., 1999).

Criticisms of Conventional Smoking Research

Much of the early research on smoking onset was guided by the social influences model (Evans, 1984; Flay et al., 1983) drawn from social cognitive theory (Bandura, 1977) in which the major determinants of adolescent smoking include parental, sibling, peer, and perhaps media influences, which operate through the mechanisms of modeling, direct peer pressure, cultural norms, and social climate (Best et al., 1988; Health Canada, 1995). Over the past decade, challenges to the social influences model have emerged (Brynin, 1999; Gorman, 1996; Leventhal & Keeshan, 1993; Poland, 1995; Rugkåsa et al., 2001) in part because the effectiveness of programs based on this model has been limited and, in some instances, counterproductive for some subgroups (Palinkas, Atkins, Miller, & Ferreira, 1996; Winkleby, Fortman, & Rockhill, 1994), girls in particular (Abernathy & Bertrand, 1992).

From critical and feminist perspectives, conventional smoking research based on a social cognitive and behavioral perspective has been criticized for focusing predominantly on individual level factors and the immediate social environment, particularly parents and peers (Daykin, 1993; Greaves, 1987; Health Canada, 1995). The research has ignored structural factors in the broader social and cultural context, such as the relative powerlessness that women may experience in their home, school, and work environments (Health Canada, 1995). These structural factors are also likely to have an important influence on the development of smoking. Furthermore, as Poland (1995) points out, the social influences approach, with its focus on social skills training and decision making, appears to assume that adolescents are not socially competent and are unable to act rationally or make good decisions. He argues, however, that there is evidence to suggest "in specific circumstances, accession to peer group pressure may be a particularly rational demonstration of social competence rather than of deviance or irrationality" (p. 3).

Thus, arguments in the literature appear to suggest that, in prevention research, we need to pay greater attention to the structural conditions in society that contribute to smoking, but at the same time we also need to improve the conceptualization of the individual within the social context to account for the human agency of adolescents (Leventhal & Keeshan, 1993). Adolescents are not passive recipients of social influences from the external context, as implied in social influences approaches to smoking prevention, but actively regulate the world around them in relation to the meanings these influences hold for them. The agency of young people has not been given serious consideration in the research based on a social cognitive perspective (Rugkåsa et al., 2001).

The emerging ecological perspective in health promotion (Green, Richard, & Potvin, 1996) also emphasizes the transactional and reciprocal nature of the relationship between the individual and the social context. That is, "the larger economic, political, cultural and organizational forces in society shape the everyday lives of individuals and groups while the everyday actions of individuals produce, reproduce and transform those same structural forces" (Eakin, Robertson, Poland, Coburn, & Edwards, 1995, p. 6). Thus, we need to develop our understanding of the meanings that adolescents make of the world, taking into consideration the environments within which the development of their behavior takes place.

Smoking Influences in the School Environment

In attempting to explore beyond the immediate peer and family environment as influences on smoking, researchers have begun to study the relationships of adolescents with their school environments using concepts like "school bonding" and "school climate." Trickett and Doherty Schmid (1993) emphasize that adolescents bring into the school their problems that originate in other contexts, but the way the school manages these difficulties can exacerbate existing problems or even create new ones. On the other hand, the school context can also moderate the effects of family environment influences on smoking. Wade and Brannigan (1998) found that among adolescents with low family attachment, a strong school attachment inhibited risk taking. Thus, both home and school are important social contexts that may contribute to or inhibit the development and maintenance of smoking.

Researchers have found that school bonding and school climate are inversely related to problem behavior (Coker & Borders, 2001; Eggert, Thompson, Herting, Nicholas, & Dicker, 1994; Simons-Morton, Crump, Haynie, & Saylor, 1999), although very few researchers have looked specifically at smoking in relationship to bonding or climate. The concept of school bonding comes out of social control theory (Hirschi, 1969) and social development theory (Hawkins & Weis, 1995), which propose that attachment to family and school and a belief in the legitimacy of the social order are important elements in establishing a social bond (Simons-Morton, Crump, Haynie, & Saylor, 1999). Thus, relationships of adolescents with family and school, and the climate within the school itself, are important considerations in the development of particular behaviors, including smoking. School climate consists of the attitudes, values, beliefs, and norms that underlie the organizational practices and the operation of a school (McEvoy & Welker, 2000).

It was found in a cross-national study by the World Health Organization (Nutbeam & Aaro, 1991) that young people were more likely to smoke if alienated from school and the values that schools represent. They were also least likely to be affected by smoking prevention education. Patterns in the data suggested that, in some countries, female smokers may be particularly alienated from schools, but the study did not explore these gender differences in depth. Bryant, Schulenberg, Bachman, O'Malley, and Johnston (2000) also found a relationship between cigarette smoking and school bonding but did not detect any gender differences.

Purpose

Based on the review of the literature presented above, there appears to be a need to continue the exploration of gender differences in smoking, particularly with respect to the influence of school context (i.e., school bonding, school climate) and the relationships among students, teachers, school administrators, and parents. We had the opportunity to use an existing data set, which contained specific measures of these concepts, to address this research question. Thus, the purpose of this study was to explore gender differences in the relationships between cigarette smoking and adolescents' perceptions of (a) school climate and (b) their relationships with the school and significant adults in their lives, particularly those in positions of authority. In this article, we report on the preliminary descriptive findings.

Method

A secondary data analysis was conducted to address the study purpose. We used the data set from a survey carried out with students in selected secondary schools in BC, Canada in 1995 (Institute of Health Promotion Research, 1995).

Sample and Sampling Procedures

The original study, from which the data for the secondary analysis was derived, involved a cross-sectional student survey conducted in 20 secondary schools across the province, each of which self-selected to participate in a pilot project to develop, implement, and evaluate a substance misuse prevention program. The stratified sample included urban, rural, and remote schools from a range of socioeconomic levels in each of five provincially designated regions of the province. Unfortunately, the city of Vancouver (the largest urban area in the province) declined to participate in the original prevention project because the school district was implementing its own prevention program. Therefore, Vancouver was not represented in the survey. Smoking and drug use rates are known to be lower in Vancouver than in the rest of the province (Mc-

Creary Centre Society, 1993); thus our data are not representative of the population as a whole. However, other municipalities in the Greater Vancouver area did participate, and the smoking and drug use rates in the areas of the province included in our sample were comparable with the rates from the same areas found in another population-based student survey conducted prior to ours (McCreary Centre Survey, 1993).

The sample included 8,179 students in grades 8 to 12. Of these, 51% were female, and 49% were male which closely parallels the population distribution. The response rate was 87%. Both students and their parents gave informed consent for participation. The original research project as well as the secondary analysis reported here received ethical approval from the respective university ethics committees.

Classrooms were sampled proportionally based on sample size calculations that would allow the detection of significant grade by gender, or smoking by gender differences. From two to four classrooms per grade in each school were selected, depending on the size of the school. In consultation with each school's principal, a subject area was selected in which all or most of the school population was enrolled. Classes in this subject were chosen randomly to participate in the survey. The school-based prevention worker in each school coordinated the survey administration using a standard protocol that provided detailed instructions for data collection. The protocol was reviewed carefully with each prevention worker prior to survey administration.

Measures

The survey instrument contained a number of standardized measures of known reliability and validity. New measures were also developed for the original study through an extensive consultation process with youth and experts. The entire instrument was reviewed by experts, pilot tested in one school, revised on the basis of focus group feedback from students, tested again in five schools, subjected to psychometric analyses to confirm reliability and validity, and then finalized.

Only those variables related to the study purpose were selected from the original data set for the secondary analysis. These included the measures related to cigarette smoking, school climate, school bonding, relationships with administrative personnel, and relationships with parents.

Smoking. The smoking measures used were developed and validated by the Waterloo Smoking Prevention Projects (Best et al., 1984, 1995; Cameron et al., 1999; Flay et al., 1983, 1994; Santi, Best, Payne, Brown, & Cameron, 1992) and used over many years in an ongoing series of studies by a well-known and respected research team at the University of Waterloo in southern Ontario. The reliability of these measures is well established and they are comparable with those used in other national and international studies. Students were asked about the amount smoked. For our purposes, we classified students as "nonsmokers," "irregular smokers," and "daily smokers." Nonsmokers included those who said they had never smoked, those who had smoked only once or twice in their life, and those who had not smoked at all in the past 12 months. Daily smokers included those who smoked at least one cigarette a day. All others were classified as irregular smokers.

School Climate. Students were asked about the extent to which they agreed or disagreed (on a five-point Likert scale) with a series of 20 questions about the social climate of their school. Cronbach's alpha, the reliability coefficient, was .78 for this school climate scale. In the original study, factor analysis produced three distinct subscales: general school climate, teacher climate, and political climate (Institute of Health Promotion Research, 1993, 1995). General school climate, which had a generally low reliability score ($\alpha = .32$), included items related to general aspects of the school climate and culture such as school spirit, safety in the school, and parent participation. The teacher climate score ($\alpha = .88$) was derived from items that related to attitudes and beliefs about teachers, whether students felt respected by teachers, the quality of teaching, and the students' general relationships with teachers. The political climate subscale ($\alpha = .70$) included items about students' experience of having influence and power in the school and the extent of their participation in rule making and school governance.

School Bonding. A variety of measures of school bonding have been reported in the literature, each encompassing somewhat different constructs (Eggert et al., 1994; Simons-Morton, Crump, Haynie, & Saylor, 1999). The common focus of these scales, however, is on characterizing the nature of the relationship the student has with the school and particularly whether students "like"

Method of Analysis

Cronbach's Alpha

Reliability refers to the dependability or consistency of a measure. A particular kind of reliability, *equivalence reliability,* is of concern when researchers use an index or scale—that is, multiple indicators that are combined to operationalize a single construct (in this case, school climate). For the index or scale to be reliable, all the items should measure the same underlying construct. *Cronbach's alpha,* also called the *reliability coefficient,* tests for equivalence reliability by determining the inter-item correlations of a scale or index. Alpha coefficients range in value from 0 to 1; the higher the score, the more reliable the scale. Most researchers consider either .7 or .8 to be an acceptable reliability coefficient. MacDonald and Wright report that the reliability coefficient for their school climate scale is .78, indicating an acceptable degree of equivalence reliability. Note the value of Cronbach's alpha for other scales and indexes in this article and in other quantitative studies throughout the book.

their school. Our data set did not contain a comprehensive measure of school bonding such as those used in other studies. It did, however, contain an item that seemed likely to be a good proxy measure of bonding in that it asked students to describe what their relationship with the school was like. In this single item measure, students were asked to complete the sentence, "The school and I are like . . ." with one of the following choices: "good friends," "friends," "distant relatives," "strangers," or "opponents."

Feelings about School Administrators. Related to the concept of school bonding is the nature of students' relationships with adults in the school who are in positions of authority over them. The teaching climate measure described above captures the nature of students' relationships with teachers. The survey also asked students how they felt about the school administrators (i.e., the principal and vice principal). Responses included, "Really don't like," "Don't like," "Neither like nor dislike," "Like," and "Really like."

Relationships with Mother and Father

Students were asked to respond to a set of 17 statements about their relationships with their mother (or female guardian) and father (or male guardian). For each statement, students were asked to indicate whether it was "never true," "rarely true," "sometimes true," "usually true," or "always true" for each of the parents. Items included statements that related to trust, involvement of the parent in the adolescent's life, ability of the adolescent to make her or his own decisions, and willingness of parent to change unfair rules. The reliability scores for these two scales were: relationship with mother ($\alpha = .86$) and relationship with father ($\alpha = .91$).

Data Analysis. We analyzed the data using the Statistical Package for the Social Sciences (SPSS for Windows). Frequency counts for daily smoking rate were calculated by grade and gender. Cross tabulations were run by gender and smoking status on school bonding and feelings about school ad-

ministrators. Chi-square analyses were conducted to determine whether the differences between males and females and between smokers and non-smokers on these variables were significant.

The two school climate subscales were standardized and composite scores were derived for each of these in three steps. First, each individual item was standardized across the entire sample so that the mean was 0 and the standard deviation was 1. Second, items for each subscale were averaged to obtain a single score. Third, this composite score was then standardized across the entire sample, again so that the mean was 0 and the standard deviation was 1. Thus, the average score on each of the climate subscales, for all schools combined, is 0. A very low climate score would be -1 and a very high score would be $+1$. Approximately 68% of the students will have an individual score ranging between -1 and $+1$. This means that for each subgroup examined (e.g., female smokers), the scores are presented in relation to the average for the entire population of students. Scores above 0 represent positive climate scores in relation to the average, whereas scores below 0 represent a negative school climate, relative to the average. Composite scores were also calculated for the two scales that dealt with relationships with mothers and fathers in the same way that composite scores were calculated for the school climate measures discussed above.

For each of the measures on school climate and relationships with parents, mean scores were calculated by gender and smoking status. Means were compared using analysis of variance with post hoc comparisons to determine whether the differences among subgroups were statistically significant. A reliability coefficient (Cronbach's alpha) was calculated for each of the continuous measures (i.e., school climate scale and its three subscales and the scales relating to relationships with mother and father).

Results

To simplify the presentation of the data that follow, only the results for daily smokers and

Method of Analysis

Chi-Square

Chi-square (χ^2) is a popular statistic for determining the relationship between two categorical variables. In this article, MacDonald and Wright attempt to understand some potentially important influences (perceived climate at school, relationship with school, and relationship with key adults in their life) on cigarette smoking among adolescent girls. They examine the relationship between four sets of variables: (1) school bonding and smoking status for females (Figure 2), (2) school bonding and smoking status for males (Figure 3), (3) feelings about school administrators and smoking status for females (Figure 4), and (4) feelings about school administrators and smoking status for males (Figure 5).

Because the chi-square procedure is the same in all four figures, we will examine only Figure 2 in depth here. Figure 2 compares female daily smokers and nonsmokers on how they perceive their relationship with the school. (Note that smoking status was actually divided into three categories: daily smokers, nonsmokers, and irregular smokers. The authors include only the first two groups in the figures, but the statistics are based on all three groups.) The percentages included on the bar graph in Figure 2 indicate that of students who consider themselves to be strangers at their school, almost 54 percent are daily smokers, and just under 32 percent are nonsmokers. Of those who say that they have good friends at

school, roughly 24 percent smoke daily, and about 61 percent do not smoke.

The chi-square value is the key to interpreting the figure. These values are not intuitive—their meaning comes only when they are compared to values of the statistic that have been calculated and are reproduced in tables. The actual chi-square value for this figure is not presented in either the text or figure. However, within the text, the authors report on the probability level that the relationship found between the two variables (school bonding and cigarette smoking) is due to chance (that is, the two variables are not really related). A $p \le .001$ means that there is at least a 99.9 percent probability that the relationship really exists; a $p \le .01$ means that there is at least a 99 percent probability that the relationship really exists, and a $p \le .05$ means that there is at least a 95 percent probability that the relationship really exists. If the probability is reported to be not significant, that means that we do not have sufficient confidence to conclude that the relationship really exists. In this figure, the χ^2 is reported to have a probability of $p \le .01$. That means that we have at least 99 percent confidence that a relationship really exists between school bonding and cigarette smoking among females. Girls who have a distant relationship with their school are more likely than those who have a close relationship to smoke cigarettes. For Figures 3 through 6, you should be able to determine what two variables are being studied and the level of probability that the two variables are related.

nonsmokers are discussed. The scores for irregular smokers fall consistently midway between the scores of daily smokers and nonsmokers.

Smoking Prevalence

As demonstrated in Figure 1, the daily cigarette smoking rates among the BC youth who participated in this study appear relatively high in comparison to population smoking rates elsewhere in Canada and the United States, particularly among girls in grades 9, 10, and 11. In these grades, 35% or more of girls report daily smoking. Recall, however, that the schools participating in this project self-selected and may have done so because of

a perceived problem with tobacco and other drug use. Nonetheless, the higher prevalence rate among adolescent girls in comparison to boys is consistent with national and international trends.

School Bonding

In Figure 2 we compare female daily smokers and nonsmokers on how they perceive their relationship with the school. Because irregular smokers are not represented in this graph, the percentages do not add to 100. Of the girls who say that their relationship with the school is like that of "strangers" or "opponents," 53.8% are daily smokers while only 31.7% are nonsmokers. In

Method of Analysis

Analysis of Variance

The analysis provided in Figures 6 through 10 is based on the use of *standardized scores* and the statistical test, *analysis of variance.* Using standardized scores leads to data that are intuitively meaningful. Figure 6 can be used as an illustration. Scores for perceived general school climate were obtained from student responses (from strongly agree to strongly disagree) to a series of twenty questions. Composite scores were created and then standardized. This means that the mean composite score was set at zero. A score higher than zero indicates a subgroup (e.g., female smokers) who were higher than the average for all students on that measure. A score below zero indicates a subgroup who were lower than the average for all students on that measure.

In Figure 6 (perceived general school climate), male nonsmokers had a standardized score of .4 and females nonsmokers had a score of .15; both groups had more positive feelings about school climate than students in general. Male smokers had a standardized score of −0.3, and female smokers had a score of −0.17; both groups of smokers had more negative feelings about school climate than the average student. Is this difference sufficiently large that we can conclude that there really is a difference in perceived general school climate among smokers and nonsmokers? (Note that smoking status was actually divided into three categories: daily smokers, nonsmokers, and irregular smokers. The authors include only the first two groups in the figures, but the statistics are based on all three groups.) The researchers use the analysis of variance technique to answer this question.

Analysis of variance enables us to determine if there is sufficient variation among three or more groups so we can conclude that an actual difference does exist (or whether the differences in variation among groups is not sufficiently large to give us confidence that the groups really are different). Using the same explanation for level of probability as discussed in the chi-square insert earlier in this chapter, the authors report that the results of the analysis of variance are significant at the .01 level ($p \leq .01$). This means that there is at least 99 percent probability that differences in perceived school climate really do exist among daily smokers, nonsmokers, and irregular smokers.

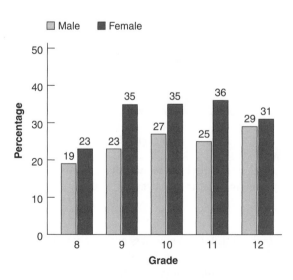

Figure 1 **Daily Cigarette Smoking by Grade and Gender**

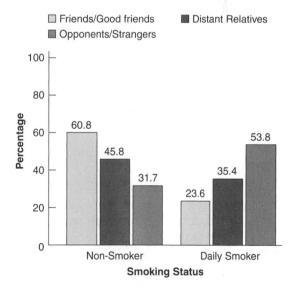

Figure 2 **School Bonding by Smoking Status for Females**

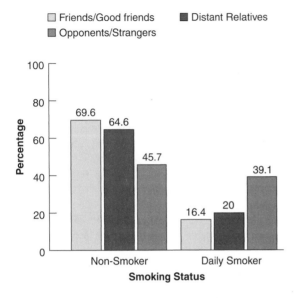

Figure 3   **School Bonding by Smoking Status for Males**

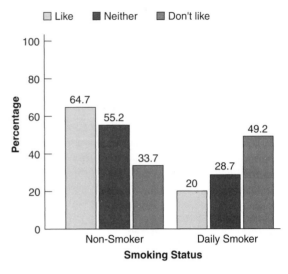

Figure 4   **Feelings about School Administrators by Smoking Status for Females**

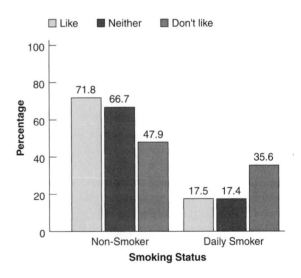

Figure 5   **Feelings about School Administrators by Smoking Status for Males**

other words, girls who feel either distanced from the school or that they have an adversarial relationship with the school are more likely to be smokers than nonsmokers ($p \le .01$). By contrast, adolescent males who feel an adversarial or distanced relationship with the school are more likely to be nonsmokers (see Figure 3; $p \le .01$). In summary, girls who smoke are much more likely than boys who smoke or girls who do not smoke to perceive that their relationship with the school is oppositional and distanced (53.8% versus 39.1%; $p \le .01$).

Feelings about School Administrators

Figure 4 demonstrates that girls who smoke are more likely than girls who do not smoke to dislike their school principal and vice principal (49.2% versus 33.7%; $p \le .01$). Of the girls who smoke, only 20% say that they like the school administrators, in contrast to the 65% of nonsmoking girls. Males show the opposite pattern (see Figure 5). More nonsmoking males dislike their school administrators when compared with smoking males (47.9% versus 35.6%). As with school

attachment, female smokers are much more likely than male smokers or female nonsmokers to dislike the school administrators. Note again that irregular smokers are not included in this graph and therefore the percentages will not add to 100.

School Climate

As indicated in Figure 6, nonsmokers of both sexes report more positive perceptions of the general social climate in the school than smokers. Male smokers, however, report more negative perceptions than female smokers (−.3 versus −.17;

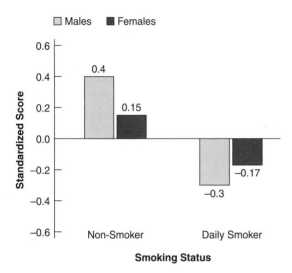

Figure 6   **General School Climate by Smoking Status**

$p \leq .01$). Figure 7 presents the differences between females and males and smokers and nonsmokers in relation to students' perceptions about the teaching climate in the school. Again, male smokers report consistently more negative beliefs about the teaching in the school and their relationships with teachers than either female smokers or male nonsmokers ($p \leq .01$). Female smokers also report more negative perceptions of teaching climate than their nonsmoking female peers.

Political climate reflects students' perceptions of their relative power in the school setting. As indicated in Figure 8, girls who smoke daily report extremely negative perceptions of political climate relative to both male smokers and female nonsmokers ($p \leq .01$). In other words, girls who smoke regularly do not believe that they have much say in decisions that affect their lives in the school while nonsmoking girls perceive substantially more power to affect decisions. Political climate scores are also negative for male smokers, but not as negative as for female smokers. Thus, it appears that adolescent female smokers feel particularly powerless and disenfranchised in their schools in comparison to either males or nonsmokers.

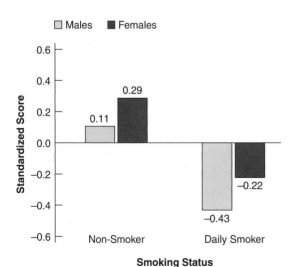

Figure 7   **Teacher Climate by Smoking Status**

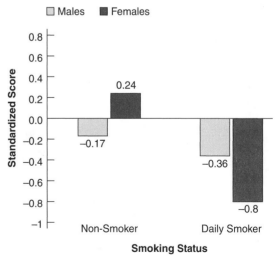

Figure 8   **Political School Climate by Smoking Status**

Relationships with Mothers and Fathers

Figure 9 presents perceptions about female and male adolescents' relationships with their mothers with respect to smoking status. For both girls and boys, those who smoke daily perceive more negative relationships with their mothers than do those who are nonsmokers. There is virtually no difference between males and females with respect to their maternal relationships for both smokers and nonsmokers. Similarly, there is only a small nonsignificant difference between male and female nonsmokers with respect to their relationship with their fathers (see Figure 10). The major difference emerges with respect to the relationship that girls who smoke daily perceive they have with their fathers. Female smokers report significantly more negative perceptions of their paternal relationship than male smokers ($p \leq .01$). The paternal relationship is also more negative for female smokers than their maternal relationship (−.39 versus −.27).

Summary

Research to date has demonstrated clearly that cigarette smoking by adolescents is a very complex behavior. Adolescents take up smoking for many reasons, and these reasons differ by age, gender, social class, economics, and geography. The data from this study provide important new evidence that adolescent girls who smoke are more likely than either males (both smokers and nonsmokers) or their nonsmoking female counterparts to experience powerlessness and alienation in their school environment and to feel considerably less attachment to the school. These girls report little control over many aspects of their schools that influence their daily lives and thus their experience of schooling. Female smokers are also more likely than male smokers or female nonsmokers to be engaged in oppositional, distanced, and generally unsatisfactory relationships with most of the important adults in their lives, particularly those who are in positions of relative power and authority. They dislike school administrators much more than their nonsmoking female counterparts and even more than male smokers. Both male and female smokers report more negative relationships with parents than nonsmokers. Adolescent female smokers, however, perceive particularly negative relationships with their fathers, one in which they

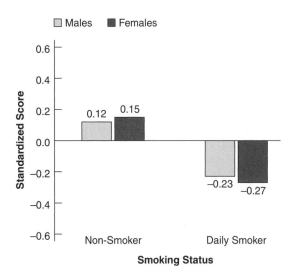

Figure 9   **Relationship with Mother by Smoking Status**

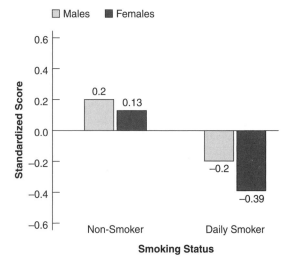

Figure 10   **Relationship with Father by Smoking Status**

perceive trust and honesty to be lacking and little paternal involvement in their lives. They see rules as unfair and feel little control over decisions that affect them. Thus, female smokers feel powerless in two important domains of their lives: home and school.

Discussion

The limitations of this study do not allow us to draw causal inferences. The data are cross sectional and not representative of the population as a whole. The findings may not be generalizable to other parts of Canada or other countries with different social and cultural circumstances and with a different population make-up. We can, however, draw from other research and theory to help us put these data into a context for interpretation that might deepen our understanding, provide direction for future research, and guide health practitioners. The finding of most importance in this study, and the one that begs for explanation, is that adolescent girls who smoke regularly experience more powerlessness and alienation in their home and school lives, and their relationships with significant adults in their world are more oppositional and distanced.

Social development or social control theories are gaining increasing support in the literature as an explanation for "problem behavior" among adolescents, which includes smoking (Hawkins & Weis, 1995; Hirschi, 1969; King, Connop, King, & Mercer, 1996; Kumpfer & Turner, 1990–1991). There are some variations on the theory, but for the most part, the problem begins with either school misbehavior or academic difficulties. If misbehavior is the starting point, then academic difficulties follow closely, with subsequent alienation from the school and its core mission and values, as well as conflict with parents. The next step in the trajectory is association by the adolescent with other "deviant" peers in efforts to find the support and caring they are not finding at home or in the school. The price of admission to these tightly knit peer groups is engagement in problem behavior, including smoking.

Our data are not inconsistent with social development or social control theory and could, in fact, be interpreted as providing some support for these theories. It is important, however, to deconstruct this theory for its unexamined assumptions and its limitations to determine whether the explanation is adequate. A major limitation is that social development theory does not explain the gender differences or the high degree of alienation and powerlessness felt in the schools by adolescent girls who smoke, relative to males. In fact, social development theory would suggest that males, given their greater likelihood to "misbehave," experience a higher degree of alienation. The particular significance of smoking to adolescent girls within social development theory is not explained.

There are two implicit assumptions in social development theory that warrant challenge from a critical feminist perspective. The first implicit assumption is that explanations for oppositional behavior can be found in the "dispositional characteristics" (Best et al., 1995; Santi et al., 1996) of individual students. Rebellion, rejection of authority, and related oppositional and problem behavior are viewed as personal characteristics rather than as mediated by the wider societal relations of class, authority, gender, and power. In ignoring the larger sociocultural context inhabited by these rebellious students, an implicit "blame the victim" ideology appears to be operating (McLaren, 1989).

The second assumption is that the existing social order, the school's mission, and its values are inherently "good." As Poland (1995) points out, rules of social conduct are designed to control social behavior and to bring it into line with the values and approved behaviors of the dominant majority. It is the consensus of the majority that legitimizes these values (Arnot, 1994). Thus, if the social order and existing school values are "good," then any rebellion against these values or rejection of authority must be "bad."

These challenges to social development theory lead us to a somewhat different perspective on the powerlessness and oppositional relationships experienced by adolescent female smokers. The "problem behavior" of smoking may be less a reflection of the particular characteristics of the individual adolescent, and more the product of the reciprocal and transactional relationship between the individual and her social context, in this case her home and school environments. This leads us to question the nature of the school values and the social order from which the adolescent female smoker is distanced. How do these values and the existing social order relate to the experiences of powerlessness among adolescent girls and their smoking behavior?

McLaren (1986) argues that the school system is tacitly structured to reinforce and reward middle-class values, attitudes, and behaviors. Within this system, girls are subject to officially sanctioned, although not necessarily explicit, codes of neatness, diligence, application, femininity, and passivity. Many girls, particularly those outside the middle-class mainstream, actively resist this code of behavior. We also know that smoking is more prevalent in working-class populations. Within this context, therefore, smoking may be a particularly effective gesture of resistance and control for girls, such as those in this study who felt a lack of control over important aspects of their lives.

McLaren (1989) defines resistance as "oppositional student behavior that has both symbolic, historical and 'lived' meaning and which contests the legitimacy, power and significance of school culture in general and instruction in particular" (p. 143). For the most part, organized resistance in schools is restricted to the privileged class of students, not to those youth who are outside the mainstream, including those who are poor, working class, or who belong to other marginalized groups. Resistance among these students usually is not overt, nor does it occur through recognized channels. Rather, resistance in these groups is "tacit, informal, unwitting and unconscious" (McLaren, 1986). Seen in this way, smoking is a gesture of resistance that takes place within a broader discourse of resistance (Eakin et al., 1995).

As a form of resistance to authority in general, smoking among disenfranchised adolescents makes sense in a society that constantly limits the auton-

omy of its youth (Eakin et al., 1995), girls in particular (Health Canada, 1995). As girls come to understand that there are limits on and cultural expectations for their behavior, they feel less control over their lives (Greaves, 1987; Greaves & Barr, 2000). This is consistent with our finding that girls who smoke do experience powerlessness and a lack of control in their lives.

Two decades ago, Jacobson (1981) argued that smoking among young women was influenced by the social context of being female, and one way that women could maintain control over their personal lives was by smoking. More recently, Daykin (1993) argued that normal attempts of young women to gain independence may be undermined by societal and familial expectations regarding femininity and the general lack of control in their lives. Adolescent girls may see smoking, which is viewed as an "adult" behavior, as one means to assert control. In resisting the discourse of femininity, smoking becomes a powerful symbol. Adolescent girls seek to create a "bad girl" image within this "girl poisoning culture" (Torn, 1999). Similarly, Michell and Amos (1997) have said that, "Girls, in contrast to boys, may be using smoking as a symbol of social identity, which incorporates attributes such as rebellion and resistance that marks them out as different than the middle ground of 'good girls' who have adopted more adult approved feminine identities" (p. 1868).

The school environment can be implicated in the process of resistance. Walker (1992) suggests that the current organization and structure of schools actually encourages smoking and other drug use. These behaviors are prohibited by adult authority, yet schools informally sanction their use among adults or at least they have done so until recently. Schools provide a "venue for close peer relationships and social networks and an implicit culture of deception and risk taking that appears designed to support a culture of resistance" (p. 47).

Implications for Health Practitioners

Generic, gender-neutral school-based programs for smoking prevention are unlikely to be broadly effective. Health professionals who work in schools, and in other settings with adolescents, need to advocate for more broadly based programs that incorporate our developing understanding about smoking by attending to a wider range of influences on smoking initiation and maintenance, particularly those in the social environment. At the very least, school programs need to provide students with a language and concepts that allow them to articulate their own experiences of powerlessness and the relationship of smoking to that experience. Not all girls smoke for the same reasons. Girls on different rungs of the social ladder will have different reasons for smoking, and the meaning of smoking in their lives will be different (Michell & Amos, 1997). Not all smoking can be explained by the analysis presented above. The place to start, however, is with the experiences and understandings of the young women themselves.

Perhaps the most important work to be done is not in relation to smoking prevention programs at all. If the "problem" is framed not as a problem of smoking behavior but in terms of the social, cultural, and economic contexts within which smoking develops, a very different focus is implied. If adolescent girls feel powerless to influence decisions in their school and home lives, and feel alienated from the important people in those settings, then perhaps the focus needs to be on the structure and organization of those settings, and not on the behavior of the girls themselves.

Practitioners also need to recognize the reality of resistance and the role it plays in the lives of adolescents. In particular, we need to be aware of the potential for resistance to our smoking prevention strategies because it is possible that we may be further entrenching that resistance. Professional attempts to stop girls from smoking may render that behavior an even more powerful symbol of resistance (Eakin et al., 1995).

REFERENCES

Abernathy, T. J., & Bertrand, L. D. (1992). Preventing cigarette smoking among children: Results of a four year evaluation of the PAL program. *Canadian Journal of Public Health, 83,* 226–229.

Aloise-Young, P. A., Graham, J. W., & Hansen, W. B. (1994). Peer influence on smoking initiation during early adolescence: A comparison of group members and group outsiders. *Journal of Applied Psychology, 79*(2), 281–287.

Altman, D., Carol, J., Chalkley, C., Cherner, J., DiFranza, J., Feighery, E., Forster, J., Gupta, S., Records, J., Slade, J., Talbot, B., & Tye, J. (1992). Report of the Tobacco Policy Research Study Group on access to tobacco products in the United States. *Tobacco Control, 1*(Suppl), S45–S51.

Amos, A. (1996). Women and smoking. *British Medical Bulletin, 52*(1), 74–89.

Arnot, M. (1994). Male hegemony, social class, and women's education. In L. Stone (Ed.), *The education feminism reader* (pp. 84–104). New York: Routledge.

Ary, D. V., & Biglan, A. (1988). Longitudinal changes in adolescent cigarette smoking behavior: Onset and cessation. *Journal of Behavioral Medicine, 11*(4), 597–604.

Bandura, A. (1977). *Social learning theory.* Englewood Cliffs, NJ: Prentice-Hall.

Bertrand, L. D., & Abernathy, T. J. (1993). Predicting cigarette smoking among adolescents using cross-sectional and longitudinal approaches. *Journal of School Health, 63*(2), 98–103.

Best, J. A., Brown, K. S., Cameron, R., Manske, S. M., & Santi, S. (1995). Gender and predisposing attributes as predictors of smoking onset: Implications for theory and practice. *Journal of Health Education, 26*(2), S52–S60.

Best, J. A., Flay, B. R., Towson, S. M. J., Ryan, K. B., Perry, C. L., Brown, K. S., Kersell, M. W., & d'Avernas, J. R. (1984). Smoking prevention and the concept of risk. *Journal of Applied Social Psychology, 14*(3), 257–273.

Best, J. A., Thomson, S. J., Santi, S. M., Smith, E. A., & Brown, K. S. (1988). Preventing cigarette smoking among school children. *Annual Review of Public Health, 9,* 161–201.

Blane, D., Hart, C. L., Davey-Smith, G., Gillis, C. R., Hole, D. J., & Hawthorne, V. M. (1996). Association of cardiovascular disease factors with socioeconomic conditions during childhood and during adulthood. *British Medical Journal, 313,* 1434–1438.

Bryant, A. L., Schulenberg, J., Bachman, J. G., O'Malley, P. M., & Johnston, L. D. (2000). Understanding the links among school misbehavior, academic achievement, and cigarette use: A national panel study of adolescents. *Prevention Science, 1*(2), 71–87.

Brynin, M. (1999). Smoking behavior. Predisposition or adaptation? *Journal of Adolescence, 22,* 635–646.

Cameron, R., Brown, S., Best, A., Pelkman, C. L., Madill, C. L., Manske, S. R., & Payne, M. E. (1999). Effectiveness of a social influences smoking prevention program as a function of provider type, training method, and school risk. *American Journal of Public Health, 89*(12), 1827–1831.

Chassin, L., Presson, C. C., Sherman, S. J., Corty, E., & Olshavsky, R. W. (1984). Predicting the onset of cigarette smoking in adolescents: A longitudinal study. *Journal of Applied Social Psychology, 14*(3), 224–243.

Cohen, J., Ferrence, R., Jackson, L., Poland, B., Pope, M., Kellner, F., & Greaves, L. (1996). *Gender differences in the predictors of the acquisition of smoking by adolescents.* Toronto, Canada: Ontario Tobacco Research Unit.

Coker, J. K., & Borders, L. D. (2001). An analysis of environmental and social factors affecting adolescent problem drinking. *Journal of Counseling and Development, 79*(2), 200–208.

Conrad, K. M., Flay, B. R., & Hill, D. (1992). Why children start smoking cigarettes: Predictors of onset. *British Journal of Addiction, 87,* 1711–1724.

Crisp, A. H., Sedgwick, P., Halek, C., Joughlin, N., & Humphrey, H. (1999). Why may teenage girls persist in smoking? *Journal of Adolescence, 22,* 657–672.

Crisp, A. H., Stavrakaki, C., Halek, C., Williams, E., Sedgwick, P., & Kiossis, I. (1998). Smoking and the pursuit of thinness in schoolgirls in London and Ottawa. *Postgraduate Medicine, 74,* 473–479.

Daykin, N. (1993). Young women and smoking: Toward a sociological account. *Health Promotion International, 8,* 95–102.

Doherty, W. J., & Allen, W. (1994). Family functioning and parental smoking as predictors of adolescent cigarette use: A six year prospective study. *Journal of Family Psychology, 8*(3), 347–353.

Eakin, J., Roberston, A., Poland, B., Coburn, D., & Edwards, R. (1995). *Young girls' smoking: A critical social science perspective.* Toronto, Canada: Ontario Tobacco Research Unit.

Eggert, L., Thompson, E., Herting, J. R., Nicholas, L. J., & Dicker, B. G. (1994). Preventing adolescent drug abuse and high school drop out through an intensive school-based social network development program.

American Journal of Health Promotion, 8(3), 202–215.

Evans, R. I. (1984). A social inoculation strategy to deter smoking in adolescents. In J. D. Matarazzo, S. M. Weiss, J. A. Herd, & N. E. Miller (Eds.), *Behavioral health: A handbook of health enhancement and disease prevention* (pp. 765–774). New York: John Wiley and Sons.

Flay, B. R., d'Avernas, J. R., Best, J. A., Kersell, M. W., & Ryan, K. B. (1983). Cigarette smoking: Why young people do it and ways of preventing it. In P. Firestone & P. McGrath (Eds.), *Pediatric and adolescent behavioral medicine* (pp. 132–181). New York, Springer.

Flay, B. R., Hu, F. B., Siddiqui, O., Day, L. E., Hedeker, D., Petraitis, J., Richardson, J., & Sussman, S. (1994). Differential influence of parental smoking and friends' smoking on adolescent initiation and escalation of smoking. *Journal of Health and Social Behaviour, 35,* 248–265.

French, S. A., Perry, C. L., Leon, G. R., & Fulkerson, J. A. (1994). Weight concerns, dieting behavior, and smoking initiation among adolescents: A prospective study. *American Journal of Public Health, 84*(11), 1818–1820.

Fried, J. L. (1994). Women and young girls . . . high risk populations for tobacco use. *Health Values, 18*(1), 33–40.

Gorman, D. M. (1996). Etiological theories and the primary prevention of drug use. *Journal of Drug Issues, 26*(2), 505–520.

Graham, H., & Der, G. (1999). Influences on women's smoking status. *European Journal of Public Health, 9*(2), 139–141.

Greaves, L. (1987). *Background paper on women and tobacco.* Ottawa: Health Canada.

Greaves, L., & Barr, V. (2000). *Filtered policy: Women and tobacco in Canada.* Vancouver: BC Centre of Excellence for Women's Health.

Green, L. W., Richard, L., & Potvin, L. (1996). The ecological foundations of health promotion. *American Journal of Health Promotion, 10*(4), 270–281.

Griffin, K. W., Botvin, G. J., Doyle, M. M., Diaz, T., & Epstein, J. (1999). A six-year follow-up study of determinants of heavy cigarette smoking among high-school seniors. *Journal of Behavioral Medicine, 22*(3), 271–284.

Hawkins, J. D., & Weis, J. G. (1995). The social development model: An integrated approach to delinquency prevention. *Journal of Primary Prevention, 6*(2), 73–97.

Health Canada. (1995). *Women and tobacco: A frame-work for action*. Ottawa, Canada: Author.

Health Canada. (1999). *Youth and tobacco: Lessons learned from the tobacco demand reduction strategy* [H39–465/1999E]. Ottawa, Canada: Author.

Hirschi, T. (1969). *Attachment to the school: Causes of delinquency*. Berkeley: University of California.

Hobbs, F., Ferrence, R., Pope, M., Poland, B., Ashley, M. J., & Pederson, L. (1997). *Tobacco and women's health: Influences on smoking cessation in women*. Toronto, ON: Ontario Tobacco Research Unit.

Institute of Health Promotion Research. (1993). *Student survey report, Fall 1993*. Vancouver, BC, Canada: University of British Columbia.

Institute of Health Promotion Research. (1995). *Student survey report, October 1995*. Vancouver, BC, Canada: University of British Columbia.

Jacobson, B. (1981). *Beating the ladykillers: Women and smoking*. London: Pluto Press Ltd.

Jason, L. A., Ji, P. Y., Anes, M. D., & Birkhead, S. H. (1991). Active enforcement of cigarette control laws in the prevention of cigarette sales to minors. *Journal of the American Medical Association, 266*(22), 3159–3161.

Johnston, L. D., O'Malley, P. M., & Bachman, J. G. (1993). *National survey results on drug use from Monitoring the Future Study, 1975–1992*. Rockville, MD: National Institute on Drug Abuse, U.S. Department of Health and Human Services.

Johnston, L. D., O'Malley, P. M., & Bachman, J. G. (2000). *Cigarette use and smokeless tobacco use decline substantially among teens* (Press release). Ann Arbor: University of Michigan News and Information Services.

King, A. J. C., Connop, H., King, M. A., & Mercer, T. (1996). *Adolescent female smoking: Influence of home, school and peers*. Toronto, Canada: Ontario Tobacco Research Unit.

King, A. J. C., Wold, B., Tudor-Smith, C., & Harrel, Y. (1996). *The health of youth: A cross-national study*. Copenhagen: World Health Organization.

Kumpfer, K. L., & Turner, C. W. (1990–1991). The social ecology model of adolescent substance abuse: Implications for prevention. *The International Journal of the Addictions, 25*(4a), 435–463.

Laugesen, M., & Scragg, R. (2000). *Trends in cigarette smoking and purchasing by fourth-form students in New Zealand, 1992, 1997 and 1998*. Wellington: New Zealand Ministry of Health.

Leventhal, H., & Keeshan, P. (1993). Promoting healthy alternatives to substance abuse. In S. G.

Millstein, A. C. Petersen, & E. O. Nightengale (Eds.), *Promoting the health of adolescents: New directions for the twenty-first century* (pp. 260–284). New York: Oxford University Press.

Lloyd, B., Lucas, K., & Fernbach, M. (1997). Adolescent girls' constructions of smoking identities: Implications for health promotion. *Journal of Adolescence, 20*, 43–56.

Lucas, K., & Lloyd, B. (1999). Starting smoking: Girls' explanations of the influence of peers. *Journal of Adolescence, 22*, 647–655.

Makomaski Illing, E. M., & Kaiserman, M. J. (1999). Mortality attributable to tobacco use in Canada and its regions, 1994 and 1996. *Chronic Diseases in Canada, 20*(3), 111–117.

McCracken, G. (1992). *Got a smoke? A cultural account of tobacco in the lives of contemporary teens*. Toronto, Canada: Ontario Ministry of Health.

McCreary Centre Society. (1993). *Adolescent Health Survey*. Vancouver, BC, Canada: Author.

McCreary Centre Society. (2001). *Adolescent health survey II fact sheet: Lighting up*. Burnaby, BC, Canada: Author.

McEvoy, A., & Welker, R. (2000). Anti-social behavior, academic failure and school climate: A critical review. *Journal of Emotional and Behavioral Disorders, 8*(3), 130–140.

McGee, R., & Stanton, W. R. (1993). *A longitudinal study of reasons for smoking in adolescence*. *Addiction, 88*, 265–271.

McLaren, P. (1986). *Schooling as a ritual performance: Towards a political economy of educational symbols and gestures*. London: Routledge & Kegan Paul.

McLaren, P. (1989). *Life in schools: An introduction to critical pedagogy in the foundations of education*. New York: Longman.

Michell, L., & Amos, A. (1997). Girls, pecking order and smoking. *Social Science and Medicine, 44*(12), 1861–1869.

Murray, M., Kiryluk, S., & Swan, A. V. (1985). Relation between parents' and children's smoking behaviour and attitudes. *Journal of Epidemiology and Community Health, 39*, 169–174.

Nutbeam, D., & Aaro, L. E. (1991). Smoking and pupil attitudes toward school: The implications for health education with young people. Results of the WHO Study of Health Behaviour among Schoolchildren. *Health Education Research, 6*(4), 415–421.

Palinkas, L. A., Atkins, C. J., Miller, C., & Ferreira, D. (1996). Social skills training for drug prevention in high-risk female adolescents. *Preventive Medicine, 25,* 692–701.

Pierce, J. P., & Gilpin, E. (1996). How long will today's new adolescent smoker be addicted to cigarettes? *American Journal of Public Health, 86*(2), 253–256.

Poland, B. (1995). *Substance abuse and smoking prevention with adolescents: An explanation of Friere's critical pedagogy.* Working Paper Series No. 7. Toronto: Ontario Tobacco Research Unit.

Pope, M., Ashley, M. J., & Ferrence, R. (1999). The carcinogenic and toxic effects of tobacco smoke: Are women particularly susceptible? *Journal of Gender-Specific Medicine, 2*(6), 45–51.

Rugkåsa, J., Kennedy, O., Barton, M., Abaunza, P. S., Treacy, M. P., & Knox, B. (2001). Smoking and symbolism: Children, communication and cigarettes. *Health Education Research, 16*(2), 131–142.

Santi, S., Best, J. A., Payne, M. E., Brown, K. S., & Cameron, R. (1992). A comparison between instructional experience and performance of teachers and nurses delivering a smoking prevention program. *Canadian Journal of Public Health, 83*(6), 433–436.

Santi, S., Cargo, M., Brown, K. S., Best, J. A., & Cameron, R. (1996). Dispositional risk factors for smoking-stage transitions: A social influences program as an effect modifier. *Addictive Behaviors, 19,* 369–380.

Sarigiani, P. A., Ryan, L., & Petersen, A. C. (1999). Prevention of high-risk behaviors in adolescent women. *Journal of Adolescent Health, 25,* 109–119.

Seguire, M., & Chalmers, K. (2000). Late adolescent female smoking. *Journal of Advanced Nursing, 31*(6), 1442–1429.

Simons-Morton, B., Crump, A. D., Haynie, D. L., & Saylor, K. E. (1999). Student-school bonding and adolescent problem behavior. *Health Education Research, 14*(1), 99–107.

Simons-Morton, B., Crump, A. D., Haynie, D. L., Saylor, K. E., Eitel, P., & Yu, K. (1999). Psychosocial, school, and parent factors associated with recent smoking among early-adolescent boys and girls. *Preventive Medicine, 28,* 138–148.

Skinner, W. F., & Krohn, M. D. (1992). Age and gender differences in a social process model of adolescent cigarette use. *Sociological Inquiry, 62*(1), 56–82.

Stanton, W. R., & Silva, P. A. (1991). Children's exposure to smoking. *International Journal of Epidemiology, 20*(4), 933–937.

Sussman, S., Dent, C. W., Flay, B. R., Hansen, W. B., & Johnson, C. A. (1987). Psychosocial predictors of cigarette smoking by white, black, Hispanic, and Asian adolescents in southern California. *Morbidity and Mortality Weekly Report, 36*(4S), 11S–16S.

Tonn, H. (1999). *Smoking room: Cigarettes and the creation of community among girls who smoke.* Unpublished master's thesis, University of Victoria, Victoria, British Columbia, Canada.

Trickett, E. J., & Doherty Schmid, K. (1993). The school as a social context. In P. H. Tolan & B. J. Cohler (Eds.), Handbook of clinical research with adolescents (pp. 173–202). New York: John Wiley and Sons, Inc.

United States Department of Health and Human Services (USDHHS). (1994). *Preventing tobacco use among young people: A report of the surgeon general.* Atlanta, GA: USDHSS, National Center for Chronic Disease Prevention and Health Promotion, Office on Smoking and Health.

Urberg, K. A. (1992). Locus of peer influence: Social crowd and best friend. *Journal of Youth and Adolescence, 21*(4), 439–450.

Wade, T. J., & Brannigan, A. (1998). The genesis of adolescent risk-taking: Pathways through family, school, and peers. *Canadian Journal of Sociology, 23*(1), 1–19.

Walker, R. (1992). The solution or the problem? The role of schools in drug education. *Health Promotion Journal of Australia, 2*(1), 43–49.

Winkleby, M. A., Fortman, S. P., & Rockhill, B. (1994). Cigarette smoking trends in adolescents and young adults: The Stanford Five-City Project. *Preventive Medicine, 22,* 325–334.

Marjorie MacDonald is the Associate Director for Graduate Education in the School of Nursing at the University of Victoria. Her responsibilities focus on the development and implementation of a new Ph.D. in Nursing program and on a new Masters of Nursing Advanced Nursing Practice. Her research interests are in the areas of adolescent health, school and community health promotion, primary health care and public health, advanced nursing practice and education, and health care policy and political action. Her methodological interests include qualitative methods, particularly grounded theory; collaborative and participatory research methods; and mixed method evaluation research.

Nancy E. Wright is a senior instructor in the School of Nursing at University of Victoria. She teaches undergraduate nursing students in practice and theory courses both on-campus and via distance education. She is interested in primarily qualitative research methods, particularly grounded theory. She recently completed a study called "Navigating the House of Mirrors: How Women Make Sense of Menopause Information."

An interview with . . .

Marjorie MacDonald

How did you become interested in the topic of smoking among adolescent females?

I became interested in this topic when I was studying for my master's degree at the University of Waterloo in Ontario. After graduation, I worked as project director on a major smoking prevention research headed up by researchers at the University of Waterloo. When my own adolescent girls grappled with the decision "to smoke or not to smoke" my interest was rekindled. My doctoral work involved an evaluation of a school-based substance abuse prevention program, of which there was a smoking component. I am currently trying to develop a more extensive research program related to smoking by adolescent girls in marginalized populations. Nancy's interest was more peripheral—she was interested in adolescent health more generally but saw this as an opportunity to learn more.

What made you choose this particular methodological approach—that is, secondary analysis of survey data?

When I was out in the field gathering qualitative data for our school-based prevention project evaluation, I observed that school administrators appeared to relate much differently to male adolescent smokers than to female smokers. Since I was only gathering observational data in six schools, I did not know whether this was just an idiosyncratic observation or might be more widespread. I put the question aside for a time, but it haunted me, and later when I had the opportunity, I reviewed the data available in a survey data set and found that there were several questions related to my observation about relationships between female adolescent smokers and the authority figures in their lives. The method, therefore, was chosen partly for pragmatic reasons, because it was the most efficient and inexpensive way to answer my research questions.

Were there any particular challenges or difficulties in using secondary data to examine your research question?

There were no insurmountable challenges because I was very familiar with this data set, having worked with it previously. Generally, getting to know a data set takes some time and a lot of "dry runs" before you figure out what you are doing. My knowledge of the data set sped things up enormously. At the same time, the major challenge in doing a secondary analysis is that the available measures are not always as relevant to the secondary study as they might have been for the original study. For example, the "school bonding" measure did not have as many items as other measures in the literature. Nonetheless, the results we obtained suggest that our single item measure was a good indicator of the more complex school bonding scales that are available.

How did you come to collaborate on this project? What do you see as advantages and/or disadvantages in collaborating as a result of your experience?

When we decided to do the study, I applied for a small research grant from the Canadian Social Sciences and Humanities Research Council, administered through our university. The grant allowed us to provide some support for a graduate student to work on the project, and that student was Nancy. At the time, we were co-members of a research seminar group that was using grounded theory as a research method and we felt we could work well together. And it was a topic we were both interested in pursuing—me from a more theoretical perspective, and Nancy from a more pragmatic learner's perspective. Nancy had some experience working on adolescent health research with another colleague so she was an ideal partner. It's all history from there. The major benefit for me was that I had some very capable help to complete the project in the midst of a very busy schedule. The major benefit for Nancy was that she had a unique learning opportunity.

Were there any unexpected events, problems, or developments that you faced in doing this research? What were they, and how did you deal with them?

No, there were no real problems or unexpected events. That is probably one of the advantages of doing a secondary analysis. Problems often arise in the initial study during conceptualization and during data collection. The data set we used was already established and had been cleaned and verified and so was ready to use.

Were your findings expected or unexpected? What do you see as the main contributions and implications of your research, say, for policies and programs addressed to that problem?

Although our initial observations suggested that school administrators might deal differently with female smokers than with males, we were very surprised at the marked gender differences with respect to the relationships between adolescents and the authority figures in their lives, particularly school administrators and parents. More surprising, however, was the finding that adolescent female smokers are much more likely than male smokers to feel disempowered in their school environments and to feel considerably less attachment to their schools than male adolescent smokers. The fact that girls in this study were more likely than boys to be engaged in oppositional, distanced, and generally unsatisfactory relationships with important adults in their lives, particularly those in positions of relative power and authority, was somewhat surprising. The strong gender differences, which have not been explored adequately in the literature, have significant implications for policy and programs. Gender neutral smoking prevention programs are the norm, at least in Canada, and these findings suggest that this may not be the best practice.

What were the ethical challenges or issues involved in your research? How did you deal with them?

The major ethical challenge in secondary analysis is that the participants do not usually consent to have their data used for a second study that was not envisioned initially. However, the full benefits of the data were never realized in the original study, because the particular question we asked in this study was not explored. Students in this study gave generously of their time to complete the survey, and we believed that using the data to its full potential honors more completely the contributions made by the students who participated in the original study. We did apply for and receive ethical approval from our university's human subjects review committee for this secondary analysis.

What were the most frustrating and most satisfying aspects of doing this research?

I can't say that there really was anything frustrating about doing this research. The most satisfying aspect of the experience was in finding something that had not been previously reported in the literature, and yet jibed with our personal experience.

If you were to do this research again, what might you do differently?

We would actually do this particular research the same, but now plan to do a follow-up qualitative study to explore in more depth the nature of "resistance" as understood by adolescent girls who smoke.

What important lesson drawn from this research experience can you share with students?

Secondary data analysis is a valuable tool for "mining" existing data sets, provided one asks appropriate questions given the data on hand, and has access to appropriate measures of the variables in question. It is an excellent way for students to learn about data analysis with "real" data, and it often reveals surprising findings that were not anticipated by the original researchers. It is an excellent way to do a master's thesis when funds are short.

Questions to Think About

1. According to MacDonald and Wright, in what ways does previous research on adolescent smoking fall short? What makes their study a *feminist* analysis of girls' smoking?

2. Describe the process by which they selected their sample. What kind of sampling was used at each stage? What are some strengths and drawbacks of the sample?

3. What are the gender differences that MacDonald and Wright found in factors that help to explain smoking? Did their results surprise you? How?

4. In her interview, MacDonald says that they plan to do a follow-up study that is qualitative. What might such a study look like (sample, measures, etc.)? How do you think it might add to what we learn from their quantitative study?

5. What are all the variables that MacDonald and Wright include in their analysis? Which ones seem to you to be most difficult to measure? How do they measure each one, and how do they assess the reliability and validity of each?

Rebellion, Modernity, and Romance

Smoking as a Gendered Practice in Popular Young Women's Magazines, Britain 1918–1939

Penny Tinkler

In Britain, the feminization of the cigarette is a 20th-century phenomenon. Prior to 1900 few women smoked, but during the 1920s and 1930s smoking amongst women increased dramatically. Set in the context of the increased prevalence of smoking among women during the interwar years, and negotiations around the meanings of gender and gender relations in this period, this article examines some of the ways in which popular young women's magazines represented smoking as a gendered practice. An examination of the fiction and illustrations featured in popular magazines, as well as articles and advertisements, reveals that representations of women smoking were employed in the interwar years to convey and develop key gender issues—these were rebellion, modernity, and heterosexual intimacy.

Introduction

In Britain, the feminization of the cigarette is a 20th-century phenomenon. Prior to 1900, few women smoked (Hilton, 2000, pp. 139, 143; see also Havelock Ellis's comments cited in Jeffreys, 1985, p. 106). In 1914, the editor of *Girls' Friend,* a magazine aimed at young working girls in their late teens, confidently claimed that "[t]he time has gone by when the notion of a woman indulging in a cigarette filled most of us with something like genuine horror" (26 September 1914). Although the editor painted a rather misleading picture of public acceptance of women smoking (see Graves & Hodge, 1991, p. 43), this reference does suggest the increased prevalence of the practice during the Edwardian period. However, the number of women who smoked was small. In 1920, the annual per capita consumption of manufactured cigarettes by females aged 15 and over in the UK was too low to record (Wald et al., 1988, Table 2.1, pp. 13–14). During the 1920s and 1930s, smoking amongst women increased dramatically. On the eve of the Second World War annual per capita consumption amongst women aged 15 and over had reached 500 cigarettes (Wald et al., 1988, Table 2.1). A diversity of sources provide further evidence that smoking amongst women was increasingly common during the interwar years.[1]

The increased prevalence of smoking among British women during the interwar years does not, however, reveal the meaning attached to this practice. Recent studies suggest that prior to the First World War the cigarette was widely perceived as a masculine product, and smoking by women had associations with deviant womanhood, that of the prostitute, actress, "New Woman" (Hilton, 2000, p. 143) or "mannish" lesbian (Garber, 1993, pp. 155–156; Jeffreys, 1985, p. 106). It is not clear whether such attitudes characterized the 1920s and 1930s. This is a particularly interesting question in the context of the strain that the First World War put on conventional views of gender and sex roles, the introduction of female suffrage (1918 and 1928) and various negotiations around the meanings of gender and gender relations during the interwar years (Braybon & Summerfield, 1987; Tinkler, 1995).

Although since 1981 there has been much research on contemporary aspects of women's smoking (e.g, Daykin, 1993; Graham, 1993; Greaves, 1996; Jacobson, 1981, 1986; Oakley, 1989; Ritchie, 1990), little is still known about its historical dimensions. Fascinating histories of to-bacco and smoking have been published (e.g., Goodman, 1994; Hilton, 2000), but insight into the history of women and smoking in Britain is still in its infancy (Hilton, 2000; Tinkler, 2001; on women smoking in the North American context, see Howe, 1984; Ernster, 1985; Schudson, 1984).

Set in the context of the increased prevalence of smoking among women during the 1920s and 1930s, this article examines popular young women's magazines as a means of exploring some of the ways in which women's consumption of cig-arettes was represented as a gendered practice. In her guide to feminist stylistics, Mills points out that in producing a text a range of choices have to be made, and that every text that has been pro-duced could have been done so differently (Mills, 1995, p. 144). Drawing upon, and adapting, this idea to include pictures as well as text, this article works from the premise that all representations of cigarette smoking are the outcome of conscious or unconscious selections. Representations are, therefore, revealing about the meanings with which women's smoking was imbued. This article focuses, in particular, on the ways in which fiction and illustrations portrayed cigarette smoking as a meaningful practice. Features on smoking are also considered, as are advertisements which are dis-cussed more fully in Tmkler (2001). The research revealed that representations of women smoking were employed in gender-specific ways to convey and develop several key themes: rebellion, moder-nity, and heterosexual intimacy. Each of these themes is addressed in turn in the following dis-cussion. An account of the research on which this paper is based and an overview of representations of smoking in young women's magazines provides the necessary context for this discussion.

Representations of Women Smoking in Young Women's Magazines

Papers that targeted young women aged 15–25 years in the period 1918 to 1939 were identified drawing upon studies of girls' and women's maga-zines by Tinkler (1995) and White (1970). Utiliz-ing classifications developed by White and Tinkler, magazines were differentiated by the social class of the intended reader, whether working-class, upper-working/middle class or middle/upper-class. Mag-azines were also differentiated by the occupation of the intended reader. There were papers for un-married young women in full-time paid work, usually aged between 15/16 years and early 20s. These magazines heralded their readers as "work-ing," "business" or "modern girls" (Tinkler, 1995). There were also papers for women who were mar-ried and usually engaged in unpaid domestic and child-care work and, in the case of middle-class women, a range of leisure activities (White, 1970). A sample of magazine titles drawn from each group of publications was identified. A selection if issues[2] from each of these magazines was exam-ined in detail in terms of the following: (a) illus-trations of women smoking; (b) cigarette advertisements; (c) articles on smoking; (d) fiction that featured women who smoked.

Women who smoked were increasingly visible throughout the 1920s and 1930s in magazines that addressed upper-working-class and middle-class young women, such as *Girls' Friend* (1899–1931), *Girls' Favourite* (1922–1927), *Miss Mod-ern* (1930–1940), and *Mabs Weekly* (1931–1936). These papers targeted "modern girls" in their late teens and early 20s who were employed in office and sales work. Snippets on the "modern girl" in these magazines were frequently illustrated by sketches of young women smoking, and there were also occasional articles on smoking. Fiction, which was the mainstay of these magazines, often featured heroines who smoked, and the accompa-nying illustrations usually reflected this. In some cases, pictures presented heroines smoking even though there was no mention of this in the accom-panying text. Cigarette advertisements were regu-larly featured in the monthly *Miss Modern* (at least one a month), but they were absent from the weekly magazines for young working women. It is likely that weekly magazines, targeted at a rela-tively poor group of women, were not regarded by tobacco manufacturers as a viable advertising out-let. *Woman* magazine, which was launched in

1937 for upper-working-class and middle-class young wives and mothers, was a weekly color-illustrated magazine with a wide circulation (White, 1970, p. 117). This paper attracted much advertising copy including advertisements for cigarettes (two or three a week, 1937–1939). Women who smoked were also visible in the feature illustrations and fiction in *Woman. Vogue*, a magazine packed with fashion plates and advertising targeted at fashionable upper-middle-class and upper-class young women, also regularly featured images of women smoking. In contrast to magazines for upper-working-class and middle-class readers these depictions were restricted to cigarette advertisements and illustrations that accompanied various features. Fashion illustrations and also photographs, for example, frequently depicted a glamorous model holding or smoking a cigarette. In contrast, magazines for working-class readers, for example *Peg's Paper* (1919–1940), *Poppy's Paper* (1924–1934), and *Silver Star* (1937–1960), did not usually address their readers as smokers, nor did they depict women smokers in their pages; possible reasons for this will be discussed shortly.

Depictions of cigarettes and of women smoking were presented as highly meaningful in fiction of the 1920s and 1930s, and cigarettes were used to facilitate the telling of stories in diverse ways. Cigarettes were use in the text and illustrations to convey character and to establish context and atmosphere. The depiction of women smoking in illustrations, especially where the text did not mention cigarettes, suggests that smoking was perceived as a convenient visual shorthand for conveying information about character and interpersonal relationships. Depictions of women smoking were also sufficiently novel as to serve as the facilitators of narrative action. Incidents involving women smoking were, on occasions, the central focus of a story or, more usually, an element in the unfolding of events. Fictional women smokers were, however, never the norm; heroines, hedonists, and evil women were more likely to be nonsmokers than smokers throughout the 1920s and 1930s.[3]

A Rebellious Gesture

In the early to mid-1920s, the depiction of women holding or smoking cigarettes was deployed as a symbol of rebellion. This connotation derived in part from the specific meanings that were already inscribed in the cigarette relating to gender, social class, and sexuality and the juxtaposition and interplay of these meanings with the femininities of fiction heroines.

"The Taming of Miranda Temple" (*Girls' Favourite*, 19 May 1923) provides a rare example of an early 1920s serial in which the central female character was portrayed smoking. Described as "unladylike," the 17 year-old daughter of wealthy Colonel Temple was presented as beautiful and as spoilt: "[t]he fiery sparkle in her dark eyes, and the defiant pose of the head bespoke quick temper and impatience of control" (p. 363). Following an act of unusually bad behaviour, Colonel Temple decided that his daughter should no longer be educated at home by a governess, but that she should be sent to a large girls' boarding school to complete her education and, he hoped, to be "tamed." Before boarding the train on her journey to her new school, Miranda purchased sweets and Turkish cigarettes.

On the train Miranda encountered Phil Carruthers who was traveling to the boys' boarding school. When she offered him sweets and cigarettes, he declined on the grounds that, due to his training in athletics, "luxuries like chocolates and fags are banned" (p. 366). Phil's reply indicated that adolescent boys smoked; it also suggested that Miranda's intention to smoke was not shocking to young men of the middle and upper classes. Before Miranda proceeded to light her cigarette she asked the permission of a third person in the train carriage.

The austere lady placed her book on her legs. "I distinctly object," she said. "I object for two reasons," continued the lady frigidly. "One reason is that this is not a smoking carriage, the other reason, although perhaps you may think it is an extraordinarily trivial one, is that I happen to be a mistress at the school to which you are going" (p. 366).

With a gesture of defiance, however, Miranda proceeded to strike a match, light her cigarette, and smoke it.

The school teacher's objection to Miranda smoking was key to this particular episode of the "The Taming of Miranda Temple," and it featured as illustration on the front cover of *Girls' Favourite*. Smoking was central to the story in that it introduced key elements of the serial's narrative and, moreover, served to crystallize impressions of some of the main characters—Miranda, the school mistress, Phil. The smoking of cigarettes emerged in this exchange as a means of establishing the relationship between Miranda and the authorities at the school for which she was destined; this relationship was, from the outset, characterized by a clash of cultures, generations, and personalities. Miranda used cigarettes as a means of establishing that she was grown up, independent, sophisticated, and modern. The purchase of cigarettes was also telling of her social class; Turkish cigarettes were expensive, and smoked principally by upper-middle-class and upper-class women, the kinds of women portrayed in *Vogue* magazine. Smoking represented the first of many ways in which Miranda rebelled against the rules and culture of the school and teachers and, in particular, their denial of her individuality and suppression of her spirit. The contrast implicit in the depictions of the young and beautiful Miranda and the school teacher was significant. Miranda smoked, but then she was from the upper-middle classes where it was increasingly the norm for stylish young women to smoke. The school teacher did not smoke, nor think it appropriate, but this was an indication that she was old-fashioned and, moreover, of a lower social class than her young prospective student. Further, and in contrast to Miranda whose (hetero-)sexuality was blossoming, the school teacher was presented as a failed woman in that she was unmarried and unmarriageable; the description of her as "austere" and as "frigid" was particularly telling (this representation was consistent with interwar criticism of the "spinster teacher" (see Jeffreys, 1985; Oram, 1989).

The author did not castigate Miranda for smoking, partly because it was quite clear that she was an inexperienced smoker. Nevertheless, Miranda's act of defiance was not openly condoned by the author, and Miranda was subsequently presented as rather foolish for proceeding to smoke her cigarette.

The smoke—everything seemed to be in conspiracy against her nowadays—went the wrong way, and she broke into a violent fit of coughing . . . Miranda smoked the cigarette down to the end—the bitter end (*Girls' Favourite*, 26 May 1923, p. 387).

In subsequent issues there was no further mention of Miranda smoking, although there were two references to deviant schoolgirls engaging in this activity, during a clandestine meeting of the "Clan Club" and during an afternoon sitting by the riverside in the sun. In both instances, smoking was associated with rebellion; "Mind they don't see you girls smoking . . . It'll mean a million lines apiece" (*Girls' Favourite*, 7 July 1923, p. 550).

Miranda's smoking was a gesture of defiance that resonated with age, social class, and sexual overtones. Smoking served as a means of challenging the school's hierarchy based on age and academic qualification, whereby school mistresses were superior to pupils, and of reinstating hierarchies of social class, whereby the schoolgirls were superior to their teachers. Smoking also worked as a vehicle, whereby girls rebelled against the school's attempt to prolong their childhood, suppress the independence associated with adulthood and the sexuality associated with womanhood. The specific depiction of smoking as a means of rebellion against the imposition of school authority, hierarchies, and enforced dependency was unusual in popular magazines. Nevertheless, many of the themes addressed in the story of Miranda were evident in the proliferation of references to smoking that appeared in magazines from the mid-1920s. Smoking was, for example, firmly established as an age marker; to smoke cigarettes signified that one was "grown up." Moreover, while the overt rebellion that characterized Miranda's smoking practices was unusual, the cigarette was commonly deployed to signify change and resistance to what had gone before. More specifically, smoking was associated with modernity (the breaking with tradition) and with the representation of generational difference. Indeed, the cigarette was often key to the representation of the "modern girl," who became both the principal character in fiction and the principal intended reader and addressee of upper-working-class and middle-class magazines throughout the 1920s and 1930s.

Smoking and Modernity in the 1920s

Following the First World War, popular magazines for upper-working-class and middle-class young working women heralded their readers as "modern girls." This appellation was a positive embrace of young women and an attempt to establish a specifically youthful female identity that publishers could subsequently identify with and cater for (Tinkler, 1995, 2000). Paid work was presented as key to the "modern girl's" identity, and as the source of the modern girls' difference from girls of previous generations (Tinkler, 1995). According to these magazines, changes wrought by the First World War had significantly shifted female ambitions. Modern girls, it was claimed, enjoyed paid work and hankered after careers. These young women wanted independence and equality with men. They enjoyed their leisure, and engaged in relaxed and friendly relations with men. Marriage was, for the modern girl, no longer perceived as the only future. Magazines that targeted young working women, or rather "modern girls," relied heavily upon visual signifiers. This was, in part, a result of the increased deployment of illustration and color by publishers in a bid to maximize the aesthetic appeal of their papers and, possibly, to distinguish them from those of their competitors. Increased dependence on visual signifiers could also have resulted from a recognition of the value of these as a means of differentiating potential audiences and of establishing reader

identification (Tinkler, 2000; White, 1970, pp. 96, 98). Indeed, visual markers provided a quickly accessible means of demarcating audiences by gender, age, and generation. For example, visible indicators of the modern girl included shingled hair and the wearing of short dresses and skirts. Smoking cigarettes was presented as another visible sign of youthful modernity (this was also the case in depictions of the Irish "modern girl," see Ryan, 1998, p. 193).

The association of cigarette smoking with modernity was a key feature of cigarette advertisements featured in young women's magazines of the 1920s and 1930s (Tinkler, 2001), it was also evident in other aspects of these papers. Illustrations for articles often depicted young modern women, perhaps an idealized reader, holding or smoking a cigarette. Fiction descriptions and illustrations also featured modern heroines smoking. Barbara, for example, was "a modern girl" who was featured in *Girls' Friend* in 1925. At 19 she had already established herself as a well-respected and "indispensable" private secretary to the head of an important firm. Although Barbara contributed £2 of her £5 weekly wage to household expenses she insisted on her independence: "she was essentially a 'modern' girl. Her spare time was her own" (21 March 1925, p. 1), and she smoked. Her father was described as extremely proud of her. Although at one point he asked her not to smoke while he was talking to her, there was no indication that the father was anything but totally approving of his daughter. The significance of the cigarette as a symbol of modernity was evident in its appearance in the opening description of the heroine. "Barbara had been sitting on the edge of the table, swinging her legs. She took the cigarette from her lips . . ." (21 March 1925, p. 1). Significantly, having served to establish the heroine's character, smoking was only mentioned once again. Smoking was similarly critical in the establishment of Sylvia Dawn, another modern young woman. The opening sentence of "The Wiles of Eve" set the scene: "Sylvia Dawn, perched on a table, a cigarette between her lips, gazed pensively at a large poster on the opposite wall" (*Girls' Friend,* 4 July 1925, p. 7). Like Barbara, Sylvia was presented as young, talented, and extremely feminine. She was also affluent, as indicated by the fact that she smoked scented cigarettes held in an amber holder. As in other stories where the cigarette was symbolic of modernity, after the initial description of the heroine smoking in a way that suggested it was a commonplace activity, there was no further reference to this practice.

Representations of women smoking cigarettes were also deployed to convey a key temporal feature of modernity. Girls' magazines placed much emphasis on full-time paid work as a key feature of modernity. They also stressed the importance of well-earned leisure and relaxation as a necessary counter to the rigor and demands of modern life in the public sphere. Smoking emerged as an important feature of relaxation and of leisure. Schudson (1984) argues that the adoption of the cigarette in the 1920s was linked to its compatability with the modern, urban pace of life; "It is the McDonald's of the tobacco trade, the fast food of smoking" (p. 199). Representations of smoking in girls' magazines suggest that the cigarette was utilized as a temporal device but in more complex ways. Smoking was presented as a form of consumption that differentiated types of time—work time and leisure time: it also facilitated a change in the tempo and quality of time in that it contributed towards the production of a relaxed leisure experience. *Girls' Friend,* for example, which addressed modern business girls throughout the 1920s, featured small sketches or motifs that depicted a young woman smoking while reclining or curled up amidst plump cushions. Often the young woman had a cup of tea or coffee at her side and/or an open book. This remained a popular motif in the 1930s as seen in a photo of a young woman in an easy chair, smoking whilst reading *Woman* magazine (*Woman,* 26 June 1937, p. 10).

Occasional articles reinforced the view that smoking was an appropriate activity for modern young women. For example, in an article entitled "Should Girls Smoke?" (*Girls' Favourite,* 18 March 1922), a fictional group of friends were presented as discussing this burning question while "puffing away merrily." The consensus was that it was acceptable for girls to smoke if they enjoyed it. The girls were adamant, however, that it was "absolutely ridiculous for girls to smoke just for mere affectation . . . It is only 'swank,' and in some cases fear of being thought old-fashioned" (p. 164). Excessive smoking was also described as inappropriate: "There is a girl I know who smokes fifty cigarettes a day, . . . it is perfectly horrid when a girl lets a habit get hold of her like that" (p. 164). While in this instance excessive smoking was disapproved of specifically, the speaker also seemed to voice a wider concern about the ways in which addictions compromised a girl's/woman's self-control that was crucial to the maintenance of feminine standards of conduct.

Although modern girls smoked, fiction indicates that this was not regarded as an appropriate activity for old-fashioned girls. Indeed, fiction often utilized the shock value of old-fashioned girls smoking to facilitate narrative action. Ruth, for example, was a young woman who, after a period of high living in London, had retreated to a quiet life in the Sussex Downs (*Girls' Friend,* 5 September 1925). The reason for this was never made clear. In her London life, Ruth had dressed in sumptuous clothes, danced the nights away, wined, dined, and smoked; she had been a "modern girl." In Sussex, she assumed the guise of a lonely spinster attired in sensible skirt, blouse, and cardigan. Ruth's friends and neighbors just assumed that she was an old-fashioned spinster type; they had no idea about her "gay" past. Although Ruth rejected many aspects of her modern lifestyle when she moved to the country, she nevertheless continued to smoke a cigarette after dinner while she read her book before retiring to bed. Indeed, the cigarette served as a link between Ruth's past and present lives and as an indicator that Ruth was still modern at heart. When her friend discovered that Ruth even kept cigarettes in the house she was quite shocked. Eventually, however, Ruth was compelled to emerge once more in her modern, sophisticated guise. Before she could retire back into anonymity Ruth won the heart of a wealthy and successful man who then proposed to her.

The incongruity of an old-fashioned young woman smoking was also employed, although to a different end, in "The Mischief Maker." In this story about Virginia Browne, a private secretary in a firm that handled secret government work (*Girls' Favourite*, 19 May 1923), smoking was used to facilitate the drama. Following a warning that she must end her friendship and blossoming romance with Jimmy Carrington, the junior partner of the firm at which she worked, Virginia attempted to discourage her suitor by being seen by him at a party flirting and smoking. It is quite clear to the reader, however, that Virginia was not a smoker, as she had to try not to cough when she puffed at her cigarette. Jimmy was quite shocked to discover that Virginia smoked, "I suppose there's no harm in smoking. It's her affair, but—" (p. 381). Jimmy's reluctance to outrightly criticize Virginia was a sign of his affection for her; it was also an indicator that smoking among women was increasingly accepted. However, his comment conveys implicitly that he did not regard smoking as appropriate feminine behavior or, as Virginia's rival put it, that "it doesn't look nice" (p. 381). Although Barbara and Sylvia with their bobbed hair and short skirts could legitimately smoke, the ultra-feminine, curly-haired and rather old-fashioned Virginia could not. The image of Virginia with her soft locks smoking a cigarette was discordant; it was inconsistent with images of both the modern girl and her Victorian predecessor. The fact that *Girls' Favourite* had, in previous years, accepted women who smoked, indicates that the difference in the treatment of Barbara and Virginia cannot be attributed to an increased acceptance of women smoking.

Social class was key to early 20th-century representations of smoking amongst girls and women. The cigarette was, from its first appearance in women's magazines of the early 1920s, firmly associated with middle-class and upper-class lifestyles. It was a symbol of affluence and of sophisticated femininity. Cigarette advertisements that were common in the upper-class magazine

Vogue in the early 1920s, and which proliferated in middle-class women's magazines by the 1930s, explicitly associated smoking with middle- and upper-class models of glamorous and fashionable young womanhood. Fashion plates in *Vogue*, which presented cigarettes as a fashionable accessory offered a further articulation of these class associations, and, moreover, consolidated the links between cigarettes, fashion, and modernity. The failure of early magazine advertisements to target working-class girls/women as potential smokers can be interpreted as a sign that tobacco manufacturers did not regard working-class women's magazines as a successful advertising outlet. However, working-class women were not depicted smoking in magazine fiction and magazines for working-class girls rarely depicted their readers or their female fiction characters as smokers. One possible explanation for this overt class distinction in fiction is that the association between prostitution and smoking continued to overshadow the working-class female smoker at least until the late 1930s. The reclassification of smoking in social-class terms from an activity associated with working-class prostitution to one equated with middle-class and upper-class lifestyles was key to the increased appearance of women smoking in magazines. The increased popularity of smoking among women was also quite probably predicated on the association of the cigarette with middle- and upper-class lifestyles and ideals of femininity.

Smoking was also, significantly, not associated with bad or evil female characters in interwar magazine fiction. This was consistent with cinemagraphic representations of female smokers in the 1920s and 1930s. Dale's study of 40 Hollywood motion pictures revealed that 12 of the pictures featured heroines who smoked and only one featured a "villainess" who smoked (Dale, 1935, p. 171); indeed, "the *heroine* smoked more than either the *villain* or the *villainess*" (p. 173, italics in original). The association of cigarettes with bad women was clearly incompatible with the attempt by tobacco companies to redefine smoking as an appropriately feminine activity. More precisely, the evil or bad woman was, in terms of her social class and/or her sexuality, representative of the associations which tobacco manufacturers were probably keen to dispel. Evil and bad women were invariably portrayed as sexually deviant in that they transgressed the boundaries of appropriate feminine behavior and, more specifically, that they rejected a passive and monogamous heterosexuality. Evil and bad women invariably had no scruples, and they deliberately flirted with men, utilizing their looks and charms to manipulate men to their own, usually materialistic ends. The link between the cigarette, deviant female sexuality, and money was perhaps too closely associated with working-class prostitution for evil characters to be featured smoking.

Lorraine Greaves, in her overview of the history of women smoking in North America, claims that "cigarette smoking in the 1920s became a symbol of women's freedom in the dominant culture and a challenge to Victorian mores. Smoking became firmly allligned with dress reform, bobbed hair, nightclubbing and suffrage" (Greaves, 1996, p. 19). Smoking, Greaves continues, was also a way of signalling women's equality with men: "If equality was understood as being 'equal to' men, then it followed that women should be allowed to do whatever men could" (p. 20). In the British context, smoking was undoubtedly presented and perceived as a challenge to Victorian models of femininity (on Victorian models of femininity, see Dyhouse, 1981; Gorham, 1982). Cigarettes and cigars had traditionally been equated with men and masculinity. Smoking also had associations with the "mannish" lesbian following Havelock Ellis' description of the "female homosexual" in *Sexual Inversions* (Garber, 1993, pp. 155–156; Jeffreys, 1985, p. 106). As Garber points out, the cigarette was a crucial prop in the proof of masculinity, and subsequently, was much used by female impersonators (Garber, 1993, p. 156). A portrait of a tomboyish schoolgirl from *Girls' Reader* ("Madcaps Three," 22 January 1910) offers a good example of the role of the cigarette as a masculine marker: "Her hair was cut short, she wore stand-up linen collars, while the general cut

of her garments helped out the masculine idea. In addition she often carried a silver mounted walking stick, [and] smoked cigarettes . . ." Given the masculine associations of the cigarette, women who smoked could be interpreted as laying claim to rights that were traditionally the perogative of men. Indeed, smoking explicitly challenged the polarized gender differentiation that rationalized the prevailing gender hierarchy. Smoking also served to differentiate the current generation of young women from their predecessors.

Popular magazines acknowledged that smoking could be interpreted as a sign that women had more freedom and greater equality with men. Issues of equality and freedom were often utilized in early cigarette advertisements such as those featured in *Vogue* 1920–1930, which either explicitly mentioned women's "new-found" freedom or which, less commonly, depicted women on their own in public. In the latter case, cigarette smoking by women was associated with women's increased independence (from men and family) and mobility (especially outside the home). Such motifs were unusual in the 1930s, and women, whether portrayed on their own or in company, were invariably located explicitly or implicitly within a heterosexual framework (Tinkler, 2001). Although magazines presented smoking as a sign of women's increased equality with men, an important distinction was drawn between a modern appearance and leisure practices on the one hand and, on the other, political equality. In the early 1920s, modern young women did not have the vote; full adult female suffrage was not granted until 1928. Sexual equality was even more remote and less easily attainable. Consistent with the limits placed on independence and equality, popular magazines for young women drew an important if somewhat hazy distinction between, on the one the hand, the modern girl and, on the other, masculine women, lesbians, and feminists. The independence and new-found status of the modern girl was carefully distanced from masculinity and male privileges.

In an examination of popular girls' magazines 1920–1950 (1995), I argued that representations of the "modern girl" were a product of the editorial negotiation of different sets of interests. On the one hand, there were the publishers whose principal aim was to increase sales and maximise profits. To maintain and boost sales, magazine editors were compelled to engage with their intended readers' concerns, interests, and aspirations, and to avoid directly challenging the reader or her self image. Editors were, however, also constrained by prevailing ideologies of feminity and of adolescent female development. Editors were constrained, in particular, by the significance attached to the age of their intended female readership that was bound up with the "heterosexual career" (Tinkler, 1995, pp. 3, 74–75). Where a publisher targeted a readership deemed to be entering heterosexual relations, heterosexuality was a crucial consideration in deciding magazine content and the cultural management of particular topics. The treatment of paid work and courtship in girls' magazines was shaped by the editor's negotiation of these factors (Tinkler, 1995, pp. 75, 94–96). Magazine representations of young women smoking reveal similar negotiations at work. Indeed, women's smoking was carefully presented in ways that simultaneously celebrated modernity but that eschewed manliness and any challenge to heterosexual age and gender relations.

In a rare diatribe against women smoking, the feared significance of smoking for gender identity and gender relations was articulated quite clearly. The author of "This Cigarette Business" (*Girls' Favourite*, 4 December 1926), detailed the ways in which smoking killed romance by arguing that women who smoked lost their femininity and their distinctiveness from men, which was the foundation of gender relations, romance, and marriage.

[H]ow can he get the proper atmosphere when, on bending to extract the kiss that seals the bargain, he finds that her waving locks are perfumed with stale smoke instead of the sweet, subtle perfume that he has been given to expect, and that her answering kiss might be that of his best boy charm for fragrance? (p. 411)

The author proceeded to describe the results of women smoking revealing the association between smoking, masculinity, and lesbianism:

she might soon grow into a mannish, nicotine-stained and perfumed travesty of her former dear little self, lolling inelegantly on chair-arms, viewing the world through a cloud of smoke and cynical remarks. She might even—terrible thought—call me "old thing!" (p. 411)

Even in articles where smoking was presented as acceptable, the spectre of "mannish" women nevertheless lurked in the background, and readers were warned against emulating male smoking practices. In "Copy-Cattishness!" (*Girls' Favourite*, 23, October 1926), readers were explicitly cautioned against aping men. Careful not to be dismissed as old-fashioned, the author did not chastize readers who smoked but advised them to feminize the masculine activity that they adopted; "You may smoke, you may crop, you may be independent—only give it the girlish touch! He likes to see you have a cigarette—if you only do it to keep him company—if you manipulate it daintily, with a certain air of "I'm not used to this, you know!" . . . He doesn't like you to look professional, as it were. You lose all your charm then. That is *his* prerogative!" (p. 271, italics in original).

The thin line between acceptable and unacceptable smoking was drawn in relation to the perceived threat that the smoking woman posed to masculinity and gender relations. Hence, in "Dreams!," a story about a 29-year-old career woman named Daisy, who "scorned the girl who threw up a career to be a household drudge," smoking was presented rather differently than in the story about teenaged Barbara, discussed earlier. Daisy was presented as rejecting marriage and motherhood in preference for a career, and she was also portrayed as attempting to emulate male authority. Daisy's friend, Carrie, thought that "Daisy looked wonderful when she was smoking, her shingled head flung back, her hands in her velvet jacket pocket, laying down the law" (*Girls' Friend*, 15 March 1930, p. 3). Although Daisy's friend Carrie was impressed, other employees at the firm regarded Daisy as bossy and, it is implied, somewhat ridiculous. The author, it would seem, was also unimpressed by Daisy's behavior and she was painfully punished in the story for going too far. When she eventually fell in love and dreamed of marriage, home, and a family, she was rejected by the man she loved in favor of the ultrafeminine Carrie. Whereas smoking contributed to the modernity of both Barbara and Sylvia ("modern girls" discussed earlier) who were portrayed as young and as potentially marriageable (they both fall in love and accept proposals of marriage), Daisy was 29 and, in the context of the interwar years, she would have been regarded as a spinster. Daisy's smoking could not, therefore, be linked to an acceptable form of feminine modernity, one that was safely contained within heterosexual relations. Instead, her smoking represented an attempt to usurp the privileges of masculinity and it was, therefore, portrayed as a travesty of femininity. This moral tale and other fiction revealed the boundaries of gender norms in the 1920s. Some flexibility of gender norms was acceptable and, indeed, consistent with modernity. The line was drawn, however, at behavior that could not be accommodated within the prevailing gender hierarchy. Women who transgressed the boundaries of feminine conduct were subsequently perceived as a threat, and dealt with harshly.

Magazines accepted that girls smoked but, in an attempt to reduce the political significance of this activity, they promoted a specifically feminine mode of smoking. Modern girls could smoke, but this activity was carefully circumscribed in ways that restated and reinforced patriarchal gender relations; the "girlish touch" was indispensable. Encouraging young women to smoke only to accompany men was another strategy of containment. Indeed, to keep men, especially brothers, company was presented as a particularly good reason why women should smoke. As Peggy explained, "when my brothers come home in the evening they like me to light up with them" (*Girls' Favourite*, 18 March 1922, p. 164). Reinforcing the prominence of the male perspective on girls

who smoked, the brother of one of the girls joined the conversation and contributed the last word on the subject. His contribution forcefully restated the social role of women smoking and, more specifically, its heterosocial significance: "Smoke! I should jolly well think they should! . . . We like our sisters and girl friends to keep us company" (p. 164). He went on, however, to specify that girls should only smoke at home: "most of us men don't like to see girls of whom we think a great deal—our girl chums and our sisters—smoking in public places. I don't know how to explain it, but it seems to take the girlish freshness away from them. There should be moderation in all things" (p. 164). Keeping men company was, in fact, a form of servicing. As such, women's smoking could be interpreted as an extension of traditional feminine behavior, and therefore, embedded safely within conventional hierarchical gender relations. Other ways to which women could play a servicing role in male smoking rituals were outlined by the author, mentioned earlier, who condemned women smoking: "I should love her to provide me with lights, and blow out my matches, and, on those occasions when I favoured a pipe, fill it for me" (*Girls' Favourite*, 4 December 1926, p. 411).

Smoking and Heterosexual Intimacy

Greaves (1996) asserts that by the 1940s cigarettes had become a "crucial erotic prop and a way of increasing one's attractiveness to men" p. 21). The heterosexual significance of smoking was, however, established in Britain during the 1920s when smoking among women was still in its infancy. Indeed, I would argue that the heterosexualization of smoking was quite central to its increasingly high profile in representations of women prior to the Second World War; whether this was a significant factor in women's actual motivations for smoking is, of course, another matter. From the early 1930s the association between smoking and heterosexual attractiveness and heterosexual relations was a crucial feature of cigarette advertising targeted at women (Tinkler, 2001). Magazines contained some criticism of smoking; for example, the article that declared that smoking spoiled romance because a woman became increasingly masculine. Generally, however, magazines acknowledged that readers smoked, and they accepted the cigarette as an important symbol of modernity. As we have seen, however, the meanings, and gender significance, of women's smoking was contained in various ways. The location of women's smoking within a heterosexual framework can be interpreted as a further means by which the significance and implications of female smoking were circumscribed.

By the mid-1920s there were frequent references in articles to women smoking to accompany men. In some contexts, smoking was actually presented as the polite thing to do. This convention was also evident in fiction which, during the late 1920s and 1930s, provided graphic examples of the place of cigarettes in heterosexual relations. Smoking was used, for example, to denote heterosexual intimacy. Interestingly, the heroine was frequently portrayed in illustrations with a cigarette even where the text did not specifically mention the woman smoking. For example, in "A Girl and Her Secret" (*Girls' Friend*, 5 September 1925), Ruth was described talking to Gerald Fielden who offered her a cigarette. There was no mention in the text of her accepting one, although the large illustration that accompanied the story showed Ruth seated beside Gerald under a tree in the garden with a lighted cigarette in her hand, smoke trailing upwards. This scene was typical of the way in which smoking was established as a visual indicator of heterosexual intimacy (see also *Girls' Friend*, 18 July 1925, p. 16). In the late 1930s, smoking in the company of a man remained highly significant, although the contexts were often quite different. For example, Nicole and Philip, both widowed with a young child, were depicted sitting together smoking quietly while their respective children got to know one another (*Woman*, 3 July 1937, p. 12).

The cigarette was also, from the 1920s, increasingly established as an important facilitator of heterosexual romance. This stemmed from the hetero-erotic significance that was graphically associated with women's smoking practices. The following extract from "That Dreadful Miss Cardew" provides a good example of the hetero-erotic significance of smoking and the role of the cigarette in fostering sexual attraction and heterosexual romance.

> He rose and handed her his case. She took a cigarette and slipped it between her lips, waiting for him to give her a light. For a moment he hesitated, for there was something in the way her soft, red lips closed round the cigarette that covered him with confusion . . . He lighted a match and held it to her cigarette, and again he noticed how red and curved were her lips (*Girls' Friend*, 16 May 1925, p. 8).

This extract set out smoking rituals whereby a man provided a cigarette for a woman that he then lit; this act required the physical proximity of the couple and the woman's dependence on the man for a light. The lighting of the cigarette brought the couple closer together, the cigarette highlighted the sensuality of the woman's lips, this was further illuminated by the light from the match. This smoking ritual was presented as highly erotic, and as a means of arousing passion between a woman and a man. In this way, smoking practices were depicted as a way of fostering the development of romantic heterosexual relationships. Similar themes emerged and were developed in the following scene from *Mabs Weekly*.

> The window behind them was wide open, and the breeze from the sea made the match-flare flicker between them, and Simone put her hand over Thurston's to make a shield for it. She could feel his eyes upon her, and presently she looked up with slow deliberation, but the smile died from her lips as she saw the expression of his face, for it was as if he said "I love You!" (17 October 1931, p. 7).

Representations of smoking practices were often clear indicators of the level of intimacy reached by a couple. In "Strangers To-day" (*Woman*, 25 September 1937) the growing feeling between Belling and Audrey was indicated by shifts in their smoking practices. At the outset, Audrey was depicted smoking alone in the hotel lounge. When Belling first approached Audrey he offered her a cigarette and then, when she accepted, he leant forward to light it for her. She then offered him a cigarette and he lit both their cigarettes. Within 24 hours, and in the final scene in which Belling confessed that he had fallen in love with Audrey, he lit a cigarette for Audrey and passed it to her before he lit one for himself.

Smoking facilitated the introduction of a flame into representations of close encounters between the sexes. Although the lighting of a cigarette was also used to illuminate scenes between women, it was in the context of heterosexual romance that it was most popularly employed. A flame served as a technical device that facilitated the action by providing illumination. It also served as a symbol of love and sexual attraction; a flickering flame, for example, was used to symbolize the awakening of passion. In the above extract from *Mabs Weekly*, it was significant that Simone placed her hands over those of Thurston to protect the flame that symbolized their newly sparked love. Flames also provided convenient illumination of the face, high lighting attractiveness, and rendering emotion visible. The moment of illumination was the subject of the illustration selected for "Strangers To-day" (*Woman*, 25 September 1937). Indeed, in this story Belling was described as deliberately offering a lone woman a cigarette in order to sneak a glimpse of her face that was otherwise hidden by the shadows in the dimly lit hotel lounge. Belling was, however, "unprepared for the lovelines the flame revealed" (p. 8).

Conclusion

In interwar young women's magazines smoking was presented, and actively utilized, as a highly meaningful practice. The meanings with which women's smoking was imbued served to convey character, establish context, and facilitate fictional drama. Throughout the 1920s magazine representations of women smoking were strongly

associated with social change and, to a lesser degree, with growing up. Attitudes towards change were, however, ambivalent. On the negative side, smoking was associated with the complete disruption of pre-World War 1 gender identities and gender relations. These postwar images of women smoking resonated with overtones of masculinity, and they were associated with women challenging traditional gender hierarchies and usurping male privileges. In a more positive vein, representations of women smoking were utilized to convey growing up and a safer form of social change, one that was associated with a carefully circumscribed form of female modernity or youthful rebellion. In relation to modernity, in particular, the disruptive and therefore dangerous gender associations of women's smoking were contained through heterosexual relations and romance. Indeed, throughout the interwar period one of the increasingly significant ways in which women's smoking was deployed (and established as a feminine practice) was in the context of successful heterosexual relations. In fiction, in particular, smoking practices were presented as hetero-erotic, and they were used to foster the development of heterosexual relationships by highlighting female sexuality and heterosexual passion.

ENDNOTES

1. Evidence that women smoked appears in contemporary surveys, for example, Mary Agnes Hamilton's study of 1936 (cited in Alexander, 1989, p. 246); also, Graves and Hodge (1991, p. 43). Autobiographical references are also telling, for instance, the description of "Jane" in Vera Brittain's (1928) *Testament of Youth* (cited in Alexander, 1989, p. 262). Letters printed in magazine correspondence features during the 1920s also suggest that some young women were smokers; see, for example, *Girls' Friend*, 4 April 1925, p. 4. The proliforation of portraiture that depicted women holding or smoking a cigarette is also revealing. See also evidence presented in Hilton (2000).

2. The sample magazines were: *Girls' Friend, Girls' Favourite, Miss Modern, Mabs Weekly, Peg's Paper, Poppy's Paper, Sliver Star, Woman, Vogue*. Each magazine was examined at roughly 5-year intervals to in-

clude, where possible, the beginning, middle, and end years of each decade. For each magazine, six weekly issues or three (bi-)monthly issues were examined for each sample year. Additional issues were examined for context and to follow through particular types of representations.

3. Although in the 1920s, men were often described as smokers of pipes, cigars, and cigarettes, their smoking was not presented in young woman's magazines as particularly significant relative to smoking by women. The mode of tobacco consumption was, nevertheless, an important indicator of masculine style, age, social class, and character. A discussion of representations of male smoking in women's magazines is, however, beyond the scope of this paper.

REFERENCES

Alexander, Sally. (1989). Becoming a woman in London in the 1920s and 1930s. In David Feldman & Gareth Stedman Jones (Eds.), *Metropolis—London: Histories and representations since 1800* (pp. 245–271). London: Routledge.

Braybon, Gail, & Summerfield, Penny. (1987). *Out of the cage: Women's experiences in two World Wars.* London: Pandora Press.

Dale, Edgar. (1935). *The content of motion pictures.* New York: The MacMillan Company.

Daykin, Norma. (1993). Young women and smoking: Towards a sociological account. *Health Promotion International, 8,* 95–102.

Dyhouse, Carol. (1981). *Girls growing up in late Victorian and Edwardian England.* London: Routledge & Kegan Paul.

Ernster, Virginia L. (1985, July). Mixed messages for women, a social history of cigarette smoking and advertising. *New York State Journal of Medicine, 85,* 335–340.

Garber, Marjorie. (1993). *Vested Interests: Cross-dressing & cultural anxiety.* Harmondsworth: Penguin.

Goodman, Jordan. (1994). *Tobacco in history. The cultures of dependence.* London: Routledge.

Gorham, Deborah. (1982). *The Victorian girl and the feminine ideal.* London: Croom Helm.

Graham, Hilary. (1993). *When life's a drag: Women, smoking and disadvantage.* London: HMSO.

Graves, Robert, & Hodge, Alan. (1991, originally published in 1940). *The long week-end: A social history of Great Britain 1918–1939.* London: Cardinal.

Greaves, Lorraine. (1996). *Smoke screen: Women's smoking and social control.* London: Scarlet Press.

Hilton, Matthew. (2000). *Smoking in British popular culture 1800–2000.* Manchester: Manchester University Press.

Howe, Holly. (1984, May/June). An historical review of women, smoking and advertising. *Health Education, 43,* 3–9.

Jacobson, Bobbie. (1981). *The ladykillers: Why smoking is a feminist issue.* London: Pluto Press.

Jacobson, Bobbie. (1986). *Beating the ladykillers: Women and smoking.* London: Pluto Press.

Jeffreys, Sheila. (1985). *The spinster and her enemies: Feminism and sexuality 1880–1930.* London: Pandora.

Mills, Sara. (1995). *Feminist stylistics.* London: Routledge.

Oakley, Ann. (1989). Smoking in pregnancy: Smokescreen or risk factor? Towards a materialist analysis. *Sociology of Health & Illness, 11,* 311–335.

Oram, Alison. (1989). "Embittered, sexless or homosexual": Attacks on spinster teachers, 1918–1939. In Lesbian history group (Ed.), *Not a passing phase: Reclaiming lesbians in history 1840–1985* (pp. 99–118). London: The Women's Press.

Ritchie, Jane. (1990). Women and smoking: A lethal deception. *Women's Studies International Forum, 13,* 201–208.

Ryan, Louise. (1998). Negotiating modernity and tradition: Newspaper debates on the "modern girl" in the Irish Free State. *Journal of Gender Studies, 7,* 181–197.

Schudson, Michael. (1984). *Advertising, the uneasy persuasion: Its dubious impact on American society.* New York: Basic Books.

Tinkler, Penny. (1995). *Constructing girlhood: Popular magazines for girls growing up in England, 1920–1950.* London: Taylor & Francis.

Tinkler, Penny. (2000). "Material girl"? Adolescent girls and their magazines, 1920–1958. In Maggie Andrews & Mary M. Talbot (Eds.), *All the world and her husband: Women in twentieth-century consumer culture* (pp. 97–112). London: Cassell.

Tinkler, Penny. (2001). "Red tips for hot lips": Advertising cigarettes for young women in Britain, 1920–1970. *Women's History Review.*

Wald, Nicholas, et al. (1988). *UK stroking statistics.* Oxford: Oxford University Press.

White, Cynthia. (1970). *Women's magazines 1693–1968.* London: Michael Joseph.

Penny Tinkler is a senior lecturer in the Department of Sociology at the University of Manchester. Trained as a historian within a social science framework, her research is largely archival. She has written extensively on aspects of twentieth-century girlhood and young womanhood including *Constructing Girlhood: Popular Magazines for Girls Growing Up in England, 1920–1950* (Taylor & Francis). She is currently researching the feminization of smoking in Britain and writing a book, *Smoke Signals: Women, Smoking and Visual Culture in Britain,* on smoking and visual culture to be published by Berg.

An   interview   with . . .

Penny Tinkler

How did you become interested in this topic?

This is a rather strange story. I received a mysterious letter from a law firm requesting a meeting to discuss a research/business proposal. Out of curiosity I agreed to the meeting. After much beating about the bush, it became clear that I was being offered funding from the tobacco industry to undertake research on the history of women and smoking. At the time I had never even contemplated doing research on this topic, although I had written about various aspects of leisure for girls and young women and completed a book on popular magazines from 1920–1950. To cut a long story short, I declined the offer and my contact disappeared, never to be seen or heard from again. However, the seed was sown. The topic dovetailed neatly with my interests in the twentieth century history of girls and women in Britain and the social construction and articulation of gender and gender relations, particularly as they are cross-cut by age and social class. The topic was also quite fascinating. When did cigarette smoking become respectable for women from different social groups? Were the two World Wars catalysts for the growth in smoking amongst women? How did smoking become a respectable feminine practice? What insights could attitudes towards women smoking offer into gender, age and class relations?

What made you choose this particular approach—that is, a content analysis of representations in magazines?

My approach is actually a combination of content and textual analysis. When I started this work there was very little literature available on women and smoking and the field offered umpteen possibilities. As with most research, my choices were shaped by both intellectual and practical considerations. On the practical side, I needed to start with something quite discreet, doable, and publishable, and because I already had considerable experience working with representations in girls' and women's magazines, this seemed a possibility. These practical considerations neatly dovetailed with intellectual ones as well. Three aspects of the history of smoking suggested that a study of magazine representations would be a fruitful place to begin my research. First, advertising was frequently cited as key to the increased popularity of the cigarette in the twentieth century, and from experience I knew that some popular magazines carried cigarette advertising and other representations of women smoking. Second, the growth in popularity of smoking amongst women in Britain and North America during the 1920s and 1930s was widely attributed to its significance as a symbol of emancipation—and emancipation was a key theme of young women's magazines of the 1920s. Third, the history of women's smoking was characterized by shifts in the social-class composition of smokers, with the earliest smokers being from the upper classes, and I knew that magazines were targeted at women from across the social-class and age spectrums.

How is it that you settled on this sample and timeframe?

I was already familiar with most magazines produced in Britain for girls and women from 1900–1970 and [I knew] where to locate them (British Library), and I was able to construct a list of popular magazines that targeted different groups of girls and women, mainly by occupation and by social class. The research originally involved a detailed survey of issues from twenty magazine titles across the entire period 1900–1970. My aims were to discover the *extent* to which representations of women smoking occurred in girls'/women's magazines; the *forms* (adverts, fiction, illustrations, and so on) of these representations; and the *specific ways* that women smokers were presented. I looked at several issues from each magazine title at five year intervals and included, where possible, the first and last years that the title ran. I focused on illustrations of women smoking, cigarette advertisements, articles on smoking, and fiction that featured women who smoked. Why five year intervals? This allowed me to sample magazines at a reasonable interval for picking up on patterns and changes. However, I also supplemented the sample with other issues, which allowed me to cross-check my analysis. I used a basic form of content analysis, noting changes and patterns over time and between magazines, and combined this with detailed textual/image analysis. My interpretation also required consideration of the broader context (the co-text and co-images, page spread, magazine content), and other contextual information about the period, the experiences of women during this time, and the production of different types of magazines.

The timeframe for this particular article, dealing only with the inter-war years (1918–1939), was not planned when I began the research, but rather emerged as I began to work through the magazines. As I collected data, my initial research questions became more refined and new angles emerged. One angle concerned cigarette advertising targeted at women—I have since published an article on this. Another related to the meanings and significance of early representations of women smoking in magazines and the observation that only after WWI did the woman smoker become visible in women's magazines. The article that is reprinted here came from my surprising discovery of representations of women smokers in magazines for upper-working-class/lower-middle-class young women, at a time when smoking was commonly associated with upper-class women. I was particularly struck by the prominence of smoking in some inter-war magazines. How was this relatively novel, and often controversial, practice represented? What did this practice mean? How, if at all, was smoking represented as a feminine practice? I decided to investigate this further—hence, the focus of this paper.

You identify three key themes in the representations of women and smoking in the magazines you analyzed. How did you arrive at those?

As I collected my data I kept notes on possible themes and ideas. I had noted that smoking was clearly associated with modernity and with heterosexual romance in the inter-war period and was used to make a statement about gender, change, and continuity. But there was also the fascinating serial about Miranda Temple, as well as a few other references to smoking as a gesture of adolescent rebellion. Equipped with these ideas I revisited all my inter-war magazine material, checking the occurrence of the three themes and looking to see if others emerged. Initially I doubted whether the theme of adolescent rebellion was sufficiently important to warrant special attention, but because I found the Miranda Temple story so unusual and interesting I decided to analyze it anyway. In the process of doing this—I always find that writing helps me unravel themes and connections—the links between Miranda's smoking and that of so-called emancipated working "modern girls" became clearer and the former then helped crystallize my thinking on the latter. Of course my material presented themes other than rebellion, modernity, and romance; social class was one such theme which was not as central to my interests. I often find that as I work through one set of interests my thoughts and questions on other, often related, points are thrown into relief.

What was the most frustrating or difficult aspect of doing this research?

Overall this research was relatively straightforward, but this was because I am already experienced at working with magazines—I know where to find them, the practicalities of using the archives efficiently, techniques for recording and analyzing the representations. In the past I encountered a range of mainly practical problems doing this type of research, and even now I get caught out occasionally. One of the main problems I've encountered researching magazines is using the archives and libraries efficiently. I have to plan my research visits with great care to maximize my time with the materials. Magazines are collated into volumes and to see one of these you must submit a request form. Usually it takes an hour or longer for a request to be processed, so it is very easy to end up twiddling your thumbs and losing valuable time. I usually work out what I want to look at before I visit the archives and order several volumes in advance. However, sometimes I still find myself with a pile of unhelpful volumes and a long wait before more material can be delivered, which is frustrating. Another problem that I have encountered on a few occasions is the delivery of the wrong volume. One periodical that has a particularly convoluted history has caused me numerous problems and so now every time I order a volume or two I request another magazine just in case!

Another aspect of this type of research that can cause headaches is the method of collecting data. In any research project involving magazines, I note the date of every magazine issue that I look at. I then copy all references to smoking, making sure to include page references (sloppy referencing causes real headaches—it really is a timely and expensive problem in archive research). Longer features on smoking, fiction, and illustrations were photocopied where possible. Working in this way allows me to return to, and go over, the material as new ideas, or even doubts, emerge. Of course with visual images it is really helpful to have copies to analyze in your own time. From past experience I have found that I frequently want to check my interpretation of material, or even to re-use it, and that, in the absence of detailed notes (and ideally, photocopies), I have found it difficult to recreate and reanalyze the context. Plus, you can't photocopy everything you want, even if you can afford it, because of rules about how much of a periodical you can photocopy. So I still have to do a lot of writing. In the past I have taken notes in long hand—not all of these are easy to read and what seemed straightforward when I made the original set of notes is sometimes less clear when revisited several months or years later because my writing is terrible. I've now converted to using a laptop for this work. Even with photocopies and detailed notes, there are always occasions when I wish I had taken *more* notes about contextual features. Having my own copies of the magazines would be ideal but this is not feasible for several reasons, not least because many of these magazines were printed on poor quality paper that has not stood the test of time. I also encounter difficulties trying to reproduce images in my publications, as I cannot usually reproduce all the images I would like because of costs and the difficulty, in some cases, of securing permission.

Were your findings expected or unexpected? What do you see as the main contributions of your research?

When I started this research, little attention had been directed at how and why smoking became established as a feminine practice and amongst which groups of girls/women. My research on women and smoking contributes to an understanding of the processes by which a relatively modern practice—the smoking of cigarettes—became established as a feminine one in Britain. Whilst my broad findings in this article were not unexpected, I did not anticipate all the subtleties of how smoking was meaningful in gender-specific ways. One interesting feature of the research process was that I sometimes found myself expecting certain female characters to smoke on the basis of assumptions I have about women smokers today. For example, when I came across a story about a wild young woman in the mid-1920s who rode motorcycles, I was very surprised that she was not described as a smoker. The ways in which my assumptions surfaced during the research process were very illuminating and showed how established certain ideas about women smokers have become.

What was the most satisfying aspect of doing this research?

It was exciting to find evidence of women's smoking in the magazines and I derived great satisfaction from teasing out the subtleties of the representations. But while the deconstruction work is great, the best bit is when the material is being synthesized and starts to become meaningful.

Were there ethical challenges or issues involved in your research? How did you deal with them?

The main ethical issue is integrity in the presentation and interpretation of the material. For me this requires keeping good records of my materials and being careful about their use and interpretation. I like to use plenty of illustrations (quotes and images) as evidence—to try to make transparent, as far as possible/feasible, the materials that have informed my observations and conclusions. Of course these illustrations add interest, too. But illustration is not sufficient evidence. The context of representations (text and image) is crucial to the interpretation of sources because meanings are context dependent and it is critical that context is attended to carefully. When I am unsure about the context of representations that are key to a point I want to make, I revisit the original magazines.

If you were to do this research again, what would you do differently?

Within the time and finance constraints that I had to work within, I would not do anything differently. If I had lots of funding and time, well. . . dream on.

Questions to Think About

1. How did Tinkler operationalize her variables—that is, identify the themes and categories that organize her data? How does she assess the validity and reliability of her measures? What are the main differences in how quantitative and qualitative researchers conceptualize and operationalize their measures?

2. Compare and contrast Tinkler's findings with those of MacDonald and Wright. In what ways are they similar or complementary with regard to what they tell us about women and smoking? In what ways do they differ?

3. What are some of the distinctive challenges that Tinkler faced in the collection of data? How did she deal with them?

4. Describe Tinkler's sample. What were her main considerations in selecting it? How generalizable do you think her findings are?

5. Describe how you might go about doing a study in which the research question is similar to Tinkler's, but that uses a quantitative rather than qualitative approach.

chapter 4

Experimental Research

Experimentation is the research technique that is at the core of scientific investigation because it offers the most powerful way to test causal relationships—that is, to determine that one variable (the *treatment* or independent variable) is truly affecting another (the *outcome* or dependent variable). The reason is the amount of control that researchers have in experimental research—control over the nature and timing of the independent variable and control for outside factors that might also have an impact on the dependent variable and thus confound interpretation.

Despite its obvious advantages, the experimental method does have some limitations in social science research. The three most important limitations are that it is only appropriate for micro-level studies (it is difficult to study large social forces with this method), that it allows one to examine only a very limited number of variables at a time, and that it can be difficult to study a large or representative sample (making generalizability difficult).

Despite these limitations, there are research questions for which the experimental method is very appropriate and useful. Two are illustrated in the articles that we include here, each of which also exemplifies one of the major kinds of experimental design: the laboratory experiment and the field experiment. Laboratory experiments are conducted in very controlled conditions that are established within a laboratory or some other specially created location. Unlike field experiments, which take place in natural settings, lab experiments maximize the control of the researcher in assigning subjects to groups, administering the pretest and posttest (measures of the outcome variable), and determining exactly what the treatment variable will be and how and when it will be administered. On the other hand, to the extent that laboratory experiments are conducted in artificial environments in which subjects know that they are being studied, the issue of *reactivity* (that is, respondents behaving in an abnormal way when they know they are being studied) is a concern. Thus, laboratory experiments may leave us wondering if the results of the experiment—say, the way people behaved when they were subject to the treatment—would be the same if the situation occurred naturally in their everyday environment.

In the first article, John Zipp's classroom provides a good laboratory in which to examine the effectiveness of a teaching technique, and the experimental method is the most logical research technique to use for this study. Zipp wants to determine if one specific technique (his use of group discussion) does, in fact, help to achieve a clearly identifiable and measurable learning outcome: students' understanding of the impact of social structure on decisions about marriage. Specifically, he wants to know if it leads to greater learning than traditional lecture, which is what the control group experiences. Like all conscientious professors, Zipp wants to teach effectively. Although instructors may find out something about their teaching effectiveness in a variety of ways—course evaluations, student performance on examinations and papers, and personal observations and impressions—none of these sources offers the same ability to determine the specific effects of a particular teaching strategy on student learning. In his interview, Zipp not only talks about the process of designing and implementing this study, but he also emphasizes how important it is for instructors to engage in the "scholarship of teaching and learning"—conducting research on curriculum and pedagogy and on how they influence student learning.

The study described in the second article is an example of a field experiment in which researchers use a real-world setting. Field experiments involve either inserting some manipulation (the treatment variable) into the everyday course of events and then observing any influences on people's behavior, or simply measuring the outcomes of a naturally occurring change in the social world. The study by Richard Scribner and Deborah Cohen is an example of the latter. Their goal is to assess the effectiveness of strategies to curb underage drinking. They note that most efforts have focused on young people themselves (e.g., arresting them for underage drinking), and they wonder if a strategy that focuses more on discouraging retailers from selling alcohol to underage youth might be more effective. They determined that a field experiment would be best, in part because this topic can really only be studied in real-world settings.

The state of Louisiana offered a naturally occurring quasi-experimental situation. From 1986 to 1995, Louisiana's underage drinking deterrence policy only targeted the young people purchasing or using alcohol. When this strategy was changed in 1995 to permit both the citation of alcohol retailers caught selling to minors and publicity about these citations, Scribner and Cohen created an experiment around this situation. Their objective was to determine if the routine issuing of citations to retailers who violated the law (and publicity about the citations) influenced the likelihood of compliance with the law. As you will see, Scribner and Cohen conclude that this deterrence strategy of issuing citations to merchants who do not comply with the law works. Their study design relied on analysis of the effects of a naturally occurring intervention in a real-world setting. As is always the case with field experiments, they lost some of the control available in laboratory experiments, which somewhat undermined the internal validity of their study. However, they felt confident that the experiment produced genuine results because the alcohol merchants did not know they were being studied, so they behaved in ways that we can assume were normal.

Finally, note how in both articles the authors explicitly identify possible limitations of their studies and encourage the use of caution in interpreting their results. These are signs of a good scientific researcher: a willingness to be self-critical, to be honest, and to be very cautious in accepting research results. Scribner also tells us much about the politics of social research—in this case, how political pressures can be brought to bear on researchers whose investigation may challenge political office holders, corporations, and even prevailing paradigms within certain academic fields.

The Impact of Social Structure on Mate Selection

An Empirical Evaluation of an Active-Learning Exercise

John F. Zipp

The individualistic orientation of most U.S. college students presents a persistent problem for teaching sociology, especially at the introductory level where many students find it hard to understand social structure and how it shapes their lives. This paper provides an empirical evaluation of whether an active-learning exercise focused on mate selection increases student understanding of the impact that social structure has on marital choice. I fielded the experiment in an introductory sociology course—half the class participated in the active-learning exercise while the other half attended a traditional lecture. Results indicate that those who participated in the exercise were significantly more likely to learn the role that social structure plays in mate selection.

The individualistic orientation of most U.S. college students presents a persistent problem for teaching sociology, especially at the introductory level. Put simply, many students find it hard to understand social structure and how it shapes their lives (e.g., Bohmer and Briggs 1991; McCammon 1999). As Lemert (1997:138–39) remarked, social structure tends to be "invisible." Although there are no hard data on this, discussions with colleagues and reactions to an earlier version of this paper suggest that many sociologists use dating or mate selection as one way to make social structure more visible to students in introductory courses. O'Brien and Foley's (1999) recent *Teaching Sociology* article describes a dating game aimed at helping students understand the impact of social structure on their lives. I have used an exercise called "choosing a mate" (described in detail below) for seven years to do the same.

The premise underlying these and other similar exercises is that they increase student learning over and above a more traditional lecture format. Although this is eminently testable, there do not appear to be any such tests in the literature. This is a sizable shortcoming, for at least two reasons. First, without such models, more traditionally-oriented colleagues can dismiss innovative classroom practices as providing too much entertainment and too little scholarly rigor. Indeed, after I described my own exercise to one such colleague, gently implying that he might consider using it, he dismissively informed me that he "had too much material to cover" to waste his time on these "sorts of 'games.' " Second, and more generally, evidence of this sort is at the heart of the recent emphasis on the scholarship of teaching and learning (SoTL), an effort that seeks to fundamentally reshape the academy (e.g., Atkinson 2001; Boyer 1990; Hutchings and Shulman 1999). Although there are almost as many definitions of SoTL as there are practitioners, common to most approaches is the call for scholarly investigation about how various teaching methods and approaches impact student learning.

Thus, the purpose of this paper is to provide such a test. Using my own "choosing a mate" exercise; I assess whether it can improve student learning, at least in the short run, over the delivery of the same material in a traditional lecture format. To accomplish this I split my mass lecture class, with one-half the class participating in the "choosing the mate" exercise and the other half receiving a lecture on the topic. At the end of each session, students completed a short "minute paper" (Angelo and Cross 1993) about (among other topics) the most important thing that they learned in class that day. The question at hand, then, is whether students who participate in the exercise are more likely to report learning the role that social structural factors play in marital choice than are students who attend the lecture. Since exercises like this may be relatively common, it is essential that sociologists have some evidence as to their impact on student learning.

"Choosing a Mate:" Fielding the Study

Before describing the experiment, it is worthwhile to note that, for a number of reasons, the choice of whom to date and whom to marry provide good ways to illustrate the effects of social structure. First, dating and marriage are relatively salient to a large number of college students; some students are married, others are engaged, while many of the rest are actively looking for life partners. Second, as the literature on the family makes clear, social structural factors—especially race, age, religion, ethnicity, socioeconomic status, and geographical propinquity—play a key role in how one chooses a mate. This is usually discussed under the rubric of "marital homogamy," "marital similarity," or "assortative mating" (e.g., Cherlin 1999; Coltrane and Collins 2001; Kalmijn 1998). Third, even with increases in cohabitation and other family forms, projections indicate that approximately 90 percent of whites and 70 to 75 percent of African Americans will eventually marry (Cherlin 1999:248).

The main goal of this paper is to determine if this active-learning experiment enhanced students' learning about the role that social structural factors play in mate selection. There are good reasons to expect that active learning will have such an impact. Considerable literature exists affirming that active learning increases student understanding of course material, enhances critical thinking skills, and improves attitudes toward the class and relationships with classmates (e.g., Bransford, Brown, and Cockings 2000; Cross and Steadman 1996; Hamlin and Janssen 1987; Johnson, Johnson, and Smith 1991; Light, 1990; McKeachie 1999; Rinehart 1999; see also the "active-learning" Web site: http://www.active-learning-site.com). In 1984 the Study Group on the Conditions of Excellence in American Higher Education named active learning one of three key practices for good teach-

ing, and Chickering and Gamson included it as one of "seven principles" for good teaching practice (1987). In fact, in a review essay, Cross (1999: 263) referred to it as the "grand meta-principle" for student learning.

To determine the impact of this active-learning exercise, I split the class alphabetically into two approximately equal groups. Students were used to these groupings as each group had a different teaching assistant who met with them, graded their papers, and so on. The first group was the experimental group, which came to class at the normal time (9:55 a.m.), while the control group reported at 10:45 a.m. (my teaching assistants monitored the doors, keeping the control group away from the classroom until the experimental group exited). Fortunately, the groups turned out to be almost identical in size: 62 students were in the experimental group and 63 in the control group.

The experimental group received the active-learning exercise described below, while I presented the same substantive material on social structure and mate selection to the control group in lecture format. In the experimental group, I started the exercise by asking students to write down the reasons why they would marry (for those who were married, I asked them to write the reasons why they did marry). I let students know that I was referring to all forms of intimate unions, both heterosexual and homosexual. I gave students only two to three minutes to write their answers (this has always proven to be enough time), before I asked for some responses, which I recorded on an overhead transparency. Students generally listed two to five reasons, with the most common being love, companionship, money, or to start a family.

I then posed a second question: what are they looking for in a future (or current) partner? I told them to list all of the qualities they could think of; however, as I did not want gay and lesbian students to feel pressured to reveal their sexual orientations, I suggested that students not mention the sex of their intended partner.

Once again, I asked the students to write down their answers. I gave them about five minutes for this, as they generally make somewhat longer lists (some students listed up to 15 or more attributes). When they had finished writing, I asked them to form small (3 to 5 member) single-sex groups, to share their answers with their groups, and to discuss the similarities/differences among their answers. They were then asked to develop a group response that distilled their individual answers and reflected the content of their group discussion, which one member of the group would then report to the whole class.[1]

For the most part, the responses from men and women were very similar: Both wanted partners with similar interests and a sense of humor, who are educated/intelligent, romantic, faithful, sexually compatible, caring, and kind. Men were more likely to mention physical attributes, and use superlatives when doing so (e.g., men might say they want someone with "great looks" or who is "very attractive," while women were more likely to want someone "good looking" or "attractive"). Women were more given to looking for a partner who respects them, does not try to change them, and who will be financially secure—all responses that almost never occurred among men. A few students mentioned that they want to marry someone of the same religion, but in only one case did this make it onto a group's final list. Thus, with virtually no students mentioning any social structural factors, the next phase of the experiment was to formally present information on the role of race, age, religion, and social status on mate selection. Although they are very familiar to readers of this paper, in the Appendix I list some recent data on each of these social structure factors and some sources that can be accessed for updating them over time.

I offered the same substantive material on social structure and mate selection to both class groups; however, while the experimental group was first involved in an active-learning exercise, the control group received only a traditional lecture. For the latter I introduced the day's topic, the role that social structure plays in whom one chooses to marry, and presented the information contained in the Appendix. In fact, except for up-

dated statistics, recent findings, and a few other minor changes, this was virtually the same lecture that I gave numerous times to my introductory students before I developed the mate selection exercise. Making the class session somewhat interactive, I began the traditional lecture by asking students what the most important factors were in marital choice. Just as in the active-learning exercise, students focused on love, physical attraction, money, and so on.

My presentation to the control group, then, represented a more or less typical lecture: I did most of the talking, though I did ask students a fair number of questions about factors they thought important in choosing a mate. I did not tell either group about the other, but I did ask the experimental group—since they went first—not to discuss anything with members of the control group. Since the only opportunity for doing so was when they passed each other in the hallway going in and out of class, and since my teaching assistants and I monitored this transition, I am reasonably sure that each group complied with my request. At the end of each presentation I asked all students to fill out the same "one-minute" paper (Angelo and Cross 1993). They were to answer four questions: (1) What was the most important thing you learned in class today?; (2) What important question remains unanswered?; (3) Did you read the textbook chapter on "Families and Intimate Relationships?"; and (4) If you read it, how well did you understand it? (1 = "not at all" through 5 = "very well").

Since the purpose of both the active-learning exercise and the lecture was for students to understand the importance of social structure in mate selection, the indicator for success was whether students mentioned one or more social structural factors in marital choice in answer to the question, "What was the most important thing that they learned in class today?" I presented the same data on the same structural factors to both groups: race, ethnicity, class/status, education, age, religion, and geography; answers containing the impact of one or more of these were coded as "social structural." I used a similar coding scheme for the question on "what remains unanswered," with one difference: I accepted gender/sexuality as a structural question as I had not covered this explicitly in either presentation.

The open-ended questions were coded in a two-step process. First, as part of our department's undergraduate research assistantship program, two undergraduates coded each answer independently. On the first round, inter-coder agreement was 84.0 percent on question 1 and 76.5 percent on question 2. Given the rather limited training of the undergraduate coders,[2] these results indicate a reasonably solid level of reliability. In the second step of the coding process, the three of us met as a team, reviewed all coding disagreements, and collectively arrived at a single answer.

Results

The first step in discovering the exercise's impact is to find the percentage of students reporting that the most important thing they learned was the impact that social structural factors have in mate selection. Indeed, almost two-thirds of all students in the class as a whole—63.2 percent—mentioned one or more structural factors. Although this suggests that most students understood at least some of the main points of the class session, what is most interesting for this paper are the differences between the results of the experimental and control groups: 44.4 percent of the control group and 82.3 percent of the experimental group reported that social structural factors in mate selection were the most important thing that they learned in class that day.

At first blush this seems to indicate a rather dramatic impact of the active-learning exercise, but there are two major caveats. To begin with, since less than half the control group identified mate selection as the most important thing learned in class, one could question whether I downplayed it as a factor in order to increase the impact of the exercise. Although I cannot completely rule out any unconscious biases on my part, two factors mitigate against its plausibility: (1) the other class

sessions were a mixture of traditional lectures and group exercises, thus both the students and I were used to and comfortable with each format; and (2) as noted earlier, the lecture presented to the control group was basically the same one that I used for years before developing the mate selection exercise—thus it was centered specifically on the impact of social structure in marital choice.

There is a second caveat: since students were not randomly assigned to groups, differences between the experimental and control groups may be a *selection*, rather than a *treatment*, effect. The observed effect may be due not to the active-learning exercise but instead to the presence of better (or at least better-prepared) students in the experimental group who thus better understood the most important aspects of the class session. I use several measures to identify this effect: whether students read the chapter; if so, how well they understood it; and the student's overall grade in the course.[3] Interestingly enough, while there were no differences between the experimental and control groups (3.57 and 3.6 on a 1–5 scale, respectively) on how well they understood the chapter or in their course grades (each group's average was 75.4), the groups did differ on their reading of the chapter: 45.2 percent of the experimental and only 29.0 percent of the control group read the chapter prior to the class session.

To address whether the difference between the two groups was due to selection or treatment, I ran a series of logistic regression equations. My dependent variable was whether or not students reported the role of social structural factors in marital choice (0 = no, 1 = yes). There were four different independent variables: class group (0 = control group, 1 = experimental group); did students read the chapter (0 = no, 1 = yes); how well they understood the chapter (0 = didn't read it, 1 = not well, ... 5 = well)[4]; and their course grade (on a 0 – 100 scale; it ranged from 28.4 to 99.4). I ran two basic equations: social structural factors as the most important thing learned in class regressed on control vs. experimental group, grades, and alternately, if students read the chapter or how well they understood the chapter.[5]

TABLE 1   *Does the "Choosing A Mate" Exercise Increase the Likelihood that Students Report Social Structural Factors in Mate Selection?*

	LOGISTIC REGRESSION RESULTS			
	b	Odds Ratio	*b*	Odds Ratio
Control vs. Experimental Group	1.845*	6.330	1.797*	6.029
Course Grade	.011	1.011	.010	1.010
Read the Chapter	−.446	.640		
How Well Read the Chapter			−.114	.892
Constant	−.890		−.807	
−2 Log Likelihood	135.804		137.629	
Cox & Snell R^2	.159		.151	

p<.05

KEY: Dependent variable: whether students reported the role of social structural factors in marital choice (0=no, 1=yes). Independent variables: Control vs. Experimental group (0=control group, 1=experimental group); Course Grade (on a 0–100 scale); Read the Chapter (0=no, 1=yes); How Well Read the Chapter (0=did not read it, 1=not well, . . . 5=very well).

The logistic regression results (see Table 1) show that being in the experimental vs. the control group is statistically significant, net of grades and of whether (1.845) or of how well (1.797) one read the chapter. The odds ratios provide an indication of the substantial magnitude of these effects: the odds of identifying structural factors in mate selection as the most important thing learned in class were *six times higher when students participated in the active-learning exercise than when they attended a traditional lecture.* This is strong testimony to the impact of active learning as an approach to student learning.[6]

There were two other interesting sets of findings. First, in addition to coding whether students invoked social structure as the most important thing they learned in class, we coded the specific factors the two groups identified (see Table 2). As illustrated, those in the experimental group were more likely to invoke race, age, religion, and geography as impinging on marital choice, while the control group was more given to offering love and "many different factors." A close reading of the full text of students' answers indicates that those

who answered "love" reported that the most important thing that they learned was that love was not as important a selection factor as they previously thought. Thus, a sizable number of students in the control group learned part of the lecture—the limits to the role of love in mate selection—but did not move beyond this.

Finally, there were no overall differences between the control and experimental groups in "what question remains unanswered" from the class session. Both groups were equally likely to answer the question (69.8 percent of the experimental group vs. 66.1 percent of the control group) and to want more information on one or more structural factors (57.6 percent of the control group vs. 52.3 percent of the experimental group). Interestingly enough, when examining the individual factors themselves, there was one significant difference between the groups: 31.2 percent of the control group and only 2.4 percent of the experimental group reported that the question left unanswered by the class session was the role of love in marital choice. The control group was more likely to report that the major thing they

Method of Analysis

Logistic Regression

Multiple regression is a statistical test to help researchers measure the amount of influence two or more independent variables simultaneously have on a dependent variable. *Logistic regression* is a special type of multiple regression that is used when: (1) the independent variables are quantitative (e.g., numerical scores) and/or qualitative (e.g., any non-numerical variable such as gender or race), and (2) the dependent variable is dichotomous (that is, there are only two categories, such as employment status being measured as employed or not employed). The dependent variable in this article is whether students identified the role of social structure as a factor in marital choice as being the most important thing learned in class. It is a dichotomous variable—either they identified it or they did not. Zipp tested four independent variables to determine if they influenced the likelihood of identifying social structure. These variables are: (1) whether the student was in the experimental (active learning class) or control group (traditional lecture class), (2) whether the student had read the chapter, (3) how well the student understood the chapter, measured on a scale of 1 (not well) to 5 (well), and (4) the student's course grade (on a scale of 0 to 100).

Now, let's look at Table 1. The fact that logistic regression is used is indicated at the top of the table. The four independent variables are listed at the left side. There are actually two separate analyses in this table; let's examine only the one on the left (which includes the first *b* and the first odds ratio). This analysis examines the simultaneous effect of three of the independent variables (group, course grade, and reading the chapter) on the dependent variable (identifying social structure as a factor). Although everything in the table contributes to our understanding of the relationship among these variables, let's just focus on the odds ratio and the asterisk next to the *b*. Zipp most wanted to determine whether participating in the active learning exercise enhanced students' knowledge over participation in a traditional class lecture. The reported odds ratio of 6.330 tells us that students in the active learning class were roughly six times more likely than students in the lecture class to identify the influence of social structure on marital choice as being the most important thing learned in class. Is this difference in performance sufficiently large that we can be assured the active learning exercise really was better, or might a difference of this size be due simply to chance? To answer this question, look at the result signified by the asterisk next to the 1.845 value in the *b* column next to control versus experimental group. Below the table, the $p < .05$ (which should be preceded by an asterisk) indicates that the probability of this difference being due to chance is less than 5 percent. So, Zipp was very confident, and so are we, that the active learning exercise really was better than traditional lecture in conveying the importance of social structure as a factor in marital choice.

learned was that love was not as important as they thought—and they wanted to know why.

Discussion

Before turning to a discussion of these results, some qualifications need to be kept in mind. First, even though I opened the classroom discussion of mate selection by explicitly referring to all intimate relationships, over the years it is clear that most students assume I am talking about heterosexual ones. Part of this behavior surely derives from cultural norms and practices (approximately 95 percent of all unions are heterosexual [Baca Zinn and Eitzen 1999]) regarding heterosexuality. Additionally, however, I surely reinforce these norms when I use single-sex groups and tell students that they do not need to include the sex of any future mate in their responses.[7] Even though I repeatedly remind them that both homosexual and heterosexual unions are appropriate, these caveats may not be enough.

Second, I have employed this exercise at midwestern state universities where the populations

TABLE 2 *Percent of Students Reporting Each Particular Social Structural Factor in Mate Selection*

	MOST IMPORTANT THING LEARNED IN CLASS TODAY		QUESTION LEFT UNANSWERED	
	Control Group	Experimental Group	Control Group	Experimental Group
Race	22.2	66.1*	9.1	29.3
Class, Status	11.1	11.3	4.5	2.4
Education	3.2	4.8	2.3	0.0
Age	9.5	35.5*	11.4	19.5
Geography	12.0	11.3	0.0	4.9
Religion	14.3	30.6*	2.3	2.4*
Ethnicity	.8	1.6	0.0	0.0
Love	22.2	0.0*	31.2	2.4
Companionship	1.6	1.6	2.3	0.0
Many Factors	27.0	6.5*	0.0	4.9
Gender Differences	0.0	11.3	4.5	9.8
Gender	—	—	2.3	2.4
N	(63)	(62)	(44)	(41)

Note: Percentages do not sum to 100 within columns as students could give more than one answer.

*Significant difference between the experimental and control groups.

are overwhelmingly white and where blacks are the primary minority group. Because the rates of intermarriage vary by racial group, the results may vary in courses where there are substantial numbers of other minorities.

This having been said, the most important finding of this study is the overwhelming impact of the group exercise on immediate student learning over a traditional lecture. To reiterate, the odds of naming one or more social structural factors as the "most important thing" learned in class were six times higher for students who participated in the "choosing a mate" exercise than for those who attended the lecture. Since this effect is net of how well students were prepared for class that day and of their overall course performance, my results provide a clear justification for using this exercise to increase student learning—at least in the short run. Contrary to my former colleague's dismissal of this exercise as a "waste" of valuable class time,

it appears that this sort of activity is of significantly more valuable use.

It is important to emphasize that my focus was on *immediate* student learning of a key concept demonstrated in one exercise in one class session. Although the experiment found large differences between groups, my results should be seen as centering on a first step in a process that might result in longer-term and/or deeper learning. Indeed, the most persuasive evidence of learning would be if students carried this knowledge forward or if they could apply it in other settings. Unfortunately, I did not explicitly collect such data, and ask that my results be interpreted accordingly.

Despite this caveat, I have some data that bear a bit on the matter of longer-term learning. On the last day of class I asked students to complete an in-class assignment on the "most important thing they learned this semester." As can be imagined, in a survey course using computer-based tests, research papers, in-class active-learning exercises, films, Web-based discussions, and so on, student answers ranged widely. However, students in the experimental group were more likely—8.1 percent of the experimental group vs. 2.2 percent of the control group—to say that the impact of social structure in mate selection was the most important thing that they learned in the semester. These percentages are not overwhelming, to be sure, but given that students had only a few minutes to think back across the entire semester and could only provide one answer (thus, the impact of social structure on marital choice may still be something students learned, just not the most important thing), these data do suggest that the impact of the experiment may have carried a bit beyond the day of the class.

A second interesting finding concerns other differences between the groups, especially in how likely each was to be concerned with the role of love in mate selection. As reported in Table 2, the control group was significantly more likely to name the role of love in mate selection to be the most important thing that they learned in class and to want to learn more about it. This is not surprising, as love is clearly what most students in the experimental group initially named as a reason for getting married. Thus, in some ways, a sizable number of students in the traditional lecture *ended* the class at an intellectual point similar to where those in the experimental group *began* the class session. More generally, these differences may indicate that it could require group exercises of this sort to counter the strong current of individualism among U.S. college students. Whether it was participating in the small group discussions, or listening to the group reports, or a combination of both is not clear, but some aspect of this active, collective process helped students move beyond their individualistic leanings. And, since this is one of the key hurdles facing sociology instructors, it is one more reason to use these sorts of exercises.

Finally, at the most general level, this paper contributes to a small but growing literature on the scholarship of teaching and learning. SoTL contends that teaching is an intellectual exercise and that teaching products and processes need to be made public and be subject to peer review and evaluation. Although by its very nature *Teaching Sociology* has made substantial contributions to this scholarship, there has been much more emphasis on "teaching" innovations than on the impact that these have on "student learning." As Hutchings and Shulman (1999:13) noted, SoTL "is *not* synonymous with excellent teaching" (emphasis in the original), as it requires that "faculty frame and systematically investigate questions related to student learning . . ." In a modest way, the main goal of this paper has to shift the focus in teaching sociology to the link between teaching and student learning.

Appendix[8]

Data Presented in Class

Race. Although the number of interracial couples has almost quadrupled in the last 25 years, and many demographers predict a continuing increase, it is important to note that more than 97 percent of marriages occur among people of the same race. According to data from the 1998 Current Population Survey, only 2.4 percent of married couples were classified as interracial (U.S. Bureau of the Census 1998:M-3).

There are several caveats to keep in mind with this statistic. First, part of the increase in interracial marriages may be artifactual, as there may now be a greater willingness to admit being married to someone of a different race. Second, questions new to the 2000 Census allowing respondents to classify themselves in more than one racial category may very well result in an increase in the reported number of interracial marriages. Third, there are sizable racial differences in the rate of intermarriage: African Americans are the most likely to marry within their race, followed by Asian Americans and Latinos, with whites being the least likely.[9] The most common type of intermarriage is between whites and Asian Americans, with the least common between whites and African Americans (Qian 1997).[10]

Age. In 1998, the median age of first marriage was 26.7 for men and 24.5 for women (U.S. Bureau of the Census 1998: M-2). Correlations between spouse's ages range from .7 to .9, with a mean of .8. These correlations tend to be higher for first marriages (Buss 1985:47).

Religion.   Religious homogamy has declined during this century, but still exists to some degree. In the 1920s, white Protestants were 47 times more likely to marry a Protestant than a Catholic; by the 1980s, this had decreased to being only 4 times more likely (Kalmijn 1991). As recently as the 1960s, 79 percent of Catholics, 91 percent of Protestants, and 92 percent of Jews married someone of the same religion (Carter and Glick, cited in Collins and Coltrane 1995:268).

Social Status.   Educational homogamy between spouses has increased in the last 50 years, and this is especially true for college graduates. For instance, the odds of a newlywed college graduate marrying a non-college graduate fell from .415 in 1940 to .324 in 1985–87 (Mare 1991). There is a U-shaped relationship between education and marital homogamy, with homogamy being particularly strong for individuals with college degrees (Qian 1997).

In addition to these data, it is helpful to explicitly draw the links between social structure and their marital preferences. Those who study mate selection note that marital choices depend on both *opportunity* and *preference,* each of which has structural and individual components. To begin with, the opportunity to marry outside of ones' group varies with the ways in which local marriage markets are segregated. For instance, the strongest predictor of interfaith marriage is the proportion of individuals with the same religious affiliation in the locale (Lehrer 1998). Furthermore, the likelihood of marrying someone with lower education increases substantially if one lives in an area with a greater concentration of poorly educated potential mates (Lewis and Oppenheimer 2000). As Kalmijn noted (1998:403), "unmarried people do not just wander around a region looking for a spouse;" racial segregation in housing and schools, and class differences in neighborhoods place limits on whom we are likely to meet, get to know, and with whom we feel comfortable interacting. Cultural styles, which vary by race, class, and ethnicity also shape these comfort levels.

The opportunity to marry outside of one's group is also shaped by the influence of significant others, especially parents and peer group, who often provide either overt or indirect advice regarding future mates. The effect of this influence is quite obvious to students, but one often-ignored mechanism of influence is through networks: at times students meet and date people who are directly connected to their significant others. One good way to illustrate this is to ask students to think about blind dates that their friends have arranged for them. How often have these involved someone of another race (especially crossing the white-black line) or someone more than five years different in age? Needless to say, blind dates of this sort are rare occurrences, almost always preceded by a request to see if this is acceptable.

Updating Information on Social Structure and Mate Selection

Although the above is a reasonable set of data for instructors to use for this exercise, this information will need to be updated over time. Clearly, the 2000 Census will provide a host of data on marital arrangements. After that (or before, depending on when the data are available), a prime source for information is the Current Population Surveys. These are monthly surveys done by the Bureau of Labor Statistics, primarily to measure employment-related matters. However, the March survey includes an "annual demographic supplement." Based on this, the Census Bureau publishes a document, "Marital Status and Living Arrangements" (in the P-20 series). This document is updated every March, and at this writing the most recent release is based on March 1998 data. This report is available on the Census Bureau Web site at: http://www.census.gov:80/population/population/www/socdemo/ms-la.html. There also are sources for some specific tables on racial intermarriage and age at first marriage (racial intermarriage: http://www.census.gov:80/population/socdemo/ms-la/tabms-3.txt; age at first marriage: http://www.census.gov:80/population/socdemo/ms-la/tabms-2.txt)

Other information on marital homogamy with respect to religion, education, or other factors is available in three ways. First, scholarly studies on the topic tend to appear in such journals as *Demography* or the *Journal of Marriage and the Family*. A second source for this information also comes from the Current Population Surveys. In addition to the March supplement, in 1971, 1975, 1980, 1985, 1990, and 1995, the June survey has included a "fertility and marital history" supplement. The 1995 data are available online at: http://www.bls. census.gov/census.gov/cps/femarch/femarhs.htm.

Unfortunately, 1995 is the last marital history supplement planned by the CPS. The reason for this is that similar, more extensive data on marriage and fertility are being collected as part of the "Survey of Income and Program Participation" (usually referred to as the SIPP data). Begun in 1984, the SIPP contains a series of national panels lasting from 2½ to 4 years. The most recent data available are for 1996, and these are online at: http://www.sipp. census.gov/sipp/daccmain.htm. More information on the SIPP can be found on its home page: http:// www.bls.census.gov/sipp/.

NOTES

1. A few points on these groups are worth noting. First, I asked each group to leave an empty chair for me so that I could listen to some of the group's discussions. Second, even though I used single-sex groups this time, in the past I have used both mixed- and single-sex groups. A possible downside to combining single-sex groups and my desire to allow gay and lesbian students not to feel any compunction to self-identify is that this exercise may unwittingly support notions of compulsory heterosexuality (Rich 1982). Obviously, without knowing each students' sexual orientation there is no way to determine this precisely, but across seven years of exercises, I have found that very rarely do lesbian or gay students reveal their sexual orientation either in groups or in class as a whole.

2. Part of the assistantship is to train undergraduates in research, thus, this is a learning process for these students as well.

3. Students were asked to put their university computer ID on the "minute paper" form. I used this to match their course grades to their responses.

4. This is a combination of two variables: whether or not they read the chapter, and if so, how well they understood it. I needed to make this transformation because only those who read the chapter answered the question about how well they understood it.

5. I needed to alternate these due to their extremely high correlation (r = .97).

6. Since there were some initial differences in responses between men and women, it is reasonable to wonder if gender differences affect noting the importance of social structural factors in mate selection. I checked this and discovered that gender had no significant impact on my results. There were no gender differences in the composition of the experimental and control groups (53.2 percent and 49.2 percent women, respectively), and gender did not affect—either entered alone in the models or with the other independent variables— the likelihood of seeing social structure as important. Finally, the inclusion of gender in the models did not change any of the independent variables. Results are available upon request.

7. The success of this exercise does not depend on instructors telling students not to list that they are looking for a partner of the opposite sex. Interestingly enough, when I did not include this note in the game's instructions, most students did not mention 'a member of the opposite sex' as one of their criteria. This, of course, suggests how much heterosexuality is taken for granted.

8. I will restrict my presentation to data drawn from the United States, as this has been my audience. For a summary of international trends, see Kalmijn (1998).

9. Because of the disproportionate number of whites in the population, the most common type of intermarriage is between whites and a racial minority.

10. Because interracial dating has increased (e.g., in a 1997 Gallup Poll of teenagers, 57 percent have been on a date with the member of another race or ethnic group), students may resist these figures. When this has happened, I ask them to consider the difference between dating and marrying, and ask them how many interracial marriages they know personally.

REFERENCES

Angelo, Thomas A. and K. Patricia Cross. 1993. Classroom Assessment Techniques. 2d ed. San Francisco, CA: Jossey-Bass.

Atkinson, Maxine P. 2001. "The Scholarship of Teaching and Learning: Reconceptualizing Scholarship and Transforming the Academy." *Social Forces* 79: 1217–30.

Baca Zinn, Maxine and D. Stanley Eitzen. 1999. *Diversity in Families*. 5th ed. New York: Longman.

Bohmer, Susan and Joyce L. Briggs. 1991. "Teaching Privileged Students about Gender, Race, and Class Oppression." *Teaching Sociology* 19:154–63.

Boyer, Ernest L. 1990. *Scholarship Reconsidered*. Princeton, NJ: Carnegie Foundation for the Advancement of Teaching.

Bransford, John D., Ann L. Brown, and Rodney R. Coekings, eds. 2000. *How People Learn: Brain, Mind, Experience and School*. Expanded Edition. Washington, DC: National Academy Press.

Buss, David M. 1985. "Human Mate Selection." *American Scientist* 73:47–51.

Cherlin, Andrew J. 1999. *Public and Private Families*. 2d ed. New York: McGraw-Hill.

Chickering, Arthur W. and Zelda Gamson. 1987. "Seven Principles for Good Practice In Undergraduate Education." *AAHE Bulletin* (March): 3–7.

Collins, Randall and Scott Coltrane. 1995. *Sociology of Marriage and the Family*. 4th ed. Chicago, IL: Nelson-Hall.

Coltrane, Scott and Randall Collins. 2001. *Sociology of Marriage and the Family*. 5th ed. Chicago, IL: Nelson-Hall.

Cross, K. Patricia. 1999. "What Do We Know about Students' Learning, and How Do We Know It?" *Innovative Higher Education* 23:255–70.

Cross, K. Patricia and Mimi Harris Steadman. 1996. *Classroom Research: Implementing the Scholarship of Teaching*. San Francisco, CA: Jossey-Bass.

Hamlin, John and Susan Janssen. 1987. "Active-learning in Large Introductory Sociology Courses." *Teaching Sociology* 15:45–54.

Hutchings, Pat and Lee S. Shulman. 1999. "The Scholarship of Teaching: New Elaborations, New Developments." *Change* (September–October): 11–15.

Johnson, David W., Roger T. Johnson, and Karl A. Smith. 1991. *Active-learning: Cooperation in the College Classroom*. Edina. MN: Interaction Book Company.

Kalmijn, Matthijs. 1998. "Intermarriage and Homogamy: Causes, Patterns, Trends." *Annual Review of Sociology* 24:395–421.

———. 1991. "Shifting Boundaries: Trends in Religious and Educational Homogamy." *American Sociological Review* 56:786–800.

Lehrer, Evelyn L. 1998. "Religious Intermarriage in the United States: Determinants and Trends." *Social Science Research* 27:245–63.

Lemert, Charles. 1997. *Social Things*. Lanham, MD: Rowman & Littlefield.

Lewis, Susan K. and Valerie K. Oppenheimer. 2000. "Educational Assortative Mating across Marriage Markets: Non-Hispanic Whites in the United States." *Demography* 37:29–40.

Light, Richard. 1990. *The Harvard Assessment Seminars*. Cambridge, MA: Harvard University Press.

Mare, Robert D. 1991. "Five Decades of Educational Assortative Mating." *American Sociological Review* 56:15–32.

McCammon, Lucy. 1999. "Introducing Social Stratification and Inequality: An Active-learning Technique." *Teaching Sociology* 27:44–54.

McKeachie, Wilbert J. 1999. *Teaching Tips*. Boston, MA: Houghton-Mifflin Co.

O'Brien, Eileen and Lara Foley. 1999. "The Dating Game: An Exercise Illustrating the Concepts of Homogamy, Heterogamy, Hypergamy, and Hypogamy." *Teaching Sociology* 27:145–49.

Qian, Zhenchao. 1997. "Breaking the Racial Barriers: Variations in Interracial Marriage between 1980 and 1990." *Demography* 34:1263–76.

Rich, Adrienne Cecile. 1982. *Compulsory Heterosexuality and Lesbian Existence*. Denver, CO: Antelope Publishers.

Rinehart, Jane A. 1999. "Turning Theory into Theorizing: Collaborative Learning in a Sociological Theory Course." *Teaching Sociology* 27:216–32.

U.S. Bureau of the Census. 1998. *Marital Status and Living Arrangement: March 1998*. Series P-20, No. 514. Washington, DC: Government Printing Office.

**John Zipp** is professor and chair of the Department of Sociology at the University of Akron. His work is primarily in political sociology, inequality, and the scholarship of teaching and learning. His research has appeared in such journals as the *American Journal of Sociology, Social Forces, American Political Science Review, Public Opinion Quarterly, Gender & Society, Social Problems,* and *Teaching Sociology.* He won the 1980–1981 Faculty Award for Outstanding Teaching from the Council of Students of Arts and Sciences at Washington University, and is a member of the editorial board of *Teaching Sociology.*

An interview with . . .

John Zipp

What got you interested in this subject?

I have always been interested in teaching. I won teaching awards when I first started teaching. But I taught the way that I think most of us do it—we think something works because students like it or we are happy with it. Then, about seven or eight years ago, I went to an ASA [American Sociological Association] session on using groups in cooperative learning and it was just terrific. They presented a lot of good evidence on the effect that cooperative learning has on student learning. I went back to my campus and started thinking about how I could implement some of this. I thought about doing something with this [marital homogamy] exercise and I ended up using the traditional lecture, but also with students talking to each other in groups. I didn't think anything else about it. Five years ago, when I came to the University of Akron as department chair, the university had just decided to become part of the Carnegie Teaching Academy to elevate the status of teaching and learning on campus. Although it was approved by the Board of Trustees and the Faculty Senate, there were still a lot of skeptics on campus, so the dean of Arts and Sciences chose three faculty members for a steering committee. He chose department chairs with reputations as good researchers to send a signal to the campus community that this was not just about teaching, but also needed to draw those interested in research. I got on this steering committee really not knowing anything about the scholarship of teaching and learning. We read books and went to seminars, retreats, and higher education meetings and conferences, and that's when I started learning about what is called "SoTL"—the scholarship of teaching and learning. Then I realized that, like most professors, I did not really know if my teaching strategies were really working in my classes. So I thought about how anything I was doing could be tested, and I thought of this particular exercise which I had been doing for quite awhile. And, that is how I got involved.

How do you see this research contributing to the "scholarship of teaching and learning" in sociology?

I want to emphasize that this type of research is not something that should be done just by experts in this area. We all have some degree of expertise in teaching, but we are focusing much more on teaching than learning. We would never in our research studies draw conclusions that were not based on evidence, but we do that in teaching all the time. We think something works. Why? Well, students liked it, it felt good, I liked it. Or, they did well on the tests—instead of defining learning goals and some way of assessing them.

What were the advantages and disadvantages of using your own students as subjects in the research?

There are a couple of advantages. First, students are accessible. This group I saw for an hour and forty minutes twice a week. A second advantage is that oftentimes we have a bifurcated existence—teaching on one hand and research on the other. Particularly when one is teaching an introductory course, it is rare that you can bring your own research into class because the research tends to be on a narrow topic. It is hard to work that into an introductory course. So, this is a way to tie the two halves of ourselves together very nicely. Lastly, the findings of the research have real, immediate, practical advantages for you and your students. One disadvantage is that if everyone did this a lot, I wonder if students would start to see themselves as research subjects less than as students.

What were the strengths of using this technique to test the value of an active learning exercise for teaching the impact of social structure on mate selection?

The same as the experimental approach elsewhere. We do have the experimental group and control group that allow us to attribute causality. The problem in this case is that I did not have truly random assignment as one would in the classic lab experiment. I did it based on some groupings that I had used in the class up to that time so as not to arouse any suspicions or to make it impossible for students to remember what group they were in. So, I used the alphabet. It turned out that I got about the same number in each group and the groups did not look very different from each other.

What were the weaknesses of using this technique for this research?

The groups were not randomly assigned in the true sense of the word. If I did it again, I could monitor it a little better. Also, I was worried that there might be something in my delivery that would subconsciously bias the results in favor of the experimental group. If I did it again, how could I guard against that? I could film it and have people judge to see if I was giving the same material, or I could have my teaching assistants rate it to see if it was about the same.

How did the reliability check process work?

I had two undergraduate students working with me in the summer on this and another minor research project. After I had them read my proposal and I talked to them about this, I told them that we had to establish categories for coding the responses. So we went through the kinds of things that might come in as answers, without coding any, and we went through a series of demonstrations—trial runs. We established the codes and then each got half of the experimental group and half of the control, so one was not coding all of one and the other coding all of the other. They went through and did all of the codes and then I went through the codes myself. Then we went through each response, and we looked for an exact agreement or disagreement. Any time that there were disagreements, we pulled those cases out and talked through them to make sure that we were coding things the same and why we coded things certain ways, and we resolved all of the cases that were initial disagreements.

What unexpected events or developments (if any) occurred during the course of this research?

Students were wondering why I told some of the class to come early and some to come late. And I had to just tell them not to complain, that they have fifty fewer minutes of class time, and asked if anyone wants a tuition refund for the shorter class. They were a little suspicious, so I had to be sure that the teaching assistants let the first group leave early and had the second group come in late. Then, it all went well. When they found out that they were to be part of a research project, they were excited. I think students at a lot of universities do not expect that research is something that happens right around them, and so they were thrilled to be part of the project. Unfortunately, we did not get the results during the semester, so they did not know how they came out. The only other small problem was that anytime I tried to do anything innovative in class after that, they were a little suspicious. I had to keep saying "No, no, this is real!"

Could you describe any specific ethical issues that you confronted in this research?

Students as research subjects. I do not think this is true just for this research project. Students are paying tuition to come and learn. I would argue that this is part of student learning, because now I have some evidence that this works. But, you still wonder how much we are profiting at the expense of students. If you study people on welfare, are you profiting from their lives? Are we giving anything back to them? In this case, I am giving something back to students of the future, and I think these students learned more about the research enterprise. But, it does give one pause.

If you were to do this research again, is there anything that you would do differently? If so, what?

I would use existing groups. The class is now broken into about twenty, 4–6 person groups for the entire semester. These groups are balanced by gender and g.p.a. If I had to do it again, I would use these groups and carefully assign them to the experimental group and control group. Also, this study provided evidence on short-term learning, but it would be nice to have evidence on long-term learning. I would probably try to get e-mail addresses from students and contact them a year later and do a follow-up on some of these questions to see what they remember a year later.

What was most frustrating to you in doing this research? What was most satisfying?

The most frustrating thing is knowing that the scholarship of teaching and learning is still seen as having ambiguous status as research. I don't know why this is—we use the same methods, the same evidence, and so forth—it has to meet the same standards. So, I think there is still a bias against this sort of research. It is still seen as not real research, but is put in a different category. That's frustrating because I think there is a lot that we can all learn by paying attention to research on teaching and learning. Unfortunately, there is less of it in sociology than in some of the physical sciences, such as biology. That is still a little frustrating.

The most satisfying was that it was really nice to be able to do research in my mass lecture class. There are not many people who wish to teach the mass lecture introductory class. It is certainly far from what we do in our other lives as scholars. And so it was really satisfying to join those two parts of my academic self. Working with the student research assistants was really good, too. We worked on two projects that summer. One was a standard research project—they helped collect data and enter data into the computer and do a few computer runs—and the other was this. They were much more interested in this project. They had been through the intro class, they knew some of the topics, and they were really anxious to hear how the results turned out. That was really satisfying because they got a lot out of it. Last, because we have a large SoTL program on campus now, I have given lots of presentations on campus and interacted with colleagues. As a result, one of my department colleagues, who has used groups and active learning for years, is working with her teaching assistant, a master's student, to do similar research in their two sections of intro sociology this semester. This professor was talking about how she wasn't sure these in-class groups were working, so she and I met with her teaching assistant. She decided to do one class as a control group and the other class (the one with an active learning requirement) will be her experimental group. The student is going to use this as the basis for her master's degree, which I think is just great. I am anxious to hear how it turns out.

What important lesson or illustration of doing good research can you share with students from your experiences in this research project?

I think one lesson is that, while a lot of qualitative researchers talk about how you should "do research where you live," about things that you are immersed in and know a lot about, quantitative researchers haven't taken that far. I think the lesson here is that research is not something that has to happen someplace "out there" away from the rest of what we do. It can happen in your classroom, anywhere that things impact your life. There are all sorts of important things to study. This research helps me and helps my students and it shows them how research can be done. There are all sorts of things in our day-to-day lives on which we can do research—gather data systematically, test hypotheses, draw some conclusions. The world is waiting for us to study it.

Questions to Think About

1. Do you think that experimental research was the best way for John Zipp to ascertain the effectiveness of his "marital homogamy" teaching strategy? Why or why not? What are some other ways that Zipp might have found out how effective this teaching technique is?

2. Explain in what ways Zipp's study deviates from "true" or "classical" experimental design. What are some threats to the internal validity of his study as a result of those deviations?

3. What are advantages and drawbacks of using students as research subjects? Do you believe that there ought to be rules about students serving as professors' research subjects? If so, what should they be?

4. What does Zipp mean by "the scholarship of teaching and learning"? What do you think might be its contribution to strengthening teaching and improving learning in college classrooms?

The Effect of Enforcement on Merchant Compliance with the Minimum Legal Drinking Age Law

Richard Scribner and Deborah Cohen

The aim of this paper is to evaluate the effectiveness of an intervention to deter underage alcohol sales by targeting alcohol retailers instead of underage youth. A quasi-experiment using a repeated-intervention design was conducted for a random sample (n = 143) of off-sale alcohol outlets from across New Orleans. Compliance checks of off-sale outlets were conducted at baseline, two months after the intervention, and eight months after the intervention. At baseline, only 11.2% (16/143) of outlets were compliant. Following the intervention, compliance increased to 39.9% (p < .001). The increase in compliance was greatest among outlets receiving citations for non-compliance (23/45, 51.1%; p < .001); however, a significant increase in compliance (34/98, 34.7%; p < .001) was also observed among outlets that did not receive a citation but were only exposed to the media coverage of the issuing of citations. A small residual effect of the intervention persisted at eight months post intervention among the outlets receiving citations for non-compliance. The study demonstrates that a deterrence strategy composed of compliance checks and the threat of compliance checks was effective in increasing alcohol retailer compliance with the minimum legal drinking age law. Given the limited effectiveness of general deterrence strategies in targeting other illegal alcohol use behaviors, these findings suggest general deterrence strategies are less effective when the behavior targeted is influenced by physiologic and social externalities, as is the case for underage alcohol consumers, rather than by costs, and benefits, as is the case for alcohol retailers.

Introduction

Minimum Legal Drinking Age (MLDA) laws have been recognized as one of a small number of primary prevention strategies that are effective in preventing alcohol-related problems (Toomey, Rosenfeld, & Wagenaar, 1996). However, it is unclear why MLDA laws are effective. Research has shown that MLDA laws are effective with little or no enforcement (Toomey et al.), leading researchers to speculate as to the potential effectiveness of enforcement strategies targeting underage youth (Wagenaar & Wolfson, 1994; Wagenaar & Wolfson, 1995).

Also unclear is the role of deterrence when applied to alcohol-related behaviors. While economists argue that increasing the probability of arrest and the severity of punishment is the basis for deterring individuals from illegal behaviors (Benson, Bruce, Mast, & Rasmussen, 1999), economic research examining the effectiveness of legal sanctions in deterring drinking and driving behavior have been equivocal (Benson, Mast, & Rasmussen, 2000; Evans, Neville, & Graham, 1993). Benson et al. (2000) argue that the use of aggregated data by economists is not sensitive enough to detect a deterrent effect due to the fact that police efforts are modest at best. On the other hand, the influences on illegal drinking behavior may be more complex than assumed by economists, involving physiologic (i.e. physical dependence) and social (i.e. social and situational norms) externalities. Consequently, some researchers acknowledge that a broad approach is required to affect illegal drinking behavior involving the drinker, the drinking environment and alcohol availability (DeJong & Hingson, 1998).

Minimum legal drinking age laws are unique in that deterrence strategies can target either the underage youth or the alcohol retailer. Deterring underage youth from purchasing alcohol using citations and arrests represents a deterrence strategy that directly targets the population at risk, underage youth. Deterring alcohol retailers from selling alcohol to youth using fines and/or license suspensions/revocations represents a general deterrence strategy that indirectly targets underage youth by decreasing the availability of alcohol in the environment. Research demonstrates that enforcement agencies prefer targeting underage youth rather than alcohol retailers. For example, Wagenaar and Wolfson (1995) have found that 2 of every 1,000 occasions of underage drinking result in an underage arrest while only 5 in every 100,000 occasions result in action against an alcohol retailer. Unfortunately there is little in the way of data documenting which deterrence strategy is more effective. Because alcohol retailers are not subject to the physiologic and social externalities that might influence their decision to sell alcohol to underage youth, there is reason to hypothesize that deterrence strategies targeting al-

cohol retailers would be more effective than targeting underage youth.

Louisiana has had a natural experiment of sorts with regard to the two types of deterrence strategies that can be used to enforce the MLDA law. From 1986 to 1995, Louisiana employed a deterrence strategy that only targeted underage youth who purchased or consumed alcohol. Alcohol retailers were not liable under Louisiana law for underage sales. Due to the imbalance of law enforcement priorities associated with arresting underage youth versus "real" criminals and the effort required to effectively prosecute underage alcohol purchases, the law was rarely enforced. Wagenaar and Wolfson (1994) document that from 1988 through 1990 Louisiana had the lowest rate of enforcement of MLDA law of any U.S. state. In 1995 the law was changed to permit the citing of alcohol retailers who sell to underage youth. Initial efforts to target alcohol retailers with a deterrence strategy were implemented, and alcohol-related fatal crashes among underage youth fell immediately (see Figure 1). The study reported here details one of those efforts.

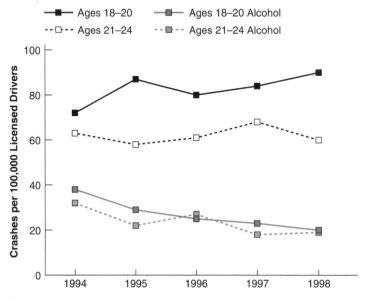

Figure 1   **Trends in Alcohol Involved Fatal and Injury Crash Rates in Louisiana among Underage Youth**

The trend in alcohol-related fatal and injury crash rates in the early 1990s both nationally and in Louisiana reflects the fact that the law has an effect whether or not it is enforced (Toomey et al., 1996). The slow decline of crash rates may also reflect a nationwide trend of fewer crashes overall due to safer highways and automobiles. However, in Louisiana, the sharp decline in alcohol-related injury and fatal crashes in 1995 stands out (see Figure 1). The 1995 drop in crash rates suggests an effect for deterrence efforts targeting alcohol retailers who sell to underage youth. The inability to sustain the low crash rates following the initial efforts to deter alcohol retailers from underage sales reflects the delay in implementing a state-wide effort in Louisiana until 1998.

This study reports on one of the ad hoc efforts to enforce the expanded MLDA law in Louisiana. The study was designed to assess the impact of compliance checks both on alcohol retailers cited for non-compliance and alcohol retailers only exposed to media coverage of the issuing of citations in the New Orleans area.

Methods

Overview

The study was conducted to evaluate the effect of a general deterrence intervention designed to increase compliance with the MLDA law among alcohol retailers. The intervention and evaluation were only conducted in the City of New Orleans. A quasi-experimental design using repeated interventions on the same population of merchants was incorporated (Cook & Campbell, 1979). The evaluation was carried out by means of compliance checks conducted at baseline (T0), five months after baseline (two months after the enforcement campaign) (T1), and twelve months after baseline (T2) (see Figure 2).

The intervention was conducted in association with the Louisiana Department of Alcoholic Beverage Control (ABC). The intervention involved a media advocacy effort around the issuing of citations to alcohol outlets failing the compliance checks at baseline. The media advocacy component was conducted two months after the baseline compliance checks and was organized around the delivery of citations by ABC agents to a sub sample of all non-compliant outlets at baseline. The event was well-covered by the media, involving a press conference attended by the Mayor and the State ABC Commissioner followed by a press "ride along" in which ABC officials delivered the citations to outlet owners. The story was covered on all three television news networks that evening, and the New Orleans major daily newspaper covered the story on the front page.

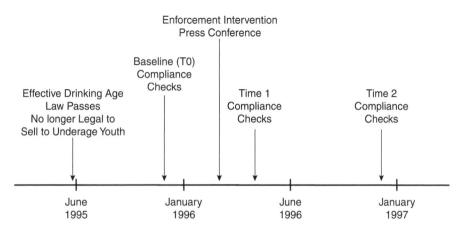

Figure 2 **Intervention Timeline**

Outlet Sample Selection

A sample of 155 off-sale alcohol outlets was randomly selected from the universe of all off-sale alcohol outlets. Over the course of the project, 12 outlets either closed down or stopped selling alcohol. As a result, only data for the 143 remaining outlets were available at all three waves. None of the outlets that stopped selling alcohol was closed due to enforcement of alcohol regulations.

Compliance Checks

Compliance checks were conducted both by State ABC agents and project staff using the same methodology. Project staff rode along with State ABC agents during their compliance checks to assure study protocols were followed. Potential youths to be used in the compliance checks were rated as to the age they looked by a panel of 5 adults. Youths who were rated 18 years old or younger were selected. The actual ages of the youths selected ranged from 17 to 22. The lower age of 18 versus 21 was used due to possible confusion with the recent change in the MLDA law in Louisiana. A total of six youths, all female, were used over the course of the project. Project staff accompanied the youths on all visits to the selected alcohol outlets. Staff witnessed the attempts to purchase either from inside the store or from outside the store if the checkout counter was visible from outside the store. If the clerk serving the youth did not ask for age identification, resulting in the sale of an alcohol product, the outlet was defined as having failed the compliance check. No other compliance checks were being conducted by any other agency over the course of the study, and the State ABC conducted no additional compliance checks during the course of the study.

Three waves of compliance checks were conducted on the same outlets at each wave. The baseline compliance checks were conducted from November 1995 through January 1996 (time 0). State ABC agents cooperated on 51 of these compliance checks. The non-compliant outlets from these 51 checks served as the basis for the media advocacy component. The second wave of compliance checks was conducted from April 1996 through May 1996 (time 1). The final wave of compliance checks was conducted from December 1996 through January 1997 (time 2). Of the 155 outlets evaluated for compliance at baseline, 143 were evaluated at all three waves.

Results

The first wave of compliance checks demonstrated low levels of compliance by alcohol retailers with the minimum legal drinking age law. At Time 0, only 16 of the 143 (11.3%) off-sale alcohol outlets visited asked for age identification before selling alcohol to our underage buyer.

Five months after the first wave of compliance checks and four weeks after the media advocacy component, the second wave of compliance checks was conducted. At Time 1, 57 of the 143 (39.9%) off-sale outlets visited asked for age identification before selling alcohol. This represented a significant increase in compliance compared with compliance at Time 0 ($p < .0001$). As expected, of those outlets that received a citation during the media advocacy component, a higher percentage of compliance 23/45 (51.1%) was observed. However, there was also a significant increase in compliance among the outlets that did not receive a citation but were only exposed to the news coverage around the issuing of citations. At Time 1, 34 of the 98 non-cited outlets visited (34.7%) were compliant, compared to only 13/98 (13.3%) of those same outlets at Time 0 ($p < .001$).

Nine months after the enforcement intervention and one year after the baseline compliance checks, the third wave of compliance checks were conducted. At Time 2, 30 out of 143 (21.0%) outlets were in compliance with the minimum legal drinking age law. This represents a small but significant difference in compliance compared with percent compliance at Time 0 ($p = .023$). However, when the changes in compliance were disaggregated into those that received a citation in the enforcement intervention and those that did not, a different picture emerges. Among those that did not receive a citation, 17/98 (17.3%) were compliant, which does not represent a significant difference between baseline (Time 0) and Time 2 ($p = 0.397$). Among

TABLE 1   *Compliance Rates for Off-Sale Alcohol Outlets throughout the Intervention*

	ALL OUTLETS (n=143)	OUTLETS CITED (n=45)	OUTLETS NOT CITED (n=98)
Time 0	16/143 (11.3%)	3/45 (6.7%)	13/98 (13.3%)
Time 1	57/143 (39.9%)**	23/45 (51.1%)**	34/98 (34.7%)
Time 2	30/143 (21.0%)	13/45 (28.9%)	17/98 (17.3%)

*p<.05 compared with Time 0; **p<.001 compared with Time 0

those that did receive a citation, 13/45 (28.9%) were compliant, a lower percentage than at Time 1 but still a small, but significant, difference between Time 0 and Time 2 (p = .011).

Discussion

This study demonstrates that the rate of compliance with the minimum drinking age law among New Orleans off-sale alcohol outlets was significantly increased following a deterrence intervention targeting alcohol retailers. The effect of the deterrence intervention was greatest among the outlets that actually received a citation for non-compliance; however, outlets that were only exposed to news coverage of the issuing of citations also significantly increased their rate of compliance. It should be noted that the effect on alcohol retailers only exposed to the media component had eroded in 9 months.

A large effect on compliance resulted from a relatively small intervention effort. We attribute the success of the enforcement intervention to the effectiveness of deterrence strategies targeting illegal behavior that is primarily influenced by economic cost-benefit realities. It should also be noted that news coverage had a deterrent effect, whether or not an outlet received any disciplinary action. The media advocacy component, which was built around the issuing of citations, attempted to frame the effort as the city and state "getting tough" on alcohol retailers illegally selling to underage youth. Given that a new State ABC Commissioner and a new Governor had recently taken office promising to be different from former administrations, outlet owners had a reason to be concerned that they may have their licenses suspended or be subject to fines. The media advocacy effort was framed to use the Governor's promise of change as an endorsement of alcohol enforcement. The media advocacy component created an effect on behavior where no effect would have otherwise occurred.

The overall low rate of compliance can be attributed to factors consistent with deterrence theory, certainty of citation and severity of punishment. New Orleans is a city known to be very permissive with regard to alcohol consumption and alcohol availability. Consequently, enforcement of liquor laws tends to be viewed as anti-business. Consistent with this general attitude, the severity of punishment for an alcohol retailer violating the MLDA law is minor. The retailer meets privately with the ABC commissioner who tailors the punishment, typically a small fine, rarely a suspension. Second, enforcement of liquor laws has never been a priority for state and city officials. Neither the State ABC nor the City of New Orleans had been involved in active enforcement of liquor laws for many years prior to the intervention. There were only three State ABC enforcement officers responsible for 5,000 alcohol outlets in the five parish region that include Orleans parish. As a result, it is likely that the perception of retailers who risk being cited for selling alcohol to minors would be low. It should be noted that in 1998 the State ABC increased the number of enforcement officers from 14 to 41 and began active enforcement, conducting compliance checks on a regular basis.

Chi-Square

Chi-square (χ^2) is a popular statistic for determining the relationship between two categorical variables. In this article, Scribner and Cohen compare the number of off-sale alcohol retailers who comply and who do not comply with the minimum legal drinking age at three points in time: (1) at the beginning of the study (baseline or Time 0), (2) five months after a wave of compliance checks (and four weeks after media attention to them) (Time 1), and (3) one year after the wave of compliance checks (Time 2). Although it is not specified in the article, the authors use a variation of the traditional chi-square statistic—the Mantel-Haenszel chi-square—that is sometimes used for data based on repeated observations. In this case, the baseline, Time 1, and Time 2 number of compliers is based on the same set of off-sale alcohol outlets.

Although the precise chi-square values are not reported in Table 1, the important information is the level of significance of the values in the table. These probability levels are located just beneath the table. A $p < .001$ means that there is greater than a 99.9 percent probability that a change has actually occurred in the number of complying outlets since the previous time frame, a $p < .01$ means that there is greater than a 99 percent probability that a

change has actually occurred, and a $p < .05$ means that there is greater than a 95 percent probability that a change has actually occurred. If no probability level is reported, that means that we do not have sufficient confidence to conclude that a change actually occurred. In this table, it is reported that there is a greater than 99.9 percent chance that between the baseline start of the study and Time 1, a statistically significantly larger number (1) of all outlets were in compliance, (2) of those outlets actually cited were in compliance, and (3) even of those outlets not actually cited were in compliance. From this, the authors conclude the compliance checks, the citations for those not in compliance, and the media report of these citations stimulated a significantly greater number of outlets to start enforcing the minimum drinking age law.

Did this effect persist for the next several months? With greater than 95 percent confidence (slightly less confidence than before), the authors found that the effect did persist for all merchants and for the cited merchants but not for the uncited merchants. Thus, a significantly larger number of the merchants that had been cited were still complying, but the effect of media attention on the citations was no longer leading a statistically significant number of uncited outlets to comply with the law.

Another issue was the deterioration of the impact of the enforcement intervention over the course of the study. Over the eight-month period between Time 1 and Time 2, the rate of compliance deteriorated from 40% to 21% overall. This finding indicates that the deterrent effect of enforcement on compliance was short-lived and suggests an effective intervention based on deterrence must be sustained, presumably to create the perception that selling to underage youth will result in a citation, which is consistent with deterrence theory.

Our study design was limited in that our measures were pre and post and the results could not be compared to a control area not exposed to the interventions. It should be noted that East Baton Rouge parish was originally selected as a control area. However, the far higher rates of compliance

(>60%) due to an active parish level ABC agency made the two parishes incomparable. The lack of a control area does not rule out the possibility that secular or seasonal trends could account for the effects of the enforcement campaign in Orleans parish. Merchant practices for checking age identification may have been different during holiday season when the first and third waves of compliance checks were conducted. In addition, a secular trend of increasing compliance following the closing of the loophole in the minimum drinking age law could account for the higher rate of compliance at the second wave of compliance checks (Time 1). The third wave of compliance checks (Time 2) with lower compliance do not support this possibility.

Another limitation of our study involves the fact that only the impact of the intervention on sales by merchants was assessed. It is possible that the interventions had an impact on youth; they might have been less likely to try to illegally purchase alcohol in order to avoid potential consequences. No data were collected on youth purchase attempts. Future evaluations of alcohol awareness campaigns should look at the impact on youth as well as merchants.

Despite these limitations, we conclude that enforcement of liquor laws can increase compliance with minimum drinking age laws and that the effect can be magnified by media advocacy associated with an enforcement effort. We also conclude the effects of enforcement are short-lived, requiring an ongoing enforcement efforts in order to be an effective PREVENTION STRATEGY.

REFERENCES

Benson, B., Bruce, L., Mast, B., Rasmussen, D. 1999. Deterring drunk driving fatalities: An economics of crime perspective. International Review of Law and Economics, 19, 205–225.

Benson, B. L., Mast, B. D., Rasmussen, D. W. 2000. Can police deter drunk driving? Applied Economics, 32, 357–369

Cook, T. D., Campbell, D. T. 1979. Quasi experimentation: Design and analysis issues for field studies. Houghton Mifflin, Boston.

DeJong, W., Hingson, R. 1998. Strategies to reduce driving under the influence of alcohol. Annual Review of Public Health, 19, 359–78.

Evans, W. N., Neville, D., Graham, J. D. 1993. General deterrence of drunk driving: Evaluation of recent American policies. Risk Analysis, 11, 279–289.

Forster, J. L., Murray, D. M., Wolfson, M., Wagenaar, A. C. 1995. Commercial availability of alcohol to young people: Results of alcohol purchase attempts. Preventive Medicine, 24(4), 342–7.

Peny, C. L., Williams, C. L., Veblen-Mortenson, S., Toomey, T. L., Komro, K. A., Anstine, P. S., McGovern, P. G., Finnegan, J. R., Forster, J. L., Wagenaar, A. C.. Wolfson, M. 1996. Project Northland: Outcomes of a community wide alcohol use prevention program during early adolescence. American Journal of Public Health, 86(7), 956–65.

Toomey, T. L., Rosenfeld, C., Wagenaar, A. C. 1996. Minimum Legal Drinking Age: History, effectiveness and ongoing debate. Alcohol Health and Research World, 20, 213–218.

Wagenaar, A., Wolfson, M. 1994. Enforcement of the legal minimum drinking age in the United States. Journal of Public Health Policy, 15, 37–53.

Wagenaar, A. C., Wolfson, M. 1995. Deterring sales and provision of alcohol to minors: a study of enforcement in 295 counties in four states. Public Health Reports, 110(4), 419–27.

Wolfson, M., Toomey, T. L., Murray, D. M., Forster, J. L., Short, B. J., Wagenaar, A. C. 1996. Alcohol outlet policies and practices concerning sales to underage people. Addiction, 91(4), 589–602.

Richard Scribner, MD, holds the D'Angelo Professorship in Alcohol Research at Louisiana State University Health Sciences Center in New Orleans. He is nationally recognized as an expert in the area of community-level prevention of alcohol-related problems. He received his advanced degrees from the University of Southern California and the University of California. His research focuses on prevention environments in which he uses Geographic Information System (GIS) technology and spatial analysis techniques to characterize healthy neighborhoods and identify community-level policies that can be used to alter the strong geographic relation between alcohol availability and alcohol problems like binge drinking, fatal traffic crashes, youth violence, sexually transmitted diseases, domestic violence, and drunk driving. Both local and national media have featured Scribner's findings and his research has been used to influence alcohol policy in communities throughout the country, including state-level policy in California and Louisiana.

Deborah Cohen, MD, MPH, is a Senior Natural Scientist at RAND Corporation. At the time of this study, she was an associate professor in the Department of Public Health and Preventive Medicine at Louisiana State University Health Sciences Center. Her expertise is in alcohol policy, substance abuse, and STD/HIV Prevention.

An   interview   with   .   .   .

Richard Scribner

What got you interested in this subject?

I have always been interested in preventive intervention associated with alcohol. Too often, researchers have focused on the individual level, but I have always thought that there had to be a structural component to this. One of the reasons that I came to Louisiana was because it is one of the most alcohol-available places with one of the highest rates of alcohol-related problems. It just seemed like a simple thing to see that relationship. Some of the first research which we did here was to document the high availability of alcohol in the New Orleans area.

What do you see as being the main contributions of your research?

The contribution of this is to add attention to the environmental component of alcohol-related problems—that the availability of alcohol is one of the factors contributing to alcohol-related problems. Also, we wanted to look at the whole area of policy, and take some of the focus off the individuals—the kids who are drinking—and put it on the politicians and what they are doing to address the high availability. After all, they are responsible for the neighborhoods being the way they are, and if we want to make changes, we have to try to change what politicians are doing. So, a focus of the research is how to get politicians and store owners to change their behavior. In addition to looking at the high rate of underage sales, we also looked at how advertising and how publicizing disciplinary actions could have a huge effect. In other words, policymakers should use that aspect of their enforcement to try to educate shop owners, and we saw that effect, which was kind of exciting. We thought it was very significant that many of the shops that had never been disciplined, or had not been disciplined in years, responded to the publicity of others being sanctioned.

What was the process by which you teamed up with the Louisiana Alcoholic Beverage Control group?

I have always wanted to go to the ABCs and deal with this. Most of the ABC officers are reduced to just processing licenses, and the idea of going out and doing this sort of study was nearly impossible. So, when we first contacted them, it was with the idea that we would be helping them by showing them how to do this study. Rather than doing proactive checks, they would only go out in response to a complaint and then do an investigation. So, we helped to create the necessary form; we created the procedure based on work that others had done, and we arranged for them to ride with us.

What were the strengths of using this technique to test the relative effects of focusing on merchants rather than underage buyers?

The strength was that it was a precursor to what enforcement officers actually do. Today, it is pretty routine to do compliance checks, but back then doing routine compliance checks was uncommon. We see the research as something that actually pushed them along in that direction. We knew this was something that people needed to do. That was demonstrated by the fact that only 11 percent of the outlets did not sell to underage youth, so that was shameful, shocking, terrible. This occurred just after a change in Louisiana law designed to reduce drinking among eighteen to twenty years olds, so we were in a period where they wanted to do something to publicize the change. The timing of this study, the fact that we worked together with the ABC and got their buy-in, and that this was a new way to address the problem were strengths of the study.

What were the weaknesses of using this technique to test the relative effects of focusing on merchants rather than underage buyers?

Our sampling was difficult. We geocoded all of the outlets and hoped that we could get the officers to accompany us to all of them. That didn't work, so we ended up with only a subsample. It turned out to be more of a convenience sample with what they wanted to do, so there are some design problems there. It was intended to be a tighter design, but we had to give in on a lot to keep the ABC with us. We wanted them in it as part of the project. Originally, we wanted to take a sample of all the outlets in the city and to stratify them by neighborhoods. It worked out that we identified where the outlets were in each census tract, and then we randomly selected the ones to be visited, but they picked and chose the ones they wanted.

What unexpected events or developments (if any) occurred during the course of this research?

The press conference that occurred to announce our findings. We didn't know that the mayor was going to be there. Because he was, every television station in the whole area showed up at the press conference. It was very unexpected and very fortunate that we got that kind of coverage. The mayor and the chief of police even rode along on a bust and that made the news, so that was something that we couldn't control and didn't expect. Another unexpected occurrence was that, only six months before the study, the state supreme court ruled that lowering the drinking age [from twenty-one to eighteen] was not age discrimination.

Also, it was pretty hairy going out to some of these sites. This is real shoe-leather research, and you are going into randomly selected poor neighborhoods in New Orleans, one of the poorest cities in America. You're there trying to keep people safe, and liquor stores are not the safest places. So, we had to change some procedures to make sure that we got there early enough in the day. And, a lot of the stores went out of business during the course of the study.

Could you describe any specific ethical issues that you confronted in this research?

A key issue was whether or not the young people entering the stores as our confederates would actually be permitted [by us] to buy the alcohol, since they were technically breaking the law. The reason that we had to buy it is that the police needed it for evidence to conduct the disciplinary action. And so, to keep it the same everywhere, whether the police were riding along or not, we just had the underage youth buy the alcohol at every site. That issue had to go through our Institutional Review Board. Ultimately, they allowed it because we were there to take it from them when they came out.

If you were to do this research again, is there anything that you would do differently? If so, what?

Back then, we were really trying to bring attention to the issue. Doing it again, we would develop and test much more specific hypotheses as to why these store owners are selling to youth. We might have surveyed the store owners who began to comply to get at why they changed their behavior, how that whole process worked. Is it the instructions that they give to their managers? Is it store policy? To really understand, you would want to get at the mechanisms of what's going on in the minds of the store owners and things like that. We would want to do much more focused research on that. This was really an exploratory study.

What was most frustrating to you in doing this research? What was most satisfying?

We had a good time doing this. It was frustrating seeing how bad the situation was. In terms of what was gratifying, we felt we contributed to raising awareness about a really important issue that had not been addressed within the city. Kind of like when you put a frog in hot water, it will stay until it boils, this issue was boiling in the city, yet there didn't seem to be awareness of the role that alcohol plays in what is going on. It was really kind of exciting to do this research, and have people say "I didn't know that." It was also gratifying to get the press attention that it got, how much we were well received. Though we did not start out to make this a piece of advocacy research, any research that focuses on public policy is going to be that, because ultimately it is supporting or criticizing a certain policy. The problem of underage alcohol sales is just so glaring.

What important lesson or illustration of doing good research can you share with students from your experiences in this research project?

This is not a methodologically tight analysis or anything like that, but it illustrates looking outside the box in the way that we focused more on the environmental than the individual level. And once you go outside the box, it is like you are stumbling around, and there are huge boulders that you are walking into. It is not hard to prove that the boulders exist, and so my point is that sometimes when you are looking at something from a different perspective, you find answers in terms of public policy, in actions of politicians.

However, we found that it was easier to get funding for continuing to look at the issue from the individual level. Our original funding agency, the Center for Substance Abuse Prevention, gave us a four-year grant, but they withdrew funding after the first year. There were lots of political pressures because we chose to emphasize the role of the environment and public policy. No one wants you pointing fingers at the powers that be—they would much rather that you point fingers at the population. Then they can just throw up their hands and say that there is nothing that we can do. When you start saying that the problem is in enforcement, that there is too much alcohol availability, people get a little antsy about that—especially when you start pointing at the alcohol industry. They absolutely hate that. They are dedicated to the proposition that there are drunks out there who are the cause of all the problems and give alcohol a bad name. And the idea that the industry has any kind of responsibility for that—they will fight that tooth and nail. That is the kind of insight that I have gotten from doing lots of expert testimony on bills in the state here, and in California, when I lived there. More and more, what we have seen is that the individual level approaches are tapped out, and it seems like what we are butting up against is that there is alcohol everywhere in the environment in which these kids live. There are billboards and advertisements on television; they are selling beer on the street corner; at every party they go to on weekends, someone is providing a keg of beer. It is tough. So, the switch to an environment approach is definitely not popular among political leaders and among the funding agencies.

Questions to Think About

1. What is the unit of analysis in this study? How was the sample selected? What were some problems the researchers faced with regard to the sample, and how might they have affected the results of the study?

2. Describe how the researchers measured *compliance*—that is, all the study protocols regarding compliance checks. What is the purpose of those protocols?

3. What are the results of their study? What implications do they have for past and future policies and programs to curb underage drinking?

4. Describe the overall design of this study, using the appropriate methodological terms. What were the advantages and disadvantages of using a field experiment to answer their research question? Are there other approaches that might be equally or more useful? Explain.

chapter 5

Survey Research

Survey research is the most commonly used data collection technique in sociology and is also used in disciplines such as political science, social psychology, economics, marketing, and communications. Most of us have participated in political polls, consumer studies, and surveys on our campuses, and telephone and mail surveys regularly ask thousands of people all over the country about everything from their opinions of the current president to their grocery buying habits. Increasingly, and much to the chagrin of legitimate social science researchers, telemarketers call us at home under the guise of survey research to keep us on the line as they try to sell us their products. That, and the increased use of caller ID technology, have significantly lowered response rates in telephone surveys in recent years. Another current trend in survey research is the use of electronic surveys, which can be cheaper and more efficient than the more conventional self-administered questionnaires, telephone interviews, and face-to-face interviews.

The unit of analysis in survey research is usually the individual, although it might be another entity such as an organization. Social scientists often use surveys to describe attitudes and behaviors of a sample. MacDonald and Wright do this in their study of adolescent smokers in Chapter 3, as does Wendy Walsh in the study about spanking in this chapter. Walsh notes that parenting attitudes and behavior are influenced by the messages that parents read and hear, and she seeks to identify the sources of information used by parents who spank and those who do not and to examine the importance that each group attaches to these messages. For her study, Walsh uses data that were collected by researchers who, in short twenty-minute interviews, asked each of 998 mothers 130 questions about childhood behavioral problems, disciplining techniques, and sources of information about parenting, along with the importance the respondents attached to them. This allowed the researchers to collect a veritable wealth of information in a relatively short period of time. This study nicely demonstrates a major advantage of survey research: That it is possible to get lots of information from a large number of people with a fairly small investment of time and money. This advantage is also noted by Thomas O'Connor, whose longitudinal study of factors that influence adults' religious involvement appears in Chapter 2. Wendy Walsh points out that telephone interviews also have the advantage of allowing respondents some sense of anonymity, which is important when the topic is a somewhat sensitive one, such as child discipline.

Although some survey research is solely for descriptive purposes, more often the aim is *explanatory*—that is, to identify factors that influence how people think and behave. This sort of causal analysis is the goal of most quantitative research. Central to sociological thinking is the assumption that our beliefs, attitudes, values, and behaviors are largely a result of different aspects of our social location. For that reason, a typical survey instrument will include questions about some attitude or behavior and also ask about the respondent's religiosity, education level, sex, age, and other factors that are thought to influence that attitude or behavior. The study of adolescents' fear of crime included in this chapter is an example of an explanatory study because the goal is to identify predictors of adolescents' fear of crime and to see if they are the same as those that predict fear of crime in adults. For this study, David May and R. Gregory Dunaway distributed self-administered questionnaires to 742 public high school students. The dependent variable in the study is fear of criminal victimization at school, and the researchers included questions to measure a number of potential independent variables, including race/ethnicity, gender, economic status, grades, previous instances of victimization at school, perceived safety at school, and perceived neighborhood incivility.

Self-administered questionnaires offer several advantages, especially over face-to-face interviews. They make it possible to collect information from a large number of people spread out over a large area at a relatively small cost, they make confidentiality and anonymity easier to achieve, and the absence of interviewers eliminates one important potential source of bias. At the same time, the absence of an interviewer means having to depend on the respondents to be motivated enough to complete and return the questionnaire and to provide thoughtful and truthful answers. As David May notes in his interview, this was problematic for them, as it became clear that a significant number of the adolescents in their study did not take the questionnaire seriously or, in his words, "blew it off." The researchers did reliability and validity checks of the data to detect inconsistent patterns that would flag questionnaires that were not completed truthfully, and the end result was a significantly smaller sample than they had hoped for originally.

Survey research presents various other challenges to researchers. One is connected with *secondary analysis,* when researchers analyze survey data that were collected by someone else at another time and typically for a different (or at least slightly different) purpose. Secondary analysis is increasingly popular, due to the ever-expanding number of state, regional, and national survey databases that are available and in light of the significant costs associated with conducting research using probability samples. A major drawback is that researchers cannot control the content and wording of questions and thus may have data that do not exactly fit their needs. Another drawback of survey research is inherent in the method: Although it allows for the collection of lots of information from sizable numbers of people, it doesn't allow for much depth, or for the "voices" of respondents to be heard. To counteract that, survey researchers sometimes include open-ended questions on their interview schedules or questionnaires, which give respondents the chance to offer insights and explanations that help researchers know if they are interpreting responses correctly. An even better alternative, but one that is not always practical, is to conduct studies that use multiple methods, both qualitative and quantitative. For example, one might follow a large-scale survey with less structured, face-to-face interviews with a selected number of respondents.

Finally, as Internet use has increased dramatically, so has the use of electronic surveys. These surveys take the form of *e-mail surveys,* with questionnaires sent to respondents' e-mail addresses and also returned electronically, or *web surveys,* for which respondents are asked to visit a designated website and complete a questionnaire that is located there. Electronic surveying will likely become more and more common because it offers most of the advantages of other techniques (quick access to many people over a wide geographic area, ease of administration by the researcher, availability of the researcher to answer questions, and relatively low cost). For surveys of well-wired groups, like students on college campuses, they already seem to be the method of choice. However, with less than half of the population linked to the Internet, broad-based electronic surveys of a cross-section of the population are still not feasible. Researchers must continue to turn to the tried-and-true methods of written questionnaires or interviews.

Spankers and Nonspankers

Where They Get Information on Spanking

Wendy Walsh

Because spanking is common, puts children at risk for harmful side effects, and is ineffective as a positive behavior management tool, it is important to identify the kind of advice families receive about the appropriateness of spanking. Using the health belief model, I examined spankers and nonspankers on the spanking messages they received from eight sources of discipline information and how important they perceived these messages to be. Data from telephone interviews with 998 mothers with children aged 2 to 14 years showed that 33% of mothers rated advice from workshops, pediatricians, newspapers and magazines, and books as "very important." Less than 15% rated parents and relatives and friends as such. Spankers perceived sources as recommending spanking, whereas nonspankers perceived sources as opposing spanking. Mothers were more likely to spank when they perceived more intense messages to spank, less intense messages opposing spanking, had younger children, and were of lower socioeconomic status.

What we read and learn from our environment influences behavior. The messages we perceive help us to determine what is normative or expected behavior. For example, public smoking was once culturally accepted and not questioned. Once the link between smoking and negative health effects was emphasized, smoking was redefined as harmful behavior, and legal controls were supported (Ferraro, 1990). Similarly, corporal punishment was once more culturally accepted than today. Because parenting attitudes and beliefs are formed in part by interaction with those in our social context and what we read, this study examines the sorts of advice families receive about the appropriateness of spanking and the importance of information sources.

Spanking Prevalence

Corporal punishment is defined as "the use of physical force with the intention of causing a child to experience pain, but not injury, for purposes of correction or control of the child's behavior" (Straus, 1994, p. 4). Six types of corporal punishment include slaps on the hand or leg, spanking on the buttocks, pinching, shaking, hitting on the buttocks with a belt or paddle, and slapping in the face (Straus & Stewart, 1999). Spanking is common; approximately 67% of all parents report using some type of corporal punishment (Straus). This figure is misleading, however, because the use of corporal punishment is strongly dependent on the age of the child. For example, spanking on bottom with a hand is a common type of corporal punishment with 72% of parents of 2- to 4-year-olds, 71% of parents of 5- to 8-year-olds, 43% of parents of 9- to 12-year-olds, and 14% of parents of 13- to 17-year-olds using this type of corporal punishment (Straus & Stewart).

Characteristics Associated with Spanking

Some adults spank more than others. The characteristics associated with spanking are the age of the child, age and gender of the parent, socioeconomic status, circumstances, and cultural norms. Younger parents are more likely to use corporal punishment than older parents (Giles-Sims, Straus, & Sugarman,1995; Straus & Stewart, 1999; Wolfner & Gelles, 1993). Mothers use corporal punishment more frequently than fathers, although the relative difference is small when time spent with the child is considered (Dietz, 2000; Wofner & Galles). Research on the relationship between socioeconomic status and the use of corporal punishment is inconclusive (Dietz; Giles-Simes et al.; Straus, 1994; Wolfner & Gelles). Parents who were hit as children are more likely to hit their children (Bryan & Freed, 1982; Graziano & Namaste, 1990; Rodriquez & Sutherland, 1999; Straus).

Not only does a parent's past history with corporal punishment influence his or her own use of it, but also cultural and subcultural norms may influence the use of spanking. For example, Greven (1991) proposed that we have perceptual blinders to corporal punishment because nearly everyone has experienced it. Perceptual blinders may be more prevalent in some geographic locations. For example, research on regional differences on attitudes and use of corporal punishment has consistently found more support and use of it in the South than in other regions (Giles-Simes et al., 1995; Straus & Mathur, 1996; Straus & Stewan, 1999).

Consequences of Spanking

A growing body of literature on spanking has focused on the potential harmful effects of corporal punishment and its ineffectiveness as a child behavior management tool. Some of the potential harmful effects of frequent and severe spankings include subsequent antisocial behavior of children (Grusec & Goodnow, 1994; McCord, 1991; Straus, Sugarman, & Giles-Sims, 1997). Some research indicates that the effects are small and vary by age of child and ethnicity (Deater-Deckard, Dodge, Bates, & Pettit, 1996; Larzelere, 1996). The excessive use of corporal punishment has been associated with a number of adult social and psychological problems, including physical aggression, delinquency, and depression (Foglia, 1997; Straus, 1994; Swinford, Demaris, Cemkovick, & Giordano, 2000). In addition, physical punishments give children pain and may teach them it is all right to inflict pain on others (McCord, 1996).

Research also indicates that spankings may work against what parents are trying to achieve. Results show that using corporal punishment

leads to greater incidences of child aggression and maladaptive behaviors (Grusec & Goodnow, 1994; Patterson & Narrett, 1990; Strassberg, Dogde, Pettit, & Bates, 1994). Research also indicates that abusive parents spank their children more often than nonabusive parents and that excessive spanking may be a risk factor for child abuse (Barber, 1992; Holden & Ritchie, 1991; Kadushin & Martin, 1981; Oldershaw, Walters, & Hall, 1989; Whipple & Richey, 1997; Whipple & Webster-Stratton, 1991). Therefore, relying on spanking may increase the potential for use of frequent and severe physical punishment.

Paralleling the increase in knowledge about consequences of spanking, approval of corporal punishment has decreased from 94% in 1968 to 68% in 1994 (Straus & Mathur, 1996), and reported use of corporal punishment has decreased from 64% in 1988 to 53% in 1992 (Daro & Gelles,1992). Nevertheless, 94% of parents of 3- to 4-year-olds still report using corporal punishment (Straus & Stewart, 1999). Thus, it is important to ask about the kind of advice families receive regarding the appropriateness of spanking.

Spanking Messages and Advice

Information about the appropriateness of spanking may be informal, such as comments from friends and relatives, or formal, such as information provided by professionals. Although parents seem to want information about child discipline, it is not clear where and what kind of information parents typically receive (Riley, Meinhardt, Nelson, Salisbury, & Winnett, 1991; Thompson, 1994). For example, a national study found 4 out of 10 parents wanted discipline information from health professionals, yet only 23% of parents reported discussing discipline with their child's pediatrician (Young, Davis, & Schoen, 1996).

In addition to the spanking advice parents receive, we know little about how consistent or strong such messages are. Perhaps the discipline message from friends and relatives creates confusion or conflict if the advice is contradictory to one's own beliefs or if information sources do not send similar messages (Edwards, 1995; Powell,

1979; Small & Eastman, 1991). The effects of discipline messages also may depend on how valued the source is and what kind of messages are provided. For example, Small and Eastman showed that, depending on the message, an information source could serve as a support or stressor. They found that when the source is valued and gives needed advice, that source is perceived as supportive. If the source has different views on child rearing from those of the parent, then that source could be a stressor. Depending on any sanctions imposed, such as parents criticizing how their child parents or a social worker removing a child from the home, the advice may have differential effects. Therefore, the current study examined spanking messages relative to the importance of the information source.

Theoretical Framework

Building on the principle that our attitudes and behaviors are formed, in part, by the environment, the health belief model (Ferraro, 1990) incorporates how community norms and opinions about the negative consequences of a behavior affect an individual's willingness to change a behavior. This framework has been used to examine the influence of community norms on smoking cessation, seatbelt safety, alcohol use, and dietary fat intake. The health belief model looks beyond the individual to consider how macrolevel norms and environmental supports encourage individuals to change behaviors (Portnoy, Anderson, & Erikson, 1989). Environmental supports include social support, availability and accessibility of services, and the mass media.

The health belief model examines how the perception of what is standard or acceptable behavior and public opinion influences an individual's behavior, positing that positive behavior change is enhanced when support networks and community structure reinforce such change. For example, the degree of support for smoking in a community was an important factor when comparing smoking attitudes in two states (Ferraro, 1990). Likewise, one of the important influences on parenting practices is accessing sources of support and in-

formation (Belsky, 1984). Because parenting attitudes and beliefs are formed in part by the influence of those in one's context and by what one reads (Richardson, Abramowitz, Asp, & Peterson, 1986), it is useful to examine the spanking advice parents receive and how important they perceive this advice to be.

Research Questions

Parents need access to a wide range of nonabusive, positive, and effective disciplinary behaviors (Baumrind, 1996). Part of the process of increasing access to information about positive parenting practices is understanding the messages from discipline information sources and their importance to parents. Using the framework of the health belief model, my objectives were to compare spankers and nonspankers on the importance of sources of discipline information, the nature of spanking advice from these sources, and the intensity of messages toward recommending and opposing spanking. The fourth objective was to assess the degree to which the message intensity of recommending or opposing of spanking was associated with the use of spanking.

Method

Participants

The data were from a study conducted in two counties in Minnesota by the University of New Hampshire (Straus & Mouradian, 1998) in 1993 to evaluate the effectiveness of a program to change attitudes and behavior about corporal punishment. The counties are thriving agricultural regions containing small manufacturing- and service-centered cities.

During a 20-minute telephone interview, 998 mothers answered approximately 130 questions about child behavior problems, discipline strategies, discipline information sources, parenting practices, personality, and family issues. Random digit dialing was used to select a sample of mothers of children aged 2 to 14. If a mother had more than one child in this age range, the child with the most recent birthday was the focus of the interview.

Mothers were chosen as the respondents because mothers have more of the day-to-day child-care responsibilities (Milkie, Bianchi, Mattingly, & Robinson's study as cited in Population Reference Bureau, 2001).

The mothers were primarily from two-parent families (93.7%) and from first marriages (85.0%). The mean age of the mothers was 37 (SD = 5.6). They had an average of two children living at home. The mean age of the focal child was 8.6 (SD = 3.7), and they were about equally divided between boys (54%) and girls (46%). Consistent with census data on the socioeconomic composition of these two communities, the sample was almost entirely White, and 48.8% had at least some college.

Measures

Importance of discipline information sources. Questions were asked about how important eight sources of information were in the mother's thinking about discipline: parents and relatives; friends; magazine and newspaper articles; child-rearing books; pediatricians; ministers, priests, or rabbis; psychologists, social workers, or counselors; and parenting workshops. Participants responded to each question on a 4-point scale (1 = not at all important, 4 = very important).

Perception of spanking message. For each of the eight sources of discipline information, participants were asked if that source recommended spanking as a way to discipline. Responses were 1 (recommended), 2 (neutral), and 3 (opposed spanking).

Message Intensity. Two spanking intensity indexes were created to capture the intensity of the message about spanking. One index was defined as the total number of sources that recommended spanking weighted by the relative importance of each source. If the source recommended spanking, the source was coded 1 and was multiplied by the relative importance of that source (ranging from 1—not important to 4—very important), and then these values were summed. The other index was defined as the total number of sources that opposed spanking weighted by the relative importance of each source. If the source opposed spanking, the source was coded as 1 and was multiplied by the relative importance of that source (ranging from 1—not important to 4 = very important), and then these values were summed. The potential range of responses for these two indices was 0 to 32.

Spanking. Participants were asked "How often did you spank, slap, or hit him/her in the past 6 months?" The possible responses ranged from 0 (never) to 6 (more than 20 times). Consistent with other research (Dietz, 2000; Straus, 1994), the responses were recoded to reflect two categories: spankers (those who spanked once or more) and nonspankers (those who did not spank) in the last 6 months. Spanking chronicity was examined to determine whether there was a difference among mothers who did not spank, spanked less than five times, and spanked more than five times. Results did not reveal significant differences between the two classification techniques.

Demographic Data. Because mothers who do and do not spank were compared, demographic data are presented separately for spankers and nonspankers. Demographic data included age of mother, age of child, number of children in household, marital status, education level, and household income. The indicators used to create the socioeconomic status score included the mother's last year of school completed, husband's last year of school completed, and household income. Indicators were converted to a z score with equal weighting.

To control for differences of spanking due to a child's age, two subsets of the sample based on the target child's age were used. Spanking prevalence trends show that the likelihood of being hit slowly declines as a child ages, with a drop in spanking at age 9 (Day, Peterson, & McCracken, 1998; Dietz, 2000; Straus & Stewart, 1999). Thus, mothers whose child was 2 to 8 years old were defined as the younger child group (n = 478) and those with a child 9 to 14 years were defined as the older child group (n = 520).

Analysis

To compare spankers and nonspankers on the importance of information sources and perception of spanking messages, chi square analyses were performed because the independent variables, importance of information source, and perception of spanking messages were categorical. To compare spankers and nonspankers and the mean scores on message intensity recommending and opposing spanking, a t test was conducted. Because the dependent variable was dichotomized, logistic regression was used to assess the degree to which message intensity either recommending or opposing spanking was associated with use of spanking.

Results

Spanking Prevalence

About one third of the mothers (35.6%) reported they spanked one or more times in the past 6 months. Possible explanations for the low percentage of mothers who reported spanking could be the time referenced; the location of the study, which is generally a low-spanking region (Straus & Mouradian, 1998); and the fact that parents of older children made up half of the sample. Just over half (54.6%) of mothers with younger children and 18.1 % of mothers with older children reported spanking. Consistent with discipline research (Day et al., 1998; Dietz, 2000; Straus & Stewart, 1999), mothers with younger children were significantly more likely to spank than those with older children, $chi^2(1, N = 998) = 144.98$, $p < .001$. In this study, the majority of mothers of 2- to 5-year-olds spanked (58.5% to 70.8%), and about half of mothers of 6- to 7-year-olds spanked (47.4% to 54.2%). A minority of mothers of children aged 8 and older spanked (11.1 % to 35.9%) in the past 6 months.

Demographic Characteristics of Spankers and Nonspankers

In the younger and older child groups, nonspanking mothers were significantly more likely to be older themselves and to have older children than were spankers (see Table 1). In the older child group, nonspankers had significantly fewer children at home than spankers. In the younger child group, nonspankers had more education than spankers, although there were no significant differences between spankers and nonspankers regarding marital status and income. In the older child group, nonspankers had higher incomes than spankers; there were no significant differences in marital status and mother's education.

Importance of Information Source

No differences between spankers and nonspankers of younger children were found in the importance of information sources (see Table 2). In this group, more than one third of both spankers and nonspankers rated pediatricians and workshops as very important sources of discipline information. More than 20% of both spankers and nonspankers rated newspapers or magazines, books, religious leaders, psychologists, and workshops as very important. In contrast, less than 15% of spankers and nonspankers rated parents and relatives or friends as very important.

In the older child group, more than 25% of spankers and nonspankers rated pediatricians as very important for discipline information. Both spankers (20.7%) and nonspankers (16.8%) also rated newspapers or magazines as very important. Less than 11% of spankers and nonspankers rated parents and relatives or friends as very important. Two differences between spankers and nonspankers were how psychologists and workshops were rated. Spankers rated psychologists as somewhat (42.3%) or very (18.3%) important, whereas 23.2% and 27.1% of nonspankers rated psychologists as such. Similarly, spankers were more likely to rate workshops as somewhat (46.8%) or very (23.4%) important compared with nonspankers (32.5% and 32.7% respectively).

Perception of Spanking Messages

In the younger child group, spankers and nonspankers perceived receiving significantly different discipline messages from all sources, except psychologists (see Table 3, p. 134). For example,

TABLE 1 *Background Characteristics for Spankers and Nonspankers by Age of Child*

CHARACTERISTICS	Total Sample (N = 998)		CHILD (2–8 YEARS)						CHILD (9–14 YEARS)					
			Spanker (n = 261)		Nonspanker (n = 217)				Spanker (n = 94)		Nonspanker (n = 426)			
	M	(SD)	M	(SD)	M	(SD)	t		M	(SD)	M	(SD)	t	
Age (mother)	37.1	5.6	33.3	4.9	35.8	5.1	5.47***		37.5	4.6	40.0	4.8	4.66***	
Age (child)	8.6	3.7	4.9	1.9	5.6	1.9	4.40***		11.0	1.7	11.9	1.6	4.63**	
Number of children	2.0	1.0	2.1	0.9	2.1	1.2	−.33		2.2	0.9	1.9	1.0	−2.26*	

	TOTAL SAMPLE	CHILD (2–8 YEARS)			CHILD (9–14 YEARS)		
	%	Spanker %	Nonspanker %	χ^2	Spanker %	Nonspanker %	χ^2
Marital status							
Married	96.7	95.8	94.5	.45	90.4	92.7	0.57
Single	6.3	4.2	5.5		9.6	7.3	
Mother's education							
High school or less	51.2	57.2	43.1	6.20*	62.5	49.3	3.67
College+	48.8	42.8	56.9		37.5	50.7	
Income							
$10–30,000	21.6	23.9	22.8	4.84	19.1	20.1	8.27*
$30–40,000	24.1	27.1	21.8		34.8	21.1	
$40–50,000	22.8	23.5	20.8		16.9	24.6	
$50,000+	31.5	25.5	34.7		29.2	34.2	

*$p < .05.$ **$p < .01.$ ***$p < .001.$

TABLE 2 *Percentage of Mothers Rating Importance of Information Source*

INFORMATION SOURCE: IMPORTANCE	Total Sample (N = 998)	CHILD (2–8 YEARS)			CHILD (9–14 YEARS)		
		Spanker (n = 261)	Nonspanker (n = 217)	χ^2	Spanker (n = 94)	Nonspanker (n = 426)	χ^2
Parents, relatives							
Not important	33.8	29.4	34.9	2.00	31.9	36.4	5.65
Slightly important	30.3	30.6	29.8		38.3	28.0	
Somewhat important	24.6	25.5	23.7		24.5	24.6	
Very important	11.5	14.5	11.6		5.3	11.0	
Friends							
Not important	32.5	32.2	30.7	2.69	29.0	34.4	5.57
Slightly important	29.1	27.5	29.3		23.7	31.1	
Somewhat important	29.7	33.3	29.3		36.6	26.1	
Very important	8.7	7.0	10.7		10.8	8.3	
Newspaper/magazine							
Not important	13.3	12.5	9.8	.93	14.1	15.4	1.22
Slightly important	23.4	20.6	21.5		27.2	25.1	
Somewhat important	43.6	44.4	46.7		38.0	42.7	
Very important	19.8	22.6	22.0		20.7	16.8	
Books							
Not important	16.1	16.7	10.4	4.51	13.5	19.2	3.39
Slightly important	22.9	20.7	22.3		27.0	23.6	
Somewhat important	39.6	41.5	41.1		34.8	38.7	
Very important	21.4	21.1	26.2		24.7	18.5	
Pediatricians							
Not important	22.6	19.1	23.1	2.70	13.5	26.7	7.24
Slightly important	14.0	10.9	14.4		15.7	15.4	
Somewhat important	31.8	32.6	28.7		37.1	31.5	
Very important	31.6	37.4	33.8		33.7	26.4	
Minister, priest, rabbi							
Not important	36.2	32.0	40.6	3.77	26.8	38.5	5.92
Slightly important	14.3	16.2	12.8		12.2	14.3	
Somewhat important	26.8	28.1	23.5		36.6	25.6	
Very important	22.7	23.7	23.0		24.4	21.6	
Psychologist							
Not important	33.1	34.6	31.2	3.72	25.4	34.8	11.37**
Slightly important	14.2	10.3	17.2		14.1	14.9	
Somewhat important	26.0	25.4	25.5		42.3	23.2	
Very important	26.7	29.7	26.1		18.3	27.1	
Workshop							
Not important	19.7	14.7	18.2	2.78	24.7	22.5	8.44*
Slightly important	11.2	11.9	10.8		5.2	12.3	
Somewhat important	35.7	39.4	32.4		46.8	32.5	
Very important	33.5	33.9	38.6		23.4	32.7	

*$p < .05$.   **$p < .01$.

TABLE 3   *Mothers' Perceptions of Spanking Message by Information Source in Percent*

INFORMATION SOURCE: MESSAGE	Total Sample (N = 998)	CHILD (2–8 YEARS)			CHILD (9–14 YEARS)		
		Spanker (n = 261)	Nonspanker (n = 217)	χ^2	Spanker (n = 94)	Nonspanker (n = 426)	χ^2
Parents, relatives							
Recommend	43.3	55.7	31.5	29.57***	54.7	39.5	8.04*
Neutral	38.5	33.3	46.0		33.7	38.7	
Oppose	18.2	11.0	22.5		11.6	21.8	
Friends							
Recommend	28.1	43.0	16.2	51.47***	36.0	23.2	15.52***
Neutral	43.6	42.6	45.6		50.0	41.9	
Oppose	28.2	14.5	38.2		14.0	34.8	
Newspaper Magazine							
Recommend	13.3	18.8	8.4	12.29**	14.5	12.2	3.79
Neutral	32.5	32.9	30.3		41.0	31.6	
Oppose	54.3	48.3	61.6		44.6	56.2	
Books							
Recommend	17.5	24.5	11.4	13.85***	31.3	13.4	25.00***
Neutral	30.6	31.9	30.3		38.8	28.1	
Oppose	51.9	43.5	58.4		30.0	58.5	
Pediatricians							
Recommend	4.4	6.5	0	18.72***	13.0	3.3	16.37***
Neutral	58.7	64.9	54.5		65.2	55.5	
Oppose	36.9	28.6	45.6		21.7	41.2	
Minister, priest, rabbi							
Recommend	11.1	15.1	4.7	15.98***	21.4	9.5	16.00***
Neutral	56.9	62.2	56.1		62.9	52.9	
Oppose	32.0	22.7	39.2		15.7	37.9	
Psychologist							
Recommend	5.1	8.7	4.1	3.76	5.3	3.7	6.48*
Neutral	49.6	54.8	49.6		61.4	44.3	
Oppose	45.3	36.5	46.3		33.3	52.0	
Workshop							
Recommend	6.0	9.8	5.3	12.92**	8.3	3.6	14.28***
Neutral	41.2	47.1	31.8		60.0	38.5	
Oppose	52.8	43.1	62.9		31.7	57.9	

*$p < .05$.   **$p < .01$.   ***$p < .001$.

55.7% of spankers and 31.5% of nonspankers responded that their parents or relatives recommended spanking. Likewise, 43.0% of spankers and only 16.2% of nonspankers responded that their friends recommended spanking.

A closer look at the messages perceived by mothers of children aged 2 to 8 years revealed some interesting distinctions between spankers and nonspankers. Messages from pediatricians were perceived differently for spankers and nonspankers.

Chi-Square

Chi-square (χ^2) is a popular statistic for determining the relationship between two categorical variables. In this article, Walsh is studying the relationship between parents' source of information about spanking and whether the parents spank. In other words, do parents who spank and those who do not get their information about spanking from the same or different sources? Table 2 is a key table. Eight possible sources of information are listed at the left side of the table with an indication of whether that source was not important, slightly important, somewhat important, or very important to each respondent. The second section of the table identifies the percentage of spankers and the percentage of nonspankers among parents of children ages two through eight who answered in each of these categories. As an illustration, for parents of children ages two through eight, 14.5 percent of spankers and 11.6 percent of nonspankers rated parents and relatives as being a very important source of information on spanking. The right section of the table provides the same information for parents of children ages nine through fourteen.

The chi-square values are the key to interpreting the table. These values are not intuitive; their meaning comes only when they are compared to table values. For now, look only to see if there is a single or double asterisk to the right of the chi-square value. If there is a double asterisk, that means we are more than 99 percent confident that spankers and nonspankers rate the source of information differently. If there is a single asterisk, that means we are more than 95 percent confident that spankers and nonspankers rate the source of information differently. If there is no asterisk, that means that we cannot be confident that this source of information is rated differently by spankers and nonspankers. In this table, none of the chi-square values for the younger age group are followed by an asterisk. This means, roughly speaking, that there is not a great difference in the way that spankers and nonspankers rate this information source. For older children, the two groups of parents rated the value of workshops differently (one asterisk, so we are more than 95 confident) and rated the value of psychologists differently (double asterisk, so we are more than 99 percent confident).

For example, 28.6% of spankers compared with 45.6% of nonspankers perceived pediatricians opposing spanking.

In the older child group, spankers and nonspankers perceived significantly different discipline messages from all sources, except newspapers or magazines. About half of spankers (54.7%) and 39.5% of nonspankers perceived their parents or relatives as recommending spanking. Slightly more than one third (36.0%) of spankers and 23.2% of nonspankers viewed their friends as recommending spanking. Similar to the younger child group, 21.7% of spankers and 41.2% of nonspankers rated pediatricians as opposing spanking.

In both the younger and older child groups, 30 to 59% of all the sources were perceived as having neutral messages about spanking. Specifically, pediatricians, religious leaders, and psychologists were most frequently perceived by mothers as neither recommending or opposing spanking. It is impossible to determine the meaning of neutral, however. This response might mean spanking was not addressed, or it might mean that information was equally balanced and parents were encouraged to use their own judgment.

Message Intensity

In the younger child group, nonspankers had significantly higher scores (M = 8.88, SD = 7.45) on the Spanking Opposition Intensity Index, which summed the sources opposing spanking relative to their importance, compared with spankers (M = 5.51, SD = 6.04), t(476) = 5.46, p < .001. Similarly, spankers had significantly higher scores (M = 4.13, SD = 4.59) on the Spanking Recommendation Intensity Index, which summed the sources recommending spanking relative to their importance, compared with nonspankers (M = 1.68, SD = 2.74), t(476) = –6.92, p < .001.

Likewise, in the older child group, nonspankers had significantly higher scores (M = 7.72, SD = 7.19) on the Spanking Opposition Intensity Index compared with spankers (M = 4.55, SD = 5.12), t(518) = 4.04, p < .001. Similarly, spankers had significantly higher scores (M = 4.10, SD = 5.12) on the Spanking Recommendation Intensity Index compared with nonspankers (M = 2.24, SD = 3.41), t(518) = –4.30, p < .001.

Predicted Probability of Spanking

Another objective of this research was to examine the degree to which message intensity was associated with use of spanking. The results of the logistic regression indicated that child's age, socioeconomic status, and both indices of spanking message intensity were all significant predictors of spanking (see Table 4). The odds ratio for child's age (.74) suggests that each additional year of the child's age decreases the likelihood of spanking by 16%. Similarly, the odds ratio of .78 for socioeconomic status (SES) suggests that each increase in SES decreases the likelihood of spanking by 12%. In addition, for each increase in message intensity opposing spanking, there is a decreased likelihood of spanking by 5% (odds ratio = .95). Finally, the odds ratio of 1.12 suggests that for each increase in

TABLE 4   *Spanking Message Intensity and Spanking Behavior (N = 998)*

PREDICTORS OF SPANKING	B	SE	ODDS RATIO
Child's age	–.31	.09	.74***
Socioeconomic status	–.24	.09	.78**
Opposition intensity	–.05	.01	.95***
Recommendation intensity	.12	.02	1.12***

**p < .01.   ***p < .001.

message intensity recommending spanking there is a 12% increased likelihood of spanking.

Discussion

Because parenting attitudes and beliefs are formed in part by the influence of those around us and also by what we read (Richardson et al., 1986) and because few studies have investigated which parenting resources are perceived most helpful by parents (Thompson, 1994), I examined the advice mothers receive about the appropriateness of spanking and the perceived importance of these information sources. Using the health belief model (Ferraro, 1990), spankers and nonspankers were compared on the importance of and spanking message received from eight sources of discipline information. I also compared spankers and nonspankers on the spanking message intensity and assessed the degree to which spanking message intensity was associated with reported use of spanking.

Importance and Spanking Message of Information Source

Spankers and nonspankers with both younger and older children rated the importance of discipline information sources similarly. Discipline advice from workshops, pediatricians, newspapers and magazines, and books was rated by more mothers as at least somewhat important. In contrast, informal sources, such as parents and relatives or friends, were rated by more mothers as not important or slightly important. This is consistent with other research (Clarke-Stewart, 1978; Riley et al., 1991; Stolz, 1967) that found professional people, parenting books, and newsletters were influential sources on parenting in general.

Perhaps parents, relatives, and friends were perceived as less important sources because mothers want to feel independent about how they discipline their children, dislike these models in general, or disagree with the advice. Mothers may value discipline advice from sources that they perceive as more objective and expert than advice from family and friends. For example, Riley et al. (1991) found mothers rated a parenting newsletter as "very

---

Logistic Regression

Multiple regression is a basic statistical test to help researchers measure the amount of influence two or more independent variables have on a dependent variable. Logistic regression is a special type of multiple regression that is used when: (1) the independent variables are quantitative (e.g., numerical scores) and/or qualitative (e.g., any non-numerical variable such as gender or race), and (2) the dependent variable is dichotomous (i.e., there are only two categories, such as employment status being measured as employed or not employed).

The dependent variable in this study was whether the parent spanked. It is a dichotomous variable—either they spanked or they did not. Walsh tests four (independent) variables to determine if they influence spanking: (1) the child's age, (2) socioeconomic status, (3) the intensity of messages received opposing spanking, and (4) the intensity of messages received favoring spanking. Let's look at Table 4. The four independent variables are listed at the left side. The β stands for beta and tells us how much influence each of the variables individually has on the dependent variable. A minus sign means the variables are inversely related (that is, as one goes up, the other goes down). The highest absolute number in this column identifies the independent variable that has the largest influence on spanking. The −.31 for child's age means that it has the greatest influence. It can be interpreted that for every year that a child's age increases, spanking decreases by .31 units (i.e., parents were more likely to spank younger children).

Next, let's examine the odds ratio and the asterisks next to it. Walsh wanted to determine the influence of these variables on the likelihood of spanking. Any odds ratios below 1.0 means that the odds of spanking go down as that independent variable goes up. With each one-year increase in child's age and each increase in socioeconomic status and in intensity of messages opposing spanking, spanking decreases (that is, spanking is less common for older children, in high socioeconomic groups, and for those receiving more intense messages opposing spanking). The effect is the opposite for ratios 1.0 or higher. So, as the parent receives more intense messages favoring spanknig, spanking increases.

Finally, we can be confident that each of these variables really does influence spanking behavior. We have greater than 99 percent confidence that socioeconomic status influences spanking (the double asterisk) and greater than 99.9 percent confidence that the other three variables influence spanking (each has a triple asterisk).

---

useful" more often than any other source, including relatives and friends. It also is possible that mothers incorporate advice from their own parents without explicitly recognizing it. If this holds true, then the mothers in this sample may draw from their own experience of being parented (Edwards, 1995).

Spankers and nonspankers perceived different messages about the appropriateness of spanking. Spankers perceived sources as recommending spanking, whereas nonspankers perceived these sources as opposed to spanking. These results may be interpreted several ways. For example, because a family's environment is a source of child-rearing ideas (Powell, 1979), perhaps the social networks of mothers who do and do not spank provide different messages about spanking. Another explanation could be that mothers perceive discipline messages as reaffirming their own parenting practices, such that they tend to hear and remember information that matches what they already do or believe. This idea would lend support to the "specificity hypothesis," which contends that when faced with a particular problem, individuals will seek others with similar experiences as sources of support (Suitor, Pillemer, & Keeton, 1995). Extending this research to the present findings, it would seem likely that parents associate with people who may hold the same beliefs, such as beliefs about discipline techniques.

In contrast to the specificity hypothesis, the health belief model (Mikanowicz, Fitzgerald,

Leslie, & Altman, 1999) suggests that cues in one's environment affect behavior. Perceived community and cultural norms often influence an individual's behavior. For example, educational messages and mothers' perception of the community's social norms about the health benefits of breast-feeding were important considerations in mothers' infant feeding decisions (Guttman & Zimmerman, 2000). Likewise, perceived messages about spanking may affect mothers' discipline decisions. Without longitudinal data, however, it is not possible to determine explicitly whether such messages influence discipline actions or vice versa.

Although there were differences in spankers' and nonspankers' perceptions of spanking messages, there also were similarities. At least 30% of both groups perceived messages from newspapers and magazines, books, psychologists, and workshops as opposing spanking. Given that so many mothers perceive a fairy large percentage of sources as opposing spanking, it is curious that these mothers still spank. It may be that Belsky's (1984) process parenting model, indicating that there are a number of influences on how information is incorporated, is applicable here. According to Belsky, for example, the personal characteristics of the parent are one of the most influential factors for competent parenting. Therefore, perhaps it is the combination of perceiving messages opposed to spanking and parents' personal characteristics, such as readiness to incorporate information into their behavior, that is critical to consider when examining the association of messages and behavior.

Message Intensity

In addition to having different perceptions about the appropriateness of spanking, spankers and nonspankers also had different spanking message intensities. Spankers scored higher than non-spankers on the index that summed the sources recommending spanking relative to the importance of the sources. Similarly, nonspankers scored higher on the index that summed the sources opposing spanking relative to the importance of the

sources. These results reinforce the association between information and child-rearing ideas (Tracy, 1990; McKenry, Kotch, & Browne, 1991).

Spankers had similar scores on both the recommendation and opposition indexes, whereas nonspankers had more messages that opposed spanking. In addition, increases in the recommendation index were associated with increases in the odds of spanking, whereas increases in the opposition index were associated with decreases in the odds of spanking. It may be that mothers need to perceive many more messages that oppose spanking to experience a substantial reduction in spanking. Thus, these findings are consistent with the health belief model, suggesting that perceptions of what is appropriate behavior are associated with behavior.

Limitations

A number of limitations of this research are noted. First, because these are cross-sectional data, it is impossible to establish any causal direction. It cannot be said that spanking messages result in the use of spanking because it also may be that use of spanking results in greater attention to certain spanking messages. Another limitation is that the data are from mothers only. Future research should gather information from all caretakers to better understand the family context of information sharing and discipline action. Additionally, because the time frame for recall was the past 6 months, mothers might have forgotten how often they spanked.

Another issue is the way in which mothers were classified as spankers or nonspankers, resulting in the potential for misclassification. For example, although nonspankers responded that they did not spank the target child during the past 6 months, these mothers may have spanked at some point or may have spanked another child, so the estimate of the number of mothers who actually spank may be conservative. In addition, because of social desirability to underreport, these are lower bound estimates. Finally, because the sample was primarily White and from two Midwestern cities, the findings are not generalizable. Spanking attitudes and behavior vary by geographic location and ethnicity (Dietz, 2000; Giles-Sims et al., 1995; Straus & Mathur, 1996).

Implications for Parent Education Programs

The findings shed some light on mothers' perceptions of sources and importance of discipline advice and suggest concrete ways to provide information to mothers. Mothers valued discipline advice from parenting courses or workshops, pediatricians, newspaper and magazine articles, and parenting books. As such, parenting information can be fairy easily disseminated to a wide audience, and the majority of those reading it would see it as valuable. This implies that those responsible for parenting workshops and those who write for the popular press have the potential to educate parents about alternatives to spanking.

These findings reaffirm the benefits of publishing articles about positive parenting practices and suggest that initiating a community public awareness campaign about alternatives to spanking would be valuable. In addition, it may be beneficial to target efforts to provide research-based discipline information to parents of young children and those parents with limited education.

These results also highlight another important area. It may be beneficial to give such discipline information not only to parents, but also to other professionals in the community. For example, parent educators could send pediatricians, religious leaders, and psychologists research-based information for dissemination. Because 50% to 59% of mothers perceived these professionals as neither recommending nor opposing spanking, these professionals might benefit by having such information.

Pediatricians, in particular, could play an important role in dissemination efforts. For example, 63% of mothers perceived pediatricians as somewhat or very important information sources; yet only 37% of mothers perceived that pediatricians opposed spanking. These results suggest that pediatricians' role in distributing information about discipline should be enhanced. For example, in addition to giving parents printed material, pediatricians could discuss child discipline and link parents to parenting resources in their community. Pediatricians may be an underdeveloped and valuable resource for educating parents about alternatives to spanking that is easily accessible to parents.

Conclusion

This research contributes to the knowledge illustrating how child-rearing ideas from many sources are associated with behavior. This study also adds to our understanding of how mothers perceive discipline messages. By increasing our understanding of what information sources are important, we can develop ways to make positive discipline approaches more accessible to parents.

REFERENCES

Barber, J. G. (1992). Evaluating parent education groups: Effects on sense of competence and social isolation. Research on Social Work Practice, 2, 2838.

Baumrind, D. (1996). The discipline controversy revisited. Family Relations, 45, 405–414.

Belsky, J. (1984). The determinants of parenting: A process model. Child Development, 55, 83–96.

Bryan, J. W., & Freed, F. W. (1982). Corporal punishment: Normative data and sociological and psychological correlates in a community college population. Journal of Youth and Adolescence, 11, 77–87.

Clarke-Stewart, K. A. (1978). Popular primers for parents. American Psychologist, 33, 359–369.

Daro, D., & Gelles, R. J. (1992). Public attitudes and behaviors with respect to child abuse prevention. Journal of Interpersonal Violence, 7, 517–531.

Day, R. D., Peterson, G. W., & McCracken, C. (1998). Predicting spanking of younger and older children by mothers and fathers. Journal of Marriage and the Family, 60, 79–94.

Deater-Deckard, K., Dodge, K. A., Bates, J. E., & Pettit, J. E. (1996). Physical discipline among African American and European American mothers: Links to children's externalizing behaviors. Developmental Psychology, 32, 10651072.

Dietz, T. L. (2000). Disciplining children: Characteristics associated with the use of corporal punishment. Child Abuse and Neglect, 24, 1529–1542.

Edwards, J. (1995). "Parenting skills": Views of community health and social service providers about the needs of their "clients." Journal of Social Policy, 24, 237–259.

Ferraro, K. E. (1990). Health beliefs and proscriptions on public smoking. Sociological Inquiry, 60, 244–263.

Foglia, W. D. (1997). Perceptual deterrence and the mediating effect of internalized norms among inner-city teenagers. Journal of Research in Crime and Delinquency, 34, 414–442.

Giles-Sims, J., Straus, M. A., & Sugarman, D. B. (1995). Child, maternal, and family characteristics associated with spanking. Family Relations, 44, 170–176.

Graziano, A. M., & Namaste, K. A. (1990). Parental use of physical force in child discipline. Journal of Interpersonal Violence, 5, 449–463.

Greven, P. (1991). Spare the child: The religious roots of punishment and the psychological impact of physical punishment. New York: Knopf.

Grusec, J. E., & Goodnow, J. J. (1994). Impact of parental discipline methods on the child's internalization of values: A reconceptualization of current points of view. Developmental Psychology, 30, 4–19.

Guttman, N., & Zimmerman, D. R. (2000). Low-income mothers' views on breastfeeding. Social Science and Medicine, 50, 1457–1473.

Holden, G. W., & Ritchie, K. L. (1991). Linking extreme marital discord, child rearing, and child behavior problems: Evidence from battered women. Child Development, 62, 311–327.

Kadushin, A., & Martin, J. A. (1981). Child abuse: An interactional event. New York: Columbia University Press.

Larzelere, R. (1996). Implications of the strongest studies for discriminating effective vs. counterproductive corporal punishment. Pediatrics, 98, 824–828.

McCord, J. (1991). Questioning the value of punishment. Social Problems, 38, 167–179.

McCord, J. (1996). Unintended consequences of punishment. Pediatrics, 98, 832–834.

McKenry, P. C., Kotch, J. B., & Browne, D. H. (1991). Correlates of dysfunctional parenting attitudes among low-income adolescent mothers. Journal of Adolescent Research, 6, 212–234.

Mikanowicz, C. K., Fitzgerald, D. C., Leslie, M., & Altman, N. H. (1999). Medium-sized business employees speak out about smoking. Journal of Community Health, 24, 439–450.

Oldershaw, L., Walters, G. C., & Hall, D. K. (1989). A behavioral approach to the classification of different types of physically abusive mothers. Merrill Palmer Quarterly, 35, 255–279.

Patterson, G. R., & Narrett, C. M. (1990). The development of a reliable and valid treatment program for aggressive young children. International Journal of Mental Health, 19, 19–26.

Population Reference Bureau. (2001). American families resilient after 50 years of change. Washington, DC: Author.

Portnoy, B., Anderson, D. M., & Erikson, M. P. (1989). Application of diffusion theory to health promotion research. Family and Community Health, 12, 6371.

Powell, D. R. (1979). Family-environment relations and early childrearing: The role of social networks and neighborhoods. Journal of Research and Development in Education, 13, 1–11.

Richardson, R. A., Abramowitz, R. H., Asp, C. E., & Peterson, A. C. (1986). Parent-child relationships in early adolescence: Effects of family structure. Journal of Marriage and the Family, 48, 805–811.

Riley, D., Meinhardt, G., Nelson, C., Salisbury, M. J., & Winnett, T. (1991). How effective are age-paced newsletters for new parents? A replication and extension of earlier studies. Family Relations, 40, 247–253.

Rodriquez, C. M., & Sutherland, D. (1999). Predictors of parents' physical disciplinary practices. Child Abuse & Neglect, 23, 651–657.

Small, S. A., & Eastman, G. (1991). Rearing adolescents in contemporary society: A conceptual framework for understanding the responsibilities and needs of parents. Family Relations, 40, 455–462.

Stolz, L. M. (1967). Influences on parent behavior. Stanford, CA: Stanford University Press.

Strassberg, Z., Dogde, K. A., Pettit, G. S., & Bates, J. E. (1994). Spanking in the home and children's subsequent aggression toward kindergarten peers. Development and Psychopathology, 6, 445–461.

Straus, M. A. (1994). Beating the devil out of them: Corporal punishment by parents and its effects on children. Boston: Lexington/Macmillian.

Straus, M. A., & Mathur, A. (1996). Social change and change in approval of corporal punishment by parents from 1968 to 1994. In D. Frehsee, W. Horn, & K. D. Bussmann (Eds.), Family violence against children: A challenge for society (pp. 91–105). New York: de Gruyter.

Straus, M. A., & Mouradian, V. E. (1998). Impulsive corporal punishment by mothers and antisocial behavior and impulsiveness of children. Behavioral Sciences and the Low, 16, 353–374.

Straus, M. A., & Stewart, J. H. (1999). Corporal punishment by American parents: National data on prevalence, chronicity, severity, and duration, in relation to child, and family characteristics. Clinical Child and Family Psychology Review, 2, 55–70.

Straus, A., Sugarman, D., & Giles-Sims, J. (1997). Spanking by parents and subsequent antisocial behavior of children. Journal of Pediatrics and Adolescent Medicine, 151, 761–767.

Suitor, J. J., Pillemer, K., & Keeton, S. (1995). When experience counts: The effects of experiential and structural similarity on patterns of support and interpersonal stress. Social Forces, 73, 1573–1588.

Swinford, S. P., DeMaris, A., Cemkovick, S. A., & Giordano, P. C. (2000). Harsh physical discipline in childhood and violence in later romantic involvements: The mediating role of problem behaviors. Journal of Marriage and the Family, 62, 508–519.

Thompson, R. A. (1994). Social support and the prevention of child maltreatment. In G. B. Melton and

F. D. Barry (Eds.), Protecting children from abuse and neglect foundations for a new national strategy (pp. 40–130). New York: Guilford Press.

Tracy, E. M. (1990). Identifying social support resources of at-risk families. Social Work, 35, 252–258.

Whipple, E. E., & Richey, C. A. (1997). Crossing the line from physical discipline to child abuse: How much is too much? Child Abuse and Neglect, 21, 431–444.

Whipple, E. E., & Webster-Stratton, C. (1991). The role of parental stress in physically abusive families. Child Abuse and Neglect, 15, 279–291.

Wolfner, G. D., & Gelles, R. J. (1993). A profile of violence toward children: A national study. Child Abuse and Neglect, 17, 197–212.

Young, K. T., Davis, K., & Schoen, C. (1996). The Commonwealth Fund survey of parents with young children. New York: Commonwealth Fund.

Wendy A. Walsh is a research associate at the Crimes against Children Research Center at the University of New Hampshire. She is currently working on a multisite evaluation of children's advocacy centers. She has been conducting evaluation research and examining how systems respond to child abuse for nearly ten years. Projects include program evaluations of child protective services and child welfare risk assessment systems, and a study on the prosecution of child abuse. Her other projects include a study of families who avoid corporal punishment and a study of unwanted sexual experiences on college campuses.

An interview with . . .

Wendy Walsh

What got you interested in this subject?

I have always been interested in social norms and how behaviors become accepted and then taken for granted—how these behaviors become generally accepted in our society. Even when research shows that these behaviors may not be positive or not be the most optimal, they are still socially accepted behavior. When I started reading about corporal punishment generally, I was fascinated that so many parents were spanking their children in our society, and yet much of the research shows that there are more effective ways to discipline children. I became curious about where parents were getting information about discipline, and, more specifically, where they were getting information about spanking.

How did previous research on spanking influence this research project? How do you see this research contributing to the understanding of spanking children?

First of all, I read a lot of previous research on parenting influences, such as parents who receive parenting newsletters have more positive interactions with their children, and much of this research shaped my research questions. As I started to read more, I found limited research on what those messages were saying, such as whether the message was advocating for or against spanking. So, previous research helped shape my research questions but then also challenged me to look further where there were some gaps in our knowledge.

I would say this research contributes to our understanding of the spanking of children by highlighting the importance of examining the messages that parents receive about discipline and also of the importance of increasing the number of messages about positive methods of discipline. It was really interesting to me how parents rated pediatricians as a valued information source, but yet many said they were not getting a lot of information about spanking or discipline from their pediatricians or from other professionals. These individuals were rated as being very important, but [the parents] were not receiving that much information from them.

What were the advantages and disadvantages of using a telephone interview survey to study this subject?

I see the main advantage of using the telephone survey to be the sense of anonymity provided to parents. As you talk to parents, they are very unclear about where that line is between spanking and child abuse. There is some hesitation for parents to talk about this because they are not sure whether they have crossed that line. Using a telephone survey makes parents feel less vulnerable or maybe just more comfortable in talking about how they are interacting with their kids.

One of the disadvantages would be the inability to develop any kind of rapport or connection with the parent. You are limited somewhat in the types of questions that you can ask when you use a telephone survey, so you cannot ask that many in-depth questions.

What unexpected events or developments, if any, occurred during the course of this research?

The only thing I can think of is some of the interpretation of the categories or responses was a little challenging, in part, I think, because this was secondary data analysis. For example, parents were asked to interpret messages received as either recommending spanking, having a neutral message, or opposing spanking. Once I started doing the analysis, it was a little unclear how parents were defining the neutral message. I'm not sure if this was unexpected, or whether it is just one of those challenges you get in interpreting data.

In the formulation of the questions, were there any issues about questions that might be overly personal?

One of the factors was the ordering of the questions and where you put questions that might be more sensitive for some parents to answer. So there was some strategizing as to how to be sensitive and also how to be ethical in that you do not want to start off a survey by asking more intrusive or intimidating questions.

If you were to do this research again, is there anything that you would do differently? If so, what?

One thing is that I would like to have done a multiple methods study. It might mean having a telephone interview survey but then also asking parents if they would be willing to participate in a subset where in-depth, face-to-face interviews were conducted. That way you can get more in-depth answers to specific questions. Another possibility—one can always dream big—would be to do a longitudinal study in which you would ask to talk to parents over multiple months or over a longer time frame. In addition, one could also give certain groups of parents particular information about discipline and other information to another group of parents. Then, you could keep surveying them so you could really assess if behavioral changes are occurring because they are receiving certain types of information.

What was most frustrating to you in doing this research? What was most satisfying?

One of the most frustrating things was being somewhat limited by some of the questions that were asked, and again this might have been because as I got into the data, I wanted to ask these parents more and more questions to understand the context, the particular situation, and I felt a little bit limited by the types of questions that were in the survey. I would say the most satisfying thing was that some of the findings have some specific application. By finding that the parents wanted to receive certain kinds of information from pediatricians, and so realizing that pediatricians may be an untapped resource for providing discipline information to parents, it was satisfying to think about how this information could be used to help parents.

What important lesson or illustration of doing good research can you share with students from your experiences in this research project?

I would say to read beyond the specific topic or specific area of interest. It is important to try to see things from different perspectives, and once you start reading in different areas, you can find new ideas to bring to your own project. One of the things I did was to start reading public health related research about the messages that people receive about smoking or about eating well or even about whether to wear a seat belt or not, and whether those messages change people's behavior. So I was able to extend some of this public health information to parents, and it helped me to look at parenting and discipline from a different perspective. So, I would say that it is always important to get outside the box, to shift how you see the world.

Questions to Think About

1. Describe in detail the sample that provided data for Walsh's study. What are some of the strengths and limitations of this sample? How do you think some of her findings might have been different if her sample had been more diverse with regard to variables such as gender, social class, ethnicity, region of the country, and so on?

2. List all the variables that Walsh examines in her study and briefly describe how each is measured. Do you detect any potential sources of measurement bias? Explain.

3. Walsh says that she would have liked the chance to ask the parents more questions, and even to be able to conduct some in-depth, face-to-face interviews. What are some questions that you would include in follow-up interviews with parents in this study? Why?

4. What are some contributions and implications of Walsh's results? Specifically, how might the results of her research be useful to professionals working in areas such as parenting education, family services, and public health information?

Predictors of Fear of Criminal Victimization at School among Adolescents

David C. May and R. Gregory Dunaway

Adolescent crime at school, as well as adolescent fear of crime at school, have increasingly become serious social problems. Although many studies have been conducted examining the predictors of fear of crime among adults in various settings, fear of criminal victimization among adolescents at school has been practically ignored. Using a representative sample of 742 high-school students from a southeastern state, this study examined the predictors of adolescent fear of crime at school in an attempt to determine whether they are similar to predictors of adult fear of crime. Results indicate that, although the predictors of fear among adolescents are, in many cases, similar to those of adults, there are important differences. As expected, youths with lower levels of perceived safety at school and youths who perceive their neighborhoods as exhibiting signs of incivility were more likely to be fearful of criminal victimization at school. Interestingly, however, there were important differences between adolescents and adults regarding the effects of race, gender, and victimization experience and fear of crime. The results from this study indicate that the effects of race and victimization experience on fear of crime vary by gender: Namely, Black males were more fearful than White males, and female victims of crime were more fearful than females who had not been victimized by crime. This study suggests that the phenomena that underlie fear of crime among adults are somewhat different than those of adolescents.

In 1998, the United States witnessed horrific shootings at schools across the country. Despite recent reports that the crime rate has slightly decreased (Federal Bureau of Investigation 1999), crimes such as these continue to create an impression among the general public that violence is rampant. Thus, in the face of statistics showing that violent crime rates are receding from previous highs, Americans are increasingly wary and, in many cases, continue to be fearful of crime and violence.

Part of this wariness and fear may be attributable to the fact that the crime rate, although decreasing slightly overall, continued until very recently to rise among adolescents (Maguire and Pastore 1996). Further, in 1986, firearms became the second leading cause of death among youths aged 15 to 19 (Fingerhut, Ingram, and Feldman 1992) and are now the leading cause of death for Blacks and Hispanics (both male and female) and the second leading cause of death for Whites in that same age group (Federal Interagency Forum on Child and Family Statistics 1998).

The growth of criminal activity and violence among youth is particularly pronounced in places where youth spend much of their time—the school. Recent homicides in Colorado, Oregon, Virginia, Mississippi, Kentucky, Arkansas, and Pennsylvania schools are unsettling, yet obviously not isolated incidents and appear to be increasing (Arndt 1995). Kachur and his associates (1996), examining school-associated deaths between 1992 and 1994, uncovered 85 deaths resulting from interpersonal violence. Furthermore, it appears that the problem of school violence, and particularly the problem of weapons at school that aggravate the violence, is not going away. Of high school students, 18.3 percent admitted that they have carried a weapon of some sort to school in the past 30 days; 5.9 percent indicated that the weapon was a firearm (Kann et al. 1998). Additionally, almost 1 in 25 students (4.2 percent) was victimized by a violent crime at school in 1995, an increase of over 20 percent since 1989 (Chandler et al. 1998).

Given the likelihood of being exposed to crime and violence at school—both directly and indirectly—it is somewhat surprising that little attention has been paid to understanding the extent to which youth fear crime, particularly in the school environment, and what factors contribute to such fears. In an extensive review of the fear-of-crime literature, Hale (1996) noted that children and adolescents have generally been neglected by fear-of-crime researchers and advocated that fear of criminal victimization among these groups be an ". . . important research priority" (Hale 1996: 100).

With the recent media attention dedicated to violent crime and its implications on the school setting, it is crucial that social scientists examine the impact that violent crime has had on adolescents, particularly in the places where they spend most of their time—schools. Thus, the purpose of this study was to examine determinants of fear of criminal victimization among, adolescents at school to determine if the predictors of fear of criminal victimization (gender, race, etc.) among adolescents are the same as those among adults.

Adult Fear of Crime

Research ascertaining the extent and the determinants of fear of crime has become a substantial area of study within the field of criminology. In fact, studies examining fear of crime date back more than three decades. Some scholars have even argued that fear of crime is a more severe problem than crime itself (Clemente and Kleiman 1976). Since its inception, the General Social Survey has asked respondents, "is there any area right around here—that is, within a mile—where you would be afraid to walk alone at night?" In 1994, 47 percent of respondents answered yes, the highest percentage responding affirmatively since 1983 (Maguire and Pastore 1996: 151). Even though there is some controversy over whether this question is a valid measure of fear of crime (see Ferraro 1995), Americans are experi-

encing heightened anxiety about their personal safety. This concern about safety and potential criminal victimization has dramatically affected the lives of many people. Fearful individuals may not travel at night or may avoid certain areas that they consider "dangerous," and they may engage in myriad other avoidance behaviors and adaptive strategies (see Hale 1996 and Ferraro 1995 for review). Further, fear of crime may contribute to a host of negative psychological states (Hale 1996).

In addition to the research examining consequences of fear of crime, a large body of research has also examined its predictors. In the 30 years that have passed since fear-of-crime research emerged (Baumer 1978; Clemente and Kleiman 1976, 1977; Garofalo 1979), several variables have consistently been found to be associated with fear of crime among adults.

There are a number of individual level variables that are associated with fear of crime among adults. Numerous studies have consistently indicated that females, non-whites (particularly African Americans and Hispanics), individuals with lower levels of income and education, and urban residents are more likely to experience fear of crime (Baumer 1985; Chiricos, Hogan, and Gertz 1997; Ferraro 1995; Hale 1996; LaGrange and Ferraro 1989; LaGrange, Ferraro, and Supancic 1992; Parker 1988; Parker and Ray 1990; Parker et al. 1993; Thompson, Bankston, and St. Pierre 1989; Warr 1984, 1990; Will and McGrath 1995). Furthermore, there is evidence to suggest that victimization experience and a greater perception of risk of victimization are positively related to fear of crime (Arthur 1992; Chiricos et al. 1997; Ferraro 1995; Hale 1996; Parker and Ray 1990; Thompson et al. 1989).

In recent years, research interest has moved away from individual background factors of fear to more structural-level predictors. The most significant of these is perceived neighborhood incivility. LaGrange, Ferraro, and Supancic (1992) defined incivilities as ". . . low-level breaches of community standards that signal an erosion of conventionally accepted norms and values" (p. 312). Nearly all the studies examining community characteristics and fear of crime have reported a significant positive relationship between incivility and fear of crime (Bursik and Grasmick 1993; Covington and Taylor 1991; Taylor and Covington 1993; Will and McGrath 1995). Some researchers have argued, however, that incivilities indirectly affect fear of crime through elevated perceived risk of criminal victimization (Ferraro 1995; LaGrange et al. 1992; Rountree and Land 1996).

Adolescent Fear of Crime

Despite the abundance of research examining fear of crime among adults, there has been scant attention paid to examining fear of crime among adolescents. Given research on adult fear of crime that has argued that fear of crime is heightened when individuals perceive themselves to be more vulnerable and likely to be victimized, it is plausible that adolescents might realistically assess their chances of being victimized by crime as being greater and would subsequently experience higher levels of fear of crime than their adult counterparts (Ferraro 1995; Parker 1988).

Nevertheless, the large majority of studies examining adolescent fear of criminal victimization, and particularly adolescent fear of criminal victimization at school, are descriptive, indicating that many students are fearful of being victimized by crime at school but failing to provide explanations for this fear. Approximately 30 percent of junior high students and 22 percent of senior high students were at least sometimes afraid another student would hurt them at school (Parents Resource Institute for Drug Education 1996), and 7 percent of eighth graders reported staying home from school during the previous month out of fear of crime (National Education Goals Panel 1993). Further, 22 percent of students in Grades 3–12 reported that because of violence or the threat of violence at school, they were less eager to attend school (Metropolitan Life 1993).

In addition, it appears that levels of fear of criminal victimization at school are increasing. The proportion of students who ". . . sometimes or most of the time feared they were going to be attacked or harmed at school" increased 50 percent between 1989 and 1995 and the percentage of students who ". . . avoided one or more places at school for fear of their own safety" increased 80 percent during the same time period (Kaufman et al. 1998: vii).

Although previous studies have examined the extent of adolescent fear of criminal victimization at school, there has been virtually no research on the determinants of adolescent fear. A review of the literature yielded three published works on the topic (see Hepburn and Monti 1979, Parker and Onyekwuluje 1992, and Wayne and Rubel 1982). The studies conducted by Wayne and Rubel (1982) and Hepburn and Monti (1979) purported to measure fear of crime among students; however, both studies are somewhat dated and include measures of fear of crime that may not be considered conceptually appropriate (see Ferraro and LaGrange 1987; Ferraro 1995).

The remaining study by Parker and Onyekwuluje (1992), though limited, is still the most pertinent to this area. Using a small, urban, and racially homogeneous sample, Parker and Onyekwuluje (1992) determined that none of the demographic variables (i.e., gender, income status, and education) examined in the analysis had a statistically significant effect on fear of crime among adolescents. Clearly, the lack of statistical significance may be due, at least partly, to a small sample size (112 respondents), as well as a lack of variation on some key causal variables. Thus, it is difficult to make definitive statements about juvenile fear of crime on the basis of this study.

In this study, we sought to address this void in the literature. Using a large and representative youth sample, we examined an array of factors that have been found to be related to adult fear of crime. Anticipated determinants include demographic, contextual, and experiential characteristics of adolescents. In the absence of previous research on adolescent fear of crime, we hypothesize that the factors that affect adult fear of crime will be similar for juveniles.

Method

The Sample

Our sample consisted of 742 public high school students (Grades 10–12). The respondents were part of the 1997 Mississippi High School Youth Survey, conducted by the Mississippi Crime and justice Research Unit at the Social Science Research Center at Mississippi State University. The data were gathered from schools randomly selected within four geographically distinct areas of the state. Students were administered a survey consisting of items relating to their experiences and attitudes with crime (e.g., criminal victimization and fear of criminal victimization). Of the students eligible to participate in the study, our response rate was 88.6 percent.[1] In general, the sample's demographic characteristics are representative of the adolescent population within the state of Mississippi.

Dependent Variable

Fear of Criminal Victimization at School

Within the literature on fear of crime, a serious debate has been documented regarding how to operationalize the concept of fear and crime. Early measures of fear of crime were critiqued either for being too general or for not distinguishing between one's actual fear of crime and the perception of risk of being victimized by crime (see Ferraro and La-Grange 1987). Ferraro (1995) and Warr (1984) suggested that the most appropriate measures of fear of crime are indices composed of questions asking respondents whether they are fearful or afraid of various scenarios. We thus used multi-item scale of fear that taps fear of crime in and around the school environment. Students were asked to what extent they agreed or disagreed (coded 6 = *strongly agree,* 5 = *agree,* 4 = *somewhat agree,* 3 = *somewhat disagree,* 2 = *disagree,* and 1 = *strongly disagree*) with the following statements: "I am afraid to go to school because I might become a victim of crime," "I am afraid to stay late after school because I might become a victim of crime," "I am afraid to attend school events (i.e.,

football games, dances, etc.) because of fights," and "There are places at school where I am afraid to go (i.e., bathroom, cafeteria, gym, etc.) because I might become a victim of crime." We conducted item analysis on the index and used Cronbach's alpha to determine its reliability. The construct demonstrated an internal reliability of .708.

Independent Variables

Race or Ethnic Origin

The respondent's race or ethnic origin was determined by the question "How do you describe yourself?" As over 97 percent of the sample consisted of White or African American respondents, only they were included in the study. Race/ethnicity was coded as African American (1) and White (0). There were 316 (42.6 percent) Blacks and 426 (57.4 percent) Whites in the sample.

Gender

Gender was determined by the question "What is your sex?" Males were coded 1 and females were coded 0. There were 425 females (57.3 percent) and 317 males (42.7 percent) in the sample.

Economic Status

The measurement of social class or economic status among adolescents is a controversial issue. Adult fear-of-crime research typically measures socioeconomic status through individual income or education. Given that adolescents do not have income in the same way as would reflect socioeconomic status for adults and that education among adolescents does not vary greatly, adolescent class cannot be directly measured for adolescents. Additionally, adolescent reporting of parental/family income is often unreliable. Braithwaite (1981) contended that defining economic status, particularly among adolescents, should be ascertained by distinguishing between those who fall below the absolute poverty line and those who are above it. Adolescents are generally knowledgeable about whether their family is at or below the poverty line because they are familiar with the receipt of public assistance funds. Consequently, following Brownfield's (1986) measure, economic status was determine by the question "In the past year, has your family received some form of public assistance (such as WIC, AFDC/welfare, or food stamps)?" There were 121 respondents (16.3 percent) in the sample who responded affirmatively to this question. Those respondents who responded affirmatively were coded 1, and their counterparts who did not respond affirmatively were coded 0.[2]

Grade

Respondent's grade was determined by the question "What grade are you currently in?" Tenth graders were coded 1, 11th graders were coded 2, and 12th graders were coded 3. There were 264 10th graders (36.1 percent), 229 11th graders (31.3 percent), and 239 12th graders (32.7 percent).

Criminal Victimization at School

The variable victimization experience was obtained by determining if respondents had ever "had someone threaten to hurt me at school." In those studies where victimization experience exhibited an association with fear of criminal victimization among adults (Arthur 1992; Thompson et al. 1989), victimization by violent crime typically has a stronger association with fear of criminal victimization than victimization by other types of crime. Forty-one percent of the sample (306 respondents) answered that someone had threatened to hurt them at school. Those who answered affirmatively were coded 1, and those who responded negatively were coded 0.

Perceived Safety at School

Recently, fear-of-crime researchers have determined that those individuals who perceive themselves to be most at risk are also the most fearful (see Ferraro 1995 for discussion). As we included no indicators that measured perceived risk adequately, we were not able to directly examine this relationship. Instead, borrowing from Williams, Dingh, and Singh (1996), we used a proxy to measure perceived risk. Williams et al. (1996), in their study of defensive adaptations to fear of crime, suggested that overall perceptions about safety and security affected one's level of fear. Thus, we used a perceptual measure assessing adolescents' level of safety in school. The variable perceived safety at school was obtained by examining responses to the statement "I feel safe from crime at my school." The student was given a choice between six Likert-scale responses ranging from *strongly disagree* (coded 6) to *strongly agree* (coded 1). Those who scored high on the variable thus perceived the school environment to be a less secure environment.

Perceived Neighborhood Incivility

The exogenous variable perceived neighborhood incivility was obtained by constructing an index that used responses to statements concerning how the respondent viewed their neighborhood. Students were asked to what extent they agreed or disagreed (coded *strongly agree* = 6; *agree* = 5; *somewhat agree* = 4; *somewhat disagree* = 3; *disagree* = 2; and *strongly disagree* = 1) with the following statements: "My neighborhood is noisy and the streets always seem to have litter on them," "There are gangs in my neighborhood," "There are drug dealers in my neighborhood," "I feel safe from crime in my neighborhood," and "My neighborhood is getting worse and worse all the time." We conducted item analysis on the index and used Cronbach's alpha to determine its reliability. The construct demonstrated an internal reliability of .825.

Table 1 presents the percentage distributions for the dichotomous variables and the means and standard deviations for the categorical variables and scales used in this study.

Statistical Method

We examined multivariate models in which adolescent fear of crime was regressed on several independent variables, including race, gender, grade, economic status, victimization experience, perceived neighborhood incivility, and perceived safety at school.[3] As several of the variables in question (perceived safety, perceived neighborhood incivility, and fear of criminal victimization)

TABLE 1   *Table of Means and Standard Deviations for Adolescent Sample*

VARIABLE	
Independent	
Race (%)	
Black	42.6
White	57.4
Gender (%)	
Male	42.7
Female	57.3
Grade (%)	
10th	35.6
11th	30.9
12th	32.2
Economic status (%)	
Yes	16.3
No	87.3
Victimization experience	
Yes	41.2
No	58.4
Perceived safety at school	
m	3.16
SD	1.44
Perceived incivility	
m	13.24
SD	6.41
Dependent	
Fear of criminal victimization	
m	7.72
SD	3.43

have been demonstrated to have associations with both race and gender, we used race–gender subgroup mean substitution to allow continuity in sample size across models.

The results of the linear regression model regressing adolescent fear on the independent variables are presented in Table 2. The model explained 17.7 percent of the variation in fear of criminal victimization at school. Perceived neighborhood incivility emerged as the best predictor for adolescent fear of crime, as those who perceived their neighborhoods as exhibiting signs of

incivility were more likely to be fearful than those youth who did not have that same perception (ß = 0.247, p < .001). Perceived safety at school was the next best predictor of adolescent fear of criminal victimization at school, as those youths who perceived school as an unsafe environment were more likely to be fearful than those youth who did not have the same perception (ß = 0.241, p < .001). Further, students in lower grades were significantly more fearful than those students in higher grades (ß = −0.099, p < .01). Contrary to research examining fear of crime among adults, gender, race, economic status, and victimization experience did not have a statistically significant effect on adolescent fear of crime at school. Thus, it appears at first glance that the dynamics driving fear of crime among adolescents may be somewhat different than those driving fear of crime among adults.

The results presented in Table 2 indicate that gender and race, two of the strongest predictors for adult fear of crime, have nonsignificant associations with fear of crime among adolescents. As

TABLE 2   *Impact of Perceived Safety at School on Adolescent Fear of Crime Controlling for Prior Criminal Victimization, Perceived Neighborhood Incivility, and Selected Background Variables*

VARIABLE	B	SE	ß	t
Black	.334	.272	.048	.221
Male	−.236	.236	−.034	.318
Poor	−.325	.333	−.035	.328
Grade	−.415	.141	−.099	.003
Perceived neighborhood incivility	.132	.021	.247	.000
Victimization experience	.374	.236	.054	.113
Perceived safety at school	.573	.083	.241	.000
constant	4.830	.472		.000

Note: N = 742, F(7,734) = 22.577, p < .001; R^2 = .177

Multiple Regression

Multiple regression is a basic statistical test to help researchers measure the simultaneous influence of two or more independent variables on a dependent variable. For example, research may show that both gender and age individually influence the likelihood of individuals getting an adequate amount of exercise. Multiple regression will help us understand the influence of gender and age taken together on exercise level. Because human attitudes and behaviors are shaped by many factors, multiple regression helps us to determine the total influence of two or more factors. Multiple regression uses variables that are measured at the ratio level, that is, on a numerical scale with zero meaning none. For example, if we ask someone how many hours of television he or she watches in an average week, we would receive a number and, if someone said zero that would mean they do not watch any television. If a variable has only two categories (e.g., gender is either male or female), it can be treated as a numerical variable by assigning one category a zero and the other a one (e.g., a male could be zero, a female could be one).

The dependent variable in this article is the fear of criminal victimization at school perceived by adolescents. The authors test for the possible influence of several independent variables, including race or ethnicity, gender, economic status, current grade level, previous criminal victimization at school, perceived safety at school, and perceived neighborhood incivility. This last variable is especially interesting because it suggests that the situation in which one lives might affect fear at school. Let's look at Table 2, a key table. All of the independent variables are listed in the far left column. Notice that the column lists black, male, and poor. These were all variables with two categories and the identified group

is the one that was scored as a one. The table tells us several things about the influence of these variables on fear of criminal victimization at school, but we will focus on just three items. First, the third column is headed by a β, which stands for beta. The coefficients in this column tell us how much influence each of the variables individually has on the dependent variable. A minus sign means the variables are inversely related (that is, as one goes up, the other goes down). The highest absolute number in this column identifies the independent variable that has the largest influence on fear of victimization. The .247 for neighborhood incivility means that it has the greatest influence. It can be interpreted that for every one-unit increase in neighborhood incivility, fear increases by .247 units. The lowest absolute number (that is, ignoring the + or − sign) in this column is .034 for male. It carries a minus sign, so for every one-unit change in gender (from female to male), fear decreases by .034 units—that is, females have slightly more fear.

The final column reports probability levels based on a *t*-test. Any number in this column .05 or below identifies a variable that we are at least 95 percent sure really influences level of fear. Perceived neighborhood incivility, perceived safety at school, and grade level are three variables that we are sure influence fear. We are not convinced that variables with a probability level higher than .05 really do influence fear. All of the other variables are in this category. Finally, R^2 (reported at the bottom of the table below the line), roughly speaking, tells us how much influence all of these variables together have on level of fear. Its possible range is 0 to 1.0. In this case, the value is .177, which means that these variables explain just under 18 percent of the level of fear. These variables are very important, but there are additional variables not studied in this research that also influence fear level.

indicated by previous adult fear-of-crime research, race and gender also tend to be associated with both neighborhood incivility and perceived risk (see Ferraro 1995). Consequently, the lack of a significant association between race or gender and adolescent fear of crime may be the result of an interaction between these variables and some of the

other predictor variables. To check for possible interaction effects, we computed a number of product terms and analyzed them as to their impact on fear of crime. Though not presented here, the results revealed that there were no statistically significant interaction effects between either race or gender with economic status, respondent's grade, victimization experience, perceived neighborhood incivility, or perceived safety at school.

The analysis did, however, reveal a statistically significant interaction effect between race and gender. The results of the linear regression model regressing adolescent fear of crime on perceived safety at school, perceived neighborhood incivility, the demographic variables, and the product term representing the interaction between race and gender are presented in Table 3. With the addition of the product term to the model, the explained variation in fear of crime among the adolescents in this sample increased to 18.3 percent. Perceived safety at school became the best predictor of fear of crime, as those who perceived their schools to be unsafe environments continued to be significantly more likely to be fearful than those youth who did not have that same perception ($ß = 0.242$, $p < .001$). Those adolescents who perceived their neighborhoods as exhibiting signs of incivility continued to be significantly more

fearful of crime than those adolescents who did not ($ß = 0.238$, $p < .001$), whereas youths from lower grades remained significantly more fearful than their counterparts from higher grades ($ß = -0.101$, $p < .01$). With the addition of the product term to the model, the effect of gender ($ß = -0.100$, $p < .05$) became statistically significant, with females more likely to be fearful.

To further explore the interaction between race and gender, we analyzed separate models for males and females. Table 4 includes the effects of the predictor variables for both male and female adolescent fear of crime. With regard to race, it appears that the race effect is only significant for male adolescent fear of crime. Specifically, Black males are more fearful than White males. Additionally, the analysis revealed varying effects between predictors of male and female fear of crime at school. Specifically, males in lower grades were significantly more likely to be fearful, whereas the effect of grade on fear of criminal victimization at school was not statistically significant for females. Additionally, prior victimization experience and perceived safety at school were found to significantly affect female adolescent fear but not male adolescent fear. Neighborhood incivility continued to be a significant predictor of both male and female adolescent fear of crime.

Discussion

Fear of crime, as a research topic, has enjoyed a high level of interest among criminologists and criminal justice policy analysts and practitioners. Although much is known regarding patterns and trends of fear of crime, as well as the correlates of individual fear of crime, the vast majority of research on fear of crime has focused on adult populations. Thus, despite this plethora of research, very little is known about fear of crime among adolescents. We find this a peculiar omission in the literature given that youth are much more likely to actually experience crime through participation, victimization, and observation.

The purpose of this study was to partially address this void in the literature by examining fac-

TABLE 3 *Impact of Gender–Race Interaction on Adolescent Fear of Crime Controlling for Perceived Safety at School, Prior Victimization Experience, Perceived Neighborhood Incivility, and Selected Background Variables*

VARIABLE	B	SE	ß	t
Black	−.122	.335	−.018	.716
Male	−.692	.306	−.100	.024
Poor	−.245	.334	−.026	.462
Grade	−.423	.141	−.101	.003
Perceived neighborhood incivility	.127	.021	.238	.000
Victimization experience	.394	.235	.056	.094
Perceived safety at school	.577	.083	.242	.000
Race × Gender interaction term	1.101	.473	.123	.020
Constant	5.071	.482		.000

Note: $N = 742$, $F(8,733) = 20.549$, $p < .001$; $R^2 = .183$

TABLE 4 *Impact of Perceived Safety at School, Prior Victimization, Perceived Neighborhood Incivility, and Selected Background Variables on Adolescent Fear of Crime by Gender*

VARIABLE	B	SE	ß	t
Females				
Black	−.212	.346	−.030	.542
Poor	−.026	.409	−.003	.949
Grade	−.169	.185	−.040	.362
Perceived incivility	.113	.028	.203	.000
Victimization experience	.623	.310	.087	.045
Perceived safety at school	.877	.109	.364	.000
Constant	3.692	.603		.000
Males				
Black	1.096	.427	.161	.011
Poor	−.512	.561	−.049	.360
Grade	−.764	.212	−.189	.000
Perceived incivility	.134	.032	.263	.000
Victimization experience	.042	.351	.006	.906
Perceived safety at school	.174	.125	.074	.164
Constant	6.331	.699		000

Note: For females, N = 425. $F_{(6,418)} = 20.711$, $p < .001$, $R^2 = .229$. For males, N = 317, $F_{(6,316)} = 11.071$, $p < .001$, $R^2 = .176$.

tors that may be linked to adolescent fear of crime. Guided by research on the determinants of adult fear of crime, we examined the effect of a set of factors on adolescent fear, including both background and experiential and perceptual measures. Using a large and representative sample of Mississippi youth, we assessed the impact of selected background and perceptual variables on fear of crime among adolescents.

Our findings suggest that there is a great deal of similarity in the determinants that affect both adult and adolescent fear of crime. Specifically, adolescents who perceive their immediate community environment as exhibiting signs of incivility are likely to have higher levels of fear. Further, adolescent fear of crime was positively affected by perceived safety at school—a proxy for perceived risk of victimization. Both neighborhood incivility and perceived risk have been consistently shown to affect adult fear of crime (see Ferraro 1995 for review). Additionally, when controlling for a gender–race interaction, females were found more likely to be fearful of crime. Typically, research on adult fear of crime has found that females have greater levels of fear.

On the other hand, actual criminal victimization, a significant predictor for adult fear of crime in many studies, was found not to demonstrate a significant effect on adolescent fear of crime in the pooled sample. Also, unlike previous research on fear of crime, socioeconomic status was not found to affect adolescent fear. This finding may, as intimated earlier, be more of a result of how juvenile economic status was measured rather than a unique attribute of juvenile fear of crime. Finally, the variable of grade in school was found to be inversely related to fear of crime. In other words, adolescents were less likely to fear crime as they matriculated through high school.

Our research also suggests that male and female adolescent fear is influenced differently. The effect of race operates differently for males and females. We find that African American male adolescents were more fearful of crime at school. On the other hand, no race effect was witnessed for females. This study also uncovered that although previous victimization experience was not significant in the pooled sample, it did have a statistically significant impact on female fear of crime. Further, perception of safety was found to be an important factor in predicting female, but not male, fear of crime.

The differential effects of victimization and safety by gender may be a result of a specific type of crime that is both feared and experienced more by females—sexual assault. In fact, some have argued that the specific fear of rape by women is the dominant factor that explains gender differences for fear of crime (Ferraro 1995; Warr 1990). Though our measures of both fear of crime and victimization experience did not specifically ask about sexual assault, it is possible that women may be taking into account that particular offense.

Ferraro (1995) suggested that the effect of victimization by crime may be different for females than for males. Female victims of crime, no matter what type of criminal victimization they are exposed to, may realize that criminal victimization makes them particularly vulnerable to rape. Whether women are victims of rape or some other crime, this victimization often forces women to realize that they are particularly vulnerable to sexual assault, a vulnerability not often faced by male victims of crime. According to Gordon and Riger (1989) and Ferraro (1995), this shadow of sexual assault may cause particular emotional damage for female crime victims that often endures for years. This emotional damage resulting from victimization by crime may cause female victims to have subsequently greater levels of fear of crime and to react to that fear in different ways; Thompson, Bankston, and St. Pierre (1991) demonstrated that, among adult females, victims of crime are more likely to own handguns than their nonvictim counterparts. Although this study failed to examine gun possession among females, it is quite possible that the emotional turmoil caused by victimization among adult females is similar among adolescents, thus explaining the differential effect of victimization by gender in this study.

Generally, our overall findings suggest that factors that affect adult fear of crime are also important for adolescent fear. Further, these initial results do tend to lend support to the social vulnerability thesis, which argues that those who are regularly exposed to the threat of criminal victimization suffer severe social consequences, one of which is a heightened level of fear of crime (Rohe and Burby 1988). Those who perceive school as an unsafe environment and perceive their neighborhood as a potentially dangerous environment may experience a heightened sense of vulnerability, and, in turn, this vulnerability may translate to higher levels of fear. Moreover, previous work has suggested that women view themselves as more vulnerable to victimization (see Ferraro 1995 for review). Our finding that Black males are more likely to be fearful of crime is consistent with actual victimization patterns that indicate that young Black males have the highest rate of criminal victimization (U.S. Department of Justice 1996). Further, the effects of grade also support the social vulnerability argument. Here, presumably, younger adolescents have higher levels of fear. Clearly, it can be argued that younger adolescents may perceive themselves as being more vulnerable to a number of victimizations, from minor hazing by upperclassmen to more serious victimization.

We began this study by noting that relatively little is known about the factors that contribute to adolescent fear of crime. This study has intimated that fear of crime, whether adolescent or adult, shares many of the same predictors. Still, this study was based on data that may not be generalizable to adolescent populations outside of the state of Mississippi. Therefore, additional studies on adolescent fear should seek to replicate these findings. In addition, other factors that affect adolescent fear of crime must be examined. Our models only accounted for a modest amount of variation in adolescent fear. Given that our study concentrated on school fear, as well as experiences within the school context, it would, perhaps, be useful to examine victimization experiences and safety perceptions in a larger context. Fear of crime within school is only one dimension of overall adolescent fear. Thus, fear of crime in other environments is likely to affect specific fears. Further, attention needs to be paid to the cultural context of adolescents and its relationship to fear of crime. Popular culture and media directed specifically at adolescents often contains violent content that may raise fears about being victimized. Finally, fear-of-crime research in general may want to consider a life-course approach in order to understand when fear of crime develops in individuals and whether fear of crime is constant across one's life span.

NOTES

1. To be eligible to be administered the survey, students under the age of 18 had to provide a parental consent form indicating that their parent approved of the child's participation in the study. Of students in the schools, 64.8 percent returned parental consent forms.

The response rate was also affected by students who were absent on the day of the survey administration, as well as those who chose not to participate.

2. We also used father's education as a proxy measure for economic status. As the association between father's education level and fear of crime was nonsignificant, we chose to use receipt of public assistance instead.

3. Adolescent fear of crime at school was also regressed on a number of community contextual variables (i.e., percentage poor, percentage Black, school size, and median income). As none of the variables had a statistically significant effect on adolescent fear of crime at school, they are not included in the models in this study.

REFERENCES

Arndt, Randolph C. 1995. *School Violence in America's Cities*. Washington, DC: National League of Cities.

Arthur, John A. 1992. "Criminal Victimization, Fear of Crime, and Handgun Ownership Among Blacks: Evidence from National Survey Data." *American Journal of Criminal Justice* 16(2):121–141.

Baumer, Terry L. 1978. "Research on Fear of Crime in the United States." *Victimology* 3(3,4):254–64.

———. 1985. "Testing a General Model of Fear of Crime: Data from a National Sample." Journal of Research in Crime and Delinquency 22(3):239–55.

Braithwaite, John. 1981. "The Myth of Social Class and Criminology Reconsidered." *American Sociological Review* 46:36–57.

Brownfield, David. 1986. "Social Class and Violent Behavior." *Criminology* 24:421–37.

Bursik, Robert I., Jr., and Harold G. Grasmick. 1993. *Neighborhoods and Crime: The Dimensions of Effective Community Control*. New York: Lexington Books.

Chandler, Kathryn A., Christopher D. Chapman, Michael R. Rand, and Bruce M. Taylor. 1998. *Students' Reports of School Crime: 1989 and 1995*. NCES 98-241/NCJ-169607, Washington, DC: U.S. Departments of Education and Justice.

Chiricos, Ted, Michael Hogan, and Marc Gertz. 1997. "Racial Composition of Neighborhood and Fear of Crime." *Criminology* 35(1):107–31.

Clemente, Frank and Michael Kleiman. 1976. "Fear of Crime among the Aged." *The Gerontologist* 16(3):207–10.

———. 1977. "Fear of Crime in the United States: A Multivariate Analysis." *Social Forces* 56(2):519–31.

Covington, Jeanette and Ralph B. Taylor. 1991. "Fear of Crime in Urban Residential Neighborhoods: Implications of Between- and Within-Neighborhood Sources for Current Models." *Sociological Quarterly* 32(2):231–49.

Federal Bureau of Investigation. 1999. *Crime in the United States—1998*. Washington, DC: U.S. Department of Justice.

Federal Interagency Forum on Child and Family Statistics. 1998. *America's Children: Key National Indicators of Well-Being*. Washington, DC: U.S. Government Printing Office.

Ferraro, Kenneth F. 1995. *Fear of Crime: Interpreting Victimization Risk*. Albany: State University of New York Press.

Ferraro, Kenneth and Randy LaGrange. 1987. "The Measurement of Fear of Crime." *Sociological Inquiry* 57(1):70–101.

Fingerhut, Lois A., Deborah D. Ingram, and Jacob J. Feldman. 1992. "Firearm and Nonfirearm Homicides among Persons 15 Through 19 Years of Age." *Journal of the American Medical Association* 267(22):3048–53.

Garofalo, James. 1979. "Victimization and the Fear of Crime." *Journal of Research in Crime and Delinquency* 16(1):80–97.

Gordon, Margaret T. and Stephanie Riger. 1989. *The Female Fear*. New York: Free Press.

Hale, Chris. 1996. "Fear of Crime: A Review of the Literature." *International Review of Victimology* 4:79–150.

Hepburn, John R. and Daniel J. Monti. 1979. "Victimization, Fear of Crime, and Adaptive Responses among High School Students." Pp. 121–32 in *Perspectives on Victimology*. Beverly Hills, CA: Sage.

Kachur, S. Patrick, Gail M. Stennies, Kenneth E. Powell, William Modzeleski, Ronald Stephens, Rosemary Murphy, Marcie-Jo Kresnow, David Sleet, and Richard Lowry. 1996. "School-Associated Violent Deaths in the United States, 1992 to 1994." *Journal of the American Medical Association* 275(22):1729–33.

Kann, Laura, Steven A. Kinchen, Barbara I. Williams, James G. Ross, Richard Lowry, Carl V. Hill, Jo Anne Grunbaum, Pamela S. Blumson, Janet L. Collins, and Lloyd J. Kolbe. 1998. "Youth Risk Behavior Surveillance—United States, 1997." *Morbidity and Mortality Weekly Report* 47(SS-3).

Kaufman, Phillip, Xianglei Chen, Susan P. Choy, Kathryn A. Chandler, Christopher D. Chapman, Michael Rand, and Cheryl Ringel. 1998. *Indicators of School Crime and Safety, 1998*. NCES 98-251/NCJ-172215, Washington, DC: U.S. Departments of Education and Justice.

LaGrange, Randy L. and Kenneth F. Ferraro, 1989. "Assessing Age and Gender Differences in Perceived Risk and Fear of Crime." *Criminology* 27(4): 697–719.

LaGrange, Randy L., Kenneth F. Ferraro, and Michael Supancic. 1992. "Perceived Risk and Fear of Crime: Role of Social and Physical Incivilities." *Journal of Research in Crime and Delinquency* 29(3):311–34.

Maguire, Kathleen and Ann L. Pastore, eds. 1996. *Sourcebook of Criminal Justice Statistics, 1994.* Washington, DC: U.S. Department of Justice, Bureau of Justice Statistics.

Metropolitan Life. 1993. *Survey of the American Teacher, 1993: Violence in America's Public Schools.* New York: Louis Harris and Associates.

National Education Goals Panel. 1993. *The National Education Goals Report 1993.* Washington, DC: National Education Goals Panel.

Parents Resource Institute for Drug Education. 1996. *1995–96 National Summary, Grades 6–12.* Atlanta, GA: Author.

Parker, Keith D. 1988. "Black-White Differences in Perceptions of Fear of Crime." *The Journal of Social Psychology* 128(4):487–98.

Parker, Keith D. and Anne B. Onyekwuluje. 1992. "The Influence of Demographic and Economic Factors on Fear of Crime Among African-Americans." *The Western Journal of Black Studies* 16(3):132–40.

Parker, Keith D. and Melvin C. Ray. 1990. "Fear of Crime: An Assessment of Related Factors." *Sociological Spectrum* 10:29–40.

Parker, Keith D., Barbara J. McMorris, Earl Smith, and Komanduri S. Murty. 1993. "Fear of Crime and the Likelihood of Victimization: A Bi-Ethnic Comparison." *The Journal of Social Psychology* 133(5): 723–32.

Rohe, William M. and Raymond J. Burby. 1988. "Fear of Crime in Public Housing." *Environment and Behavior* 20(6):700–20.

Rountree, Pamela Wilcox and Kenneth C. Land. 1996. "Perceived Risk Versus Fear of Crime: Empirical Evidence of Conceptually Distinct Reactions in Survey Data." *Social Forces* 74(4):1353–76.

Taylor, Ralph B. and Jeanette Covington. 1993. "Community Structural Change and Fear of Crime." *Social Problems* 40(3):374–94.

Thompson, Carol Y., William B. Bankston, and Roberta St. Pierre. 1989. "Parity and Disparity among Three Measures of Fear of Crime: A Research Note." *Deviant Behavior* 13:373–89.

———. 1991. "Single Female-Headed Households, Handgun Possession, and the Fear of Rape." *Sociological Spectrum* 11(3):231–44.

U.S. Department of Justice. 1996. *Criminal Victimization in the United States, 1994.* Bulletin NCJ-158022, Washington, DC: U.S. Department of Justice, Bureau of Justice Statistics.

Warr, Mark. 1984. "Fear of Victimization: Why Are Women and the Elderly More Afraid?" *Social Science Quarterly* 65:681–702.

———. 1990. "Dangerous Situations: Social Context and Fear of Victimization." *Social Forces* 68(3):891–907.

Wayne, Ivor and Robert J. Rubel. 1982. "Student Fear in Secondary Schools." *Urban Review* 14(3):197–237.

Will, Jeffry A. and John H. McGrath Ill. 1995. "Crime, Neighborhood Perceptions, and the Underclass: The Relationship Between Fear of Crime and Class Position." *Journal of Criminal Justice* 23(2):163–76.

Williams, J. Sherwood, B. Krishna Dingh, and Betsy B. Singh. 1996. "Urban Youth, Fear of Crime, and Resulting Defensive Actions." *Adolescence* 29(114): 323–31.

David C. May is an associate professor and Kentucky Center for School Safety Research Fellow in the Department of Correctional and Juvenile Justice Services at Eastern Kentucky University. He has published numerous articles in the areas of causes of juvenile delinquency and adolescent fear of crime and a book that examines the relationship between adolescent fear of crime and weapon-related delinquency. He is presently coauthoring another book examining the antecedents of gun ownership and possession among adolescent male delinquents.

R. Gregory Dunaway is Professor of Sociology and Director of Sociology Graduate Studies at Mississippi State University. His research interests include criminological theory, rural crime and justice, inequality and crime and justice, corrections, and criminal justice policy. Currently, he is involved in a number of research projects including an evaluation of Mississippi's Drug Court Program, a survey of Mississippi's juvenile detention facilities, and a study on rural crime and justice. His work has been published in outlets such as *Criminology, Justice Quarterly, The American Journal of Criminal Justice, Research in Crime and Delinquency, Journal of Quantitative Criminology,* and *Sociological Spectrum.*

David May

What got you interested in this subject?

The idea of fear of crime came about from my interest in guns. My master's thesis focused on reasons for gun ownership among adults, including the influence of fear of criminal victimization—that some people own guns for self-protection. As I read the literature on fear of criminal victimization, I discovered that there is much literature about adults but very, very little about adolescents. I thought that was interesting because later adolescents are often the target of crimes. So, I began conducting research on the fear of crime among adolescents, hoping to make a contribution.

How do you see this research contributing to understanding of adolescent fear of criminal victimization?

It really is one of the first pieces to look exclusively at fear of criminal victimization among adolescents and to ask specific questions of kids about their fears. The questionnaire asks about their fear in a variety of scenarios. Most of the literature that had been conducted up to that time focused at a more global level, like "I am afraid to walk alone in my neighborhood at night." This is what the General Social Survey still uses. So, this research really made two contributions: (1) It extended the literature about fear of crime among adolescents, and (2) it improved the methodology that was used in studying fear of criminal victimization.

What were the advantages and disadvantages of using data from the Mississippi High School Youth Survey?

One disadvantage of using the Mississippi High School Youth Survey was that it was administered in public high schools, and whenever you use students as your research subjects, it introduces special obligations and issues. Institutional Review Boards look very closely at methodology and typically require parental consent for each student's participation. Usually, if you are just using adults who have been randomly selected, you do not have this extra obligation. So, it makes it a much more tedious process, and, in many cases, a much more difficult process. Another disadvantage of using data from the Mississippi High School Youth Survey is the fact that some people think that fear, being an emotion, cannot really be measured accurately through survey research. They argue that some kind of measurement of physiological change is necessary, and we did not have the capability of doing that in the public high schools without incurring incredible cost. So, to me, those were the two disadvantages.

The main advantage of using the data from the high school youth survey was that we were able to collect the data in about four or five days by surveying the kids pretty much all day in different classes. That is a fairly quick data collection process. Plus, because it was in a survey format, it made the analysis much easier than if it would have been done using some qualitative technique like open-ended interviews. So, the main advantages were speed and administration.

What prompted such a high response rate?

Probably the main reason for the high response rate was that the survey was conducted as part of an anti-drug task force that was active in these communities. They were already well aware of the idea that crime is a problem. Incorporating this survey into the work of the anti-drug task force gave added credibility to it and made it more acceptable to parents. We sent the parental consent forms to the teachers who then passed them on to the students to take home to their parents. In every case, the teachers were really good about reminding the students to return the signed parental consent forms. Those were the two main contributors to the high response rate.

What were the strengths of using survey research to examine adolescent fear of crime at school?

The use of survey research allowed us to tap into a wide variety of attitudinal and behavioral measures. We were pretty much unlimited in scope because the teachers had agreed to give us an entire class period and we had the kids as a captive audience. We designed the questionnaire to take 30 to 45 minutes, which provided us with considerable data about fear and about a number of related subjects. The data set has now been used for several research articles.

What were the weaknesses of using survey research to examine adolescent fear of crime at school?

I have already referred to the problem of not being able to include any physiological change in our measurement of fear. While the best measure of fear might be able to be taken in a physiological laboratory, social scientists have pretty much accepted that survey research is a legitimate method to measure fear.

What kind of response did the students have to being surveyed?

This was my first experience with surveying adolescents, though I have now done several more. I have found that you generally have a certain percentage of the students who really enjoy it and appreciate the opportunity that they have to give their opinion. Then, there may be a slightly larger percentage who completely blow it off and you can tell that they are doing it just to get it done. That is an important reason for doing validity and reliability checks to look for patterns in answers, so that you know which ones are answering it seriously. That is part of the survey design.

What unexpected events or developments, if any, occurred during the course of this research?

I was surprised by the number of students who did not take it seriously. At the point at which we were doing this survey, I anticipated that everyone would take it seriously. That was a realization for me. The second surprise was the very time-consuming process of getting parental consent.

Could you describe any specific ethical issues that you confronted in this research?

Perhaps not as much with this project, but it has been my experience since that time that the whole idea of parental consent is handled differently by different researchers. Unfortunately, there are some researchers who don't want to deal with institutional review boards and thus find ways to get around securing parental consent by using the school system to administer the survey. So the whole idea of parental consent and efforts to avoid having to get parental consent is an ethical issue.

If you were to do this research again, is there anything that you would do differently? If so, what?

There are a couple of things that I would do differently. First, I would make maximum effort to get a much larger sample. Even though we had over 700 students responding, I would like to have had a much better cross-section of every district in the state. In the ideal world, our sample would have been three to four thousand students who represented all of the districts in the state. In this project, we sent letters to the superintendents asking them to allow their schools to participate, and there were a couple of areas in the state that were not represented as well because the superintendents did not allow us to be there. Second, at the time of this project, I did not know about the concept of implied consent from parents—that is, where you send a letter home, state that a survey will be being administered at the school, and to notify the school if you do not want your child to participate. Otherwise, we will give them the survey. That would make the administration process a lot easier while still meeting the ethical obligation.

What was most frustrating to you in doing this research? What was most satisfying?

The most frustrating thing about the research was the relatively small sample because we could have had many more respondents if all of the superintendents would have cooperated. The most satisfying aspect of the survey was, as a graduate student, that we really got to get out there and get our hands dirty with research. It is one thing to read about research and another to actually do

it. So, I was involved from the very outset, from contacting the superintendents, to writing the letters, to designing the survey, to administering the survey, to analyzing the data, so I received a really good feel as to what goes into
that type of research. I think it has made me a better researcher because I
started at the very beginning, went all the way through the process, and came
out with an eventual publication from it. So it was a very gratifying experience
in that regard.

What important lesson or illustration of doing good research can you share with students from your experiences in this research project?

The important lesson about doing good research that I would share with students is that you are not always going to find the results that support your hypothesis, but good research will allow you to state with confidence what
relationships do or do not exist. My realization over the years is that I don't
feel comfortable saying anything about research findings until I have read the
research and until I have seen how it was done. You can say with confidence
that if a good research design is used, then the relationships that the authors
have found probably exist in most situations, but you cannot say that with
confidence when the research is less than good.

Questions to Think About

1. What are the independent and dependent variables in this study and how is each
   one measured? Which variables presented particular challenges, and how did
   May and Dunaway deal with those challenges?

2. Describe May and Dunaway's sample. What are some categories of adolescents
   who are not included in the sample? Do you think that including them would
   have affected the results of the study? How?

3. What are some methods other than survey research that could be used to study
   adolescent fear of crime? What might be their strengths and limitations compared
   to using survey research?

4. Briefly summarize May and Dunaway's findings. What are some additional research questions that they suggest should be pursued in light of their results?
   Choose one that is of interest to you and develop a research design to study it.

chapter 6

Nonreactive Research
Content Analysis, Accretion Measures, and Using Existing Statistics

Social and behavioral scientists face a peculiar problem that is not faced by scientists in other disciplines: We study human beings. And because humans are social beings who take others into account in their behavior, reactivity is a common problem that threatens the validity of our research. *Reactivity* refers to the fact that when people participate in an experiment, fill out a questionnaire, or welcome a researcher into their social group, their behavior is affected in some way. *Nonreactive* (or *unobtrusive*) research methods include a mix of approaches that have one important feature in common: Those being studied do not know they are being studied. The researcher examines evidence of people's behavior or attitudes, rather than interacting directly with those being studied. In this chapter we include articles representing three of the most commonly used kinds of nonreactive research: content analysis, accretion measures, and the use of existing data.

Content analysis is an approach that examines written, visual, or spoken text. It is particularly appealing because the choices about what to analyze are diverse and rich—from textbooks to television shows, conversations to song lyrics, and including visual images of all kinds such as wedding photos, cartoons, advertisements, and campaign posters. In the first article reprinted here, Melvin Thomas and Linda Treiber choose a popular kind of text to study—magazine advertisements—and look for evidence of racial and sexual stereotyping. However, they go beyond previous studies of this sort by focusing on the interplay of race and gender, and by looking at magazines for African Americans as well as the more commonly studied magazines aimed at whites. In contrast to Penny Tinkler's qualitative content analysis of representations of women's smoking in magazines (Chapter 2), Thomas and Treiber use a quantitative approach. Their results are summarized in tables that report the proportional representation of each race–sex group across "status image" and "product promise" categories.

They go on to test for statistically significant differences across those race–sex categories, which would indicate the continued existence of stereotyping in the ads they study.

Another kind of nonreactive research is *accretion measures,* techniques in which researchers systematically examine things that people leave behind that can yield insights into their behaviors, attitudes, and values. Carol Hagen and her colleagues analyze an unusual kind of accretion measure, what they call "catastroffiti"—private graffiti left in public places after a disaster, in this case the Red River Valley Flood of 1997. What began as the need to tag flood-damaged property developed into a fascinating array of notes, drawings, and symbols that adorned furniture, appliances, houses, debris, and billboards throughout the areas hardest hit by the flooding. The researchers conclude that such catastroffiti is an important means by which community members recover from the disaster, achieve cohesion, share social and political commentary, and express a range of emotions in a "free arena of discourse." Hagen and her colleagues use a qualitative approach, coding their observations into dominant themes and summarizing their findings in words, not numbers. Although they draw on previous research on graffiti in public bathrooms to help them identify organizing themes, their research is largely exploratory and descriptive rather than explanatory. They close by expressing the hope that other researchers will follow their lead and undertake similar analyses of a community's cultural expressions following a disaster.

The third article in this chapter illustrates a popular and unmistakably quantitative kind of nonreactive research: analysis of existing, usually "official," statistics. In their study that examines the viability of the deterrence hypothesis that states that the death penalty deters homicide, Sorensen and his colleagues neatly illustrate some of the distinctive advantages and disadvantages of using existing data, including official statistics. One common drawback, for example, is that researchers must identify and compensate for deficiencies and limitations of data that have been collected by others for other purposes. In this instance, the Houston Police Department failed to report homicide information in 1983. This is a potentially serious source of bias in this study because Houston is not only the largest jurisdiction in Texas, but also the one responsible for the greatest number of homicides in the state. As a result, the authors must limit their analysis to the years from 1984 on. Limitations of the data also force the researchers to turn to alternative sources of data for some of the many different control variables that are known to influence homicide rates and that must be included in their models. Of course using existing data has many advantages as well. In this study, existing data are the best kind for addressing the research question. Another advantage that Sorensen notes is that because the data are "official," they are familiar and equally accessible to researchers on both sides of the death penalty debate. Thus, results can be readily replicated and researchers are not as subject to accusations of ideologically motivated bias in this highly politicized area of death penalty research.

Because nonreactive research methods do not often involve humans directly, they allow researchers to avoid some of the ethical problems related to privacy and avoiding harm to participants. That is not always the case, however, as Carol Hagen reveals in her description of the care that she and her colleagues took to conceal the identities of the creators of the graffiti that they studied. Sometimes other ethical issues may simply take center stage instead. For both Jon Sorensen and Linda Treiber, one important ethical concern had to do with the potential consequences of their research findings. Sorensen raises particularly troubling questions about the possible consequences of research findings related to the death penalty: Will they be used to justify killing? Or somehow contribute to the deaths of innocent citizens? It seems that social scientists, like other scientists, must be ever mindful not only of possible harm to research participants, but also of other more far-reaching potential consequences of their work.

Race, Gender, and Status

A Content Analysis of Print Advertisements in Four Popular Magazines

Melvin E. Thomas and Linda A. Treiber

In this article, we consider the continuation of race–gender stereotypes in advertising images by way of the product's suggestive messages, specifically, connotations of higher or lower social status and promises of intangible social rewards (e.g., friendship, appearance, romance). We examined 1,709 advertisements in magazines whose primary reading audiences differ by race and/or gender: Life, Cosmopolitan, Ebony, and Essence (1988–1990). For the analysis we created and then compared three dimensions of status (affluent, trendy, and everyday) and five product "promises" (celebrity identification, sex–romance, appearance, marriage–family, and good times) as they are modeled by and presented to male, female, Black, and White readers in the magazines examined. We hypothesized that these status-image portrayals differ by race and gender. We found that most ads make use of positive (i.e., high-status) images of Blacks and Whites and women and men and that differences between magazines are more pronounced than differences between models. Some patterns in the use of status and product promises may be suggestive of continued, though subtle, stereotyping.

We examined the prevalence of race and gender stereotypes in print media through a comparative content analysis of contemporary magazine advertisements. Existing studies have tended to confine the analysis to women vis-á-vis men or Blacks vis-á-vis Whites, overlooking the potential for interaction effects or combined race–gender stereotyping. Our research provides insight about race and gender assumptions through an examination of these combined effects. Our comparisons are based on the frequency and patterns of status images and product promises as embodied by Black and White and male and female models. For the analysis, we created and then compared three dimensions of status (affluent, trendy, and everyday) and five product "promises" (celebrity identification, sex–romance, appearance, marriage–family, and good times) as they were modeled by and presented to male, female, Black, and White readers. We hypothesized that the conventional stereotypes identified in previous studies have been transformed into subtler presentations that become apparent in group-to-group comparisons.

The goal of selling products is met by harnessing visual cues that link the material object with a level of social prestige and implicitly promise intangible social rewards (e.g., friendship, beauty, romance), providing a slice of life to consumers (Packard 1961; Williamson 1978; Berman 1981). Advertisements link products with status and rewards, targeted to both specific and mass audiences (Berman 1981).

A number of works in the fields of gender, race, sociology, and psychology have dealt with media images of Blacks, women, and other groups. In the area of gender, for example, researchers have demonstrated that women are depicted as dependent and decorative (e.g., Courtney and Lockeretz 1971; Pingree et al. 1976; Goffman 1976), unemployed homemakers and care givers (e.g., Culley and Bennett 1976; Tuchman 1979; Craig 1992; Leppard, Ogletree, and Wallen 1993), and sex–beauty objects (e.g., Venkatesan and Losco 1975; Bretyl and Cantor 1988; Signorielli 1992). Similarly, scholars have noted the "invisibility" or "tokenism" of Blacks, along with more active stereotypical characterizations such as domestic, sidekick, hyper-sexed, or athletic (e.g., Chapko 1976; Culley and Bennett 1976; Staples and Jones 1985).

Many early studies focusing on gender representations surveyed only magazines intended for White readers; consequently, Black magazines have rarely been the subject of media analysis. Black magazines are as likely as not to be included in the media mix; for example, Barthel (1988) included *Essence* (but not *Ebony*) in her study of gender and advertising, and Belknap and Leonard (1991) did not survey any Black magazines.

There is some evidence that media images of Blacks and women are improving (Saunders and Stead 1986; Sullivan and O'Connor 1988; Allan and Coltrane 1996; Coltrane and Allan 1996), yet the extent to which stereotypical hierarchy still exists in contemporary advertising needs further exploration. We enhance the insights of previous analyses by focusing on the interplay of race and gender in print advertisements.

Method

We surveyed 1,709 full-page ads from four different magazines using 1988–1990 issues for the months of February, July, September, and December. The unit of analysis was the full-page magazine print advertisement. Only ads depicting Black or White human models (i.e., no product-alone ads) were considered; ads depicting more than one status, race, and/or gender were categorized. Originally, our intent was to consider Black models in White-audience magazines separately, and vice versa. Unfortunately, because of the severe race segregation of the ads, none of the publications contained sufficient numbers of ads featuring models of the "opposite" race to make such an analysis possible.

As we surveyed the ads, we attempted to describe a detailed impression of high or low status. To do this, we relied on the methodology of the subfield of visual sociology–anthropology as articulated by Ball and Smith (1992) and illustrated in the works of Williamson (1978), Barthel (1988), and Ewen (1988). This method allowed us to look at subtleties in the visual data and to discern the visual image as situated in a social context (i.e., as the creation of a group of individuals with a particular purpose in mind). For consistency and reliability in categorizing the ads, we used a comprehensive list of visual cues as an aid for objective identification of the categories of ads.

The ads studied were published in magazines whose readership was predominantly Black (*Ebony*), White (*Life*), Black and female (*Essence*), or White and female (*Cosmopolitan*). The comparative emphasis of this study precluded us from selecting magazines from a newsstand at random; instead, we matched Black and White publications in terms of content. The choice of the four months reflects significant period themes in the popular culture that are incorporated into advertising campaigns (e.g., February, Black History month and Valentine's Day; July, the height of summer; September, back to school, and December, holiday season).

Each advertisement surveyed was tallied in as many categories as deemed applicable; however, not all ads embodied a combination of categories. Some ads with subtexts did not have identifiable status images. For example, the face-alone model used to sell cosmetic products (i.e., appearance subtext) cannot be grouped into a status image, for there are no status "clues" such as clothing, hairstyle, and jewelry. We evaluated 1,599 status-image and 1,709 product-promise advertisements for this project. In addition to cell frequencies and percentages, the chi-square statistical procedure was used for all tabulations.

Status Images

Within this framework, we conceptualized three status images in print advertising: *affluent, trendy,* and *everyday.* Table 1 summarizes the characteristics of model appearances used in identifying the three status-image categories.

Affluent status images are commonly associated with wealth, elite style, and taste. In terms of presentation, affluent ads tend to be visually simplistic; viewers immediately recognize the implications of the upper class elegance and lifestyle.

TABLE 1 *Appearances, Words, and Backgrounds Associated with Five Status Images*

APPEARANCE	ASSOCIATED WORDS	BACKGROUND/ACTIVITIES
	Affluent	
Black-tie tuxedo/gown	International	Mansion, estate, private yacht/jet,
Diamonds	Exclusive	private beach
Fur coats/stoles	Continental	Penthouse/limousine, Paris/Rome
Upswept hair		
Conservative suits	Elegance	Tennis/racquetball, golf course,
(blazer-style; knee-length skirts)	French	sailing/marina
		Opera/theater, restaurants
		(linen/crystal/marble)
Conservative colors	Classic	Bayside tables
(navy, beige, burgundy,	Sterling	Drawing room
gray, gold/pearls)	Quality	Executive suite
Pumps/oxfords	Savoir faire	
Chin-length hair; "clean cut"	Style	
	Taste	
	Trendy	
High fashion	Modern	Dancing/aerobics
(asymmetrical/layered/glitter/fringe/	Avant garde	(bungee-jumping, skate
studs leather/fur, double-breasted	Unique	boarding, dating/flirting)
oversized suits, short skirts)		
Spike heels/	Flair	
high boots	Hot	Rapping
Colors (fluorescent	Cool	Houseboats
fuschia/yellow/teal/orange)	Nouveau	Futuristic
Jewelry excessive/metallic	New	Apartments
Wild/geometric hair	Fresh	Discotheques
Beards/facial hair	New	Dance concerts
	Today	
	Tomorrow	
	Cutting edge	
	Everyday	
Casual clothes sweats/jeans/flannels/	Honesty	Sand castles
polos/sweaters/bathrobes	Reliability	Snowball fights, biking/picnics
Sneakers	Dependability	Families, weddings, recitals/sports
Blue collar	Nostalgia	Station wagons, graduations
Plain jeans/white T-shirt	Just like . . .	Kitchen/backyard
	Neighbors	Front porch
	Family	Studio apartment, balcony/patio
	Common concerns/worries	
Blue collar/pink collar	Salt of the Earth	Construction site
(plain jeans; white T-shirts; ill-	Unaffected/unpretentious real	Typing pool
fitting clothes; no jewelry; plain		Repair garage
shoes; plastic shoes, accessories)		Local bar/pool hall

Affluent images also depict executive status, embodying power and conservatism.

As opposed to the classic style of affluent status images, *trendy* models present a more fashionable "in-crowd" appearance. Trendy advertisements use unconventional elements of page design: silhouetted or floating figures, close cropping, reverses, or fluorescent colors. We considered trendy a high-status image; usually only those with a reasonable disposable income can devote the resources to following fashion trends.

Everyday status refers to men and women dressed and posed to evoke the "average" person. Unlike the high-status images, everyday images do not perpetuate an ideal of physical beauty, style, and material luxury unattainable for most of the population. Clothing is casual rather than elegant or cutting edge, and the models are well groomed and attractive rather than stunning.

Because everyday models have pedestrian concerns like getting dishes clean or keeping diapers dry, they are often posed in common environments performing everyday activities. Everyday models have working- or middle-class occupations as opposed to professional or executive-level jobs.

Product Promises

We also assessed the implicit promise or advertising subtext of the commodity. In our examination of contemporary product promises in advertisements, we identified five popular subtexts: good times, appearance, sex–romance, family–marriage, and celebrity identification.

Good times is depicted by three or more models involved with one another and noticeably having fun. From young people frolicking on the beach (Newport) to urban sophisticates enjoying their "Party Bacardi," the promise is one of having the time of one's life, surrounded by friends.

Appearance promises operate on the expectation that a product will make its user more attractive—younger, thinner, sexier, more beautiful or powerful—common subtexts aimed at both men and women. Readers gaze on the faces or bodies of attractive men and women and are en-

couraged to believe that using the advertised product will result in their looking like the model(s).

The *sex–romance* subtext depicts a male model and a female model who are physically intimate and reciprocally adoring one another. This differs from the *appearance* subtext in that the couple's relationship is reciprocal (in the appearance promise, one partner is admiring, the other condescending to be admired). Sex–Romance couples are usually situated in a romantic atmosphere.

Family–marriage associations are conveyed by images of men and women in traditional, recognized "family" behaviors such as recording a ballet recital, supervising a Little League practice, or having family meals.

Celebrity identification messages build on the identification with and trust in a famous person. The intention of the advertiser is to imply that the user of such a product is in good company with rich, famous, notorious, or high-achieving people.

Analysis

Each magazine ad for the designated period was sorted into a status image or product promise according to the described criteria. These data were then analyzed by computing simple row percentages for the three status images, across race and gender lines; the chi-square procedure was used to determine if the resulting distribution was statistically significant. Column percentages enabled us to consider the proportional representativeness of each race–sex group in the three status images. We then concentrated on the magazines themselves, considering percentage distributions of status images and product promises by each publication.

Findings

Status Images

As can be seen in Table 2, racial differences became apparent only in the context of race–gender groups. For example, White women modeled the high-status (affluent) image most frequently

TABLE 2 *Model's Race/Sex Group Across Status Images (N = 1,599)*

GROUP	AFFLUENT	TRENDY	EVERYDAY	TOTAL
White women				
%	35	34	31	100
n	235	230	205	670
White men				
%	36	17	47	99
n	96	45	127	268
Black women				
%	31	31	38	100
n	118	117	141	376
Black men				
%	34	21	45	100
n	96	60	129	285
Total *n*	545	452	602	1,599

Note: $\chi^2(6, N = 1,599) = 48.9, p < .001.$

(35 percent), followed by trendy (34 percent) and everyday (31 percent). Black women portrayed everyday status most frequently (38 percent), followed by affluent and trendy (both at 31 percent); they were, therefore, slightly more likely than White women to model lower status.

Both racial groups of men portrayed everyday status most frequently, followed by affluent, then trendy. Black men were slightly more likely than White men to appear as trendy in magazine ads (21 percent for Black men vs. 17 percent for White men). Black men were less likely than White men to model the affluent status (34 percent for Black men vs. 36 person for White men).

It seems clear that advertisers rely on high-status images (i.e., affluent and trendy) more frequently than low-status images (i.e., everyday) to sell products. Female models of both races more frequently embodied the trendy status than their male counterparts. The everyday status was more commonly portrayed by men.

Although all four publications "flattered" their reading audience with a greater number of high-status presentations, there were differences in the distribution of status categories between them that were statistically significant, as shown in Table 3.

Life, a general interest magazine aimed at Whites, used the affluent image almost 50 percent of the time. Trendy images were used least frequently in this publication. In *Cosmopolitan,* the images were nearly evenly divided between status groups. However, in *Ebony* and *Essence,* magazines targeted to Blacks, images representing the everyday status were dominant.

The frequency differences between magazine images suggest that advertisers found certain images more appropriate or effective for specific race–gender audiences; they hypothesized that Black women are more likely to respond to everyday images than White women and that Black general readers are less likely to respond to affluent images than White general readers. By the same logic, we can also surmise that trendy images are seen as more effective for White women than for Black women.

Next, we analyzed status images by race and gender. The results are given in Table 4. When comparing White women and Black women across status categories, the results were nonsignificant. White women and Black women were shown with similar frequency in the status categories. Similarly, when we compared White men

TABLE 3 *Magazines across Status Images (N = 1,599)*

MAGAZINE	AFFLUENT	TRENDY	EVERYDAY	TOTAL
Life				
%	47	17	36	100
n	63	22	48	133
Cosmopolitan				
%	34	32	34	101
n	260	249	260	760
Ebony				
%	33	27	40	100
n	141	116	173	430
Essence				
%	30	24	45	99
n	81	65	121	267
Total *n*	545	452	602	1,599

Note: $\chi^2(6, N = 1,599) = 29.02, p < .001$.

and Black men across status categories, the results were also nonsignificant. However, when we compared White men with White women, we found a significant difference in status categories, $\chi^2 (2, N = 940) = 35.327, p < .001$. White men and White women were portrayed significantly differently in status categories; White men were more likely to be portrayed as everyday status and less likely to be portrayed as trendy status when compared with White women. Similarly, when we compared Black men with Black women across status categories, we found significant differences as well $\chi^2(2, N = 661) = 8.79, p < .012$. Black men were portrayed less often as trendy and more often as affluent than Black women. Therefore, it seems that both gender and race influence status images in magazine ads.

Product Promises

The final exploration in our analysis involved product promises as they are conveyed among the four magazines. As can be seen in Table 5, *Life*'s prevailing promises are good times (30 percent), followed by family–marriage (28 percent). *Ebony*'s product promises are most often

sex–romance (28 percent), followed by family–marriage (24 percent). It is notable that the sex–romance subtext is seldom used in ads in *Life*, which caters to a predominantly White audience (13 percent), but sex–romance was the most frequently occurring product promise in *Ebony* (28 percent), which caters to a predominantly Black audience.

Cosmopolitan, a magazine geared to White women, was dominated by appearance messages (54 percent), followed by sex–romance (21 percent). In *Cosmopolitan*, marriage and family product promises were rarely found. In contrast, *Essence*, a magazine geared to Black women, contained a more proportionate percentage of appearance ads (30 percent), with family–marriage being the next most frequently occurring subtext (26%).

It is also interesting to observe which subtexts were not present in the magazines. For example, as previously stated, advertisers did not sell products by promising sex–romance in *Life* as often as in the other publications, and the family–marriage subtext was rare in ads in *Cosmopolitan*. Also important is the fact that in both women's magazines, the good times product promise was rare.

Method of Analysis

Chi-Square

Chi-square (χ^2) is a popular statistic for determining the relationship between two categorical variables. In this article, Thomas and Treiber are studying the relationship between four sets of variables: (1) A model's race and sex and the status image portrayed (Table 2), (2) the primary audience of four magazines and status images of models (Table 3), (3) bivariate categories of race and sex and the status image portrayed (Table 4), and (4) the primary audience of four magazines and the main type of product promise made in the magazine (Table 5).

Because the chi-square procedure is the same in all four tables, we will examine only Table 2 in depth here. In Table 2, the race and sex of the model in the advertisement is in the left-hand column (the independent variable), and the status image of the model (whether affluent, trendy, or everyday) is listed across the top (the dependent variable). Within the cells of the table are both the number in the category and its percentage. For example, of the 670 white female models, 235 (35%) portrayed an affluent status, whereas 205 (31%) portrayed an everyday status. Of the 376 black female models, 118 (31%) portrayed an affluent image, and 141 (38%) portrayed an everyday image. The question asked by this table is whether the status image portrayed by print models varies by race and sex.

The chi-square values are the key to interpreting the table. These values are not intuitive—their meaning comes only when they are compared to values of the statistic that have been calculated and are reproduced in tables. The chi-square values in these tables are presented at the bottom of the table (along with degrees of freedom and the total number of models studied). After the value of the statistic, the authors report the level of probability that the relationship found between the two variables is due to chance (that is, the two variables are not really related). A $p<.001$ means that there is greater than a 99.9 percent chance that the relationship really exists, a $p<.01$ means that there is greater than a 99 percent chance that the relationship really exists, and a $p<.05$ means that there is greater than a 95 percent chance that the relationship really exists. If the probability is reported to be not significant (ns), we do not have sufficient confidence to conclude that the relationship really exists. In this table, the χ^2 is reported to have a probability of $p<.001$. That means that we have greater than a 99.9 percent confidence that a relationship really exists between the race and sex of the model and the status image portrayed. In looking at the percentages in the table, one can see that the differences between men and women tend to be greater that the differences between blacks and whites.

For Table 3, the four sub-tables in Table 4, and Table 5, you should be able to determine what two variables are being studied, the reported chi-square value, and the level of probability that the two variables are related.

The distribution of product promises across magazines was statistically significant, χ^2 (12) = 275.67, $p < .001$.

Discussion and Conclusions

We hypothesized that analyzing which race–sex type models a particular status image within a magazine would yield insight into the continued presence of stereotypical assumptions. *Life* favored affluent images, but *Cosmopolitan* contained more trendy images than any other magazine. The Black magazines, *Ebony* and *Essence*, by contrast, most frequently published everyday images. We did not find in these print advertisements any gross stereotypes that support ideologies of patriarchy and White supremacy (e.g., Warren 1978; Staples and Jones 1985).

Nevertheless, a few patterns did emerge that support the idea of the continuation of gender and racial stereotypes in media images. These are subtle and as such support the interpretation that although media images do not actively or conspiratorially support sexism and racism, they nonetheless represent, reflect, or resonate with the cognitive dispositions of those who create them and believe such images will have some persuasive effect on those who view or read them.

TABLE 4 *Race/Sex Models across Status Images*

	AFFLUENT	TRENDY	EVERYDAY	TOTAL
White women and White men (n = 940)[a]				
White women				
%	35	34	31	
n	235	230	205	670
White Men				
%	36	17	47	
n	98	45	127	275
Total				
%	35	29	35	
n	333	275	332	940
Black women and Black men (n = 661)[b]				
Black women				
%	31	31	38	
n	118	117	141	376
Black men				
%	34	21	45	
n	96	60	129	285
Total				
%	32	27	41	
n	214	177	270	661
White women and Black women (n = 1,046)[c]				
White women				
%	35	34	31	
n	235	230	205	670
Black women				
%	31	31	38	
n	118	117	141	376
Total				
%	34	33	33	
n	353	347	346	1,046
White men and Black men (n = 555)[d]				
White men				
%	36	17	47	
n	98	45	127	270
Black men				
%	33	21	45	
n	96	60	129	285
Total				
%	35	19	46	
n	194	105	256	555

[a] $\chi^2(2) = 35.327, p < .001.$
[b] $\chi^2(2) = 8.97, p < .012.$
[c] $\chi^2(2) = 5.19, ns.$
[d] $\chi^2(2) = 1.775, ns.$

TABLE 5   *Magazines across Product Promises (N = 1,709)*

MAGAZINE	CELEBRITY ENDORSEMENT	APPEARANCE	SEX ROMANCE	FAMILY MARRIAGE	GOOD TIMES	TOTAL
Life						
%	12	16	13	28	30	100
n	15	20	16	34	37	122
Cosmopolitan						
%	13	54	21	7	5	100
n	111	452	173	58	45	839
Ebony						
%	15	23	28	24	10	100
n	66	104	125	107	45	447
Essence						
%	15	30	20	26	9	100
n	44	91	61	78	27	301
Total *n*	236	667	375	277	154	1,709

Note: $\chi^2(12) = 275.67$, $p < .001$.

Status-image distributions suggest that men are rugged, "real," average and normal (everyday), whereas women are fashionable, glamorous, young, and perhaps frivolous (trendy). Beauty–glamor messages are aimed relentlessly at women, more so for White women than for Black women.

It would seem from the distributions in these four magazines that the desirability of high status and promise of intangible rewards such as appearance and sex–romance are powerful. However, sex–romance product promises seemed to be considered more appropriate or effective for Black audiences. This finding may represent the vestiges of stereotypical thinking about Black sexuality. Advertisers who hold to this view, subliminally or actively, may find themselves reasoning that if their product promises sex, it will sell more successfully to a predominantly Black audience. Or they may have accepted stereotypical thinking that Whites, particularly Whites who read *Life,* are more sophisticated, intellectual, and conservative.

We did not see women in evening gowns draped across the hoods of cars or otherwise used as stage dressing for products. We did not see many ads where women were staring passively and adoringly at the men they accompanied. Nor did we see a particularly large group of images of women posed with downcast eyes and folded hands to look demure; instead, female models were "empowered," meaning they looked directly at the camera (viewer) in active stances and a variety of settings. Even everyday female models were not overwhelmingly suggestive of homemakers, and women seen as affluent were clearly executives with large desks and private offices, not secretaries in the typing pool. Whether selling lipstick or pickup trucks, advertising aimed at women was thought to work more effectively by connoting youth and fashion instead of real life or business savvy. Men, in contrast, were most often portrayed as real-life characters.

These lingering stereotypes became visible largely because of the comparative nature of this analysis. Most images in all four magazines were high status; it is only by comparing *Life* with *Ebony,* for example, that we discovered the disproportionate selling of sex–romance to Blacks and the subtle overuse of affluent images for whites.

The use of high-status associations keeps some stereotypical ideas from seeming obvious or insulting. As a result, within the contained universe of *Ebony* magazine, it is hard to perceive any one particular presentation as deliberately or malevolently intended because the advertisement is obviously about attractive, well-groomed people. However, given the legacy of structural racism and sexism, and a media still largely controlled by Whites, especially men, it is not surprising that stereotyping persists.

Racial and gender stereotypes endure as exaggerated, over-simplified images used to sell products. We have demonstrated that magazine advertisements differentially use these superficial images when targeting products to women, men, Blacks, and Whites. The use of stereotypical images in magazine advertising confirms to the readership that subordinate groups should remain in a lower status. In this study, both gender and race were found to be strong underlying principles of organizing everyday experience. One of the tragic characteristics of media-generated stereotypes is their ability to generate self-fulfilling prophecies, although stereotypes in ads often provide an incorrect image of race and gender.

REFERENCES

Allan, Kenneth and Scott Coltrane. 1996. "Gender Displaying Television Commercials: A Comparative Study of Television Commercials in the 1950s and 1980s." *Sex Roles* 35:185–203.

Ball, Michael S. and Gregory W. H. Smith. 1992. *Analyzing Visual Data. Qualitative Research Methods Series 24*. London: Sage.

Barthel, Diane. 1988. *Putting on Appearances. Gender and Advertising*. Philadelphia: Temple University Press.

Belknap, Penny and Wilbert M. Leonard, II. 1991. "A Conceptual Replication and Extension of Erving Goffman's Study of Gender Advertisements," *Sex Roles* 25:103–18.

Berman, Roy. 1981. *Advertising and Social Change*. Beverly Hills, CA: Sage.

Bretyl, D. and J. Cantor. 1988. *Putting on Appearances*. Philadelphia: Temple University Press.

Chapko, Michael. 1976. "Black Ads Are Getting Blacker," *Journal of Communications* 26:175–78.

Coltrane, Scott and Kenneth Allan. 1996. "New Fathers and Old Stereotypes: Representations of Masculinity in 1980's Television Advertising" *Masculinities* 2:43–66.

Courtney, Alice E. and Sarah Wernick Lockeretz. 1971. "A Woman's Place: An Analysis of the Roles Portrayed by Women in Magazine Advertisements." *Journal of Marketing Research* 8:92–5.

Craig, R. Stephen. 1992. "Women as Home Care Givers: Gender Portrayals in OTC Drug Commercials." *Journal of Drug Education* 22:303–12.

Culley, James D. and Rex Bennett. 1976. "Selling Women, Selling Blacks." *Journal of Communication* 26:160–74.

Ewen, Stuart. 1988. *All Consuming Images: The Politics of Style in Contemporary Culture*. New York: Basic Books.

Goffman, Erving. 1976. *Gender Advertisements*. Cambridge, MA: Harvard University Press.

Leppard, Wander, Shirley Matile Ogletree, and Emily Wallen, 1993. "Gender Stereotyping in Medical Advertising: Much Ado about Nothing." *Sex Roles* 29:829–38.

Packard, Vance. 1961. *The Status Seekers*. New York: Pocket Books.

Pingree, Suzanne, Robert Parker Hawkins, Matilda Butler, and William Paisley. 1976. "A Scale for Sexism." *Journal of Communication* 26:193–200.

Saunders, Carol S. and Bette A. Stead. 1986. "Women's Adoption of a Business Uniform: A Content Analysis of Magazine Advertisements." *Sex Roles* 15:197–205.

Signorielli, N. and M. Leavs. 1992. "Children, Television, and Conceptions about Chores, Attitudes, and Behaviors." *Sex Roles* 27:337–56.

Staples, Robert and Terry Jones. 1985. "Culture, Ideology and Black Television Images." *Black Scholar* 16:10–20.

Sullivan, Gary L. and P. J. O'Connor. 1988. "Women's Role Portrayals in Magazine Advertising: 1958–1983." *Sex Roles* 18(3–4):181–88.

Tuchman, Gaye. 1979. "Women's Depiction by the Mass Media." *Signs* 4(3):528–42.

Venkatesan, M. and Jean Losco. 1975. "Women in Magazine Ads: 1959–71." *Journal of Advertising Research* 15:48–54.

Warren, Denise. 1978. "Commercial Liberation." *Journal of Communication* 28:169–73.

Williamson, Judith. 1978. *Decoding Advertisements: Ideology and Meaning in Advertising*. London: Marion Boyars.

Melvin E. Thomas is an associate professor of sociology at North Carolina State University. His research focuses on racial inequality, quality of life, and the sociology of religion. He has published book chapters as well as numerous articles in journals such as *American Sociological Review, Social Problems,* and *Sociological Quarterly.*

Linda A. Treiber is a doctoral candidate in sociology at North Carolina State University in Raleigh, NC. She also holds a master's in community health nursing. Her dissertation research focuses on social inequality and workplace hazards. Other interests include the social construction of chronic illnesses, with a particular focus on diabetes. As a follow up to this piece, she is again collaborating with Dr. Melvin Thomas on a study of advertisements and race, class, and gender images in men's lifestyle magazines.

An   interview   with . . .

Linda A. Treiber

How did you get interested in the topic of race and gender stereotyping in ads?

I've always been a magazine junkie. Ever since I was an adolescent, I would hoard the *Cosmopolitan* and the *Seventeen* magazines—impossible to throw them away. When I moved from place to place, I would always have a big stack of magazines that I would have to part with regretfully. I gave them to doctors' offices because I couldn't bear to throw them out. So I've always really liked magazine ads and I've always been the sort of dreamy person that thought "If I buy this product, it will make me the person in the ad." First I saw *Killing Us Softly* and that really hammered home the gender message. Then I saw *Ethnic Notions,* the Marlon Riggs film about images of blacks. It starts during the slavery period and shows how blacks were portrayed as happy, then as brutes; it gets into the whole idea of using stereotypical images of African Americans to sell products. So those two films really piqued my interest in the idea of gender stereotyping and race stereotyping in ads.

How did you end up with this particular topic and research approach?

I was Dr. Melvin Thomas's teaching assistant the first year I came to N.C. State and he had already started this research; it was already in place. I had selected the *Ethnic Notions* film to show to his Soc 305 class, Race and Ethnic Relations, and we started to talk about how interesting this was; and he talked about his project that was already in progress and invited me to join him. (Initially there was another graduate student involved who dropped out of the project). When he asked if I was interested, I jumped at it. He already had some of the data collected and the research design was in place, but some of the categories we analyzed had not really emerged yet—how we [were] actually going to categorize the ads. It was the first time that I had even actually used content analysis. I think in my mind the paradigm was already there, but to methodically and systematically use the method—I hadn't before. It won't be the last time I use it; I really like it.

How did you like collaborating? Were there particular difficulties or benefits with that?

I was already collaborating a lot with Melvin because I was going to his class twice or more a week. So we were already spending some amount of time together, and bouncing ideas off each other was great for me. He has always been a good mentor for me and I was very happy to be able to see a different viewpoint. He always listened to my views, and I appreciated that he respected my opinions and didn't lord it over me that he was a professor and I was a graduate student. I always felt that I got a lot of respect and I gained a lot from my association with him.

In your article, you note that there have been many different studies of race and gender stereotyping. What makes your approach different, and why did you decide to look at it the way that you did?

Well, you see interaction effects of race and gender all the time in regression models, and we thought it would be interesting to see if there are similar interaction effects in advertising. So we were trying to find a way to capture that. We picked the magazines we did in an effort to control for race and gender, especially with the *Essence* and *Cosmopolitan* magazines—*Essence* is aimed at young African American women and *Cosmo* is aimed at young white women, basically. Then we compared them with two general interest magazines: *Life* (which has since gone by the wayside), a general interest magazine for whites, and then *Ebony*, a similar magazine for African Americans. We tried to kind of match them in terms of audience. It was sort of difficult, because as the different categories emerged and we started to sort the magazines ads into different categories, we'd find a new category that we didn't have on the list. We would have to ask: Is this really a new category, or does it overlap with the existing category that we'd identified? So that was a real challenge. Some categories we had in mind ahead of time. For example, I was impressed with a book by Diane Barthel, *Putting on Appearances*, that came out in the 80s and was about gender in advertising. Some of her ideas and her methodology influenced us; that's where we got the idea of "product promises." Since we knew we wanted to use class as one of the variables, the status variable was pretty much always there; we wanted to see if the ads differed in terms of social class and appearance. Then we started to see these "trendy" images more and more and there was really no other way to fit them in. It takes money to buy trendy clothes, but they really weren't affluent images. They weren't class or old money, they were really just kind of "trendy."

How did you make other decisions about your sample, such as sample size?

We decided to divide them up by significant month of the year. I'm not completely certain how we decided the number—four magazines for each year. I think that was already determined when I came onto the project. But I do know that they were selected to include the significant holidays—Valentine's Day, Christmas, etc.

How long did it take you to collect all the data?

My part of it took about a year, but that's possibly because I was a first year graduate student, so a lot of my attention was given to my theory, methods, and introductory statistics courses—plus I was a teaching assistant, which kept me very busy. So it took a while. I spent most of my first summer doing it. Also, it took me longer than I expected because I tend to underestimate how long it takes to produce a good product.

Were there any unexpected events or developments that you had to deal with?

The hardest thing was trying to nail down discrete categories and then, just dealing with the sheer volume of ads. Each one had to be tagged and set aside in the appropriate pile or piles. Some ads would fit into two categories, so then we had to copy each of them and stick it in another pile. So just the paper thing was a challenge—finding a big enough, clean work space. Getting the magazines wasn't a problem, as the person who was in on the project originally had left us all the magazines.

Were your findings expected or unexpected? What do you think the implications are of your findings—for understanding racism and sexism, the media, and so on?

The first thing that surprised me was how few African Americans were pictured in ads in predominantly white magazines. You might expect to see that in 1967, but not twenty years later. So that surprised me right off the bat. The rest of it: I was somewhat surprised to see more sex/romance targeted at African Americans than at whites, though when you think about these negative stereotypes about African Americans' sexuality, it wasn't that surprising. But when it started to emerge, I was a little surprised. I was also surprised at how almost all the magazines put forth such affluent status images. I guess that is because we all want to become something better than we are; that is part of buying the product. We believe if we purchase these things, they will improve our appearance and social status in some way. But I was still surprised that was the overarching category. What sticks most strongly in my mind is how these stereotypes have changed somewhat, yet are still so salient. This is one point in the film *Killing Us Softly*, the idea that magazines and ads are so subtle and we think we are immune, but we are not. Another implication that I'm starting to get interested in is the idea that from a conflict oriented point of view, we are seen as "dupes of capitalism" and advertising is working us to consume more and more. But I also see this other side: that we really consent to this, that we really want to feel better about ourselves. They create the desire, but that we really do feel better when we buy. So the implications that I see are that stereotypes have continued, we are not immune even though we think we are, and the other side of the consumption/exploitation debate that says that even though these images are being forced on us and we seem to be controlled by advertisers, we also consent to it. That is an idea that I am relating to my dissertation research, on the labor process and occupational health and safety. We do have agency, in the structure/agency debate. The structure is magazine ads and capitalist advertisers getting us to buy products and use up our wages and work more so we can afford the products, but then on the other hand we do make the choice. On some level we do this because we try to improve our image and status and shape our identities based on products, and some of it does give us pleasure and joy.

Do you see any ethical issues in your research?

Not really. There were no human subjects issues to worry about. We had easy access to magazine ads, no consent to worry about . . . it is ideal in that sense. I always worry about presenting a particular negative finding, which might sometimes reinforce negativity in people's minds when they read it. Constantly talking about discrimination, for example—Does that reinforce the idea that things are inevitable and keep people from thinking of the possibility of change? I do think about that.

What was the most frustrating or difficult aspect of doing the research?

The most frustrating was the logistics of handling all the ads, then the discreteness of the categories. Sometimes they would overlap, and originally we had more categories and then we had to narrow the categories because they weren't mutually exclusive.

What was the most satisfying thing about the research experience?

Because it was my first publication, seeing the proofs and seeing it in the journal was satisfying. While I was looking at syllabi preparing to teach an introductory course last summer, I found one that used our article for a content analysis project. Then I found a citation for us in a textbook. So that was satisfying, too.

If you were to do this research again, what would you do differently?

I think I would try to expand the sample to include all the months of the year. Other than that, not much. If we expanded the months, would the categories change? Would our findings still be valid?

Are there any important lessons that you draw from this that would be useful to share with students?

I share this with my own students every time I teach Principles of Sociology because we have one class that is devoted to magazine ad categorization. I show *Ethnic Notions* and *Killing Us Softly,* then I lug about a hundred pounds of magazines to class, provide them with lots of little sticky tabs, and say "Let's go through all these magazines and see if we can find examples of the kind of things we saw in the films." Then, I adapted the assignment on the Web that uses our article (by Dr. David Cotter at Union College), so now students do a hands-on kind of content analysis with the magazines that I provide. Then later they do an assignment where they choose two issues of the magazine at least ten years apart and look for changes. So they have our article on reserve as a reference, and the films to look at. I did this the first time this summer, and it was very exciting . . . and very popular with students. They found great things in the magazines. Then I also tell them they can keep the magazines if they want, so I got rid of all these magazines.

My aim would be for students to use what they know, and combine it with the sociological information that they acquire from what they read for their sociology classes. We all see things like advertising, but if you apply a method and theory to it, you can come up with original results on your own. Some of my students have done that, and it has been very rewarding for me to see a small idea just blossom.

Questions to Think About

1. Describe the sample that Treiber and Thomas selected. According to Treiber, what would she do differently with regard to sampling if she were to do this study again? Do you think that her results would be different? Why or why not?

2. How did Treiber and Thomas construct the coding categories for their variables "status images" and "product promises"? Can you think of ways that their decisions about how to define and measure these constructs might have influenced their results? Explain.

3. What were the major results of the Treiber and Thomas study? Did any of these surprise you? Why?

4. Do you think that you could adapt Treiber and Thomas's research design and measures to analyze race and gender stereotypes in advertisements in some other medium (e.g., television)? Describe how you might go about doing such a study.

Graffiti on the Great Plains

A Social Reaction to the Red River Valley Flood of 1997

Carol A. Hagen, Morten G. Ender, Kathleen A. Tiemann, and Clifford O. Hagen, Jr.

Superficially, graffiti and disasters seem unrelated. Nevertheless, following the Red River Valley flood of 1997, a private form of graffiti emerged in public spaces in the twin cities of Grand Forks, North Dakota and East Grand Forks, Minnesota. Five thematic categories of graffiti emerged through the analysis of photographed images. The emergence and content of the graffiti appear to be directly related to residents' flood experiences. Initially, this graffiti provided a functional symbolic cue to demarcate flood-damaged property. However, the intended purpose of tagging property evolved into a community discourse of flood-recovery through graffiti that included the reaffirmation of the ethos of the community. We label such graffiti *catastroffiti* as a unique typology related to natural disasters.

Graffiti is traditionally not associated with disasters. However, the emergence of graffiti after the Red River Valley (RRV) flood of 1997 and other disasters, such as Hurricane Andrew in southern Florida, presents evidence that a relationship does exist. The print media have recorded isolated examples of graffiti following natural disasters, yet there is little systematic examination in the scholarly literature, sociological or otherwise, that specifically addresses this phenomena.

*The views expressed in this paper are those of the authors and do not reflect the position of the institutions with which they are affiliated. An earlier version of this paper was presented at the Annual Meeting of the American Sociological Association, San Francisco, California, August 21–25, 1998.

The graffiti on the Upper Great Plains that followed the RRV flood provided a functional symbolic cue to demarcate flood-damaged property. For some, the initial tagging of property was an act of conformity, meant to appease requests by public officials by identifying contaminated property for community disposal. However, sociologists recognize that behavior is not always reflective of its consequence (Merton, 1967). Graffiti ultimately served as a medium of communication that subverted the attempts of public officials to impose a specific definition on the situation. Community members used graffiti to express their frustration and the strain involved in recovering from a devastating flood. As such, the intended purpose of tagging property evolved into a community discourse of flood-recovery through graffiti including the reaffirmation of the ethos of the community. The essence of this discourse, heretofore unexamined in the disaster literature, is revealed through a variety of themes that emerged from our analysis.

In the remainder of this paper we describe the context and content of graffiti that blanketed Grand Forks, North Dakota, and East Grand Forks, Minnesota, after the RRV flood of 1997. In addition, we suggest the emergence of graffiti, an otherwise rare phenomenon in this region, to be a cultural manifestation of the collective strain experienced by these neighboring communities as a direct result of the flood. Further, the participation in the activity of graffiti served citizens as a social, political, and perhaps, psychological voice for coping with aspects of the flood. Finally, we offer a new term—catastroffiti—to describe the emergence of graffiti-like messages that may follow a disaster.

Literature Review

Graffiti Literature

Graffiti is a medium of expression and an outlet for stress (Abel & Buckley, 1977; Reisner & Wechsler, 1974). Through anonymity, graffiti allows the writer to express his or her feelings with little emotional risk. Therefore, a person normally constrained by social norms or personal inhibition is free to self-express in ways not otherwise possible (Abel & Buckley, 1977).

By most definitions graffiti is a criminal act that usually results in the defacing of public or private property visible to the public (Grant, 1996; Lachmann, 1988; Rudin, 1996). Moreover, the debate over whether graffiti should be considered art or vandalism is ongoing (Abel & Buckley, 1977; Ferrell, 1993a, 1993b, 1995; Raymond 1989; Rudin, 1996). Some argue that the presence of graffiti is a sign of urban decay (Black, 1997; Grant, 1996, Kriegel, 1993; Rudin, 1996). In an effort to reverse this trend, some communities have sanctioned graffiti by hiring graffitists to create public murals (Castleman, 1982; Romo, 1992).

Graffiti is often categorized as private or public (Abel & Buckley, 1977; Melhorn & Romig, 1985). Private graffiti is associated with latrinalia, or bathroom graffiti. It reflects the attitudes of the community in which it is found (Abel & Buckley, 1997; Melhorn & Romig. 1985). Moreover, its content appears to reflect cultural and gender differences (Melhorn & Romig, 1980; Otta, 1993; Otta, Santana, Lafraia, Hoshino, Teixeira, & Vallochi, 1996).

Public graffiti is associated with urban areas and usually labeled as the work of lower socioeconomic status, inner city youths (Ferrell, 1993a, 1993b, 1995; Grant, 1996; Lachmann, 1988; Melhorn & Romig, 1985). However, Lasley (1995) suggests that this social profile is a stereotype and that today's graffitist can be of any age, sex, race, or socioeconomic status, and that modern works of graffiti are not limited to urban environments. While still rare in small towns and rural areas (Gross & Gross, 1993), the rise of sub-

urban graffiti has become a common theme in more recent literature (Black, 1997; Lasley, 1995).

The study of graffiti and graffiti subcultures is multi-disciplinary. The majority of the literature focuses on the content of graffiti itself, makes cross-cultural comparisons, or focuses on the subcultures and careers of graffitists (Otta et al., 1996). A systematic examination of graffiti associated with communities, but especially rural ones, following a disaster is novel in the literature.

Disaster Literature

Discussion of graffiti in the disaster literature is noticeably absent. To date, we located only one reference to the existence of post-disaster graffiti. In an ethnographic study describing stages of recovery following Hurricane Andrew in southern Florida, Smith and Belgrave (1995) quote one phrase of graffiti with no attempt to discuss its meaning or significance.

Literature on coping and natural disasters or other stress producing experiences focuses on the effects or outcomes of coping (Carver & Scheier, 1994; Smith, 1996). General coping responses are typically categorized as "active" or "avoidant," "emotion-focused," or "problem focused," and research has focused on the efficacy of these coping strategies (Carver & Scheier, 1994; Smith, 1996). The literature does address the use of humor and religion as part of coping processes, but does not discuss specific behaviors, like graffiti, as coping techniques.

Reviewers of the sociological literature on disaster stress the over-abundance of studies on flood prevention and policy (Quarantelli, 1994). Sociologists are urged to fill voids in this literature that overlooks a variety of phenomena associated with disasters including popular culture and disaster. Although Quarantelli (1994) does not specifically address the participation of disaster victims in the activity of graffiti, he argues that sociologists should investigate the rise in other deviance-related activities associated with disasters. This paper contributes to this literature by linking the cultural expression of graffiti and disaster.

The Red River Valley Flood

The upper mid-western United States and Manitoba, Canada experienced one of the harshest winters in their history during the 1996–97 season. With eight blizzards, the last of which caused power outages nearly statewide, North Dakotans and north-western Minnesotans looked forward to spring. Despite perfect thawing conditions, the saturated ground, ice jams, and floating debris set the stage for one of the worst floods in the nation's history in terms of per capita damage and the relocation of people (University of North Dakota Alumni Review, 1997).

The Red River Valley flood 1997 was unlike other floods. First, the river rose very slowly past the flood stage. Although residents of Grand Forks and East Grand Forks and other volunteers spent weeks making and stacking sandbags to raise the level of the dikes, the spring-like weather and warnings about floods that did not occur in previous years contributed to a collective denial that a flood would happen. Second, this flood is unusual in that there was no loss of life directly related to this disaster. Third, the flood ultimately affected every resident of Grand Forks and East Grand Forks and nearly everyone in the city limits was evacuated. Indeed, this was one of the largest mass evacuations of any U.S. city (University of North Dakota Alumni Review, 1997).

After the Flood

Upon their return, residents initially had the problem of meeting basic survival needs. Smith and Belgrave (1995) describe a process of "getting by" and "digging out" after Hurricane Andrew that parallels the events that occurred in Grand Forks and East Grand Forks. In the "getting by" phase, people concentrated on their basic survival needs. After these needs were met, residents began to assess their flood-related losses: losses ranged from entire homes and their contents to the loss of minor personal effects. Eighty percent of the homes in Grand Forks suffered flood damage (*Grand Forks Herald*, 1997); only eight homes in East Grand Forks were spared by the flood (Fee, 1997). Consequently, most residents were forced to "dig out" their basements and remove flood damaged property. In the words of Smith and Belgrave (1995), residents began to "reconstruct the intimate territory of everyday life" (p. 250). At the instruction of city leaders, residents placed this rubbish on the berm, the grassy and sometimes tree-lined area between the sidewalk and the curb, for removal. Rubbish included any items touched by contaminated river water that could not be sanitized or which were otherwise corroded and destroyed. Thus, furniture, large appliances, furnaces, personal items, toys, and building materials were placed on the berm. Automobiles destroyed by flood water were hauled away for disposal from wherever they had floated.

Graffiti first appeared during the digging out phase of the flood, in the days prior to when refuse was cleared from the berm and hauled away in dump trucks. Graffiti tagging major household appliances in Grand Forks and East Grand Forks was sanctioned by city officials in response to rumors of, and for the deterrence of, possible theft and resale of flood damaged goods to unsuspecting buyers. However, graffiti continued to appear—especially on severely damaged homes after the berms had been cleared.

Method

A Procedural Note

In his study of prolonged trauma following the flood in Logan County, West Virginia, Erikson (1976) noted that some situations are simply too pressing to allow for objectivity, at least early on in a research project. He argued that "the traditional methods of sociology do not really equip one to study discrete moments in the flow of human experience" (Erikson, 1976, p. 13). Our study describes the reactions of people during a brief period after a disaster. Our attempts to understand one phenomenon in the Red River Valley following the flood were inextricably linked to our own social situations. We experienced the flood on a personal level and concomitantly thought about the human dimensions of the flood in a sociological manner. Thus, this study is hypernaturalistic because as researchers, we intimately interacted with the context of our data collection. We describe the emotional context of data collection elsewhere (Ender, Hagen, Hagen, Morano-Ender, & Tiemann, 1998).

Qualitative researchers have commented on "messy texts" where the situation and the collection of data allow for vague, difficult, emotionally intense, and subjective perceptions to be chronicled (Marcus, 1994). This speaks to our situation as researchers who were initially connected to the flood emotionally and who are now connected more objectively. On one level, we were victims situated in the affected community who understand what it means to have survived this particular disaster. On another level, we are researchers who visually captured images of the aftermath of others' trauma. We essentially vacillated between the two roles.

Our fieldwork reflects what Adler and Adler (1987) refer to as an opportunistic feature of research and our role as "complete membership researchers." They argue that "rather than neglecting 'at hand' knowledge or expertise, they (opportunistic researchers) should turn familiar situations, timely events, or special expertise into the objects of study" (p. 69). Moreover, they note the potential dangers with opportunistic research in that the conflict between the roles of member and researcher can become "near-schizophrenic in its frenzied multiple focus" (Adler & Adler, 1987, p. 70). As issues emerged where these roles were in direct conflict, the role of recovering disaster victim was considered before the role of researcher. Once we processed the issues that affected us personally as disaster victims, we were able to more easily move into the role of researcher. In doing so, we believe we have reconciled the role conflicts that researchers have noted as social consequences of a disaster (Fritz, 1961).

The Visual Sample

Eventually, the condemned homes and trailers and graffiti on berms would be cleared. Therefore, we made a concerted effort to photograph the graffiti in its context. The data are captured on 148 photos including 50 photos that contain more than one source of graffiti. A total of 290 selections of graffiti represent the overall sample. Two-thirds of the sample comes from Grand Forks, North Dakota and one third from East Grand Forks, Minnesota. Approximately half of the graffiti in the sample appeared on homes and garages, about 30 percent tagged household items, and the remaining 20 percent appeared on sign-boards placed on the berm, in the yard, on the porch, or leaned against a home. Most graffiti were done with spray paint, but some graffiti that appeared on homes was written with mud.

In the Field

On May 27, 1997, approximately five weeks after the flood and during the first weeks evacuated residents returned to Grand Forks and East Grand Forks, we began to comb the city in cars, on foot, and on bicycles. We took color photographs of graffiti on berms and on houses and trailers (two photos were reproduced from a personal video recording). We each started in a location where we knew graffiti existed. Next, we traveled through the streets in search of graffiti. The combination of closed and impassable streets and the presence of clean up crews and heavy machinery made it difficult to be as systematic as we would have liked.

Access to severely damaged neighborhoods was difficult because roads were heavily damaged and access was restricted.[1] We approached these neighborhoods at various times of the day to secure photographs.[2] After rigorously combing the streets of Grand Forks and East Grand Forks for new graffiti for several weeks, we had reached a point of saturation.[3] For confirmation, the research team compared our independently collected data and noted considerable duplication of materials.[4]

Category Construction and Coding Procedures

Although public in form, we consider catastroffiti to be consistent with the characteristics of private graffiti. Therefore, we relied upon the latrinalia literature for guidance as we created categories of catastroffiti (see Abel & Buckley, 1977; Melhorn & Romig, 1985; Otta, 1993; Otta et al., 1996). We began with 19 categories and individually coded each piece of graffiti according to the most dominant theme. When we met to compare and discuss coding, we reached consensus on how each piece of graffiti should he coded. Next, we collapsed these 19 categories into five more useful categories to facilitate analysis and discussion. The final categories are humor, social and political commentary, frustration, drawings, and "other."

Results

Humor

Humor is the dominant theme in catastroffiti. The situations in which it appeared were diverse, but four sub-categories of humor emerged. The subcategories are jocular, sarcastic, satirical, and miscellaneous humor.

Jocular Humor. The jocular humor category refers to graffiti characterized by simple, comical, and light-hearted messages directed at the effects of the flood. This form of graffiti is illustrated by "LOOK MOM I CLEANED MY ROOM." This particular piece of graffiti was painted on a refrigerator that sat on the berm. Another example, "1-800-BIG-MESS," was painted on the picture window in a home that had been almost completely submerged in the flood. "This is what happens when your brain is on flood" was written in large blue letters on the side of a severely damaged home and appears to be a take off on a popular anti-drug slogan from the late 1980s.

Sarcasm. Sarcasm, the second largest subcategory of humor, is typified by both cynical and matter-of-fact sorts of statements. Cynical humor was expressed in many creative ways. "Are we having fun yet? Keep it up!" was painted across a tabletop and "next time the party is at your house," on the side of a severely damaged home are good examples. "Th Th That's all folks," the finale to many Warner Brother's cartoons, appeared on a headboard of a bed, while "sight seer free zone" was on a large piece of peg board propped up against a streetlight. In each case, we interpreted the text and context of the humor to express thinly veiled cynicism.

Satirical Humor. Satire is a form of humor that relies on irony or sarcasm to expose human foibles. It is also used to ridicule or discredit others. Graffiti of a satirical form was often directed at government agencies and their personnel, but it was primarily directed at those involved in flood prediction, prevention, and rebuilding efforts. One example of satirical graffiti was "49 FEET MY ASS!" This message, written with fluorescent orange paint on the side of a house, was hard to miss—especially since it was visible to traffic on the adjacent major thoroughfare. Adding impact to the message was the fact that the damaged house was adjacent to a dike that had been fortified to 52. This message appeared to be directed at city officials and at the National Weather Service as they had assured residents that the Red River would crest at 49 feet. A related example, "Have a seat X 49 feet. Yeah Right," was painted on a recliner that awaited disposal on the berm. A third example jabbed at city officials who said that money that was allocated by voters to build a controversial, multi-purpose events center called the Aurora, could not legally be reallocated for flood recovery efforts. One resident addressed this situation by writing "Free donation 4 the Aurora" on a large piece of plywood on top of a pile of flood-damaged debris.

Miscellaneous Humor. The content of the miscellaneous humor category is disparate. Although humorous, this graffiti did not neatly fit into the other categories and it made up less than one percent of the total number of cases in the humor category. This category contains statements as diverse as "Help us Noah!" on a water heater and "We said a Bud not a flood" on a piece of plywood found leaning against a pile of debris, to "Fuck me floating," a derivation of the slang expression "Fuck me running." The latter example appeared on the side of a severely damaged house and is unique in that someone attempted to censor the expletive by covering it with white paint. Despite their efforts, the expletive was readable because the red paint in which it was written bled through.

Social and Political Commentary

Much of the graffiti represented social and political commentary in relation to one's flood experience. With the exception of "I think the mayor did great," all of the political commentaries had negative messages directly related to the flood. The handful of politically oriented messages were directed at the mayor of Grand Forks, the City Council, the Federal Emergency Management Agency (FEMA), the National Weather Service, and the U.S. Congress. One piece of graffiti located on the berm of a gutted house addressed the Congressional delay in signing a disaster relief appropriations bill. It said: "Hey, Congress! Spend Your Break Here!" Other examples include: "She [the mayor] lied to us" and "PAT OWENS (the mayor) YOU KNEW 53ft," "FUCK YOU CITY councel" [sic], "I SURVIVED the Flood—But FEMA SUNK ME!!!" and "FEMA Housing" (a sign located on a small tool shed).

Those who predicted the river crest were also targeted. For example, "100 year flood MY ASS!" was painted on the corner of one condemned house. Another house bore the inscription "CITY corp NO BRAINS" referring to job performance of the Corp of Engineers and their crest predictions. Another graffitist sarcastically referred to the final river crest and said "So, What was the crest? 60'–70'?"

Social commentary appeared more than three times as often as political commentary. Two-thirds of the social commentary expressed negative sentiments over the loss of security and control. It also expressed residents' anguish. Examples of loss of control and security which appeared on household items included "THE END," "GOODBYE RRV," "WE HAVE NO CONTROL," and "SHOW ME THE POWER." Others wrote about their loss of control on the sides of their homes: "129? Didn't I use to live here?" "This X was my house . . . I think?!?" "Why?" and "UFF-DA" an

upper-Midwest linguistic term with Norwegian roots that is loosely translated as an expression of exasperation, and also the bittersweet "THIS WAS HOME SWEET HOME," all exemplify this theme. Much of this type of graffiti was a public means to express personal anguish. Many people wrote on items on the berm and directly on their homes. Statements such as "FLOODS SUCK," "THIS SUCKS," "DOES THIS SUCK OR WHAT?" and "FLOODS BITE" reveal their discontent.

The remaining one-third of social commentary graffiti had a positive message. Many offered encouragement words and slogans. Examples include: "NEVER GIVE [with an arrow pointing up]," "Don't Worry! Be Happy!" and "WE ARE *BACK*!" Others offered encouragement through the expression of personal philosophies like "You are more than the sum of your possessions" and ". . . with all its shame, drudgery, and broken dreams . . . it is still a beautiful world. . . ."

Frustration

A common emotion with which people who live through natural disasters must cope is frustration. The problem is, of course, where to direct it. One affect of frustration is a raging debate in local newspapers and at town meetings. Others offer their political and social commentary through graffiti. As we previously noted, some people directed their frustration toward the river while others focused on government officials and federal agencies. This graffiti typically expressed the belief that residents were lied to about the magnitude of the flood or they had been mistreated by these organizations.

The majority of the graffiti that we interpreted to express frustration, and occasionally anger, was directed at sightseers and looters. "Sightseer GO AWAY," "We Shoot Looters," "Stay Out," and "Don't Make My Loss Your Gain," were just some of the sentiments expressed about the post-flood situation. Unlike these particular graffitists, others took well-known phrases and modified the meaning slightly to make them relevant to the flood. "We FOUGHT the FLOOD . . . AND THE FLOOD WON" and "RATS" exemplify this trend.

In some cases, manifestations of frustration over the flood's destructive power had a humorous edge. "TOURIST ATTRACTION CENTER" is one example. In other instances, feelings of powerlessness, sadness, and resignation were palpable. "This was home," "My ROOM WAZ HERE," "We Miss You RIVERSIDE [name of a neighborhood]," as well as "SAD," "Angry," "whatever," and "Why?" exemplify these feelings. Perhaps the most poignant message of frustration was spray painted on a sheet of plywood. It said: "We've been dragged through the fire. We bragged about that fire. But suddenly we're tired. Could it be that loss can weigh?"

Drawings

In a departure from the literature, we did not categorize drawings as sexual or non-sexual in nature because only two of the 60 drawings that we documented were sexual in nature. The more logical division for this graffiti was to sort it into symbols and sketches.

Symbols.   Arrows constituted the overwhelming majority of symbols. Arrows either enhanced the nature of a message or they directed the viewer's attention to a particular location. For example, an arrow was included on a sign that said "yard sale." It pointed to a pile of clearly damaged household items placed on the berm for disposal. Other symbols included peace signs, hearts, and the anarchy sign.

Sketches.   Smiling and frowning faces were spray painted on houses and rubbish. Some sketches appeared alone while others accompanied written messages. Moreover, some graffitists took poetic license with the traditional smiley face. For example, one smiley face had buck-teeth and a large nose and one frowning face had steam rising from the top of its head.

A few "other" types of sketches also appeared in the two communities. While crude in their construction, they included depictions of stairs, bricks in a wall, a hand, and male and female genitalia. Interestingly, there were no repeats of any particular sketch in this subcategory of drawings.

Other Types of Graffiti

Other types of graffiti are a broad but salient category. Other graffiti fell into two main categories: city sanctioned graffiti and billboard graffiti.

City Sanctioned Graffiti.   This was the largest subcategory of other graffiti types. City authorities asked residents to use graffiti for two reasons: to stop pilfering and to allay concerns that damaged and potentially dangerous items would be taken from berms and sold to unsuspecting buyers. City sanctioned graffiti appeared most frequently on appliances followed by furniture, building supplies, and on some condemned houses. The text people chose to tag their rubbish included the words "flood," "flood 97" or "flood damaged" and these words surfaced throughout the city.

"Toast," like its companion phrases "contaminated" and "out of order," indicated that an item was damaged or dangerous.[5] Regardless of word choice, the graffiti indicated that an item had been defiled by flood water. Other graffitists indicated that an item was ruined through symbols. Squiggly lines and Xs were used to deface formerly valued property such as furniture and some household appliances and a lone X was visible on the side of a garage.

Billboard Graffiti.   The intention of some graffitists appeared to be the protection of their property from theft. Others used it as a means to communicate with the processions of sightseers in cars and buses who drove though devastated neighborhoods to see the results of the flood. While some simply looked, others videotaped or photographed the homes and the piles of personal items on the berm. This led some residents to use sheets of ply-wood and other large surfaces as billboards. "Not responsible for accidents" served as a threat directed toward perceived gawkers. Two other graffitists had a different intention as they referred to ongoing, but friendly, school rivalries. One addressed the competition between two local high schools. The inscription on their refrigerator door said "GFC [Grand Forks Central] #1 Red River Bites." The other graffitist painted "NDSU

[North Dakota State University] Bookstore" on a plywood board and propped it against a pile of flood-tainted books and magazines.

Billboard communiqués were typically specific and lengthy. In contrast, messages such as "Luv" (washer/dryer). "The End" (washer and dryer), "Stop" (side of house), "Welcome" (cement steps on house), "ND Doc" (refrigerator door), "Hello" (stove top), and "Hot Stuff" (dresser) were terse and sometimes ambiguous.

Discussion and Conclusion

In the Red River Valley, catastroffiti was a method of ephemeral cultural expression. The messages contributed to a community discourse that reflected loss, coping with loss, recovery, and hope. Catastroffiti was a social reaction to the post-flood devastation of Grand Forks and East Grand Forks. Officially tagged flood-damaged property appeared side by side with messages that were consistent with those in the extant graffiti literature (see Abel & Buckley, 1977; Gadsby, 1995; McMenemy & Cornish, 1993; Melhorn & Romig, 1985; Otta, 1993; Otta et al., 1996, Phillips, 1996). Further, catastroffiti proved to be short-lived as both cities began their removal of debris from the berms within two weeks of its initial appearance. Within eight weeks, most evidence of personal loss had vanished from the berms, and catastroffiti on condemned houses was erased with their demolition and removal.

Unlike other unsanctioned graffiti, catastroffiti is not strictly anonymous. The artists' works, we presume, appeared in front of or upon their own property. In addition, there seemed to be an unwritten moral code regarding what constituted acceptable catastroffiti. This explains three documented incidents of the "white-washing" of offensive graffiti. Regardless of the graffitist's motivation, catastroffiti seemed functional. On the one hand, it placated fears about berm looting. As a result, most residents complied with the directive to mark their property appropriately. On the other hand, many residents took tagging contaminated property a step farther by marking their property

with reflective text. Functionally, this extension of sanctioned catastroffiti facilitated a community discourse and allowed residents to express their frustrations, sadness, hopes, and survival. It may also have reaffirmed the community ethos and promoted some form of community solidarity.

In his classic study, Robinson (1966) characterized North Dakotans as having an inferiority complex. More recently, it was argued that North Dakotans do not have a negative mind set as a cultural characteristic, but they do project negativity in response to circumstances beyond their control. For example, North Dakotans distrust outside corporations because they see them as self-serving. Stofferahn (1992) refers to the negative mind set as a "subjective appraisal of an objective condition" (p. 74). The definition of the situation of the flood as an objective reality and responding to it through the emotional spray-can of catastroffiti is consistent with this notion. Yet the saliency of humor in the graffiti suggests a collective, conscientious attempt to be positive in order to cope with the aftermath of disaster. Indeed, evidence is emerging that suggests humor is a useful coping response to situational stress (Hall & Rappe, 1995; Martin, Kuiper, Olinger, & Dance, 1993).

Perhaps North Dakotans are hardier than scholars have thought.

We encourage researchers to document catastroffiti in other communities following a disaster.[6] The general absence of graffiti in Grand Forks and East Grand Forks after the initial outbreak suggests that catastroffiti was a direct social reaction to the flood and its effect on people. The literature on graffiti suggests that this is unusual—new graffiti replaces old graffiti in metropolitan areas (Melhorn & Romig, 1985). We provide some confirmatory evidence to the new literature on graffiti that it remains a medium of expression of discontent with a social situation and is not isolated to urban, youth populations.

These findings suggest that during a disaster, community cohesion and recovery are dependent upon one another and that they are created by many different factors. In this study, residents contributed to the recovery process through the mundane act of tagging damaged property. How-ever, what also occurred was the voicing of emo-tions in a free arena of discourse. As these findings suggest, humor, frustration, social and political commentary, and even drawings reflected resi-dents' sentiments and desires. For the Upper Great Plains, our findings suggest that disaster relief workers should recognize the functional nature of catastroffiti and avoid negative sanctions against it. Regardless of the methods used in future disas-ter research, catastroffiti when present might prove a viable predictor of the community's reaction. Are these findings a cultural anomaly in the disaster lit-erature? We challenge others to document similar cultural forms of expression that capture the senti-ments of a community following a disaster.

NOTES

1. We were sensitive to the fact that personal effects from residents' backstage area were exposed on the front stage—the berm. Like Rathje and Murphy (1992) whose "Garbage Project" focused on disposed of household refuse, we argue that items placed on the berm are abandoned and public. Therefore, it is not an ethical violation to study garbage. Also like Rathje and Murphy (1992), we attempted to protect residents' anonymity by not recording names, addresses, or other personal information in the photograph.

2. Survivors of Hurricane Andrew reported anger to-ward "tourists" who came to view and photograph the devastation. As they put it, "the appearance . . . of empty-handed voyeurs . . . in their automobiles gawking at the misery of others for their own entertainment and continual helicopters were part of the problem" (quoted in Smith and Belgrave, 1995, p. 255). Thus, as re-searchers we felt uncomfortable taking photographs as it further violated the personal space and tragedy of others.

3. The research team discussed, but decided against, interviewing the creators of the catastroffiti. Because we experienced the flood ourselves and had attempted to create some sense of normalcy, we knew that locating and interviewing people would have been intrusive and difficult (many had moved from the area or were living in transitional housing) at this time. Additionally, many residents had already been bombarded by surveys that originated from both public and private agencies. We felt the field was too sociologically contaminated.

4. We could not determine whether the catastroffiti that appeared in Grand Forks was comparable to that which may have appeared in the smaller city of East Grand Forks as most of those berms were cleared before we had access to them. However, we did record the graffiti that appeared on residents' homes in East Grand Forks.

5. "Toast" and a small contingent of other descriptive terms quickly entered the local vernacular or "flood-speak" after the flood (Baker, 1997).

6. Smith and Belgrave (1995) report only one incident of graffiti. "We still need help" (p. 246) appeared on the side of an abandoned tract home two years after Hurri-cane Andrew.

REFERENCES

Abel, E. L., & Buckley, B. E. (1977). *The handwriting on the wall: Toward a sociology and psychology of graffiti*. Westport, CT: Greenwood.

Adler, P. A., & Adler, P. (1987). *Membership roles in field research*. Sage University Paper series on Qual-itative Research Methods (Vol. 2). Newbury, CA: Sage Publications, Inc.

Baker, T. (1997). Floodspeak. *Graduate Grapevine Graduate Student Newsletter, 58*, 4.

Black, T. (1997). The handwriting's on the wall: Cities can win the graffiti war. *American City and County, 112*, 22–25.

Carver, C. S., & Scheier, M. F. (1994). Situational cop-ing and coping dispositions in a stressful transaction. *Journal of Personality and Social Psychology, 66*, 184–199.

Castleman, C. (1982). *Getting up: Subway graffiti in New York*. Cambridge, MA: MIT Press.

Ender, M. G., Hagen, C. A., Hagen, C. O., Jr., Morano-Ender, C. A., & Tiemann, K. A. (1998). Sociologist as rubbernecker: Photographing the aftermath of the Red River Valley Flood of '97. *North Dakota Quar-terly, 65*, 276–285.

Erikson, K. T. (1976). *Everything in its path: Destruc-tion of community at Buffalo Creek*. New York: Simon and Schuster.

Fee, K. (1997). Stauss: EGF recovery moving at good pace. *Grand Forks Herald*, November 2, A16–17.

Ferrell, J. (1993a). [Review of the book *Moscow Graf-fiti: Language and Subculture*]. *Social Justice, 20*, 188–192.

Ferrell, J. (1993b). *Crimes of style: Urban graffiti and the politics of criminality*. Boston: Northeastern Uni-versity Press.

Ferrell, J. (1995). Urban graffiti: Crime, control and resistance. *Youth & Society, 27,* 73–92.

Fritz, C. E. (1961). Disaster. Pp. 651–694 in R. K. Merton & R. A. Nisbet (Eds.), *Contemporary social problems: An introduction to the sociology of deviant behavior and social disorganization.* New York: Harcourt, Brace & World, Inc.

Gadsby, J. (1995). Looking at the writing on the wall: A case review and taxonomy of graffiti texts. http://www.graffiti.org/faq/critical.review.html.

Grand Forks Herald. (1997). 200 Days of recovery: Statistics tell the tale. *Grand Forks Herald,* November 2 (Special Supplement), 10.

Grant, C. M. (1996). Graffiti: Taking a closer look. *The FBI Law Enforcement Bulletin, 65,* 11–15.

Gross, D. D., & Gross, T. D. (1993). Tagging: Changing visual patterns and the rhetorical implications of a new form of graffiti. *A Review of General Semantics, 50,* 150–164.

Hall, M. N., & Rappe, P. T. (1995). Humor and critical incident stress. Pp. 289–294 in L. A. DeSpelder & A. L. Strickland (Eds.), *Readings in death and dying: The path ahead.* Mountain View, CA: Mayfield.

Kriegel, L. (1993). Graffiti: Tunnel notes of a New Yorker. *The American Scholar, 62,* 431–436.

Lachmann, R. (1988). Graffiti as career and ideology. *American Journal of Sociology, 94,* 229–250.

Lasley, J. R. (1995). New writing on the wall: Exploring the middle class writing subculture. *Deviant Behavior: An Interdisciplinary Journal, 16,* 151–167.

Marcus, G. E. (1994). What comes (just) after 'post'?: The case for ethnography. Pp. 563–574 in N. K. Denzin & Y. S. Lincoln (Eds.), *Handbook of Qualitative Research.* Newbury Park, CA: Sage.

Martin, R. A., Kuiper, N. A., Olinger, L. J., & Dance, K. A. (1993). Humor, coping with stress, self-concept, and well-being. *Humor, 6,* 89–104.

McMenemy, P., & Cornish, I. M. (1993). Gender differences in the judged acceptability of graffiti. *Perceptual and Motor Skills, 77,* 622.

Melhorn, J. J., & Romig, R. J. (1985). Rest room graffiti: A descriptive study. *Emporia State Research Studies* (Fall), 29–45.

Merton, R. K. (1967). *On theoretical sociology: Five essays, old and new.* New York: The Free Press.

Otta, E. (1993). Graffiti in the 1990s: A study of inscriptions on restroom walls. *The Journal of Social Psychology, 133,* 589–591.

Otta, E., Santana, P. R., Lafraia, R. M., Hoshino, R. L. Teixeira, R. P., & Vallochi, S. L. (1996). Musa latrinalis: Gender differences in restroom graffiti. *Psychological Reports, 78,* 871.

Phillips, S. A. (1996). Graffiti definition: The dictionary of art. http://graffiti.org/faq/graf.def.html.

Quarantelli, E. (1994). *Draft of a sociological disaster research agenda for the future: Theoretical, methodological and empirical issues.* Unpublished paper presented at the World Congress of Sociology, Germany.

Rathje, W., & Murphy, C. (1992). *Rubbish!: The archeology of garbage.* New York: Harper-Collins.

Raymond, C. (1989). Scholar finds art, social tradition in graffiti that many dismiss as chaotic scribbling. *The Chronicle of Higher Education, 36,* A4–A6.

Reisner, R., & Wechsler, L. (1974). *Encyclopedia of graffiti.* New York: MacMillan Publishing Company, Inc.

Robinson, E. B. (1966). *History of North Dakota.* Lincoln, NE: University of Nebraska Press.

Romo, R. (1992). Borderland murals: Chicano artifacts in transition. *Aztlan, 21,* 125–154.

Rudin, S. (1996). Art crimes. http://www.wm.edu/SO/JUMP/spring96/graffiti.html.

Smith, B. W. (1996). Coping as a predictor of outcomes following the 1993 Midwest flood. *Journal of Social Behavior and Personality, 11,* 225–239.

Smith, K. J., & Belgrave, L. L. (1995). The reconstruction of everyday life: Experiencing Hurricane Andrew. *Journal of Contemporary Ethnography, 24,* 224–269.

Stofferahn, C. W. (1992). Do rural North Dakotans have a negative mind set? *Great Plains Sociologist, 5,* 68–76.

University of North Dakota Alumni Review. (1997). Flood facts. *University of North Dakota Alumni Review,* June, 3.

Carol A. Hagen was finishing up her master's degree in sociology at the University of North Dakota in Grand Forks during the early stages of this research project. Her husband and coauthor, Clifford Hagen, was finishing up his bachelor's degree in criminal justice. As a result of the flood, they lost their home and lived for three months in a small camping trailer before moving to Kentucky to continue their formal educations. Currently, Carol is working on her doctoral dissertation through the University of

Kentucky and is a research analyst for the Substance Abuse Research Group at Westat Incorporated in Rockville, Maryland. Her research interests include substance abuse, domestic violence, juvenile delinquency, disaster research, and qualitative research methods.

Morten G. Ender is currently the Sociology Director and an associate professor of sociology in the Department of Behavioral Sciences and Leadership at the United States Military Academy, West Point. He recently published the book *Military Brats and Other Global Nomads: Growing Up in Organization Families* (Praeger Publications, 2002). His next book will feature the role of sociology at military academies around the world. He is currently studying representations of military children in American cinema. He was formerly an assistant professor of sociology and peace studies at the University of North Dakota, where he participated in this research project.

Kathleen A. Tiemann is professor of sociology at the University of North Dakota. Her areas of specialization are gender and sexualities, research methods, social problems, and teaching sociology. Recent publications include two books of readings for undergraduate classes in introductory sociology and social problems. Her current research includes a study of rural lesbians' lives and an examination of graduate departments of sociology and their chairpersons.

Clifford O. Hagen, Jr., is a Juvenile Electronic Incarceration Program Probation Officer for the county of Spotsylvania in Virginia. He is also a part-time adjunct instructor at Germanna Community College where he teaches criminal justice. Clifford was an undergraduate at the University of North Dakota at the beginning stages of this research project. He graduated from the university with a bachelor's degree in criminal justice, and he went on to earn a master's degree in criminal justice from Eastern Kentucky University. Hagen's research interests include deviant subcultures, disaster research, juvenile justice, and juvenile gangs.

An interview with . . .

Carol Hagen

How did you become involved in this research?

After the flood, we started seeing the graffiti popping up all over and we started thinking "Wow! This is data!" We got very excited—going out at all hours, snapping pictures, trying not to be seen. We weren't sure what we were going to do with it at first, but we were both interested in deviance and we had never read anything about this, so we knew it was worth studying. At first it was just me and my husband. But we began thinking that, since we had never published anything, we should get someone on board who had. Mort [Ender] had actually been one of my professors, and I was acquainted with Kathy [Tiemann], though I had never actually been her student. I mentioned this to Mort, who told me that he and Kathy had also been talking about the graffiti. The next thing we knew, the four of us were meeting together. We agreed that we saw four papers that could come out of our work, and we each agreed to take the lead on one of them. Mine was the first, because they credited me with the initial idea. The process was unusual and challenging because we were all having to deal with the after effects of the flood, so sometimes we couldn't meet because we were busy trying to meet our immediate needs. It was not your normal, everyday research project. Plus, I was trying to juggle finishing my master's thesis at the same time.

Was every one of you equally affected by the flood?

No, my husband and I were probably affected the most. We had a mobile home on campus, and we were sandbagging a dike right near our home only to hear someone say "Oh, my gosh, I'm glad that's not my trailer!" and we saw this huge river of water coming around this trailer; we looked up and it was ours. We ended up losing our trailer, which was destroyed. We were able to save some of our clothes, after countless days at the Laundromat and disinfectant, but we lost almost all our furniture and anything that absorbed moisture.

You mention in the paper the challenge of vacillating between the roles of flood victim and researcher. Were there ways that being a victim of the flood affected your ability to be objective and analytical?

We were not able to be completely objective. In the paper we write about the "complete membership role;" we were part of the population, the victims. What we did was to use our experience to inform our research. For example, as we collected data, we were very careful not to offend anyone or invade anyone's privacy. Everyone was very upset about people who would come in from outside of Grand Forks to cruise and gawk, and we wanted to make sure that people were not further victimized by our data collecting. So we tried to take into account how we knew we would feel. We did talk openly with people and ask for their help, saying things like "Hey, we're really interested in this; do you know if there is any other graffiti?" It became a game among our friends and colleagues: "Oh, did you see the one over on Sixth Street? The one about the. . . ." "Yeah, yeah, got that one." "How about the one on such and such a street?" So we shared the excitement of it among our network of friends. And some people even gave us some photos. As I mentioned before, our two roles also meant that we couldn't meet consistently because we had to juggle the research with dealing with every day survival. So it was definitely not the perfect research environment.

Tell me more about how you collected your data.

We tried to be as systematic as we could in gathering our data. We would go up and down streets that had roadblocks; we'd hear of graffiti and we'd go down that street and it had been removed. So, we had to take advantage of what was there. I think we ended up getting the majority of the graffiti that appeared in Grand Forks. In East Grand Forks, we did not get as much. By the time we discovered that there was lots of graffiti in East Grand Forks, they had already started clearing a lot. This wasn't really a problem because even though Grand Forks and East Grand Forks are in two different states, the cultures are very similar and we didn't see any difference in the graffiti in those two cities.

Returning to the idea of not wanting to be invasive or to victimize the victims again: Is there anything else you did to avoid that?

When we took photographs, we tried not to include addresses, street signs, anything that would make it obvious whose house it was. Also, when we saw something that we said was "really good data," we would go at early hours of the morning so people wouldn't see us taking photographs. At one point, Mort actually went out with his one-year-old son on the back of his bike instead of using a car. We took walks instead of using cars to get photos when we could. We tried hard to be nonintrusive because most people were busy cleaning out their houses and it was a really stressful time.

What made you focus on graffiti? Did you take any other approaches or collect other kinds of data pertaining to the flood?

My husband is working right now on a paper about the criminal activity that occurred after the flood. We did another article called "Sociologists as Rubberneckers," which is an essay that describes the methods that we used. We also have an article that is coming out on the commodification associated with the flood—the production and sale of mugs, t-shirts, and so on. That is going to be in an edited volume about disaster research.

Were there unexpected events, problems, or developments that you had to deal with, and how did you deal with them?

I think the one thing we didn't quite anticipate was that when they started cleaning up, we became a bit frantic about trying to get everywhere so that we didn't miss any of the graffiti before it was cleaned up. We didn't want to miss anything. Also, getting access was difficult. We weren't expecting that streets would be completely closed. Another problem was the sightseer issue. We didn't want to give the appearance of being sightseers. We actually walked down streets when we couldn't drive down them. We also engaged our friends and family. If they knew anything or if something had been taken down and they had a snapshot or knew what it had said, we went ahead and wrote it down. At one point my father had a video camera and went surreptitiously up and down the street filming some graffiti.

Now I'd like to ask you about collaboration—what it was like to work with three other people on this project?

Well, it was really exciting to have everyone so excited about it. Because the flood did have an impact on all of us, it was nice to work with people who had some of the same emotions that we were going through. We worked together as a team to work through some of those. The same was true for ethical issues. For example, we debated for a long time about whether we should even publish a picture. Is that a violation of the person's privacy? Mort was familiar with the research on garbage, where one of the authors argues that once something is put out on the berm, it is public. We thought long and hard about this. It was good to have the team to bounce ideas off and to be so motivated, because it did affect us all directly.

What about the writing?

It was difficult in some sense. My husband and I collaborate really well together and so where his strengths are, my weaknesses are and vice versa. We assigned different sections of the paper, and when Mort and Kathy handed theirs in, I thought "They're not thinking the way we are." So we had to think about how to work in their ideas. At one point Mort said "When we get to the end, if it looks like one person wrote it, we will have accomplished what we set out to do." My job was to blend it together.

What do you see as the main contributions and implications of your findings?

I tend to think in terms of policy, and I think government agencies could learn from looking at this graffiti because it provides insight into the pulse of the community. So often when government agencies come into housing disasters, they don't consider the community and the ethos of the community. If they listen to the discourse of the graffiti, they could learn a lot about the community—how it is coping with disaster and what is needed for recovery. This can be of great value for agencies that come in to help communities after disasters. For example, the people from FEMA [the Federal Emergency Management Agency] don't always recognize the red tape that people have to deal with and how hard that is when they are under tremendous stress. I would hope that they could learn from the graffiti.

What was the most frustrating or difficult aspect of the research?

For me, the most frustrating part was not being able to capture all the graffiti. I wanted to be able to get everything on film, but they were being removed constantly. It was a losing battle; we couldn't capture everything. I didn't find a whole lot frustrating. It was more a challenge to overcome.

What was most satisfying?

To realize that we had filled a huge gap in the literature. It is exciting to see others citing us. I had people emailing me from Norway to talk to me about the article; we were cited in a paper in Australia. I also asked my coauthors some of these questions and Kathy said that the most satisfying thing for her was working with a highly motivated team. She felt that giving back to the community and making a contribution to the literature were also important.

Is there anything you would do differently if you were to do it again?

I would like to get out into the field faster. To be honest, if I did this again, I would probably sneak into the city before I should have. I would have lost more sleep walking the streets. I probably would have started in East Grand Forks if I'd known they were going to clear that first. But because we were going through so much ourselves because of the flood, we couldn't plan ahead. Maybe if we'd had a city map and marked out the streets . . . but as it was, the graffiti came and went.

Are there any important lessons from your experience that would be useful to share with students?

The main thing is that life can provide wonderful opportunities for research. Take advantage of the situation. If you see some exciting data, don't let it pass you by. Sometimes opportunities just present themselves and you don't have time to sit down and lay out a carefully thought out research design; you have to go with your gut. You have to go with what you have learned, trust your instincts, do the best you can to be as systematic as you can, but realize that sometimes you may be part of your research and to just acknowledge that and move on. You can learn and you can contribute when you are part of your research . . . it was a lot of fun. Now I have a secret desire to go and chase disasters. I don't think we could make a living doing that . . . but it would be fun!

Questions to Think About

1. Describe the process by which Hagen and her colleagues created coding categories for their data. Do their final five categories make sense to you based on what you know about their observations? Why or why not?
2. What do the authors mean by "catastroffiti"? What is the rationale for their inventing that word? What do they suggest are important implications or contributions of their research?

3. What are some of the distinct problems that Hagen and her colleagues faced in collecting data? Do you detect any possible sources of bias in their sample? Explain.

4. Explain what the authors mean when they describe their study as "hyper-naturalistic" and themselves as "complete membership researchers." Discuss the implications for issues of objectivity in disaster research.

5. Think of other accretion measures, including some on your campus, that have the potential to provide useful sociological insights. Design a study aimed at collecting and analyzing those data.

Capital Punishment and Deterrence

Examining the Effect of Executions on Murder in Texas

Jon Sorensen, Robert Wrinkle, Victoria Brewer, and James Marquart

This study tested the deterrence hypothesis in Texas, the most active execution jurisdiction during the modern era. Using monthly observations during 1984 through 1997, both the general relationship between executions and murder rates and the specific relationship between executions and felony murder rates were examined. An initial bivariate relationship between executions and murder rates proved to be spurious when appropriate control variables were included in regression models. Within a context so ideally suited for finding any potential deterrent effects, this study confirmed the results of previous ones that failed to find any evidence of deterrence resulting from capital punishment.

The dominant approach to determining the relationship between deterrence and the death penalty involves comparing the rate of homicide or some subset of homicide and either the legal status of the death penalty or the performance of actual executions within or across particular jurisdictions. The deterrence hypothesis is supported when lower homicide rates are found within time periods or jurisdictions where the death penalty has been available or in use. If homicide rates are higher in the presence of capital punishment, the alternative, or "brutalization hypothesis," is supported (Bowers and Pierce 1980). The third possible outcome is that the death penalty is found to have no influence on homicide rates.

Empirical studies of deterrence and capital punishment are best classified by their research designs. Cross-sectional designs compare homicide rates across jurisdictions. The earliest deterrence studies of this kind simply compared rates of homicide in retentionist states that have statutory provisions for the death penalty to the rates in abolitionist states without such provisions. Findings showed that retentionist states typically experienced higher rates of homicide than did abolitionist jurisdictions (Sutherland 1925). However, examination of geographical, social, and economic dissimilarities between abolitionist and retentionist states suggested that factors other than the death penalty could have influenced homicide rates.

Scholars then began making comparisons that are more specific between neighboring states, which were presumed to be comparable on such factors. These studies failed to support the deterrence hypothesis, finding that retentionist states most often experienced higher rates of homicide than did contiguous abolitionist states (Schuessler 1952; Sellin 1967). A new generation of cross-sectional studies has employed multiple regression analyses to predict the rate of homicide across jurisdictions while controlling for extraneous variables (Forst 1977; Passell 1975) and has consistently found executions to have no effect on murder rates (Cheatwood 1993; Peterson and Bailey 1988).

Longitudinal designs are used to study the influence of the death penalty in a single jurisdiction over time. The earliest of these studies examined homicide rates in jurisdictions before and after a legislative change in the legal status of the death penalty that either abolished or reimplemented capital punishment. The deterrence hypothesis would be supported if states experienced lower rates of homicide during retentionist periods and higher rates of homicide during abolitionist periods. These studies failed to support the deterrence hypothesis (Bedau 1967; Sellin 1967) because they found inconsistent changes in murder rates after legislative enactments.

More recently, the advent of sophisticated statistical techniques has influenced the methodology used in testing the deterrence hypothesis. Times series analysis, introduced by economist Isaac Ehrlich in 1975, has proven to be a superior means of testing the deterrent effect of the death penalty over time. Time series analyses typically concentrate on the effect of actual executions and enable the researcher to simultaneously control for the influence of alternative explanatory variables. In his initial study, Ehrlich claimed that executions carried out during 1933 through 1969 had resulted in a significant reduction in the number of homocides occurring throughout the United States. However, reanalyses of his work failed to find support for the deterrence hypothesis; instead, researchers concluded that the reduction in homicides observed by Ehrlich was an artifact of measurement error that resulted from inappropriate design specifications and faulty statistical analysis (Baldus and Cole 1975; Bowers and Pierce, 1975; Klein, Forst, and Filatov 1978). Recent time series analyses have confirmed the findings of Ehrlich's critics; they have failed to find evidence of a deterrent effect (Bailey 1983; Cochran, Chamlin, and Seth 1994; Decker and Kohfeld 1984).

Another recent advance in methodology has been to limit analyses to only those types of murder likely to be deterred by capital punishment. Because only certain instances of murder can result in the death penalty, many researchers have disaggregated the universe of homicides to limit the dependent variable to those that have death as a possible sentence. For example, Bailey and Peterson (1987) found that the likelihood of receiving a death sentence was not related to the killing of police officers in the United States during 1973 through 1984. The findings supported those of earlier studies that have failed to find a relationship between capital punishment and police killing (Cardarelli 1968; Sellin 1980). One limitation of these studies was that the researchers were unable to consider the certainty of punishment because very few executions had been carried out during that period.

In a later study that included a measure of the certainty of punishment, Peterson and Bailey (1991) analyzed the relationship between actual executions and the monthly rates of felony murder throughout the United States from 1976 through 1987. The researchers found no consistent relationship between the number of executions, the level of television publicity of these executions, and the rate of felony murder. A study following Oklahoma's return to capital punishment disaggregated homicides into felony murders and murders involving strangers (Cochran et al. 1994). Using an interrupted time-series design, Cochran and colleagues found no change in the rate of felony homicides over the 68 weeks following this highly publicized execution, but observed an increase in the rate of stranger homicides. This brutalization effect was recorded in another study that found an increase in several types of homicide in metropolitan areas after Arizona's first execution in 29 years (Thompson 1997).

After thoroughly reviewing the empirical literature, Peterson and Bailey (1998) concluded that the lack of evidence for any deterrent effect of capital punishment was incontrovertible. According to them, no credible empirical studies had ever been able to demonstrate that the severity, certainty, or celerity of capital punishment reduced the rate of homicide. However, they did envision situations that might present unique opportunities to engage the deterrence hypothesis.

One such opportunity presented itself in Texas in recent years. By far the most active death penalty state, Texas has accounted for more than a third of all executions in the United States since the reimplementation of capital punishment in the years following *Furman v. Georgia* (1972). In 1997 alone, Texas executed a record number of 37 capital murderers, accounting for half of the 74 U.S. executions in that year. Texas has provided an ideal natural experiment to engage the deterrence hypothesis.

One study of the effect of capital punishment on homicide rates in Texas from 1933 through 1980 found no support for the deterrence hypothesis (Decker and Kohfeld 1990). Although this study did not include the effects of any post-Furman executions in Texas, an update of their research extended the period studied through 1986. Decker and Kohfeld then found that executions were actually followed by an increase in homicide rates, supporting the brutalization hypothesis. Their studies, however, included a limited number of control variables, an aggregate measure of homicide, and the use of years the unit of analysis. Their updated study captured few of the executions that were to occur in the post-Furman era. The study reported here advances the work of Decker and Kohfeld by examining the deterrence hypothesis in Texas from 1984 through 1997, capturing the most active period of executions in a jurisdiction during the post-Furman period. It also simultaneously incorporates the methodological strengths of recent studies to provide one of the most compelling tests of the deterrence hypothesis completed thus far.

Data and Methods

To examine the deterrence hypothesis during the modern era, data that spanned the years from 1984 through 1997 were collected from official sources. The year 1984 was chosen as the beginning of the data collection period because of the availability of specific data on homicides and the onset of executions.[1] Because no executions took place until December 1982, the period before the onset of executions was eliminated from our analyses due to a lack of variance in the independent variable. Data collection was further limited as a result of the Houston Police Department's failure to report information on homicides in 1983 for inclusion in the *Supplemental Homicide Reports* (SHR).[2] Estimating the murder rate for 1983 would, to some unknown degree, bias measures of the deterrent effect of the lone execution in December 1982, particularly because no further executions were carried out until March 1984.[3] Because of these potential sources of bias, data collection began with the year 1984.

The number of executions served as the independent variable. The number of executions was tabulated from ledgers provided by the Texas Department of Criminal Justice—Institutional Division. The dependent variables included rates of murder and rates of felony murder. Information on the number of murders was collected from the Texas Department of Public Safety—Uniform Crime Reporting Division. The murder rate was based on the number of murders and nonnegligent manslaughters occurring in Texas during the period studied. Excluded from this category were negligent manslaughters, accidental homicides, justifiable homicides committed by citizens and police officers, and executions performed by the state. Murders involving burglary, robbery, or sexual assault were coded as felony murders.[4]

Information on control variables that have most often been found to be related to homicide rates in previous studies was also collected. Information related to homicide in general, including the percentage of the state population living in metropolitan areas, the percentage of the population aged 18 through 34, and the unemployment rate, were culled from the *Statistical Abstracts of the United States* (see Land, McCall, and Cohen 1990; Peterson and Bailey 1991). The number of physicians per 100,000 residents was also coded from the *Statistical Abstracts of the United States* and is included as a proxy for the availability of emergency services, which could prevent an aggravated assault from turning deadly. Other variables available in the *Statistical Abstracts of the United States* that are typically included in homicide studies are the percentage of Blacks and the percentage of divorced individuals. They were excluded from this study because both were constant over the time period studied. Furthermore, these variables were not significant predictors of homicide rates in a recent deterrence study (Peterson and Bailey 1991).

Additional information was collected from alternate sources. The percentage of murders resulting in convictions was collected from the *Annual Reports of the Texas Judicial Council* as an additional measure of the certainty of punishment. The rate of incarceration per 100,000 in the state was gathered from the Bureau of Justice Statistics. The incarceration rate was included to control for possible incapacitation effects resulting from a vast increase in Texas's prison population during the time period studied. Information on the percentage of Texas residents who are on Aid to Families with Dependent Children (AFDC) was gathered from the Texas Department of Human Resources. The direction of its expected relationships to homicide is not specified herein. Although a direct relationship between welfare and homicide rates is typically expected, a recent study found that is an indicator of available resources that act to mitigate the harshness of poverty, thereby decreasing homicide rates (DeFronzo 1997).

Control variables were also calculated from the SHR data. The percentage of homicides resulting from gunshots was included as a proxy for the availability of firearms. Temporal variables were included to account for surges and lulls in the homicide rate. A high- and low-season variable specified months that were found to be significantly higher or lower in general homicide rates. High season included the months of July and August, whereas low season included only the month of February. Because the state experienced a record number of executions in 1997, an indicator of that year was also

included as a control variable. Lagged-execution variables, T_1 to T_3, were also calculated.

Following Chamlin, Grasmick, Bursik, and Cochran (1992), the unit of analysis is the month. Although Chamlin and colleagues did not find significant macro-level deterrent effects when their data were aggregated at longer time intervals, they did find deterrent effects when lagging data in shorter temporal aggregations. A month was the shortest time interval available for which information about the dependent variables was recorded. Accordingly, although we aggregated the number of executions by month, control variables were typically observed on a yearly basis; thus, monthly figures were estimated using linear interpolation. These estimation procedures were appropriate because these variables were treated only as control variables, and not as alternative explanatory variables (Peterson and Bailey 1991).

Analysis and Findings

Figure 1 provides an overview of execution and murder rates during the time period encompassed

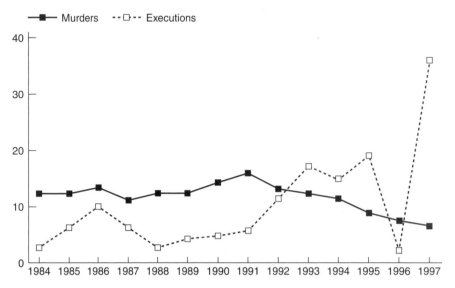

Figure 1   **Murders and Executions in Texas**

Note: This graph shows the murder rate per population of 100,000 and the number of executions per year.

by the study. This figure illustrates the episodic nature of executions. After the first execution, which was that of Charlie Brooks, was carried out in December 1982 (not included in Figure 1), the next one did not take place until James Autry was executed in March 1984. A small wave of executions, which peaked at 10 in 1986, followed. A slump in executions then occurred, with an average of four per year being carried out during 1988 through 1991. The ascendance of executions in 1992 signaled the beginning of a more substantial wave of executions, with an average of 15.5 executions per year during 1992 through 1995.

A legal challenge to Texas's procedures for speeding up the appellate processing of capital cases resulted in a moratorium on executions. With the exception of the voluntary execution of Joe Gonzalez in September 1996, executions were halted to await a decision of the Texas Court of Criminal Appeals on the legality of the new procedures. Executions resumed in February 1997, after the court's pronouncement that the expedited appellate procedures were constitutional. The next wave of executions in Texas would be of historical significance. In dispatching 37 backlogged cases, Texas reached a new record for the number of executions carried out in the state during a single year.

The rate of murder in the state from 1984 through 1991 showed no discernible trend in relation to the execution rate. Although there was a slight decrease in murder rates in 1987 through 1989 after the execution wave of the mid-1980s that could be attributed to a deterrent effect, the homicide rate only began to increase in 1990 and 1991, which was after a 2-year lull in executions during the late 1980s. Although the increase could be attributed to the earlier lull in executions and hence support the deterrence hypothesis, the considerable lag in its increase would suggest that any deterrent effect, or lack thereof, occurred only after a considerable time and is of limited significance.

The greatest amount of support for the deterrence hypothesis is found when the decrease in murder rates is paired with the increase in executions during the 1990s. During the execution wave of the 1990s, the murder rate declined substantially in the state. In the same year that the state reached a historical high in executions, the murder rate fell below what was experienced in decades. Although this seems to provide a strong support for the deterrence hypothesis, the downward trend in homicide rates does not appear to be disturbed by the moratorium on executions in 1996, as the deterrence hypothesis would predict; instead, the downward trend continued. Although a bivariate regression model (not reported in tabular form) produced a significant equation, with executions explaining 7 percent of the variance in murder rates ($b = -.046$; $t = -3.640$; $p < .001$), the estimates were not reliable due to a high degree of serial correlation (Durbin-Watson = .558). Furthermore, murder rates have been declining throughout the United States during this same period, which suggests that factors unrelated to executions were responsible for this pattern.

To test for the influence of other causal factors, control variables were included along with executions and used to predict general murder rates and felony murder rates across the monthly series of data from 1984 through 1997. In the first model, the general murder rates were regressed on executions and the control variables. An analysis of residuals from a preliminary ordinary least squares (OLS) regression model that was used to predict murder rates indicated possible heteroscedasticity. In addition, serial autocorrelation found in the original OLS equation (Durbin-Watson = 1.594) suggested the need for some type of correction. The equation was recalculated using the Newey-West variance estimator, which was specifically designed to correct for these violations of OLS assumptions (Newey and West 1987; StataCorp 1997). Because the Durbin-Watson test indicated problematic levels of autocorrelation up to the third lag, the model presented in Table 1 included Newey-West variance estimates based on a model with three lags.

As shown by the coefficients presented in Table 1, the number of executions was not related to murder rates over the 14-year period that was studied. Control variables positively related to

TABLE 1 *Newey-West Regression Model Predicting General Murder Rates*

VARIABLE	ß	SE ß	*t*-VALUE
Number of executions	.0066	.0061	1.073
Percentage in metropolitan area	.2166***	.0566	3.828
Percentage aged 18 to 34	.1989***	.0470	4.232
Unemployment rate	.0369	.0315	1.171
Physician rate	−.0013	.0110	−.122
Conviction rate	.0192*	.0093	2.068
Incarceration rate	.0001	.0004	.246
Percentage on AFDC	−.0419	.0596	−.702
Percentage of homicides involving guns	.0016	.0026	.617
High season	.1285***	.0323	3.983
Low season	−.1151***	.0253	−4.549
Year 1997	−.0176	.0603	−.292

Note: R^2 = .750. AFDC = Aid to Families with Dependent Children.

*$p < .05$ (one tailed).   ***$p < .001$ (one tailed).

murder rates included the percentage of the population in metropolitan areas, the percentage of the population age 18 to 34, the murder conviction rate, and the high season. The low season, February, was the only variable with a significant negative relation to murder rates. Inclusion of these variables produced a high degree of fit to the data with an overall R^2 of .75.

The model presented in Table 2 limits the dependent variable to felony murders. Because the Durbin-Watson statistic did not indicate a high degree of autocorrelation and because the residuals were more normally distributed, a simple OLS regression model was employed. Because models that were run with lags, T_1 to T_3, showed no difference in findings, only the nonlagged model is presented below.

Just as in the model that predicted murder rates in general, the rate of felony murder was not related to the number of executions. The same variables found to be significantly related to murder rates in general were again found to be significant predictors of felony murder rates. The percentage of the population in metropolitan areas, the percentage of

the population age 18 to 34, the murder conviction rate, and the high season were positively related to felony murder rate, whereas the low season was negatively related. One additional variable having a significant positive coefficient in the felony murder model was the unemployment rate.

Conclusions

This study found that recent evidence from the most active execution state in the nation lent no support to the deterrence hypothesis. The number of executions did not appear to influence either the rate of murder in general or the rate of felony murder in particular. At the same time, no support was found for the brutalization hypothesis. Executions did not reduce murder rates; they also did not have the opposite effect of increasing murder rates. The inability to reject the null hypothesis supports findings from the vast majority of studies on deterrence and capital punishment (Peterson and Bailey 1998). From the data presented, it appears that other factors are responsible for the variations and trends in murder rates.

Multiple Regression

Multiple regression is a statistical test to help researchers measure the simultaneous influence of two or more independent variables on a dependent variable. Because all forms of social life, including human attitudes and behaviors, are shaped by many factors, multiple regression helps us to determine the total influence of two or more factors. Multiple regression uses variables that are measured at the ratio level, on a numerical scale with zero meaning none. There are two dependent variables examined in this article: murder rates (Table 1) and felony murder rates (that is, murders involving burglary, robbery, or sexual assault) (Table 2). The authors are primarily interested in determining the effect of the number of executions on these rates in Texas. They include in their analysis other potentially influential independent variables, such as the percentage of the population between the ages of 18 and 34 and the unemployment rate.

Table 1 focuses on general murder rates. All of the tested independent variables are listed in the far left column. The table tells us several things about the influence of these variables on general murder rates, but we will focus on just three items. First, the second column is headed by a ß, for beta. The coefficients in this column tell us how much influence each of the variables individually has on the dependent variable. A minus sign means the variables are inversely related (that is, as one goes up, the other goes down). The highest absolute number (that is, ignoring the + or – sign) in this column identifies the independent variable that has the largest influence on general murder rate. The .2166 value of beta for percentage of the population in a metropolitan area means that this has the largest influence. It is positively related to the general murder rate. It can be interpreted that for every 1 percent increase in the percentage of people living in the metropolitan area, the general murder rate increases by .2166 murders per 100,000 people. The lowest absolute number in this column is .0001 for incarceration rate. It means for every one unit increase in the incarceration rate, the general murder rate increases by .0001 (that is, almost no effect whatsoever). Notice that the beta value for number of executions is just .0066, meaning that the general murder rate changes hardly at all as the number of executions increases.

The final column reports actual *t*-values. Higher numbers in this column mean that it is more likely that the relationship between that independent variable and the general murder rate really exists. This increases our ability to make generalizations. For example, the highest absolute *t*-value is −4.549 for low season (defined as February). The number of asterisks immediately to the right of the beta values tells us how sure we are that a relationship between that variable and general murder rate actually exists. One asterisk indicates more than 95 percent probability, two asterisks indicate more than 99 percent probability, and three asterisks indicate more than 99.9 percent probability. By convention, we insist on having at least 95 percent probability before concluding that a relationship really exists. We have more than 99.9 percent probability for four variables, including the negative value for low season, meaning that the general murder rate is much lower in February than in other months. However, the data do not allow us to conclude that the number of executions influences the general murder rate.

Finally, R^2 (reported at the bottom of the table below the line), roughly speaking, tells us how much influence all of these variables together have on the general murder rate. Its possible range is 0 to 1.0. In this case, the value is .750, which means that these variables explain 75 percent of the general murder rate. Thus, these variables taken together explain a substantial portion of differences in the general murder rate. We must take all of these results (ß, *t*-value, R^2) into account when assessing the impact these independent variables have on the general murder rate. The results will help us to determine which factors should be included in future studies on general murder rates.

Table 2 should be interpreted in the same manner. Which independent variable has the largest influence on felony murder rate? For which independent variable do we have the most confidence that it really relates to felony murder rate? How much of the differences in felony murder rates do these variables together explain?

TABLE 2   *OLS Regression Model Predicting Felony Murder Rates*

VARIABLE	ß	SE ß	t-VALUE
Number of executions	−.0012	.0023	−.508
Percentage in metropolitan area	.0381**	.0135	2.815
Percentage aged 18 to 34	.0251*	.0131	1.916
Unemployment rate	.0153*	.0071	2.151
Physician rate	−.0001	.0024	−.060
Conviction rate	.0057*	.0028	2.028
Incarceration rate	.0000	.0001	.176
Percentage on AFDC	−.0069	.0177	−.391
Percentage of homicides involving guns	−.0004	.0006	−.635
High season	.0240***	.0069	3.503
Low season	−.0162*	.0093	−1.746
Year 1997	.0226	.0230	.982

Note: $R^2 = .360***$; Durbin-Watson = 1.765. AFDC = Aid to Families with Dependent Children.

*$p < .05$ (one tailed).   **$p < .01$ (one tailed).   ***$p < .001$ (one tailed).

Although appropriate methodology and statistics were employed in the analysis, a number of criticisms could be raised concerning our failure to find evidence of a deterrent effect. As noted elsewhere, using the SHR to measure dependent variables presents problems of reliability and validity (Maxfield 1989). Missing data are particularly troubling when data are disaggregated to calculate felony murder rates (Peterson and Bailey 1991). Cases that are missing data on the circumstances surrounding a homicide in the SHR are likely to turn into felony murders when their circumstances are finally uncovered (Riedel, Zahn, and Mock 1985). Furthermore, it maybe that the deterrent effects of executions on potential offenders can never be adequately ascertained (Van den Haag 1975), because measuring crimes that did occur is only a proxy for how many that were prevented. We also concede that the findings are limited to the sampled time period and the jurisdiction studied.

Considering these limitations, any research that makes a claim concerning the deterrence hypothesis should be treated with caution. However, because we confirmed the findings of previous studies and because the Texas context was so uniquely suited for finding any potential deterrent effects, there is little reason to question the findings.

Once this argument is accepted, several implications can arise. Some may infer, for example, that these results suggest the repeal of the death penalty because it fails to serve the penological function that is so often offered in its defense. Others would argue that various other goals must also be taken into consideration before making this determination, such as whether the public supports its use, whether it serves the goals of retribution, whether it saves money over life imprisonment, whether it serves to provide justice to the families of victims, and whether it serves the interests of the criminal justice system in general. However, these justifications have also been challenged by research (Acker, Bohm, and Lanier 1998; Bedau 1997). Along with the steady stream of consistent findings on the failure of capital punishment in all of these areas, this study cannot help but support the abolitionist argument.

NOTES

1. Detailed information on homicides, a necessity in disaggregating felony murders from more general ones, has been routinely kept by the state since 1976 in the *Supplemental Homicide Reports*.

2. In addition to being the largest jurisdiction in Texas, Houston is the most significant contributor to the number of murders, particularly felony murders, in the state.

3. Information from Houston would be crucial in estimating statewide murder rates, especially felony murder rates, for 1983, the year immediately following the first post-Furman execution.

4. Disaggregating murders into a felony murder category was imperative, because this type of murder was eligible for capital punishment. Felony-related murders have also been the category of capital murders that have most often resulted in death sentences and eventual executions in Texas (Marquart, Ekland-Olson, and Sorensen 1994). Noncapital murders, especially those occuring in the heat of passion, should not be expected to decline in response to executions because they are not punishable by death. Death-eligible homicides, particularly those involving the premediation of felony-related murders, should reasonably be expected to decrease in response to executions if the deterrence hypothesis is correct.

REFERENCES

Acker, James R., Robert M. Bohm, and Charles S. Lanier. 1998. *America's Experiment with Capital Punishment: Reflections on the Past, Present, and Future of the Ultimate Sanction*. Durham, NC: Carolina Academic Press.

Bailey, William C. 1983. "Disaggregation in Deterrence and Death Penalty Research: The Case of Murder in Chicago." *Journal of Criminal Law and Criminology* 74:827–59.

Bailey, William C. and Ruth D. Peterson. 1987. "Police Killings and Capital Punishment: The Post-Furman Period." *Criminology* 25:1–25.

Baldus, David C. and James W. L. Cole. 1975. "A Comparison of the Work of Thorsten Sellin and Isaac Ehrlich on the Deterrent Effect of Capital Punishment." *Yale Law Journal* 85:170–86.

Bedau, Hugo A. 1967. *The Death Penalty in America*. Rev. ed. New York: Doubleday.

———. 1997. *The Death Penalty in America: Current Controversies*. New York: Oxford University Press.

Bowers, William J. and Glenn Pierce. 1975. "The Illusion of Deterrence in Isaac Ehrlich's Research on Capital Punishment," *Yale Law Journal* 85:187–208.

———. 1980. "Deterrence or Brutalization: What is the Effect of Executions?" *Crime & Delinquency* 26:453–84.

Cardarelli, Albert P. 1968. "An Analysis of Police Killed in Criminal Action: 1961–1963." *Journal of Criminal Law, Criminology and Police Science* 59:447–53.

Chamlin, Mitchell B., Harold G. Grasmick, Robert J. Bursik, Jr., and John K. Cochran. 1992. "Time Aggregation and Time Lag in Macro-Level Deterrence Research," *Criminology* 30:377–95.

Cheatwood, Derral. 1993. "Capital Punishment and the Deterrence of Violent Crime in Comparable Counties." *Criminal Justice Review* 18:165–79.

Cochran, John K., Mitchell B. Chamlin, and Mark Seth. 1994. "Deterrence or Brutalization? An Assessment of Oklahoma's Return to Capital Punishment," *Criminology* 32:107–34.

Decker, Scott H. and Carol W. Kohfeld. 1984. "A Deterrence Study of the Death Penalty in Illinois, 1933–1980," *Journal of Criminal Justice* 12:367–77.

Decker, Scott H. and Carol W. Kohfeld. 1990. "The Deterrent Effect of Capital Punishment in the Five Most Active Execution States: A Time Series Analysis." *Criminal Justice Review* 15:173–91.

DeFronzo, James. 1997. "Welfare and Homicide" *Journal of Research in Crime & Delinquency* 34:395–406.

Ehrlich, Isaac. 1975. "The Deterrent Effect of Capital Punishment: A Question of Life and Death," *American Economic Review* 65:397–417.

Forst, Brian. 1977. "The Deterrent Effect of Capital Punishment: A Cross-Tabular Analysis of the 1960's." *Minnesota Law Review* 61:743–67.

Furman v. Georgia, 408 U.S. 238 (1972).

Klein, Lawrence R., Brian Forst, and Victor Vilatov. 1978. "The Deterrent Effect of Capital Punishment: An Assessment of Estimates." Pp. 331–60 in *Deterrence and Incapacitation: Estimating the Ejects of Criminal Sanctions on Crime Rates*, edited by A. Blumstein, J. Cohen, and D. Nagin. Washington, DC: National Academy of Sciences.

Land, Kenneth C., Patricia L. McCall, and Lawrence E. Cohen. 1990. "Structural Covariates of Homicide Rates: Are There Any Invariances Across Time and Social Space?" *American Journal of Sociology* 95:922–63.

Marquart, James W., Sheldon Ekland-Olson, and Jonathan R. Sorensen. 1994. *The Rope, the Chair, and the Needle: Capital Punishment in Texas, 1923–1990.* Austin: University of Texas Press.

Maxfield, Michael G. 1989. "Circumstances in Supplemental Homicide Reports: Variety and Validity." *Criminology* 27:671–95.

Newey, Whitley and Kenneth D. West. 1987. "A Simple, Positive, Semi-Definite, Heteroskedasticity and Autocorrelation Consistent Covariance Matrix." *Econometrica* 55:703–8.

Passell, Peter. 1975. "The Deterrent Effect of the Death Penalty: A Statistical Test" *Stanford Law Review* 28:61–80.

Peterson, Ruth D. and William C. Bailey. 1988. "Murder and Capital Punishment in the Evolving Context of the Post-Furman Era." *Social Forces* 66:774–807.

———. 1991. "Felony Murder and Capital Punishment: An Examination of the Deterrence Question." *Criminology* 29:367–95.

———. 1998 "Is Capital Punishment an Effective Deterrent for Murder? An Examination of the Social Science Research." Pp. 157–82 in *America's Experiment with Capital Punishment: Reflections on the Past, Present, and Future of the Ultimate Sanction,* edited by J. R. Acker, R. M. Bohm, and C. S. Lanier. Durham, NC: Carolina Academic Press.

Riedel, Marc, Margaret A. Zahn, and Lois Mock. 1985. *The Nature and Pattern of American Homicide.* Washington, DC: Government Printing Office.

Schuessler, Karl F. 1952. "The Deterrent Effect of the Death Penalty." *The Annals of the American Academy of Political and Social Science* 284:54–62.

Sellin, Thorsten. 1967. *Capital Punishment.* New York: Harper & Row.

———. 1980. *The Penalty of Death.* Beverly Hills, CA: Sage.

StataCorp. 1997. Stata Statistical Software (Release 5.0) [Computer software]. College Station, TX: Author.

Sutherland, Edwin H. 1925. "Murder and the Death Penalty." *Journal of Criminal Law and Criminology* 15:522–9.

Thompson, Ernie. 1997. "Deterrence Versus Brutalization: The Case of Arizona." *Homicide Studies* 1:110–28.

Van den Haag, Ernest. 1975. "Why Capital Punishment?" *Albany Law Review* 54:501–14.

Jon Sorensen is head of the Juvenile Justice Department at Prairie View A & M University. He has written many articles on the death penalty and is currently in the process of completing a book on that subject for the University of Texas Press. He often serves as an expert witness in death penalty trials, testifying about the probability that capital murder defendants will commit future acts of violence.

Robert Wrinkle is a professor of political science at UT Pan American. His research interests include minority politics and public policy. Currently he is working on a book-length project on minority political incorpation as well as examining the impact of September 11 on minority political trust. He has published articles in the *American Journal of Political Science, Journal Politics, Political Research Quarterly,* as well as other journals.

Victoria Brewer Titterington is an associate professor of sociology at the University of Central Florida, and was assistant professor in the College of Criminal Justice at Sam Houston University when she participated in this research. Before entering academia, her career included administrative and clinical work in community mental health, as well as corporate human resource development. Her current teaching and research interests are in aging, health, lethal and nonlethal family violence, and social deviance. Her research appears in journals including *Violence and Victims, Public Health Reports, Homicide Studies,* and the *Journal of Research in Crime and Delinquency.*

James Marquart is a professor of criminal justice at Sam Houston State University. He has long-term research and teaching interests in prison organizations, capital punishment, criminal justice policy, and research methods. He has published articles on social control and change in prison settings. His work has appeared in such journals as *Criminology, Deviant Behavior, Law and Society Review, Crime and Delinquency, Child Abuse and Neglect,* and *Ageing and Society.* One of his three books, *An Appeal to Justice: Litigated Reform of Texas Prisons,* written with Ben M. Crouch, received the Outstanding Book Award from the Academy of Criminal Justice in 1991. His most current research involves investigating underage drinking and inappropriate staff–inmate relationships in prison settings.

An interview with . . .

Jon Sorensen

How did you become interested in the topic of capital punishment?

I was a graduate student at Sam Houston in the late 1980s and in our first year as master's students, one of our professors encouraged us to get involved in the research activities of faculty members. So I went to James Marquart and asked if he had any work for me, and he said "yes, I do" and it happened to be on the Fuhrman released inmates (these were the inmates released in 1972 when the Supreme Court overturned capital punishment). And we followed up [on] their behavior. Since then the death penalty has been the focus of most of my research.

How did you end up working with these three other researchers?

One of them, Jim Marquart, was my original mentor and I asked him and he brought in Victoria Brewer. I chose Bob Wrinkle for his statistical skills. They were colleagues and I thought it was a good idea to share the work. I like collaboration; almost all my articles are coauthored. I sometimes work with lawyers and sometimes with psychologists, because people from different fields tend to have complementary knowledge. This is especially true in the death penalty area; the lawyers make it much better because they can weave in the legal aspect, which I'm not very good at.

For this article, what made you choose this particular approach and data source to examine the death penalty?

I would say that was dictated by the research question. I figured that if the death penalty has a deterrent effect, then one would see it in Texas, because we had executed quite a few people during this period of time. The use of monthly data was dictated by the research question and by the literature I had read that said you should use the smallest unit possible (i.e., disaggregate). And the variables were all ones that had been found to be most important in previous studies.

What are some of the benefits and the drawbacks or limitations of using existing statistics in sociological research?

One benefit is that it is economical. I think that's why most of the studies in this area now use existing statistics. Another is that, because they are government statistics—official records—we can't be accused of compiling them. In the death penalty research, people who are opponents of your position are suspicious of your findings, and by using the official records we can't be accused of mucking them up. The government statistics have their own problems, but they've been used enough that we know where the problems lie in terms of reliability and that sort of thing. The main problem was that, because sometimes the measures were yearly, for some of the control variables we had to extrapolate the month and that wasn't the greatest thing. Sometimes using the government statistics, too, means you have to wait until they are published. Things have changed a lot in the last five years—you can get them on the Web, you can download them—but you still might have a couple of years lag time where you are waiting for a couple of variables and you have to cut if off at some point. So I guess that was a drawback: waiting and updating at the last minute.

Were there any unexpected events or developments that you had to deal with in doing this research?

One is what they call the effect of history: 1996 was a moratorium year, when we didn't execute anybody. (Actually, there were two executed, but they volunteered.) So we went from having about twenty executions per year to nearly none. Then 1997 was a "stellar" execution year; we executed about thirty-some people, which was really unusual. I didn't know how to handle that because I felt like that would sway the results. So I included that year as a dummy variable. The funny thing was that a colleague who does this kind of research all the time suggested that if I hadn't used the 1997 dummy variable, my results might actually have supported the deterrent effect. So I went back and reran the results, and it wasn't true—they weren't significant. But that was a problem because that year came so near the end of the data series.

From what you are saying, it sounds like you always have to anticipate the responses of opponents to your research because of the political importance of this topic?

Yes. In fact, several people have asked me for this data set. I know they are re-analyzing it, but I've never seen anything written using it.

Talk about your findings, particularly what you point out in your article: The findings continue to find no support for the deterrence, yet the majority of Americans still support the death penalty.

It's funny you should mention that. There is a group of people—sociologists and lawyers—who are staunch abolitionists, and the guy who heads this group sends out mailers to keep us updated about developments. In fact, there has been a series of articles published recently that show a deterrent effect of the death penalty. There are six in all, all done within the last two years (since the publication of my article); a couple have been published already. They are all done by economists, using very sophisticated econometric techniques and panel data from states, over several years' period. They are quite sophisticated, so it is very challenging for us. We look at them closely because there has always been a "learning curve"—we have to catch up with them and their methods to figure out just what it is they are doing, and doing wrong. Sociologists are mostly on the left on the ideological spectrum and economists are mostly on the right—they emphasize free choice, that people are rational actors, and therefore that punishment deters crime—and proponents of the death penalty send around abstracts and copies of these articles that show the deterrent effect. They even lobby the legislatures. They send mass emails with this information.

Were there any ethical challenges or issues involved in your research?

I did and always have faced ethical challenges when I study the death penalty. Someone pointed out to me early on that if I find that the death penalty is not racially discriminatory, then others could take those findings and use them to justify killing people. So I've always thought about that. In this case, if I find that it is a deterrent, then it would support the execution of those who have been convicted of murder. But if I find that there is no deterrent effect, then it could also be costing innocent citizens their lives. So I always think of that when I do this research. Plus, I believe many death penalty researchers are against the death penalty and I think that colors their work. I think people push it one way or the other, not really badly—because of replication, you can't fudge the numbers too much—but I've seen several articles where people tease out suspicious sorts of relationships trying to force their positions. This happens on both sides, but mainly on the abolitionist side because about 90 percent of articles written about capital punishment are written by people who don't support it. I don't want to say they are the worst offenders; rather, there are just more of them. I've testified in capital cases and that is the first thing they ask me: "You are against capital punishment, right? You try to make the figures comes out this way, right?" The general public is very suspicious of scientists when we do studies of gun control or abortion or any of these hot-button issues. They know that statistics can lie, but they don't understand the idea of replication and that we share our data sets—it is almost an ethical obligation, now. I would be shocked and very suspicious if someone published something and wouldn't share their data. We all can be found to be wrong if we try to fudge the data. There are lots of forces that compel us not to cheat.

What was the most difficult or frustrating aspect of doing this research?

Learning to deal with the time series data and using the statistical program to check for autocorrelations was the most difficult thing. I had never run serial data—time series—so I had to learn to check and correct for things like autocorrelations. From one year to the next the state-level variables are correlated—that is, they tend to be correlated across the cases just because it is year to year from the same location. So overcoming that, learning to check for that, was complicated. But of course I had help.

What was the most satisfying about it?

The same thing. Learning to use the program and to work with a different type of data.

If you were to do it again, is there anything you would do differently?

Yes. In fact, I *have* done it again. There was an article that came out in 2001 by an economist who created a model that seemed to show that if Texas had executed people in 1996 (the moratorium year), the lives of something like 200 "innocent citizens" would have been saved. In other words, that because we didn't execute anyone in 1996, something like 200 people were killed. I looked at it and knew right away there was something wrong with that, especially because they were looking at the same data that I used; I knew that it didn't sound right. So I reanalyzed their findings; I ran several different tests and concluded that their findings were completely wrong and that there were huge problems with their model. Theirs was in a very obscure economics journal, but of course someone got a hold of it and now it is all over the Internet. Because of its findings, it was even sent to the Texas legislature.

I have an article under review for a law journal right now that that responds to the economist's paper. I reran their models three different ways, one with full data, another with yearly data from the past forty years. I used their exact techniques, but to predict the 1996 Texas homicide rate, I looked at the past few years of the Texas violent crime rates and found that there was the exact same relationship between Texas violent crime rates and U.S. rates over the past five years. In other words, whatever was happening in Texas was happening across the board: Violent crime dropped, and homicides did too. This is similar to what happened in the late 1960s when the economists came out with their first bunch of findings that the death penalty was a deterrent. At that time, homicide rates were going up and executions were going down (until they reached zero in the late 1960s) and some people concluded that those two things were causally related. But it was a spurious correlation, because it just so happens that all crime rates were going up. In 1996 in Texas, we have another spurious correlation. Violent crime rates, including homicide rates, tend to travel a little more sharply than other crime rates. They go down a little more steeply, and at the same time we happened to be executing more people than in the past. So we are getting another illusory correlation, and the failure to control for other factors leads some people to conclude that the death penalty has a deterrent effect. I can't say for sure that it is bogus everywhere, only in Texas. Anyway, I thought this was a settled issue, but research like this is reviving the deterrence idea, so now we in turn are driven to go back and challenge them. I don't challenge them as an ideologue, saying "Oh my god, they are finding support to bolster executions." Frankly, no offense, I think these guys have committed murder and they deserve to die—which is unusual for a criminologist to say. I have wavered in years past, and now I really don't have any problem with it [the death penalty]. But is it a deterrent? No, I don't think it is. Or if it is, we can't show it statistically. So, yes, I'm driven to go back and tear these guys apart not based on ideology, but based on my fascination with their research—with statistics and the advanced designs they are using with the panel data and all that. I just want to know how they did it and how they came up with these results that I'm pretty sure are not real. In fact, Texas has an undue influence on assumptions about the deterrent effect of the death penalty because it has the most executions in recent years and also a steep reduction in homicide rates. But, again, it is an illusory correlation. If we are finding there is no relationship between the two other than chance, then probably that holds true for the nation. But I haven't been able to prove that yet because I have too many other things on my plate.

Are there any lessons from the research experience that you would share with students?

I would say to be skeptical. Don't believe everything that you hear or read. Even if we think that we know something because it's been done over and over again, it is still worthwhile to check up on it every now and then. I would also say not to let politics or ideology interfere with your research. I know there are different views on that—that you should admit up front what your bias is—but I think that is also an important lesson because our judgment can be clouded. We believe what we want to believe. If the research supports that, good, but if it doesn't, we might be tempted to reject it.

Questions to Think About

1. According to the literature review in the article by Sorensen and his colleagues, what are some shortcomings of previous research that tests the deterrence hypothesis? How does their study design improve on previous ones?

2. List and briefly explain each of the variables that the authors include in their model. What are some of the problems they encounter as a result of having to rely on existing statistics for their data?

3. How challenging was this article for you to read and understand? What are the implications of that for public and political debates about the death penalty? Were your own views about the death penalty changed as a result of reading this article or Sorensen's interview?

4. Discuss the different ethical issues related to this research that Sorensen discusses in his interview. What are some of the potential pitfalls that one must be aware of when doing research on highly politicized topics such as capital punishment? What are some other current hot topics on which social scientists conduct research?

chapter 7

Field Research

When social science researchers immerse themselves in social worlds and interact with people in order to understand those worlds through people's eyes, they are doing field research. Field research is qualitative, naturalistic, and inductive in its approach. In important respects, field researchers reject some of the assumptions of quantitative approaches—that researchers much be detached, that total objectivity is possible (or even desirable), that rigor requires numbers, and that a goal of research is generalizability. At the same time, field research is very much social science research: systematic, analytical, scientific, and very demanding, both personally and intellectually.

The researchers whose articles are included in this chapter provide many insights into the distinctive features of field research—insights that challenge the common perception that field research is less rigorous, hence somehow easier, than quantitative approaches such as survey and experimental design. In fact, because the field researcher is the research instrument, she or he must possess a remarkable range of analytical, intellectual, social, and emotional skills to be successful. Selecting a site, negotiating access, making decisions about self-disclosure, building rapport, assuming an attitude of strangeness, dealing with hostile or dangerous members or settings, being an astute observer and a careful listener, carving out a role, dealing with stress, working to normalize social research, earning trust, maintaining relations, conducting field interviews, figuring out how and where to take field notes, managing crises, continually assessing the reliability and validity of one's observations, and in the end telling a true story while protecting the privacy and integrity of the people one has come to know require special skills and talents. Although it may be true that the best way to learn how to do field research is to *do* field research, we think that reading others' accounts of their research is another good way to begin to learn how to do it.

Although field researchers have some sort of plan when they enter the field—an idea of what they wish to learn and the concepts or theoretical frameworks to guide their data collection and analysis—they are participating in social settings and relationships over which they have limited control. As a result, their research almost always has an emergent quality to it, and because they never know just what will transpire in the course of the research, they must be resilient, creative, resourceful, and stand ready to respond and change course, as necessary, at any time. Often, of course, things go right. In her interview, Julie Bettie talks about her fears that her whiteness and inability to speak Spanish would make it hard to get working-class Mexican American high schoolers to talk openly with her about their lives and aspirations, but they turned out to be responsive, helpful, and anxious to have her hear their stories. Hugh Campbell had more negative experiences, which he describes in his account of an eighteen-month fieldwork experience in a pub in rural New Zealand. There he discovered an exclusionary and largely unwelcoming setting where, as an outsider, he sometimes was physically threatened, verbally assaulted, and coerced to do things (like drink more than he wanted to) in order to earn continued acceptance.

In field research, the researcher neither strives nor pretends to be an objective and distanced observer of social life, but instead deals quite openly with the ways that she or he affects and is affected by the research. Julie Bettie illustrates this nicely as she refers in her article and interview to how her own race, class background, and gender influenced everything from her choice of topic to the ways that she related and responded to the girls with whom she spoke. She also talks quite frankly about how frustrating it was to have to repress her "self" in the course of the research—for example, feeling that she could not dress and talk the way she normally might for fear of biasing the responses of her interviewees. Hugh Campbell also had to deal with being an outsider. Mia Tuan, however, had the opposite problem: she had an easy and immediate rapport with people with whom she talked. For her, the challenge was to achieve some amount of neutrality and detachment despite the fact that the experiences of the Asian ethnics she interviewed were so close to her own.

Ethical concerns always loom large for field researchers, mainly because of their involvement in the lives of the people whose social worlds they study. As a result, they are especially sensitive to research ethics and commonly dedicate a section or chapter of their published work to discussion of the ethical issues that they faced and how they dealt with them. Because qualitative research reports typically describe and quote individual people who were part of their research, researchers must build into their research plans deliberate strategies for protecting people's privacy and anonymity—changing names, mixing up characteristics or circumstances, and so on. Other more subtle ethical issues, such as that of betrayal, may emerge in the course of the research, as was the case for Julie Bettie's research in a high school. Hugh Campbell discusses at some length another kind of ethical dilemma facing some field researchers, which is when research results raise objections or create dissension in some parts of the community studied. He concludes that because he could not have presented results that did not disadvantage some segment of the community, he would simply "tell it like he saw it" and risk making some people unhappy.

The three articles in this chapter typify other aspects of field research as well. Each is written by one author, which is common in field research because collaboration is impractical. Each of the articles is part of a larger study with results published in book form. Again, this is typical of field research because the data are hard to condense to article length. Each article is immensely engaging, colorful, and readable. Finally, although none of the three researchers claims to have results that are generalizable in any meaningful way, each is actively engaged in the work of theory-building. All three studies produce evocative concepts and rich insights that underscore how thoroughly indispensable field research is to a multifaceted and deep understanding of the social world.

You know, I'm tired of the Kristi Yamaguchis and the Michelle Kwans! They're not American . . . when I look at a box of Wheaties, I don't want to see eyes that are slanted and Oriental and almond shaped. I want to see American eyes looking at me."[1]

—*Bill Handel, popular morning DJ for KFI-AM, one of the nation's most listened to talk radio stations.*

"American Beats Kwan"

—*MSNBC's erroneous headline after figure skater Tara Lipinski beat out Michelle Kwan during the 1998 Winter Olympics. Both women are Americans.*

Introduction

Multi-generation Asian-Americans (hereafter referred to as Asian ethnics) are faced with an interesting dilemma these days. While longtime Americans with roots extending back three generations or more, they are decidedly in the minority since the majority (66%) of Asians currently in this country are foreign born (U.S. Bureau of the Census, 1993). This was not the case only three decades ago when the numbers were tipped the other way; two thirds of Asian-Americans were native born back then. Thanks to changes brought about by the 1965 Immigration Act, the complexion and composition of Asian America has changed dramatically. One result of these demographic changes has been that Asian ethnics find themselves confronted with questions of ethnic and cultural authenticity, as not

being "Asian enough" in the way they conduct themselves or their lifestyles. In their interactions with non-Asians, they must contend with the expectations of others who believe them to be closer to their ethnic roots than to their American ones. Meanwhile, their interactions with and observations of Asian immigrants reveal how much they differ from their foreign-born counterparts. Many are aware that Asian immigrants look upon them as watered down, "less than" versions of themselves (Lee, 1996; Chen, 1992; Wong, 1977; Weiss, 1973).

At the same time, they also face resistance to being seen as "real" Americans as captured by the excerpts above. Even prior to the spate of recent immigration, Asian ethnics struggled to be recognized as authentically American with legitimate places in this society (Kitano, 1992; Min, 1995; Espiritu, 1992; Omi, 1993; Wei, 1993; Takaki, 1987, 1989). The World War Two internment of over 110,000 Japanese-Americans, two-thirds of whom were American born, stands as the embodiment of this disregard and blurring of national and ethnic identities.[2] Thus, while the influx of Asian immigrants has further reinforced the notion that all Asians are foreigners, the tendency to see Asian-Americans as conditional citizens has a long-standing history.

In this paper I explore what I call the "authenticity dilemma" confronting Asian ethnics today and discuss how they negotiate a social terrain where others define them as neither *real* Americans nor *real* Asians. They have not passively accepted either of these "less than" labels, however. On the contrary, I argue that Asian ethnics have and continue to actively struggle against the stereotypical labels others impose on them. As part of their resistance, many dismiss the essentialism inherent in the belief that ethnic authenticity lies solely in practicing particular cultural traditions or rigidly upholding the same values as those held in the motherland. Furthermore, they insist that uniquely Chinese-American, Japanese-American, and even Asian-American cultures have developed in this country and it is within these hyphenated spaces where their true authenticity lies.

Methodology

To explore the authenticity dilemma confronting Asian ethnics, I draw from interviews gathered for a larger study I conducted on the middle class Asian ethnic experience. Between 1994 and 1995, I led a research team in interviewing ninety-five third, fourth, and fifth generation Chinese and Japanese ethnics living in northern and southern California to: (1) determine the content, meaning, and salience of ethnicity in their lives; (2) explore the extent to which they felt that ethnicity was an optional rather than imposed facet of their identities; and (3) examine the role played by race in shaping life experiences. All the participants are well-educated and from urban areas; many are white collar professionals in fields such as medicine/health, banking, law, engineering, publishing, computer technology, education, finance, insurance, and real estate. Those who are not included are housewives, small business owners, students, and a few artists. The youngest participants were in their early 20s while the oldest were well into their 70s. Forty-eight participants are of Japanese ancestry, three of mixed Chinese-Japanese heritage, and the remaining forty-four are of Chinese ancestry.

The fact that this study was conducted in California is of special significance. Ever since Chinese were first brought in to labor in mines and railroads, California has remained the state with the largest concentration of Asian-Americans (Barringer et al., 1993; Min, 1995). It is also a particularly appropriate place for studying native-born Chinese- and Japanese-Americans; 42% of the na-

tion's native born Chinese and 36% of native-born Japanese reside there.

Clearly, California is a rich and essential site for studying the Asian-American experience. Strangely though, whether their numbers and long history have promoted greater social acceptance or the reverse—greater hostility—is not at all clear. Asian ethnics in California have the most substantive reasons to feel part of the mainstream and subsequently to feel that ethnicity is an optional part of their identity. After all, they have been present in the state since the mid 1800s, are well integrated into its social fabric, and may be found in all occupational fields. Further, California is the primary receiving state for Asian immigrants, a situation that may actually reinforce a sense of ethnic identity among Asian ethnics.

In addition, the general climate towards immigrants, both legal and illegal, is decidedly less hospitable today. With California's governor Pete Wilson stirring up tensions, increased hostilities come as no surprise. Asian ethnics who are mistaken for Asian immigrants have received some of this negativity (Horton, 1995; Saito, 1993). Possibly, such cases of mistaken identity may cause Asian ethnics to question their own levels of acceptance by the mainstream. Subsequently, because of perceived social exclusion, ethnicity may become more salient for them.

Interview Findings

"I'm not your typical American when people think American"—Not American Enough. According to classic assimilation scholars such as Park (1950) and Gordon (1954) ethnicity's salience in people's lives declines with each passing generation, a prediction based on years of researching the white ethnic experience. Today, identifying along ethnic lines or pursuing an ethnically embedded lifestyle have largely become optional facets of life for white ethnics (Gans, 1979; Waters, 1986, 1990, 1992; Zenner, 1985; Bershtel and Graubard, 1991; Lieberson, 1985; Crispino, 1980; Kellogg, 1990; Alba, 1985, 1985b, 1990, 1995; Alba and Chamlin, 1983, Bakalian, 1992; Phinney, 1990). As Alba (1990, p. 62) argues, identity choices for whites ethnics today can be capriciously based on nothing more than a "sense that it is nicer to be an X, rather than a Y."

Of course, this state of affairs did not take place overnight. European immigrants who poured into the country in the early part of the twentieth century suffered greatly at the hands of nativists who looked upon their cultures as backward and threatening to the American way of life (Higham, 1963). Nativists demanded that newcomers shed their language, rituals, and practices in exchange for an all-encompassing American identity and access to the privileges associated with that status. Clearly these immigrants paid a heavy price, but the very success with which their descendants have become one of "us" has reinforced this country's belief in its ability to assimilate and embrace diverse peoples (Alba, 1985; Gordon, 1964; Park, 1950; Park and Burgess, 1921).

As longtime Americans who are not part of the racial norm, Asian ethnics face a markedly more circumscribed set of identity options. How they choose to identify is not solely a private affair as it is for white ethnics. They experience real pressures to identify in ethnic or racial terms because these remain salient markers to others (Min, 1995; Espiritu, 1992). Most identify in hyphenated terms as Chinese-American, Japanese-American and, increasingly, Asian-American. Cathy Leong,[3] who identifies as Asian-American, explained her choice:

> For myself I have more Japanese, Korean, Filipino friends, just through work and the people we associate with, you know, my co-workers and stuff like that. So I think there's more of an emphasis on Asian-American.

As more individuals come to think of themselves as members of a general family of Asian-Americans and associate accordingly, they are more likely to embrace the pan-ethnic label to describe themselves. Since the bulk of her friends are other Asians, Cathy feels more comfortable reinforcing the racial bond while downplaying ethnic differences.

Emily Woo, who also identifies as an Asian-American, does so because it encompasses both her Chinese and Japanese roots:

Q: How do you identify yourself?

A: That's a really hard question actually. I guess as an Asian-American. I don't consider myself just Japanese, just Chinese. I don't consider myself just American. I don't know. I kinda like terminology like Asian-American and African-American because it's kinda messy . . . By blood, I'm Chinese and Japanese. By culture, I don't know if I am so much of either. I don't know . . . Mom would always tell me I used to get confused growing up. "How can I be Japanese and Chinese and American?" "Well, you are half Japanese, half Chinese, and all American."

For Emily, identifying along racial lines as an Asian-American eliminates the cumbersome task of acknowledging both components of her ancestry, a strategy white ethnics of mixed ethnic ancestry also utilize (Waters, 1990; Alba, 1990). Her rationale provides a glimpse into how future generations of mixed ethnic ancestry Asians may possibly identify.

Tony Lam, also of Chinese and Japanese ancestry, prefers to call himself an American-Asian. As the son of a career soldier and a veteran himself, he chooses to emphasize his patriotism to this country by asserting his American identity first. And yet, Tony also expressed great frustration over what could be characterized as a societal "blindspot" to the role Asian-Americans have played in defending this country:

Q: How do you identify yourself?

A: American-Asian . . . I saw that parade in '92 on Hollywood Boulevard and they had veterans marching down (pause) I tell you which group was missing. Asian. There was not one Chinese, Japanese, Filipino, Korean, Pacific Islander in uniform. Now I know they served (pause). It's either the fault of those people who plan that parade or the fault due to a lack of vigilance for an

Asian veterans organization by not insisting on it (pause) through all that hard times. I still persist that I'm an American but I'm not going to deny that I'm Asian because first thing they're not going to let me do it. I still got to (pause) about Asian culture whether I like it or not . . . You see, Caucasians must understand that they (pause) put that on us and we must learn to confront people who say those kinds of things so we should say things like, "No I don't know that. I hope you know your French food. Or, he's Scottish (pause) look, look, what are you? Okay, Armenian. Tell me about Armenian stuff. We should put that on them. I think it's fair, they got to get a taste of what they did or how dumb they sound or who's truly American. Yeah, I am American and then Asian.

Tony considers himself to be a loyal American who risked his life to defend his country. The sad irony, however, is that there are others who do not consider the U.S. to be his country. Even if he chose to identify solely as an American, he believes "they," presumably white Americans, would not legitimate his choice—"they're not going to let me do it."

Others also spoke about the pressures they experience to identify in ethnic or racial terms. Ted Uyematsu:

Q: How about identifying as just a plain old American?

A: Yeah I would, but you know (pause) there's (pause) but then again you have to realize that I'm not your typical American when people think American. In your mind you don't see a whole blooded Japanese guy you know. They conjure up some blond headed dude that (pause) but I would have no problem seeing myself but I think it would confuse certain people if I were to say that.

Ted demonstrates a clear understanding of what the typical American male presumably looks like—and he does not even come close. Subse-

quently, while he has no qualms calling himself an American Ted believes others might take issue with him since he believes white ethnics feel, to use Blumer's (1958) terminology, a sense of proprietary claim to the term. As such, he was unsure how his usage of the term would be received.

Others were even more direct in stating how inappropriate *in other people's eyes* it would be if they were to identify as Americans without any hyphenation. Rick Wubara on why he identifies as Japanese-American:

(Rick) I don't think I can be just American just for the fact that I look different from the typical American, white. (Why not just Japanese then?) Because I definitely am Americanized, an American raised in America. And I don't always agree with what Japanese, Japan stands for.

"I look different from the typical American." "I'm not your typical American." Statements such as these vividly convey the dilemma Asian ethnics, as racialized ethnics, face. They have learned by watching how others respond to them that they are viewed as outsiders to this society. Despite being longtime Americans they are not perceived as such since they do not fit the image of what a "real" American looks like (Lowe, 1996; Espiritu, 1992; Nagel, 1994; Jiobu, 1988). This, I believe, is the key difference separating the white ethnic from the Asian ethnic experience. While white ethnics must actively assert their ethnic uniqueness if they wish this to feature prominently in their interactions with others, Asian ethnics are assumed to be foreign unless proven otherwise.

"They still look at the Chinese as foreigners"— The Realization of Difference.

No one ever asks a Polish American after the first generation why they don't speak Polish or are they ashamed of being Polish because they don't speak Polish. But (they will say) that you're ashamed of being Chinese, or you don't understand Chinese culture because you don't speak Chinese. But no one ever asks that of anybody else. I mean if your grandparents speak French, and you still cook coq au vin, but no one ever demands that you also know how to speak French. And no one ever asks you, where did you come from.

The frustration Carol Wong experiences is hard to miss in this passage. She believes there is a double standard in operation. While white ethnics are free to discard their ethnic links and merge with the American mainstream after the first generation, Asian ethnics do not have this option; an assumption of foreignness stubbornly clings to them irrespective of generational status.

Carol was not alone in her way of thinking. Others concurred with her assessment of the status difference between Asians and whites. Based on their experiences with prejudice, discrimination, and stereotyping they understand that the public is unable or unwilling to distinguish between Asian ethnics and immigrants. That these respondents, residents of such diverse and cosmopolitan areas as Los Angeles and San Francisco, still feel this way is telling. Subsequently, they believe their status in this society is vulnerable to changing social, political, and economic conditions beyond their personal control (Nishi, 1989). For instance, the majority agree their lives would be affected not only if the U.S. were to go to war with their country of origin but if war were declared on any Asian country since "whites or blacks can't tell the difference between Asian-Americans and Asians." Carol Wong again:

> When there was all the whoop-to-do about Japan and all the businesses that Japan owns and all the property that Japan owns in this country, (while) England, Canada and the Netherlands own a whole lot more individually than Japan ever did. But it was this thing of the Pacific horde. And of course American car companies screwed up and they had to blame it on someone else.

References to Japan and Middle Eastern "bashing" as well as the wartime internment of Japanese-

Americans were frequently made to substantiate their views. And while not everybody believed that a mass internment sanctioned by the federal government could happen again, most agreed that hostilities from the general citizenry were likely. Friends and co-workers who knew them as individuals probably would not act differently, but strangers and nativists certainly would. As Jonathan Tse put it, "They'd see us as being evil and they'd start, it's just like what they do with the Middle East and the Soviet Union. They would all look down on us."

We see this with the recent Asian campaign finance scandal involving questionable campaign donations made to the Democratic National Committee as well. That the possible wrongdoing of a handful of Asians and Asian-Americans has cast a shadow over all Asian-American donors is an all too familiar scenario. Contributors with the misfortune of having an Asian or Asian sounding last name have had to endure intrusive questions concerning their citizenship status and other highly personal questions. As Daphne Kwok, Executive Director for the Organization of Chinese-Americans put it, "Wouldn't a more neutral approach be to investigate all contributions over $5000 and not just those targeting the APA community?"

Would the lives of white ethnics be affected if war were declared on their country or countries of origin? Most believed no. Morrison Hum, who was required to wear a badge identifying himself as Chinese during World War II, looked to the past to substantiate his opinion:

Q: If U.S. were to go to war with Europe . . .

A: Probably not, because they are considered white. I don't believe so. Like the Germans (pause) but you stand out because you are colored. It would make you feel bad too. Feel ashamed of your native country.

Whiteness, once again, is equated with being American; Asianness is not. And because Asianness is not, questions regarding their loyalty to this country are raised. This was the case during World War II and many of Asian ethnics believe this is still the case today. Daphne Kitano:

Q: If U.S. were to go to war with Europe . . .

A: No, because it didn't really happen to Germans in World War II and they were our enemies and the Italians were our enemy and it didn't happen to them, you know, which leads me to believe the obvious that it was just on the basis of color of your skin. If you weren't white and you were Japanese and even though you were American you were still the enemy. . . . I still feel there's some trend that the media is generating about how Japanese are taking over the United States or buying out everything, which is totally not the real case. They're not looking at the investments that England has in the United States, or the Canadians or Australians, the Dutch, the Germans. And I was like, you know, the media say all these things about Japanese taking over and it (pause) it's going to affect me here, a Japanese-American, because the ignorant white person isn't going to (pause) it's going to be like, "Oh you're just one of these Japanese who are trying to take over." So they don't realize the effect, the effect on how people view Asians in this country.

As for the possibility of another mass internment, opinions were mixed. About a third did not believe it could happen again. Some felt the country had learned its lesson and would not repeat the mistakes made with Japanese-Americans. References were made to how "times have changed" as indicated by interest in multicultural issues and greater respect for human rights. Others referred to the growing political power of Asian-American organizations who would fight against such actions. Still a third response, captured by Greg Okinaka's comments, suggests that the imprisonment of the spirit may be more damaging than that of the flesh:

I don't think they'd be sending mass people to prison, but if something like a war came up with the Japanese, you would be getting a lot more widespread discrimination. Its more like a mental internment than an actual physical internment, understand?

The rest either conceded internment was possible but unlikely or adamantly agreed that mass incarceration was not only possible but probable if the political situation became volatile enough.

In response to the question, *"Does it mean something different to say you are an American of Irish (any European ethnicity) descent compared to saying you are an American of Chinese or Japanese descent,"* Morrison Hum had this to say:

Yeah there is a difference. They still took at the Chinese as a foreigner. For an Irish American, they don't see him as a foreigner. I don't know how long it is going to take, but you are still looked upon as a foreigner. I think so.

Diane Okihiro chose to personalize the question by applying it to her Irish-American girlfriend and herself. Her response is revealing:

Like my girlfriend, it's kinds funny because she's of Irish descent, but people would never think that or ask where are you from because they see her as being Caucasian. And if they look at me they would say, "Oh where are you from," because I'm perceived as being Asian first. It's like girl, an Asian girl, and anything that follows after that. For my girlfriend it would be like, she's white, she's of Irish descent but it doesn't really matter. It's like way down the list of whatever.

Here Diane refers to her racial distinctiveness as featuring prominently in her interactions with strangers; she believes it is the first aspect of her identity to register with others. This, in turn, triggers the stereotype that she must be from someplace else since being Asian is not equated with being from the U.S. No one ever thinks to ask her girlfriend of Irish ancestry where she is from, however, given her white racial background combined with high degree of acculturation.

A related stereotype many Asian ethnics encounter is an assumption of Chinese or Japanese language fluency and its corollary, surprise over their fluency in English. As Terry Winters put it, "I've had this happen all my life when some stranger will come up and start speaking Japanese to me and I don't speak Japanese." Women, in particular, were more likely to recall instances where unsolicited male strangers approached with the intent of "hitting" on them or otherwise engaging them in conversation. Marilyn Tokubo:

I get offended and then there's times when somebody will come up to me in a bar and say, "Are you Japanese," and start speaking Japanese to me and actually (pause) people do this to me all the time and I don't know why it's me over anybody else. They always seem to zoom in on me and start speaking this, trying to speak Japanese.

Q: Who approaches you?

A: Whites. They'll come up and start gibber jabbering in Japanese and I'll just kind of have to laugh it off and this happens a lot and also that they assume that I know how to speak Japanese and they also want to show off their Japanese.

Far from flattering, Marilyn experiences these instances as invasions into her privacy and resents the arrogance these men display in assuming they are welcome to approach her. Popular racialized and gendered stereotypes such as the "Suzie Wong" character portraying Asian women as subservient, acquiescent, sensual, and exotic have encouraged white men in particular to view her as an object for their entertainment (Hamamoto, 1994; Kim, 1986; Fong, 1998). Also at play in situations such as these is the element of white male privilege, the sense of entitlement those in the "driver's seat" feel whether consciously or not.

Other language stereotypes abound. Michael Lowe, a manager for a chain electronics store in the Bay Area, deals with irate customers all of the time. After soothing one woman who called to complain over purchasing a faulty CD player she exclaimed, "Thank God you're an American! I'm tired of dealing with all those ching chong people!" Another respondent, Barry Sato, who spends a large portion of his day on the phone with clients, struggles with the preconceived notions of those he does business with and their subsequent reactions when they meet in person:

I think a couple of times my jaws hit the ground. Why should my English be any different? . . . Mostly I was shocked. When I met someone who I've talked on the phone with and when they saw me they'll go, "I didn't realize you were Asian." That was the first time. I was shocked. And on the other side when I met them what I really want to say was, "Oh, I couldn't tell you were black over the phone either." But I held my tongue because now let's not have a fight (laugh).

Without the benefit of sight or knowledge of his last name, Barry's client was surprised to learn he had been conducting business with a Japanese-American. Barry has since gotten used to this kind of response from his clients. He claims it does not bother him anymore; he just shakes his head in amazement over the regularity with which people cannot believe that he doesn't "sound" Japanese over the phone.

For the most part, the stereotyping Asian ethnics experience is not intended to wound or alienate. Rather, incidents are largely based on ignorance. Even when no ill will is intended, however, hurt is inflicted since, once again, they are reminded that they are viewed not as individuals but as stereotyped members of a group relegated a foreign status. The frustration comes from trying so hard to be treated as distinct individuals and then confronting thoughtless stereotypes. Tony Lam:

My closest friend happens to be Caucasian. He says, Tony, you're a good old boy like me, you know. You're just Asian on the outside but you like burgers and so forth and all that. I told him I like Caucasian women, they look pretty good to me, you know, everybody else. I like Asian too . . . so how does he see me? He sees me as an American but sometimes be has to make off-handed comments like, "Aah So," or some-thing like that and I go why do you have to bring that for? I don't go up to you and say you want to go dance country with all the other red-necks. Why can't we just be neutral?

Yet another way Asian ethnics are reminded of their marginalized status centers around the stares, comments, and even threats they receive from others who look upon them as strangers or intruders in a public place; about half have felt out of place or suddenly conscious of their racial background during a stop somewhere. Most often this occurs when they travel or visit unfamiliar places but it can also happen in their own neigh-borhoods. I personally experienced an example of this at a supermarket in the city of San Marino, an affluent suburb in southern California where many Chinese immigrants have recently moved. While standing in line to pay for my items two older white women behind me began to complain over how Asians were taking over the area. Nei-ther woman appeared concerned that I, an Asian woman, could hear everything they were saying; they either assumed I could not speak English or did not care in the least.

The experience of walking into a restaurant ("a McDonalds in the middle of nowhere") and hav-ing all heads turn to watch them was a familiar story. Sharon Young:

> (T)here are times when you go to a restaurant or you go somewhere like a business or something and you walk in and they're all Caucasians. I don't know if it's unconscious or what, but you feel like they're staring at you or they're looking or they notice. Even coming down my street sometimes which basically is all white and we've all lived here for years and still when we drive they all kinds stare at you like, "Oh my gosh, they're Asian." Like we used to experience that a lot when we went to the market and we'd go there and get all these stares, people would look at you. And you first think "Haven't you seen an Asian in your life?" God, just because you have dark hair and different skin, it's like, wake up,

you know. It's occasional, but it's still kinda sad because you still feel that.

Feeling uncomfortable while stopping in gas sta-tions, gift shops, and other stores was also fre-quently mentioned as was receiving poor service. In all of these cases, the message they received was that they were out of place or clearly did not be-long where they were. In some cases, local resi-dents were merely confused over their presence and viewed them as oddities. In other cases, hos-tility was unmistakable. Tony Lam:

> I passed this car, these two Caucasians were in the car. They were slow and I just passed them and they notice that I was Asian and drove alongside me. We drove through the entire town side by side and then they tried to hit me. At first they called me names and I rolled my window up. So then he set himself on the window of the passenger side and started to give me the finger and I ignored it and drive down the road. . . . They tried to run me off, hit me, I guess. So I sped up and got to a four corner stop . . . and I look up and I saw the driver there but where is the other fella? And I find out what he was doing. He grabbed a bottle and now he is sitting himself on the window and trying to position himself so do when they got near me he could throw the bottle. I turn my lights on. They thought I was braking and they suddenly brake and throw the bottle and miss and I drove through the lights. I drove through the stop sign taking a risk of I might be hit or arrested by the police.

Similarly, Paul Leong described the unease he felt while working in a rural part of California. While he never experienced anything close to what Tony Lam endured, he maintained an alert stance dur-ing his time there:

> When I worked in Sacramento we used to go to different places in the valley, like all white towns and stuff like that, quite a bit. And you do feel kinda conscious about how they're gonna treat

you and that kind of thing, and I think it actually has maybe socially hindered me in some ways. But I also (pause) it's a safety mechanism because you never know what's going to happen. You're out there in the middle of farmland USA and shit. You never know if Joe Bob's gonna come around the corner with a rake and shit. It's never happened yet, but I do feel very sensitive about that.

Women traveling to unfamiliar places typically encountered gendered stereotypes which were used to make sense of their presence. Patti Ito: "When I've gone to places like Oklahoma, you know, I kind of feel like they think I'm some sort of Korean bride that some army person brought back." Again, the point is that some special explanation is needed to placate local residents as to why there are "strangers" in their community.

For their psychological as well as physical survival, many Asian ethnics have honed their sensory skills to a finely tuned level. Upon entering an unfamiliar environment, their "antennae" come out looking for any signs of potential trouble to gauge the degree of safety. The price paid for such attentiveness, however, is high. As Paul Leong mentioned earlier, he has socially hindered himself by being on the lookout for trouble so intently. And yet, he feels compelled to do so because he knows in some communities he is not welcome solely because he is not white.

"When I'm around real Chinese people they don't think I'm Chinese"—Not Asian Enough.   As if being deemed inauthentically American wasn't enough, Asian ethnics must also contend with not being seen as Chinese or Japanese enough. They face societal expectations to be *ethnic* since others assume they should be closer to their ethnic roots than to their American ones. Carol Wong, a dietitian, speaks about an experience she had while on the job:

I had just moved to New York, maybe four months, and this doctor came up to me and said something to me in Chinese and I turned around

and said something like "Are you talking to me?" And he said yeah, and I said, "I don't speak Chinese." This was a Caucasian guy . . . and he starts going into this tirade like, "Are you ashamed of where you came from da da da da. And I turned around to him and I looked him straight in the face and I said, "How many Americans do you know who go around speaking Chinese? I'm not ashamed of where I come from. I come from Fresno. The place that provides you with those little red boxes of Sunmaid Raisins."

Whereas for later generation white ethnics to identify along ethnic lines is a matter of personal choice, my respondents have not found this to be the case for them; not identifying in ethnic or racial terms is problematic in their interactions with non-Asians. Asian ethnics are not free to practice symbolic ethnicity to the degree white ethnics are (Gans, 1979). Symbolic ethnicity for the latter, as Steinberg (1989, p. 63) argues, comes out of a crisis of cultural authenticity that has left later generations with only high profile symbols to champion: "People desperately wish to 'feel' ethnic precisely because they have all but lost the prerequisites of 'being' ethnic." Asian ethnics, on the other hand, are expected to "be ethnic" in spite of similar degrees of acculturation. Others consistently expect them to identify ethnically (as Chinese or Japanese) or racially (as Asian) as well as be knowledgeable about Chinese or Japanese "things" and to express dissatisfaction when they are not.

Meanwhile, Asian ethnics get it from the other end as well. That is, Asian ethnics also experience judgment from their foreign-born counterparts who see them as "too American," not knowledgeable enough about Chinese or Japanese ways. While Asian immigrants were not interviewed for this project, other studies have documented the attitudes the foreign-born have towards the native-born (Lee, 1996: Uba, 1994; Chen, 1992; Weiss, 1973). Wong's (1977, p. 6) work on intergenerational relations in New York's Chinatown is particularly noteworthy:

In dealing with the members of the community, the traditional (foreign-born) elite tend to claim that they are the "real Chinese," as opposed to the second- and third-generation Chinese Americans. A "real" Chinese means one who speaks and writes the Chinese language, interacts with other Chinese in a "humane," "Chinese" way, practices all the Chinese customs, celebrates the important Chinese festivals, etc.

My respondents are well aware of how they differ from their foreign-born counter-parts in both superficial (i.e., style of clothing, accent, how they carry themselves) as well as more meaningful ways (culture, values, beliefs, lifestyles). They are also aware that immigrants see them as less culturally authentic. Kevin Fong:

Q: How do you identify?

A: First and foremost I was born Chinese and this goes back to what my brother told me one time. He said, and I totally related with that, "You're born Chinese, but when you're around Chinese people, like when I'm around real Chinese people, they don't think I'm Chinese because I was born here and I'm kind of Americanized. And if I call myself an American, I hang around with American guys, they don't consider me American because I don't look American, I'm Chinese. So I would say that I'm Chinese-American first and foremost. I was born Chinese and I'm proud of that but I'm also proud that I'm an American of the United States.

Except for a handful whose personal histories include prolonged time spent in the motherland or who came from a family with an immigrant parent, few respondents feel comfortable identifying with the foreign-born. The vast majority see themselves as a breed apart, as clearly being related to but distinct from Asian immigrants.

As a compromise, most have chosen, like Kevin Fong, to adopt a hyphenated identity to honor their American as well as ethnic roots. Victor Ong

spoke insightfully about his decision to call himself a Chinese-American:

> Usually I say Chinese-American because I realize I'm not Chinese. People from China come over here and like, whoa, they're like a foreign species. And I'm not American because just one look and I'm apart. I used to struggle with this question a lot and to make a long story short, Chinese-American is a hybrid of its own. It's kind of like Afro-Americans. Boy, they're not African and they're not American and it's just its own species and that's the way it is.

Both Victor's and Kevin's comments aptly summarize the authenticity dilemma confronting Asian ethnics as well as hint at how they begin to address the dilemma, a topic to which I now turn.

"Where are you really from?" Playing the Ethnic Game and Other Acts of Resistance.   Most Asian ethnics have been asked the question, "where are you from," at some point in their lives. All have learned that the question really being asked is, "what is your ancestral homeland," since answering "San Jose" or "Los Angeles" usually fails to satisfy whoever is asking. Such a localized answer typically results in the response, "No. Where are you *really* from?" While some answer straightforwardly, others choose to play an "ethnic game" with their interrogator. This involves mischievously bantering with whomever is asking the question until they give up or refine their query. Dani Murayama's and Greg Okinaka's experiences provide excellent examples:

> (Dani) A lot of times people will come up to me and ask me where I'm from and I'll answer Los Angeles and they'll look at me really strange (laugh). But that's where I'm from and then they'll say. "No, no, no. Where were you born?" And I'll say Los Angeles. And then they'll ask me where my parents were born and I'll tell them the United States. And then they'll ask me where my grandparents were born and I'll tell them the United States (laugh).

(Greg) I get it all the time. I think it's kind of funny because I always say, "I'm from so and so." And then they say. "No. Where are you from?" And then you say, "Well, actually I'm from Oakland." "No. Where are you *from*?' "And then it's like, "Well, I'm from North Dakota, if you want to go there." Then it's like, "No, no, no. . . ." (laugh)

What strikes me about these passages is the insistence on the part of their interrogators to get to the *truth*, to find out where Dani and Greg are *really* from. They were not satisfied with the responses provided because they believed these two had to come from some place other than this country. Dani and Greg, for their parts, were only willing to provide opaque answers as a gesture of defiance.

Tony Lam, who also plays the ethnic game, refuses to give others the satisfaction of pigeon-holing him as a foreigner to this country:

Yeah, I get that all the time. You know what I tell them? I use the tact now. This guy (was) asking me and I could tell he's really excited (and) he's anticipating the answer. "Will it be Thailand? Will it be Japan?" He's all excited. Maybe he went to the Orient. And I tell him with a perfect look, "San Jose." And all of a sudden he has all this enthusiasm, flustered and goes, "Oh. San Jose." I'm answering honestly where I came from.

Some might think Tony, Dani, and Greg are being unnecessarily sensitive to a seemingly innocuous question. After repeatedly facing this line of questioning, however, they are marking out their own ways of defiance. After all, the answers they provide are truthful given what is being asked. Where are they from? They are from this country as are their parents and, in some cases, their grandparents and great-grandparents.

While a few experience dissonance or guilt over their seeming drift away from cultural traditions, the majority of my respondents are unapologetic about their lifestyles. The sentiment is captured well by Jan Muramoto:

I took three years of Spanish to qualify for college because it was easier, and you know, people say to me all the time, don't you feel guilty? And I say, you know, you can't live your life feeling guilty. It doesn't make me any less of an Asian person because I can't speak the language. It doesn't make me any less of a person because I don't make sushi. There are other things that I teach my children. I mean my parents didn't speak Japanese at home. They spoke English to us . . . We speak English at home. We live in this country. We speak English.

Jan is clearly defensive over her authenticity as an "Asian person" because she has been challenged on this issue before. However, she is rebelling against a static, essentialized definition which stipulates that unless she is fluent in Japanese and can make sushi she is not "really Japanese." She prefers a more fluid interpretation of culture since that is how she was brought up to understand it herself.

Respondents like Jan represent a powerful emerging voice within the Asian-American community. They are self consciously aware of how far the proverbial apple has dropped from the tree and how the resulting sapling has adapted to its own unique circumstances and soil conditions. As such, they are actively engaging in the process of cultural production and are embracing the resulting forms and practices (Nagel, 1994; Yancey et al., 1976).

"They passed on a Chinese-American culture to me, not as much a Chinese culture"—Ethnic Authenticity on Their Own Terms.   Despite all of the ways ethnicity has ceased to influence their daily lives, Asian ethnics do consider it to be a salient aspect of their identity. What matters to them, however, has increasingly little to do with cultural traditions as practiced by Chinese and Japanese nationals. Gary Hong:

My parents don't have a whole lot to pass on because my dad doesn't speak the language. The primary thing they could have passed on to me would be the language because both my grandparents and my parents don't do traditional stuff like lighting incense. We're all Christians so we don't do the Buddhist or Confucius things.

Q: So what Chinese-American things did they pass on?

A: It's not really cultural, partly social. Being Chinese-American, being Asian-American, it's a combination of ideological, cultural, social. There is that social part because there is a community there. Just because they don't do traditional things like lighting incense in a temple doesn't mean that it's not a Chinese-American community. Chinese-American community in the sense that they do things together, they all understand each other, have a common background, look out for each other, do things in the community together. That's what they passed on to me. A recognition, they brought me up in that community, playing sports, doing things with their other friends. In that sense that's what they passed on to me. They passed on a Chinese-American culture to me, not as much a Chinese culture.

The attention of respondents like Gary Hong rests squarely on the evolving cultural patterns being generated in this society by Japanese-American, Chinese-American, and other Asian-American groups. The cultural elements they feel are worth retaining are the emergent as well as re-interpreted values and practices they grew up with which weave together strands of Japanese, Chinese, and American mainstream cultures. Lisa Lowe (1996, p. 65) speaks to this theme when she writes: "The making of Asian-American culture includes practices that are partly inherited, partly modified, as well as partly invented." Gary Hong again, reflecting on his third generation father.

My dad is uniquely Chinese-American in the true sense. He's really Asian-American because he grew up in (pause) because his father passed away, he doesn't even speak Chinese. . . . I think there is a direct link there. So he does have a

background in Chinese culture because he hung out with all these Chinese people in the Bay Area in that generation in Berkeley. There are a lot of Chinese people around, so he had the culture, he knows some of the stuff. He didn't practice it but he knew it. He hung around Chinese people a lot. He's definitely Chinese but a lot of the things they did as kids were like Happy Days, American stuff. Cars, girls, and baseball. That's kinds cool. So I look at all of them as Chinese-American.

Gary makes an important observation in stressing the cultural fusion that took place for his father's generation. Without denying the historical basis of culture, it is essential not to reify it either. Traditional Chinese culture was not simply transferred over to the United States and preserved in the exact same state as when the first Chinese came over. A uniquely Chinese-American culture developed in this country and it was within this cultural context that his father grew up. In turn, an ethnic identity fashioned out of both Chinese and American elements was forged and adopted by Gary's father. What Gary's father passed on to him was not Chinese culture as traditionally defined but, rather, what Yancey et al. (1976) refer to as an emergent identity and practices centered around both Chinese and "American stuff," created and shared with co-ethnics and in some cases other Asian ethnics.

Greg Okinaka, a sansei in his 20s, was particularly insightful about the dynamic character of culture. He describes his philosophy:

I mean, I think it is very important for the next generation, the younger, the next bunch of people to realize . . . I think there's such a specific Japanese, no not Japanese, well, Asian-American (pause) culture that has evolved and that is in the process of evolving (and) that it's more important to learn about that than it is to learn about . . . I mean because the Asia, the Japan that my parents knew when they were my age was a completely different Japan than I know at my current age. And it's gonna be a different

Japan that any other generations learn fifteen or twenty years from now.

Greg is speaking of a "homegrown" culture and identity that reflect the cultural frames of reference influencing his life, and his pride as well as defensiveness around that developing identity are important features. It is more important, in his estimation, to be well versed in the culture that is evolving here in the U.S. (which is increasingly pan-ethnic in orientation) than in Japan's culture, a value he acquired from his parents and continues to uphold in his own life.

One cultural value that has been modified to reflect the boundary shifts taking place among different Asian ethnic groups includes their preference for ethnic friendships. While clearly not a new cultural value, my respondents have put their own twist on it by expanding the category pan-ethnically to include Asian-Americans more generally. Less than a fifth described their friends as consisting exclusively of co-ethnics, but more than a third have friendship circles consisting primarily of other Asian-Americans; the remainder describe their friends as being racially diverse or primarily white.

Those with predominantly Asian-American friends claim to share a special bond or sense of kinship with them which they do not necessarily experience with non-Asians. According to Barry Sato, "It was easier to hang out with Asians. Thing is when you talk about things your experiences and values seem to mesh a little bit more." References were repeatedly made to perceived similarities between themselves and their Asian-American friends based on similar upbringing, parental expectations, values, and even experiences with stereotyping and intentional prejudice, discrimination, and marginalization. These shared experiences, as Laura Nee put it, result in comfortable interactions. "There's less explaining because we were brought up pretty much the same." Whereas in the past this sentiment would have extended only to co-ethnics, today it increasingly applies to other Asian-Americans irrespective of ethnicity.

As was the case during their childhood, the activities they engage in with their Asian-American friends are not ethnically centered in any traditional sense. As later generation Americans, they are highly acculturated and participate in many of the same activities as other Californians irrespective of race or ethnicity. About a third are members of one or more organized ethnic activities. Especially popular among younger respondents are Asian-American sports leagues of which there are myriad to choose from: JAVA (Japanese-American Volleyball Association), Westside Volleyball League, and LA Asian Ski Club to name only a few. Some have also joined college fraternities and sororities and other campus groups geared to Asian-American students. For professionals, there are a wide range of business networks and employee associations to choose from where members share both class and ethnic resources (i.e., Asian Professional Exchange (APEX), Asian Business League (ABL), Asian-American Journalist Association, Young Generation Asian Professionals (YGAP), Asian Business Association (ABA), M Society, and Orange County Chinese-American Chamber of Commerce). Vo's (1996) research, for example, on the San Diego branch of the ABA demonstrates how members develop business opportunities and deal with issues such as glass ceilings in the workplace and trade with the Pacific Rim. And, of course, membership in long-standing political interest groups such as the Japanese American Citizens League (JACL) and the Organization of Chinese Americans (OCA) is common, as is church attendance in predominantly Asian congregations.

In this sense, Asian ethnics are carrying on a tradition dating back to an earlier period of racism and social exclusion. Because native born Asian-Americans were barred from participating in mainstream clubs and activities with white children, community leaders took it upon themselves to sponsor their own chapters and clubs to meet their children's needs (Chan, 1991). Many of these clubs have survived to the present day and, while no longer forced to participate in ethnically specific leagues, many choose to do so out of family tradition or sense of comfort.

Their preferences toward Asian-American friends is also extending to their dating practices. Of the forty-eight single men and women we interviewed, only four exclusively date co-ethnics.[4] The rest date interracially (mostly commonly with whites) as well as interethnically (with other Asian-Americans). That they frequently choose white partners is not surprising given their demographic dominance and availability (Sung, 1990). What is surprising, however, is how frequently they date other Asian-Americans, their casual attitudes towards doing so, and in some cases, the purposefulness of their choices. Some, in fact, do not consider it interdating since, "after all, we're both Asian." Diane Okihiro, for example, spoke of the interchangeability in her mind between Chinese-American and Japanese-American men:

I think most of the guys I've gone out with who are Chinese-American, the guy I'm with now, it's not any different. To me it's the same as being with someone who would be Japanese-American.

While at an earlier time a Japanese-American woman would have encountered stubborn resistance if she dated or married a Chinese-American man, today this union hardly raises an eyebrow among contemporary and single Asian ethnics.

I believe the matter of fact attitude my respondents have towards interethnic dating is both the producer and product of an intense boundary shift currently taking place. More and more Asian ethnics, particularly younger ones, are defining themselves pan-ethnically as Asian-Americans and identifying along racial lines (Espiritu, 1992; Shinagawa and Pang, 1996; Kibria, 1997; Onishi, 1996). They subsequently can have a casual attitude because they believe it is still "within the family," that is, the family of Asian-Americans.

This has not come about easily nor naturally, however. Pan-ethnic categories are initially created by forces beyond the control of the subsumed groups and the resulting label, in this case

Asian-American, must first be externally imposed (Espiritu, 1992). Ignoring cultural, linguistic, and oftentimes long-standing animosity between different ethnic groups, members of the dominant society have historically invoked their power to categorize others according to criteria that are convenient for them (Nagel, 1991, 1994).

Only over time do groups who were forcibly lumped together (usually on the basis of shared language or presumed racial similarities) begin to recognize the commonalties in their experiences and found alliances to protect and promote their collective interests (Omi and Winant, 1994). Eventually, the identity that was originally imposed on them, in this case Asian-American, takes on a life and meaning of its own as a new cultural base reflecting their common experiences in the U.S. is gradually constructed (Nagel, 1991, 1994). Ethnic distinctions matter less and less in the face of an emerging racial consciousness (Onishi, 1996). This does not mean they cease to think of themselves in ethnic-specific terms as Chinese- or Japanese-American or that the pan-ethnic progression is irreversible or even inevitable. The point to keep in mind is that they are more willing to see themselves as Asian-Americans in a larger variety of contexts.

From one perspective, my respondents' dating behavior may be viewed as further proof of the erosion of ethnicity's meaningfulness in their lives. Clearly, younger respondents do not feel constrained by social mores to exclusively date or eventually marry a co-ethnic. Given how many have chosen to exercise their freedom of choice, their behavior could easily be interpreted as signaling the death knell for ethnicity as fewer and fewer homogeneous couples are formed and eventually sanctioned by marriage.

Viewed from a different perspective, however, their openness to dating other Asian-Americans can also be seen as an example of a new and thriving racial salience. Increasingly, the issue is not whether they date co-ethnics, but whether they date others within the same pan-ethnic and racialized category as themselves.

Conclusion: Who Qualifies as an American?

It would only be a slight exaggeration to say that the quintessential American experience is rooted in the experience of immigration. The ability to recall an earlier time when one's ancestors travelled great and unfamiliar distances to seek a new life, the difficulties they faced, their eventual triumph over adversity, and their contributions toward building a new nation are the stuff from which we have built our cultural mythology—countless American morality tales have been written using this basic template. White ethnics today are united by this collective public memory—the journey across the Atlantic and subsequent pioneer experience are nostalgically recalled as rites of passage toward becoming an American (Alba, 1990; Bodnar, 1992).

Less clear is how the experiences of non-European origin groups fit into this public memory. The fact that African Americans were forcibly brought over on slave ships or that Native Americans and Mexicans were incorporated into this country against their will, adds a troubling element to an otherwise straightforward picture of assimilation.

Unlike these other groups, Asian America has its roots in voluntary immigration. Like their European counterparts, Chinese and Japanese immigrants freely entered this country in the nineteenth and early twentieth centuries in search of economic opportunity. Where they differed, however, was in the level of exclusion, resistance, and outright rejection they encountered. This is not to deny the rejection experienced by some European groups, most notably Irish, Italians, and Poles, but the extreme "foreignness" of the Chinese and Japanese in terms of culture, language, and phenotype so different from European and western norms, set them off for a unique degree of persecution and exclusion (Said, 1979).[5]

In short, while they did immigrate voluntarily, they were not put into the same category as European immigrants and therefore not worthy or capable of becoming "real" Americans. And so we have the World War Two Internment of innocent Japanese-Americans, racist housing covenants barring rental or sale of property to "Orientals," miscegenation laws prohibiting marriages between whites and "Mongolians," and on and on. And let us not forget the 1790 Naturalization Act which restricted citizenship eligibility to "free white persons," and which was not fully nullified until 1952.

So what becomes of groups whose experiences do not neatly fit with the collective memory of what it took to become an American? Where does that leave them today? In the case of Asian ethnics, it leaves them feeling like "guests in someone else's house," as Ron Wakabayashi, former director of the Japanese American Citizens League (JACL) puts it, "that we can never put our feet up on the table."[6] Not only do they not fit the romanticized and sentimentalized account of assimilation offered in the melting pot metaphor, their own pioneer roots, unique experiences and contributions in building this country have been and continue to be erased from collective memory. Lowe (1996) speaks powerfully to this point in her work on the Asian-American experience as she explains how and why Asian-Americans continue to be located outside the cultural and racial boundaries of the nation. As Alba (1990) argues, what it means to be an American continues to demand European ancestry. Whites continue to feel a sense of "proprietary claim" to being the "real" Americans (Blumer, 1958).

Today, Asian ethnics exercise a great deal of choice regarding the elements of traditional ethnic culture they wish to incorporate or do away with in their personal lives. They befriend whom they please, date and marry whom they please, choose the careers they please, and pursue further knowledge about their cultural heritage if they please. In this sense, ethnicity has indeed become optional in my respondents' personal lives. But in another very real way, being ethnic remains a societal expectation for them despite how far removed they are from their immigrant roots or how much they differ from their foreign-born counterparts.

NOTES

1. Sam Chu Lin, "Radio Tirade," *Asian Week*, April 5, 1996.

2. More recent examples include the 1982 killing of Vincent Chin, a second generation Chinese-American, by two angry white autoworkers who saw him as a "job-stealing Jap" and the harassment of only Asian-American campaign donors in response to charges of illegal campaign finance activities on the part of Asian nationals (Takaki, 1989; Daniels, 1972; Nagata, 1993).

3. All names have been changed to protect the anonymity of study participants.

4. As for the 47 respondents who are married, about a third have intermarried; half are with white partners (except for one Chinese-American woman who is married to a Latino) and half with Asian-Americans.

5. See Ronald Takaki's *Strangers From a Different Shore* and Bill Ong Hing's *Making and Re-making Asian America Through Immigration Policy, 1850–1990* for excellent overviews of the discriminatory treatment experienced by Chinese- and Japanese-Americans.

6. Michael Moore (1988) "Scapegoats Again," *The Progressive* 52: 25–28, 26.

REFERENCES

Alba, R. (ed.). (1985). *Ethnicity and Race in the U.S.A.: Toward the Twenty-First Century*, Routledge and Kegan Paul, London.

Alba, R. (1985b). The twilight of ethnicity among Americans of European ancestry: The case of Italians. In Alba, R. D. (ed.), *Ethnicity and Race in the U.S.A.: Toward the Twenty-First Century*, Routledge and Kegan Paul, London.

Alba, R. (1990). *Ethnicity in America: The Transformation of White America*, Yale University Press, New Haven.

Alba, R. (1995). Assimilation's quiet tide. *Public Interest* 119:3–18.

Alba, R., and Chamlin, M. B. (1983). A preliminary examination of ethnic identification among whites. *American Sociological Review* 48:240–247.

Bakalian, A. P. (1992). *Armenian-Americans: From Being to Feeling Armenian*, Transaction Publishers, New Brunswick.

Barringer, H. R., Gardner. R. W., and Levin, M. J. (1993). *Asian and Pacific Islanders in the United States*, Russell Sage Foundation, New York.

Blumer, H. (1958). Race prejudice as a sense of group position. *Pacific Sociological Review* 1:3–7.

Bodnar, J. (1992). *Remaking America: Public Memory, Commemoration, and Patriotism in the Twentieth Century*. Princeton University Press, New Jersey.

Chan, K., and Hune, S. (1995). Racialization and Panethnicity: From Asians in America to Asian-Americans. In Hawley, W. and Jackson, A. (eds.), *Toward a Common Destiny*, Jossey-Bass, San Francisco, pp. 205–233.

Chan, S. (1991). *Asian Americans: An Interpretive History*, Twayne Publishers, Boston.

Chen, H. (1992). *Chinatown No More*, Cornell University Press, New York.

Cornell, S., and Hartmann, D. (1998). *Ethnicity and Race: Making Identities in a Changing World*, Pine Forge Press, Thousand Oaks, Calif.

Daniels, R. (1972). *Concentration Camps USA: Japanese-Americans and World War II*, Holt, Rinehart and Winston, Inc., New York.

Daniels, R. (1991). *Japanese-Americans: From Relocation to Redress*, University of Washington Press, Seattle.

Espiritu, Y. L. (1992). *Asian-American Panethnicity*, Temple University Press, Philadelphia.

Fong, T. (1998). *Contemporary Asian American Experience*, Prentice Hall, New Jersey.

Gans, H. (1979). Symbolic ethnicity: The future of ethnic groups and cultures in America. *Ethnic and Racial Studies* 2:1–19.

Hamamoto, D. (1994). *Monitored Peril: Asian-Americans the Politics of TV Representation*, University of Minnesota Press, Minnesota.

Higham, J. (1963). *Strangers in the Land*, Rutgers University Press, New Jersey.

Hing, B. O. (1993). *Making and Remaking Asian America Through Immigration Policy, 1850–1990*, Stanford University Press, Palo Alto.

Horton, J. (1995). *The Politics of Diversity: Immigration, Resistance, and Change in Monterey Park, California*, Temple University Press, Philadelphia.

Hune, S. (1990). Opening the American mind and body: The role of Asian-American studies. *Change* 21:56–63.

Jiobu, R. M. (1988). *Ethnicity and Assimilation: Blacks, Chinese, Filipinos, Japanese, Koreans, Mexicans, Vietnamese, and Whites*, State University of New York Press, New York.

Kibria, N. (1997). The construction of 'Asian American': Reflections on intermarriage and ethnic identity among second-generation Chinese and Korean American. *Ethnic and Racial Studies* 20: 523–544.

Kim, E. (1986). Asian American and American popular culture. *Dictionary of Asian American History,* University of Chicago Press, Chicago.

Kitano, H. H. L. (1992). *Generations and Identity: The Japanese-American,* Ginn Press, Massachusetts.

Lee, S. J. (1996). *Unraveling the "Model Minority" Stereotype: Listening to Asian-American Youth,* Teachers College Press, New York.

Lowe, L. (1996). *Immigrant Acts,* Duke University Press, Durham.

Min, P. G. (ed.). (1995). *Asian Americans,* Sage Publications, Thousand Oaks.

Nagata, D. (1993). *Legacy of Injustice: Exploring the Cross-Generational Impact of the Japanese-American Internment,* Plenum Press, New York.

Nagel, J. (1991). The political construction of ethnicity. In Yetman, N. R. (ed.), *Majority and Minority: The Dynamics of Race and Ethnicity in American Life,* Allyn and Bacon, Boston, pp. 76–86.

Nagel, J. (1994). Constructing ethnicity: Creating and recreating ethnic identity and culture, *Social Problems* 41:152–176.

Nishi, S. M. (1989). Perceptions and deceptions: Contemporary views of Asian-Americans. In Yun, G. (ed.), *A Look Beyond the Model Minority Image: Critical Issues in Asian America,* Minority Rights Group, Inc., New York.

Omi, M. (1993). Out of the melting pot and into the fire: Race relations policy. In LEAP Asian Pacific American public policy institute and UCLA Asian-American studies center, *The state of Asian Pacific America: Policy Issues to the Year 2020,* The Editors, Los Angeles, pp. 199–214.

Omi, M., and Winant. H. (1994). *Racial Formation in the United States,* Routledge, New York.

Onishi, N. (1996). New sense of race arises among Asian-Americans, *New York Times,* May 30: A1.

Park, R. (1950). *Race and Culture: Essays in the Sociology of Contemporary Man,* University of Chicago Press, Chicago.

Park, R., and Burgess, E. (1921). *Introduction to the Science of Sociology,* University of Chicago Press, Chicago.

Phinney, J. S. (1990). Ethnic identity in adolescents and adults: Review of research. *Psychological Bulletin* 108:499–514.

Said, E. (1979). *Orientalisin.* Vintage Books, New York.

Saito, L. (1993). Contrasting patterns of adaptation: Japanese Americans and Chinese immigrants in monterey park. In Revilla, L., Nomura, G., Wong, S., and Hune, S. (eds.), *Bearing Dreams and Shaping Visions: Asian Pacific American Perspectives,* Washington State University Press, Washington, pp. 33–43.

Shinagawa, L. H., and Pang, G. Y. (1996). Asian-American panethnicity and intermarriage. *Amerasia J.* 22(2):127–132.

Steinberg, S. (1989). *The Ethnic Myth: Race, Ethnicity and Class in America,* Beacon Press, Boston.

Takaki, R. (1987). *From Different Shores.* Oxford University Press, New York.

Takaki, R. (1989). *Strangers from a Different Shore,* Penguin Books, New York.

Uba, L. (1994). *Asian Americans: Personality Patterns, Identity, and Mental Health,* Guilford Press, New York.

U.S. Bureau of the Census. (1993). *1990 Census of Population: Asians and Pacific Islanders in the United States,* CP-3-5, Washington, D.C.

Vo, L. (1996). Asian immigrants, Asian Americans and the politics of ethnic mobilization in San Diego. *Amerasia J.* 22(2):89–108.

Waters, M. C. (1986). *The Process and Content of Ethnic Identification: A Study of White Ethnics in Suburbia.* Doctoral thesis.

Waters, M. C. (1990). *Ethnic Options: Choosing Identities in America.* University of California Press. Berkeley.

Waters, M. C. (1992). The construction of a symbolic ethnicity: Suburban white ethnics in the 1980s. In D'Innocenzo, M., and Sirefman, J. P. (eds.), *Immigration and Ethnicity: American Society—"Melting Pot" or "Salad Bowl"?,* Greenwood Press, Connecticut, pp. 75–90.

Wei, W. (1993). *The Asian-American Movement,* Temple University Press, Philadelphia.

Weiss, M. (1973). Division and unity: Social process in a Chinese-American community. In Sue, S., and Wagner, N. (eds.), *Asian Americans: Psychological Perspectives,* Science and Behavior Books, Palo Alto, pp. 264–273.

Wong, B. (1977). Elites in Chinatown, New York City. *Urban Anthropology* 6(1):1–22.

Yancey, W. L., Ericksen, E. P., and Juliani, R. N. (1976). Emergent ethnicity: A review and reformulation. *American Sociological Review* 41:391–403.

Zenner, W. P. (1985). Jewishness in America: Ascription and choice. In Alba, R. D. (ed.), *Ethnicity and Race in the U.S.A.: Toward the Twenty-First Century,* Routledge and Kegan Paul, London, pp. 117–133.

Mia Tuan is an associate professor of sociology at the University of Oregon in Eugene. Her research interests include racial and ethnic identity, transracial adoption, immigrant adaptation, and racial reconciliation/mediation work. She is currently conducting a qualitative study (with Jiannbin Shiao) of Asian adoptees raised by white families, which is being funded by the Russell Sage Foundation.

An interview with . . .

Mia Tuan

How did you become interested in this topic?

Well, the work came out of my personal experiences and was a coming together of my personal interests as well as my intellectual and academic interests. I am what is known, affectionately, as a "one-point-five generation Asian American," which means that I was born elsewhere, so I am technically an immigrant, but I came at such a young age (three years old) that for all intents and purposes, my outlook on life and the way I see things is very American-based. So I think that somewhere along the line I just became very curious about the experiences of people who look like me, but had been here numerous generations, and whether or not the kinds of questions and maybe even insecurities that I had as a one point fiver were shared by people who had been here three, four, five generations. And so the research was really my way of going further into those types of questions and, on a personal level, to be able to compare what my own experiences and what, at that time, my future children's experiences might reveal.

You say in the article that this was part of a larger study that you had done?

The article was a sort of sub-chapter of a larger project, a book which was based on interviews with 100 Chinese and Japanese ethnics in California (which was also my Ph.D. dissertation).

What made you choose this particular methodological approach—semistructured, or would you call them unstructured, interviews? And what do you see as the main strengths and the limitations of that approach?

I call them semistructured. Well, partly it fits with my personality. I'm definitely someone who is more comfortable sitting across the table from somebody having what I call a "guided conversation," where I have the luxury of kind of delving deeper into themes and following up hunches and probing and following different leads, as opposed to data sets or quantitative data. So semistructured interviews fit both my own personal strengths as well as allowing me to tell the kind of tale that I wanted to tell. Allowing me to tell the richer, more personal tale is clearly the strength. The main weakness is that you are only able to tell a deep, rich tale of a set number of people. In my case, I was still pretty ambitious. I shot for 100, but certainly I can't say that I speak for the Asian ethnic experience in any kind of representative fashion.

How did you recruit participants for the study, and were there any particular challenges in gaining their trust or developing rapport with them?

At the time I was in Los Angeles—I was a graduate student at UCLA—and in many ways I was in the "heart" of what I call Asian ethnic experience because California is kind of the hub of Asian American later generations. So in that sense it wasn't that difficult, and I recruited a number of undergraduates who took a course with me and I kind of prepped them about the literature and gave them a sort of quick methods class as well. So we basically snowball sampled. We worked through both community organizations as well [as]— "Oh, I know somebody"—and kind of followed that lead up, so it really wasn't very difficult to get 100 people on board. We also sampled folks in San Francisco, the Bay area, which is where I am from as well, so that part was very smooth.

Developing trust and rapport was not an issue. People were very eager and willing to speak with us about this and seemed very pleased. The shortest interview was about an hour, the longest was three or four hours. That totally depended on how much each interviewee wanted to elaborate on their story. We interviewed them in lots of different places: homes, coffee shops, restaurants, my office. Since then I've moved onto projects where I do phone interviews, but these were all face to face. I had some undergraduates doing interviewing with me. I had most of them putting out the word and recruiting for me.

Were there any unexpected events, problems, or developments that you faced?

I don't think so. This was a smooth, meant-to-be project. Nothing out of the blue—other than coordinating. Since I wasn't doing all of the interviews, coordinating and staying on top of people. We ended up losing data because I went off to do a predissertation fellowship in Iowa and I had a student who was doing some transcription for me and he lost the interviews in the mail. So I lost four or five cases as well as the transcription machine. And so this was something that I had not anticipated. It wasn't the actual craft of doing the interviews; it was just the logistics of getting them transcribed. This was a lot of transcription and so I hired somebody. I didn't think twice about it—I just figured I would get it and it got lost in the mail.

How did you go about compiling and analyzing your data? Did you use some of the software that is available?

At the time I used a program called FolioView and I do have some stories around that. My training didn't involve any sort of software—you just go combing through with a lot of highlighters. And with a hundred interviews it was just a lot of paper. I actually went through the first third of the interviews the old-fashioned way—yellow Post-it notes and highlighters. About a third of the way through I said "this is just too much" and decided I needed to learn the software. So I switched over midstream; it was retooling.

How do you see your findings as contributing to our understanding of the Asian ethnic experience in the United States? What do you see as the implications of your research?

What I saw myself doing, theoretically, was linking the Asian ethnic experience— or what I call the racialized Asian ethnic experience—to the broader literature that is out there, which is largely based on the European or white ethnic experience. What I wanted to do was to talk about how Asians fit or don't fit into assimilation models—folk wisdom about what is supposed to happen to groups of people and their relationship to their various identities over time. That was my goal. The question of the implications of my research is a fascinating one that I am struggling with right now. The current work I am doing is what I might call a "cousin" to that earlier work. We've been interviewing Asian adoptees raised by white parents, once again kind of continuing the theme of aspects of the Asian American experience and talking to people who may look one way and face people's assumptions and expectations based on appearance, versus how they themselves understand themselves and feel inside and how they "do life." It is a complicated thing to try to figure out how Asians fit in larger race relations because the common paradigm is black/white. Typically no one knows what to do with Asians. Are they honorary whites? Are they a more permanently racially-stigmatized group? It's a big question mark. Even now, after embarking on the second project and going much further with this, I still have to say the jury is out because in some ways, they are honorary whites and in some ways, they are a stigmatized group in that race just seems to stick on in a way that is more tenacious than ethnicity. And so it is still unfolding.

Were there any particular ethnical challenges or issues involved in your research, and how did you deal with them?

Probably the biggest one is the fact that this is personal for me. As an Asian American who, obviously, has her own set of experiences and assumptions about how the world works and how I have kind of floated through daily life, I have to do my best to stay on top of those assumptions or at least acknowledge when I was surprised by something, in either a positive or negative direction. I don't think it is ever possible to be neutral, but I think the next best thing is to be very cognizant and upfront so that when people read your work, they know what your angle is. Especially now, with my current work, I am spending a lot more time debriefing at the end of a project about the trials and tribulations of the work. I pay much more attention to that now. With regard to anonymity, we did change the respondents' names; the project happened in the early 90s, and no one has come back since and raised any concerns.

What was the most frustrating or difficult aspect of doing this research?

It really was just waiting for the transcriptions and getting the data to me, managing that many cases. The projects I had done before that were always just me, 30 or 40 or 50 cases, and it was in house—I was able to stay on top of it, every quote I was looking for, I had a sense of where it was, and once I started to sort of farm it out when I was working with others, where there were interviews that I hadn't done—that was a challenge for me, to basically delegate and then try to organize and coordinate information, that was a struggle.

What was the most satisfying about the experience?

For me the most satisfying aspect was being able to fill in what I consider to be a hole as far as research focus. Up to that time, I was not aware of any extended study that has been done about Asian ethnics who have been here a long time, but are Asian—of Asian ancestry. That was very satisfying.

If you were to do the research again, what might you do differently?

If I were to do it again, I would move beyond the West Coast. Assuming the world were mine and I didn't have to worry about logistics, this would have been more than a West Coast study. I would have had a West Coast, East Coast, and perhaps a Midwest sample (if I could find them). I think I would also want to do it longitudinally, because my own thinking has shifted in ten or fifteen short years, and I'd like to see how people evolve. I've never been one to think of ethnicity as a static thing; it evolves over time and in response to life experiences, so I would like to have done that.

Is there any important lesson that you have drawn from the research that you might share with students?

It would have something to do with being open to being surprised, and acknowledging the sort of sacred responsibility that I, as a researcher, have in telling somebody else's story. If someone is willing to sit down with me, take time out of their day, to tell me about some aspect of their life, I may or may not agree with what they have to say or how they do their life, but as a researcher I have a sacred responsibility to be respectful of the people who I have spoken to, in at least trying to convey the spirit of the story that they told me. I can offer my own analysis, so I am more than just a transcriber or a documenter—I am also an analyzer. But I need to be clear about those two different roles. I think that is the main lesson that I am acquiring as I continue on my own journey as a researcher.

Questions to Think About

1. Describe Tuan's sample. Why and how does it meet her needs? Do you think her findings would have been different had she used a more nationally representative sample? How?

2. If Mia Tuan were not Chinese American, do you think there would be a difference in how she conducted her research, what people were willing to share with her, and the sort of relationship that she was able to develop with people she interviewed?

3. List three or four testable hypotheses that are suggested by Tuan's findings. Choose one and indicate how you might go about testing it.

4. How does Tuan define "Asian ethnic"? How does her study of Asian ethnics fill a hole in the research?

5. Tuan refers to her "journey as a researcher." What do you think she means by that? In what ways might one think of a field research project as a journey?

Exceptions to the Rule

Upwardly Mobile White and Mexican American High School Girls

Julie Bettie

While most high school students will obtain future social class positions consistent with their class backgrounds, a handful of students are exceptions to this rule, being either upwardly mobile working-class students (on the college preparatory track) or downwardly mobile middle-class students (on the vocational track). Highlighting predominant patterns, research typically ignores such students precisely because they are exceptions to the rule. This article, based on ethnographic research among white and Mexican American high school girls in California's Central Valley, foregrounds the experience of upwardly mobile working-class students showing how race/ethnicity, class, and gender intersect in the lives of these young women, shaping their educational mobility. Using a comparative approach, this article examines the similarities and differences between white and Mexican American working-class girls' experiences of mobility. The article first describes the various contingencies leading to the girls' mobility, then explores their subjective experience of mobility, in both cases noting the girls' different experiences according to their race/ethnicity.

While the correlation is strong between parents' socioeconomic status and a student's membership in a middle- or working-class peer group, track in high school, and academic achievement, it is imperfect. There always are at least a handful of working-class students who are college preparatory and upwardly mobile and a handful of middle-class students who are on the vocational track and downwardly mobile. Yet most school ethnographies assume working-class and middle-class categories are two clearly distinct peer groupings (Brantlinger 1993; Eckert 1989; Foley 1990; MacLeod 1995; Weis 1990; Willis 1977). Students who are exceptions to the rule are often ignored.

This article represents a portion of my larger ethnographic study of working- and middle-class white and Mexican American high school girls located in California's Central Valley (Bettie forthcoming), which demonstrates the way in which class identity is constructed and experienced in relationship to color, race/ethnicity, gender, and sexuality. Here I focus on those white and Mexican American girls from my study who were from working-class origins but who were upwardly mobile, middle-class performers in high school, en route to receiving state or university educations.

I ask what we might learn from their exceptionalism. The first obvious question is, Why are they exceptional, or what makes these students' mobility possible? I looked for reasons for each girl's exceptionality and for their ability to perform class identities other than their own. It seemed that they did so for multiple and varied reasons, but some patterns can be identified. The other question of interest is, How do they do it? How do they negotiate the disparity between the working-class identity acquired from home and the performance of a middle-class identity at school? What is the subjective experience of class passing and of "choosing" upward mobility? While the first question on causality is difficult to answer and my analysis should be considered exploratory and limited given my small sample, the second question is more readily answered using my ethnographic methodology. My goal is to show how race/ethnicity, class, and gender intersect in the lives of the young women as these social forces relate to educational mobility.

Literature Review

Consideration of upwardly or downwardly mobile students exists within the context of the broader ethnographic scholarship on the reproduction of inequality in educational sites, but too often these have been class-, race-, or gender-centric. I will consider each literature separately.

Class-Centered Research

Social reproduction theory and production theory have offered much to the study of the reproduction of class inequality in education (Apple 1982; Bernstein 1975; Bourdieu and Passeron 1977; Bowles and Gintis 1976; Foley 1990; MacLeod 1995; Willis 1977). But these studies rarely include an analysis of both gender and race/ethnicity because these are social inequalities that cannot be explained by and understood through class analysis.

Race/Ethnicity-Centered Research

Other qualitative research has examined race/ethnicity as a distinct axis of inequality but often fails to include an analysis of class or gender. One line of research, following Ogbu's (1991) ideas (Fordham 1999; Gibson 1988; Matute-Bianchi 1991), explains "minority" school success or failure in terms of the difference between students who adopt a caste-like orientation toward schooling (found among involuntary immigrants) and those who adopt an immigrant orientation toward schooling (found among voluntary immigrants) (Ogbu and Matute-Bianchi 1986). The former equate schooling with the loss of racial/ethnic identity (i.e., school success means "acting white") and develop an adaptive strategy of resistance (often resulting in school failure). The latter hold an "achievement ideology" (MacLeod 1995), believing in meritocracy and education as a route to mobility.

One problem with this approach is that the ideology of some students does not unambiguously follow their status as either voluntary or involuntary immigrants. Matute-Bianchi (1991)

found both a caste-like orientation and an immigrant orientation within the native born, non-immigrant group of Mexican American students she studied and usefully named these competing "ethnic strategies." Similarly, Mehan, Hubbard, and Villanueva (1994) found that some non-immigrant Latinos combined achievement with a critical consciousness of structural inequality rather than perceiving school success as assimilationist. Still other research shows that not all upwardly mobile Latina/Latino students equate mobility with assimilation (Flores-Gonzales 1999; Gándara 1995; Portes and Zhou 1993). Gándara (1995) found that "family stories" told to children (e.g., of coming from highly educated or well-to-do families in Mexico, or stories of lost fortunes) transmitted a disposition toward schooling and the future that worked as cultural capital (regardless of whether the stories were true or embellished).[1] In other words, having a structural rather than an individual explanation for one's class location, such as the history of colonialism and institutionalized racism assisted some working-class students' success.

While useful in thinking through the social force of race/ethnicity, these literatures too often fail to give sustained attention to the differential effects of class on achievement across racial ethnic groups (for a possible exception, see Hemmings 1996). Moreover, gender is typically ignored (for exceptions, see Fordham 1996; Gándara 1995).

Gender-Centered Research

Early feminist analyses primarily focused on the differences between women and men or girls and boys, failing to account for gender differences across race/ethnicity and class and therefore failing to analyze women as racial/ethnic and class subjects (i.e., Gilligan 1982). While many studies are now cognizant of these dimensions, others still dichotomize white middle-class girls and working-class girls of color, paying little attention to cross-racial analyses of class. Sometimes, studies address race or ethnicity and class, but only gender is theorized (Brown and Gilligan 1992; Eder,

Evans, and Parker 1995; Orenstein 1994; Pipher 1994; McLeon Taylor, Gilligan, and Sullivan 1995; exceptions include Higginbotham and Weber 1992; Luttrell 1997).

Some studies take an additive rather than intersecting analytical approach, simply presuming that boys' educational experiences and opportunities are in all cases better than girls' rather than exploring the unique set of challenges girls face. The American Association of University Women (1994) study on schooling did not compare boys' and girls' graduation rates or grades but compared them on only six subjective self-esteem measures, arguing that girls suffer from lower self-esteem than boys do in almost all cases. Although some attention was paid to racial differences (African American girls scored higher on self-esteem than Latinas and white girls but lower on the academic self-esteem measure), class differences among girls were not analyzed at all. Such studies fail to ask if working-class girls might actually have higher academic achievement than their male counterparts. There is little research to draw on in answering this question, but Gándara (1995) found that low-income Chicanas who were upwardly mobile academically outperformed their male peers, and Valenzuela (1999) found that working-class Chicanas promoted a proschool ethic among their male peers. However, even if working-class girls do have higher academic achievement than their male counterparts (and this is unknown), the possibility of pregnancy and the fact of lower-paid (than men) jobs for women with only high school degrees mediates and inhibits girls' mobility in the long run.

In short, no studies appear comprehensive enough to control for all the variables that need to be considered when examining working-class upward mobility. This ethnographic study goes beyond previous research in its comparison of the mobility experience of white students and students of color by providing attention to the simultaneous interaction of race/ethnicity, gender, and class, which are not accounted for in much of the literature on the reproduction of inequality in educational sites.

By studying both white and Mexican American girls, I am able to point to the similarity of working-class girls' educational experiences across race/ethnicity, therefore revealing how class operates independent of race/ethnicity. My comparative approach also shows the limits of the similarities between working-class girls across race/ethnicity, therefore revealing how race/ethnicity operates independent of class and why it cannot be reduced to it. Finally, I make suggestions about the salience of gender on educational mobility.

Waretown Girls

The larger study from which this research is drawn includes more than 60 girls—working- and middle-class white girls and working- and middle-class Mexican American girls—who were seniors in vocational and college prep high school tracks. Of the 60 girls formally interviewed, 11 were upwardly mobile and of working-class origin: 5 were white and 6 were Mexican American (2 immigrants and 4 children of immigrants).

It is notable that among college prep Mexican American girls in the senior class, only two were immigrants. These two girls were fluent enough in English to be successfully able to complete college prep courses. The remainder of the immigrant girls were on the vocational track. A limitation of this study is that since I am a monolingual English speaker, I could study only fully bilingual students. Therefore, I am unable to make generalizing comparisons between the experiences of these two immigrant college prep girls and their vocational track counterparts.

In labeling a student's class origin, I mean her socioeconomic status: a combination of parental occupation, income, and educational attainment. The parents of girls coded working class were those without a college education (some had vocational training). They worked, for example, as grocery store stockers, nurses' aides, beauticians, clerical workers, janitors, or truck drivers and had corresponding incomes. The parents of girls coded middle class were college educated and worked, for example, as teachers, counselors, administrators, lawyers, doctors, professors, and business owners, with corresponding incomes.

Method

The site of the ethnography is a California public high school located in an agricultural town of approximately 40,000 people that I call Waretown. Waretown High is the only high school, and it reflects the town's demography, having about 60 percent white and 40 percent Mexican American students. The majority of these students, regardless of race/ethnicity, are from working-class families, but middle-class students are a visible minority. Most of the latter are white, but a handful are third-generation Mexican American. While the town is home to one private elementary school, no private schooling options exist in Waretown above the primary school level. Thus, both middle- and working-class students are educated together in their middle and high school years.

I engaged in participant observation for one year at the high school, hanging out daily with girls in classrooms, hallways, and a variety of other social contexts. I had no official role at the school, and to gain student trust, I distanced myself from adult school personnel. I spent my time wandering about the school looking for students who had free time to talk. I introduced myself as "a student from the university" who is doing "a study of high school girls." I sometimes met students through a trusted teacher but more typically through other students, as I interviewed girls in several networks or friendship circles.

I conducted tape-recorded interviews of approximately two hours in length with all the girls and follow-up interviews with many of them. Given my whiteness and my upward mobility, I felt far closer to white working-class students in experience, but this was not necessarily reciprocated. I knew that white working-class students perceived me as "other" and Mexican American girls even more so, although I ultimately estab-

lished a rapport with both sets of girls. The fact that I was willing to speak openly and ask frank questions about race seemed to automatically engender a certain level of trust among Mexican American girls. I asked them how they felt about me as a "white girl" from the university writing a story about them, attempting to represent them. While they occasionally expressed concern that the multiple factors influencing their lives may be hard for me to understand as a cultural outsider, they also felt it was important that I include their stories. For further consideration of the effect that my own class and racialized identity had on this research and a discussion of issues of ethnographic authority, see Bettie (forthcoming).

I talked with girls at length about dating, fashion, school, work, and their families' educational and occupational histories, income, and stories of immigration. The interviews were transcribed and coded by hand. In the larger project, several themes emerged, some of which are relevant to the issues of mobility discussed here. In what follows, I address the life contingencies that led to mobility among white girls and then consider the identity negotiations involved in their process of mobility. Next, I address these same issues among Mexican American girls.

White Girls' Routes to Mobility

Events and attitudes that were linked to mobility among working-class white girls include having received a private elementary education, defining oneself in opposition to a delinquent brother, and having an interest in sports. I will discuss these factors in sequence.

Staci's membership in the prep crowd was unusual given her parents' economic and cultural capital. Her father worked "doing maintenance" at a retirement community. But the fact that her mother worked for a time in the kitchen at the private elementary school enabled Staci to receive a subsidized private elementary school education.

Like Staci, Heather also had attended private elementary school but was not subsidized, and it was difficult to understand how her parents could have afforded it. Her father worked as a mechanic and her mother as a nurses' aide. Most Waretown families in this economic category were not sending their kids to private elementary schools. As I pushed for a clearer explanation, she indicated that her parents experienced great financial sacrifice to send her to the private elementary school, even borrowing money from relatives, but they felt it was worth it. According to her, her parents wanted to segregate her from "bad influences," which was a euphemism for Mexican American students.

Likewise, Jennifer told me that while her parents had been able to afford to send her to private elementary school, they could not afford to do the same for her brother too. Instead, he attended public school in a neighboring town (primarily composed of white middle-class residents) and, once again, the reason was to avoid "bad influences." When I pressed her for the meaning of this, she hesitated but then said her brother "won't admit to being prejudiced, but he does not like Mexicans. He thinks they should all go back to their own country. . . . He's just very opinionated, very traditional like my dad."

Julie: So he doesn't like going to school in Waretown because there is . . .

Jennifer: Mexicans, and he doesn't, and I know he'd get in a lot of trouble if he was here.

Thus, the racism of relatives sometimes resulted in girls' access to private education.

At times, an individual girl's academic motivation seemed to come from defining herself in opposition to an older sibling, in each case a brother, who was labeled delinquent and whom she witnessed causing her parent(s) angst. Mandy had not attended private elementary school yet did reasonably well academically in junior high and managed to get in with the prep crowd by high school. When I asked her why she was not friends with the kids from her neighborhood and what motivated her academically, she explained,

My brother, um actually had his first child before he graduated from high school. . . . I can remember being at my aunts' and uncles' houses and they're all talkin' about my brother and me and what's gonna happen to us. And even my cousins, they used to have bets on if I was gonna get pregnant by 15 or 16. I was kind of destined to fall into my brother's footsteps, and so I think that ever since I was 10 years old, my goal was to prove everyone wrong. I was gonna graduate, I was gonna go to college, I was gonna make something big, and then I was gonna come back and say, "Well, look what I did."

Likewise, Heather explained,

My brother Ray, he's a hoodlum. . . . He had lots of problems with drugs and alcohol, and after he dropped out of school he had a really rough time. My mom, when he left the house, she just cried. . . . I just saw them [my parents] in so much agony about him the whole time. He was such a rebel. I felt bad for them. He put them through so much.

Later she added, "I'm an angel. I do my schoolwork, don't get into trouble. My parents have had enough of that." I heard this story frequently enough, among both white and Mexican American girls, that I began to suspect that working-class girls experience a certain advantage over their male counterparts as a consequence of their gender. The social pressure for girls to conform and follow rules, as part of the definition of femininity, could facilitate their doing better in school than working-class boys, for whom manhood includes more pressure to engage in risk-taking behavior and resistance to control. Girls are relatively less likely to engage in these activities or be labeled and punished as delinquents when they do so, although this was somewhat less true for Mexican American girls than white girls.

Liz articulated yet another route to mobility, explaining how early on she discovered that she was good at basketball, and it was through this sport that she began to spend time with girls who were far more privileged than herself. Through association with high achievers, she was exposed to information that helped her get ahead. Overhearing conversations about college requirements and college prep courses made her aware of the existence of two tracks in schooling and of what she was missing out on. She clung to a middle-class girl, Amber, her best friend, hoping it seemed, that she might "catch" the middle classness Amber took for granted.

Though I did not study boys, I would expect that sports as a route to mobility was more common for them, given that high schools tend to offer more support for men's than women's athletics and given that boys are more likely to choose athletics than are girls. For some girls, being athletic still conflicts with a feminine gender identity just as does entering the military (an option that has historically worked as a route out of poverty for working-class boys).

White Girls' Experience of Mobility

These girls' experiences of mobility are characterized by a nascent awareness of class distinctions, the perception that they have to work harder than their middle-class peers, an awareness of having exceeded their parents' educational level, and an associated ambivalence about the meaning of mobility.

Class is a relational identity; awareness of class difference is dependent on the class and racial/ethnic geography of the environment in which one's identity is formed. The working-class, upwardly mobile girls I met, by virtue of their location in mixed-class peer groups and the college prep curriculum track, had an earlier awareness of class distinctions than their vocational counterparts, although they did not often name those differences as being about class.

Liz was one of very few students I met who actually referred to herself as working class.

Julie: You said you were "working class" earlier. Where did you get that term; what does it mean?

Liz: I learned it in a social science class or maybe in history. Working class is like the serfs, you know, the working class are the majority, blue collar versus the college educated.

It is ironic that Liz learned this in her college prep curriculum, and it raises the question of what it might mean for working-class students (especially those located in the vocational track who will continue to be workers) to become conscious of themselves as class subjects, to learn labor history, for example. As production theory has suggested, even the smallest exposure to the knowledge of class as a structural inequality might aid those students who, due to the U.S. ideology of individualism, can only see their status as linked to their own and their parents' individual inadequacies (MacLeod 1995, in particular). My broader research showed that working-class vocational students were obscurely aware of their difference from college prep students, but they never articulated it as clearly as (college prep) Liz did.

Unlike working-class girls in the vocational track, who rarely were in mixed class settings or peer groups, these upwardly mobile girls were not as mystified by the success of preps. By virtue of class crossing, they could see the advantages their middle-class friends experienced. They were more acutely aware of the cultural differences based on class as they found themselves exposed to the children of middle-class professionals in the college prep curriculum, on the basketball court, in student government, and in middle-class homes. They could see the reasons they had to work harder, and they were less likely to attribute friends' success to some innate difference between them.

Unlike other working-class girls, who were often unclear about the distinctions between junior colleges, four-year colleges, and universities or the kinds of certificates and degrees available, these upwardly mobile girls understood the distinctions. When I asked Mandy if her mom and dad had gone to college, she said,

No. Dad was in the army, Vietnam. Now he works as a postal clerk. My mom, well, I argue this with my mom all the time. . . . She went to junior college and got an associate degree. She calls this college, but I don't. I mean it's just a certificate; she's a secretary. I'll be the first one in my family that's ever gone to a four-year college.

In addition, these girls perceived that they had to work exceptionally hard for their high school diplomas and to get into college, relative to their middle-class friends. As Staci said,

They've always been kind of handed everything, that they've never really had to think about their future, and I was always like I don't want my future to be like my parents'. . . . I don't ever want to have to worry about money, like we have all my life. . . . I want to go to college and get a good education so I can have a better life, and they have always had a good life. I work my butt off, but it just seems easier for them. It's just always everything has always kinda been there for them.

When I asked Liz (working class) and Amanda (middle class) whether they considered themselves good at school, Amanda modestly offered "pretty good" while Liz shook her head "no."

Amanda: No, you are too.

Liz: Well, I'm not. She is an amazing writer, and I mean sometimes she'll have a lot of fun in class, but she, I mean, she's an A student all the way. Everything she does is . . .

Amanda: When I do my work, I do okay, but I'm a procrastinator, and I don't apply myself.

Liz: When she applies herself, she is like great.

Amanda: But Liz's good. She works hard at it.

In a later conversation with Liz she expanded on her perception that Amanda could afford to be a bit reckless about school, procrastinate, and still do all right. She felt that Amanda took much for granted that she does not. Liz, working incredibly hard to stay on top, feels she has no room for occasional slipups the way she believes her peers do.

Moreover, these girls were aware of the fact that they exceeded their parents' educational level early on. They perceived as a handicap the fact that their parents were unable to help them with school. Mandy explained,

Ever since I've been in honors classes, I've always been around these people, you know, their parents have advanced degrees and everything else. My parents were never able to help me out with math. Once I entered algebra, that was it, that was as far as they could help me. I remember one time in this one class we had this project, we had to build something. One girl's father was an architect, and her father designed, and basically built the entire project for her. We all had these dinky little things and she's got this palace!

Later, she attempted to define her parents' lack of education as an asset:

I mean, I was never mad at my parents because they couldn't help me. I was actually happy because once we get to college you're not gonna call your parents up and say, "Hey Dad, can you design this for me?" You're on your own then. And so I've always had to work on my own with my schoolwork; it was always on my own, whereas other students, they always had their parents standing right there, you know?

Simultaneously distancing from and connecting to parents was a common theme in the discourse of these students. On one hand, they wanted to point to the importance of mobility, while on the other hand, they did not want to degrade their parents by suggesting they wanted to become someone other than who their parents were. Such a desire to distance themselves from elements of working-class community while remaining close to and respecting their parents was a difficult process to navigate and often left them speaking in contradictions. They experienced some confusion and ambivalence when they realized that their own desire for mobility implicitly might mean that something was wrong with who they and their parents are now.

These middle-class-performing, working-class girls were also readily able to see the differences between their own parents and those of their friends. They were painfully aware of the fact that their friends' parents viewed their own parents with indifference at best, disdain at worst. When I asked Liz, whose mother works in retail, if her parents and Amanda's parents knew each other, she said they did and then went on:

> Well, but my mom is not *friends* with her mom. They [Amanda's parents] are not rich snobs, like in New York or something, but her mom would see someone who helps her in a store as, well, just a clerk in the store. My mom would be [willing to be] friends with her mom, but I think her mom would be less accepting.

When I asked Mandy about what differences she perceived between herself and most of the students she takes courses with, she noted, "In an honors class once, the teacher asked how many of us had parents who went to college. All but me and three others raised our hand. I know people think differently of me . . ." I sat next to Heather at a girl's basketball game one evening. She was sitting on the bleachers with the rest of her prep friends, front and center, cheering on the team. She kept glancing at the corner of the gym. When I asked her if she was expecting someone, she whispered, "My dad said he might stop by and check the score. I hope he doesn't." In a later conversation, she said,

> Well . . . my family is a lot different than . . . my friends' families . . . [who] are real formal. . . . Like my best friend's dad owns the bank and they always have nice things. . . . I've been embarrassed, especially of my dad . . . 'cause he's a real hick-like kind of guy, wears those kind of clothes. . . . All growing up, I was embarrassed of him, and I didn't want to take him anywhere.

Where I first thought the idea of her father's attending the game represented the standard embarrassment teens experience in relationship to

having their parents near them at social events, I recognized later that its meaning went beyond this for her. In the middle-class milieu of the school, some parents are more embarrassing than others.

Mexican American Girls' Routes to Mobility

A small group of working-class Mexican American girls, mostly second generation but including two girls who had immigrated, were exceptional in that they did not identify with large peer groupings of Mexican American working-class vocational track girls but rather were upwardly mobile, in the college prep curriculum. They were more involved in school activities than their vocational counterparts, although different ones than white college preps. They took leadership roles in activities designed for "minority" students or linking them to their community, such as the Math, Engineering, and Science Achievement program for minority students; the Early Outreach Program; the Advancement via Individual Determination program; Ballet Folklórico; organizing the annual Cinco de Mayo dance; and similar programs and activities.

The experience of exceptionalism that these Mexican American girls articulated in some ways paralleled white working-class girls' accounts. But in other ways, the two groups' experiences diverged from each other, revealing the racial/ethnic specificity of their early mobility experiences. There are several events and attitudes that appear to have led to mobility among working-class Mexican American girls including having an interest in sports, defining oneself in opposition to a delinquent brother, and having an older sibling (usually a sister) in college who passed on cultural capital. Among immigrant girls, two other factors emerged: immigrating from an urban site and exposure to family stories that could have worked as cultural capital.

Like Liz, Adriana's location in the college prep curriculum seemed to be partially linked to organized sports. She showed a talent for soccer early on and received much support for it from home given that her father was a big fan. Adriana's friendship group in junior high included many of the college prep girls who tend to dominate organized sports. Like Liz, through her association with preps, she experienced the benefit of privileged treatment by teachers and counselors that is often reserved for college prep students. But while she was friendly with these girls in the classroom and on the playing field, she primarily located herself in a peer group of upwardly mobile working-class Mexican American girls.

As with white working-class girls, these young women told stories of defining themselves in opposition to delinquent brothers. Adriana said, when I asked if she were going to go to college,

> Yeah. That is my hope, because all my brothers have let my dad down. My dad . . . really like was hoping that . . . they would, you know, be somebody. . . . It's like a lot of pressure on me to be someone. . . . And I know I can do it. I mean, I want to do it, but you never know what's going to happen.

But more often, they told stories of older siblings as the source of help and inspiration to go to college. Usually, but not always, these older siblings were sisters. Generally, this was an older sister who had finally managed, albeit through a long and circuitous route that included junior college and many part- and full-time jobs, to attend a four-year school. Their desire was to help their younger sibling do it more easily by advising them on the import of getting the courses required for state or university admission completed in high school (rather than in junior college), on taking SAT tests, and on filling out applications for financial aid and admissions on time. Luisa had two older sisters attending state schools, and she had been accepted to three university campuses. I asked her if her mother had encouraged her to go to college early on:

Luisa: No, my sister did. She kind of like, she's the one who encouraged me.

Julie: Your mom didn't?

Luisa: She doesn't really want me to go away. . . . She doesn't really . . . understand what college . . . is all about.

When I asked her if she had understood the differences between attending a junior college versus a state or university institution she said,

> Yeah, just from my sister. . . . She's the one who told me what the differences were, and she helped me figure out that I wanted to go to UC [University of California] because I didn't want to go spend two years at a JC (junior college] and [then] like go for four more years because I thought that was like a waste of two years.

Although Angela did not have older siblings guiding her, she clearly saw it as her job to help her five younger siblings. When I asked her about her social life she said,

> Well, I don't spend time like I used to, with friends so much. . . . My little brothers and sister are more important than friends. They need to get ahead. And I don't want them to get behind or something. I want to help them do well.

Because she had so many younger siblings who she wanted to help, who took her energy away from her own schooling, and who would need to use the family's economic resources, I have doubts that Angela's college dream will manifest itself. Her younger siblings will probably benefit from her sacrifices.

One advantage that enabled Victoria's mobility was having siblings much older than herself, as she was born when her mother was 42. Not only were these older siblings able to advise her, but by the time she was ready to go to college, many of them were established and could help her financially.

In short, older siblings who were the first in the family to go to college turned out to be important sources of "insider" information (already known to students whose parents were college educated), provided social and cultural capital not available from parents, and sometimes even offered economic capital.[2]

Two of the girls in this group were immigrants whose families lived in poverty, and explaining their upward mobility requires additional considerations. One explanation for their achievement is that their parents had other benefits and resources. Lupita had immigrated at 13, quickly learned English, was an academic star at the school, and had been admitted to multiple University of California campuses. When I asked her why she was different from the other students in her neighborhood, she explained that while their families had immigrated from rural areas of Mexico, her family had come from an urban environment where there was greater access to education. In fact, she had an older sibling who received a college degree in Mexico.

> The majority of the immigrant families, they are totally farm workers. . . . They used to live in little towns where they didn't have high schools there. If their kids wanted to go to high school, they would have to go to another town where they have high schools. So, I mean . . . they're used to saying, "Okay, high school is the top thing that you're going to get because we have no more way to get any more education for you." And I think the difference is that we [my family] used to live in a big city, where we had all the facilities. And, I mean, my brother, he's a college graduate. So it's been like a tradition in my family to go to school.

And Angela reported that her family had been well-to-do in the United States before they were deported and later reentered: "My grandparents owned property here. They were well-off. After the war, my grandfather had to come back across the border and start from scratch all over again."

Like Gándara's (1995) upwardly mobile participants who grew up hearing family stories that worked as cultural capital by engendering in them a sense of hopefulness and deservedness that might otherwise be absent, Lupita described grandparents who were property owners in Mexico and explained that there was a family dispute over this property when these grandparents died. In her mind, her family's current state of poverty was only because of this dispute.

These immigrant girls' high aspirations, of course, will not necessarily result in higher achievement, since a variety of structural barriers can inhibit their mobility. In the case of Lupita and Angela, while cultural benefits, whether real or imagined, may have shaped their aspirations, they do not dictate their outcomes. Lupita appeared to come from an educated extended family in Mexico, and her college-educated sibling provided her with cultural capital that would likely benefit her. However, Angela, with five younger siblings, no health care, and a sick mother, is less likely to reap the benefits of her higher aspirations than is Lupita. Even though Angela was admitted to a University of California campus, she was hoping to attend a nearby junior college, saying, "That's the only place I can go because I can't afford to go away."

When I asked Adriana about her family's income, she explained,

> Oh you know how Mexican families are, a little bit from here, a little bit from there. My dad pays the rent, mom buys the food, my little brother pays the phone bill, and I'm responsible for the gas bill. My uncles fill in whatever else is needed.

Adriana cannot afford to live away from home, and her family cannot spare her economic contribution to the household.

Mexican American Girls' Experience of Mobility

These girls' experiences of mobility are characterized by an early awareness of class distinctions, an awareness of having exceeded their parents' educational level, a related ambivalence about the meaning of mobility, an acute awareness of what kinds of occupations await them if they do not finish school, and their refusal to interpret mobility as assimilation to whiteness.

As with white upwardly mobile girls, these Mexican American young women could also see the differences between themselves and the (mostly white) middle-class college prep girls more clearly than could their vocational counterparts. But where white working-class students articulated their difference from preps in the most obscure class terms, Mexican American girls articulated their difference clearly in terms of race. Luisa stated,

> I think it is harder for Mexican American students because I think most white people have like money, like their parents, they went to college, and they have money. They have an education. But you know, I'm not saying, well, you know, it's my mom's fault that she didn't go to college. She could have, you know, but I don't know, it's just like that's just what it is, kind of. The white students don't understand because, you know, their parents got to go to college, you know, had an education, they all have jobs.

Similar to white girls, Mexican American girls wanted to point to the importance of mobility yet did not want this to mean that their parents' lives were without value, thus expressing a certain amount of ambivalence toward mobility and/or the acquisition of the middle-class cultural forms that accompany mobility. This can be seen in Luisa's comment above wherein she identified her mother's limited education but then noted her mother is not to blame for this. Similarly, Adriana said,

> Well I'm proud of my parents. I'm proud of my dad, because like if anybody says anything about their parents [such as] . . . "Oh, they went to college" . . . or something like that. Like I'm proud of my dad, you know, he learned just from doing, from life. Being as poor as we were, he, you know, we're like doing good, you know.

Mobility experiences can never be understood outside of the racial/ethnic specific experience of them. These girls were also well aware of having exceeded their parents' ability. But for the Mexican American girls, unlike the white girls, the acquisition of middle-class cultural forms included becoming bilingual while their parents remained primarily Spanish speakers.

Where white girls would say generally that they did not want to struggle for money the way their parents did, Mexican American girls were cognizant of the correlation between being Mexican American and being poor; they were more likely to name the specific occupations the poorest people in their community worked and identify their motivation to escape this. Angela said,

> I don't want to be like everyone else. . . . I want something better. I hate working in the fields, that's not for me, and I don't want to do that. It is minimum wage and I don't want to work for that.

And Adriana said, "When I think about havin' to work in the fields or cannery, then I get back to studying real hard."

Unlike third-generation Mexican American middle-class girls, who sometimes felt that to be authentically Mexican one must adopt working-class cultural forms and who were downwardly mobile (Bettie 2000, forthcoming), these college prep working-class girls refused to interpret mobility as assimilation to whiteness. Adopting an ethnic strategy of "accommodation without assimilation" (Gibson 1988), they were not apologetic about their mobility and did not feel any "less" Mexican for being college bound. Moreover, their participation in school activities that were specifically linked to the Mexican American community helped them acquire college skills while maintaining their racial/ethnic identity. They were not compelled to interpret their mobility as evidence of assimilation.

The correlation of race/ethnicity with poverty promotes the belief that middle-class status and whiteness are one and the same. As a result, Mexican American students have to negotiate their educational mobility against the broader social perception that this mobility represents assimilation to whiteness. Such assimilation is resisted and gets played out as intraethnic tension in peer groups when Mexican American vocational students accuse college preps of "acting white." These working-class, upwardly mobile girls received an occasional "acting white" accusation from their working-class peers, but they interpreted this as a joke that, although painful at times, was not taken as a real challenge, and their racial/ethnic identity remained unthreatened by their college prep status.

I conclude that class is a salient factor in the formation of a bicultural racial/ethnic Mexican American identity. Consistent with Matute-Bianchi (1991), I found both a caste-like orientation and an immigrant orientation among nonimmigrant Mexican American students. But while Matute-Bianchi described these as "ethnic strategies," I suggest naming them "race/ethnic-class strategies" because of the equal salience of class. Although the girls discussed here were upwardly mobile, because they grew up working class, their identity as Mexican American was unwavering. Their Mexican identity seemed less challenged than it was for some middle-class Mexican American girls (Bettie 2000, forthcoming).

As Mariana explained, "I'm not really acting white because look at where I live and who my friends are and what I do." Mariana lived in a Mexican American neighborhood; hung out socially with other working-class, college prep, Mexican American girls; and was heavily involved in school and church activities that focused on her community.

Discussion and Conclusion

Comparing the upward mobility of working-class white and Mexican American high school girls is one way to see class, race/ethnicity, and gender are intersecting identity constructions and axes of inequality that inform the overall reproduction of inequality. This comparison goes beyond the limitations of previous research on the reproduction of educational inequality and educational mobility by attending to the simultaneous interaction of class, race/ethnicity, and gender. I have been able to illustrate similarities and differences between white and Mexican American working-class girls' experiences of mobility and thus to show how mobility is experienced in racial/ethnic-specific ways, to demonstrate how class identity (or the lack thereof) shapes the mo-

bility experience, and to consider the gender-specific experience of mobility as well.

I found some similarities between working-class white and Mexican American girls' experiences in relationship to both questions I posed: Why does mobility occur? and How is it experienced? Both white and Mexican American students defined themselves in opposition to an older male sibling. Sport was a route to mobility for those girls who did not experience gender identity conflict in relationship to it. There is some evidence that working-class girls, across race, may be more academically oriented than their male peers. Both sets of girls were aware of having exceeded their parents' academic ability early on. Both experienced some confusion and ambivalence around the distance between themselves and their parents because of this, although the experience was far more dramatic for Mexican American girls. As a consequence of their location in a college prep curriculum, both sets of girls seemed to have a greater understanding of class differences relative to other working-class girls, although this was articulated obscurely in class terms by white girls and almost solely in racial terms among Mexican American ones.

I found important racial/ethnic differences between white and Mexican American girls' experiences as well. Not surprisingly, racism sometimes informed white working-class mobility, as for the two girls whose parents' wanted them to be segregated from Mexican American students. The greater salience of race over class (in a society that lacks a discourse on class) means that white girls' mobility is less encumbered in some ways than Mexican American girls'. Mexican American students, in contrast, are pressured (though not necessarily successfully) to sacrifice racial/ethnic identity by educational curriculums that routinely work to colonize their Mexican identities, but at the same time, they may be pressured by their peer group not to "act white."

Upward mobility also may be informed by gender. In some cases, feminine norms allowed girls to forgo the delinquent paths their working-class brothers felt compelled to follow when they engaged in rituals of proving masculinity. In other cases, girls' mobility was enabled by their interest in sports and the fact that they did not experience a gender conflict in relationship to it. But there is another way in which gender is potentially salient to these girls' mobility. Both the white and the Mexican American upwardly mobile girls performed the same school-sanctioned femininity that middle-class, white, college prep girls did. That is, they wore little or no makeup and less sexualized clothing than most of their vocational track counterparts who enacted various forms of dissident femininity (Bettie forthcoming). This school-sanctioned femininity signifies middle classness to school personnel who view these girls, in contrast to many vocational track girls, as modest and tasteful, their demeanor as "nice" and "not hard." Nonetheless, a comparative study of upwardly mobile boys would be necessary to confidently argue the salience of gender on the mobility experience.

Because the nature of ethnographic methodology leads to small sample sizes, I cannot make generalizations about the reasons for mobility, and my findings here should be taken as suggestive and exploratory. But ethnographic data do allow me to elaborate on the meaning of mobility for the girls studied. The mobility experience differs, of course, for whites and people of color, as the latter often are more consciously aware of themselves as a community of people as a consequence of having in common a history of oppression based on being historically defined as a racial/ethnic group. This can be experienced as an advantage when it produces an awareness of structural barriers based on race/ethnicity and thus helps to explain the difficulty of individual achievement. It also can be experienced as a disadvantage, as when upwardly mobile students of color feel the burden of representing an entire people.

In contrast, whites often do not experience themselves as members of the racial/ethnic category white but as individuals. Without a cultural discourse of class identity, they do not readily experience themselves as members of a class community either. Evidence of this can be seen in the way white, working-class, college prep girls ex-

pressed their experience of how education was distancing them from their parents. They did not articulate this as a distancing from their working-class community; their pain was more often articulated in relationship to an individual family, not a people. For white working-class students, this can be an advantage. Their mobility is less complicated because they are not made to feel that they are giving up racial/ethnic or class belonging in the process. And while an unarticulated sense of loss, a class longing, may remain—precisely because it is unarticulated—it may be a less salient force, making their mobility somewhat less encumbered.

Although I have focused primarily on students' constructions of identity within the peer culture, this occurs within an institutional context. The influence of the structure of schooling on student identity formation and the responsibility of schools to provide the context for mobility should not be underestimated or ignored.

The possibility of, and perhaps ease of, upward mobility for white working-class students appears greater than for Mexican American girls, who were more likely to experience tracking as a consequence of counselors' perceptions and stereotypes about Mexican American students. The relationship between race and class means that counselors are likely to make assumptions that students of color are from low-income families (even when they are not) and therefore assumptions about what educational resources they need and can handle. White working-class students can escape tracking more easily because their class does not as easily appear encoded onto the body.

Social and educational policy can potentially assist social mobility. Becoming middle class requires doing well in school, and for Mexican American students, doing well in school too often means learning a colonialist history, English, and the suppression of one's own culture (Darder 1991). Schools routinely fail to provide genuine bicultural education, and consequently, the curriculum makes it difficult to embrace an identity that is both middle class and Mexican American at the same time. Therefore, school programs could promote mobility by offering a bicultural identity, the possibility of being middle class and maintaining a racial/ethnic identity of color simultaneously. As noted, upwardly mobile Mexican American students were more involved in school extracurricular programs than their vocational counterparts. They were involved in activities not dominated by white middle-class students but that specifically linked them to their culture and community.[3]

Moreover, these research findings are relevant to affirmative action policy. California's proposition 209 appropriated a discourse on class and used it to help dismantle affirmative action based on race/ethnicity. Although affirmative action without attention to class is of little help to the mass of working-class students (white and of color) who are tracked out of a college prep curriculum in junior high and early high school years, affirmative action based on race/ethnicity, class, and gender can help this handful of upwardly mobile working-class girls.

NOTES

1. Cultural capital refers to class-based knowledge, skills, linguistic and cultural competencies, and a worldview that is passed on via family and is related more to educational attainment than to occupation (Bourdieu 1984).

2. Social capital refers to middle-class forms of social support in a person's interpersonal network (Bourdieu 1984).

3. Mehan, Hubbard, and Villanueva (1994) found that students who participated in an Advancement via Individual Determination program, in particular, had higher rates of school success.

REFERENCES

American Association of University Women. 1994. *Shortchanging girls, shortchanging America: Executive summary.* Washington, DC: American Association of University Women.

Apple, Michael W. 1982. *Education and power.* Boston: Routledge Kegan Paul.

Bernstein, Basil B. 1975. *Class, codes, and control.* London: Routledge Kegan Paul.

Bettie, Julie. 2000. Women without class: Chicas, cholas, trash and the presence/absence of class identity. *Signs: Journal of Women in Culture and Society* 26 (1): 1–35.

———. Forthcoming. *Women without class: Girls, race, and identity.* Berkeley: University of California Press.

Bourdieu, Pierre. 1984. *Distinction.* Cambridge, MA: Harvard University Press.

Bourdieu, Pierre, and Jean Claude Passeron. 1977. *Reproduction in education, society, and culture.* London: Sage.

Bowles, Samuel, and Herbert Gintis. 1976. *Schooling in capitalist America: Educational reform and the contradictions of economic life.* New York: Basic Books.

Brantlinger, Ellen. 1993. *The politics of social class in secondary school: Views of affluent and impoverished youth.* New York: Teachers College Press.

Brown, Lyn Mikel, and Carol Gilligan. 1992. *Meeting at the crossroads.* New York: Ballantine.

Darder, Antonia. 1991. *Culture and power in the classroom: A critical foundation for bicultural education.* New York: Bergin and Garvey.

Eckert, Penelope. 1989. *Jocks and burnouts: Social categories and identity in the high school.* New York: Teachers College Press.

Eder, Donna, Catherine Colleen Evans, and Stephen Parker. 1995. *School talk: Gender and adolescent culture.* New Brunswick, NJ: Rutgers University Press.

Flores-Gonzales, Nilda. 1999. Puerto Rican high achievers: An example of ethnic academic identity compatibility. *Anthropology and Education Quarterly* 30:343–62.

Foley, Douglas. 1990. *Learning capitalist culture: Deep in the heart of Tejas.* Philadelphia: University of Pennsylvania Press.

Fordham, Signithia. 1996. *Blacked out: Dilemmas of race, identity, and success at capital high.* Chicago: University of Chicago Press.

———. 1999. Dissin' the standard: Ebonics as guerrilla warfare at capital high. *Anthropology and Education Quarterly* 30 (3): 272–93.

Gándara, Patricia. 1995. *Over the ivy walls: The educational mobility of low-income Chicanos.* Albany: State University of New York Press.

Gibson, Margaret A. 1988. *Accommodation without assimilation: Sikh immigrants in an American high school.* Ithaca, NY: Cornell University Press.

Gilligan, Carol. 1982. *In a different voice: Psychological theory and women's development.* Cambridge, MA: Harvard University Press.

Hemmings, Annette. 1996. Conflicting images? Being Black and a model high school student. *Anthropology and Education Quarterly* 27:20–50.

Higginbotham, Elizabeth, and Lynn Weber. 1992. Moving up with kin and community: Upward social mobility for Black and white women. *Gender & Society* 6:416–40.

Luttrell, Wendy. 1997. *School-smart and mother-wise: Working-class women's identity and schooling.* New York: Routledge.

MacLeod, Jay. 1995. *Ain't no makin' it: Aspirations and attainment in a low-income neighborhood.* 2d ed. Boulder, CO: Westview.

Matute-Bianchi, Maria Eugenia. 1991. Situational ethnicity and patterns of school performance among immigrant and nonimmigrant Mexican-descent students. In *Minority status and schooling: A comparative study of immigrant and involuntary minorities,* edited by Margaret A. Gibson and John U. Ogbu. New York: Garland.

McLeon Taylor, Jill, Carol Gilligan, and Amy M. Sullivan, eds. 1995. *Between voice and silence: Women and girls, race and relationship.* Cambridge, MA: Harvard University Press.

Mehan, Hugh, Lea Hubbard, and Irene Villanueva. 1994. Forming academic identities: Accommodation without assimilation among involuntary minorities. *Anthropology and Education Quarterly* 25 (2): 91–117.

Ogbu, John U. 1991. Immigrant and involuntary minorities in comparative perspective. In *Minority status and schooling: A comparative study of immigrant and involuntary minorities,* edited by Margaret A. Gibson and John U. Ogbu. New York: Garland.

Ogbu, John U., and Maria Eugenia Matute-Bianchi. 1986. Understanding sociocultural factors: Knowledge identity and school adjustment. In *Beyond language: Social and cultural factors in schooling language minority students.* Los Angeles: Evaluation, Dissemination and Assessment Center, California State University, Los Angeles.

Orenstein, Peggy. 1994. *School girls: Young women, self-esteem, and the confidence gap.* New York: Doubleday.

Pipher, Mary. 1994. *Reviving Ophelia: Saving the selves of adolescent girls.* New York: Putnam.

Portes, Alejandro, and Min Zhou. 1993. The new second generation: Segmented assimilation and its variants. *Annals of the American Academy of Political and Social Science* 530:74–96.

Valenzuela, Angela. 1999. Checkin' up on my guy: Chicanos, social capital, and the culture of romance. *Frontiers: A Journal of Women Studies* 20 (1): 60–79.

Weis, Lois. 1990. *Working class without work: High school students in a de-industrializing economy.* New York: Routledge.

Wiles, Paul. 1977. *Learning to labor: How working class kids get working class jobs.* New York: Columbia University Press.

Julie Bettie is an assistant professor of sociology and an affiliate of women's studies at the University of California, Santa Cruz, where she teaches courses in feminist theory and cultural studies. She is the author of *Women without Class: Girls, Race, and Identity.* She has published on race and class among girls; on class identity and male feminism; and on race, class, and gender in the television show *Roseanne.*

A n   i n t e r v i e w   w i t h . . .

Julie Bettie

How did you become interested in this research topic?

In part, it was accidental, as I wasn't really interested in education or in the Chicana experience per se when I started out. I was interested, however, in moving feminist and cultural theory forward by bringing ethnographic research to bear on how the intersections of race, class and gender are "lived out." That interest came in part from my own experience of mobility in graduate school. Much of the feminist theory about women of color spoke to me, as there were lots of claims made there that I identified with—especially the idea that we are "strangers" in this academic setting. I remember talking to a friend, a fellow graduate student and an African American woman, who described having to learn to talk like white people, and I remember thinking that I am also learning to talk in this different kind of way. For me it wasn't about whiteness [she is white], but about my working class background; my people don't talk in these obscure ways using multisyllabic words. At the same time, I wanted to be sure I understood how the difference of race cannot be reduced to class. So I was sorting through the different constructs and effects of race and class as I was immersed in cultural theory and, at the same time, experiencing mobility myself. I also felt the disjuncture between the assumption in some cultural theory that white automatically means you are middle class, and I felt a need to articulate that. So my research project came out of my theoretical interests, a political desire to form class alliance across race, and a personal desire to understand the experience that I was having. I wanted to find a site that was race and class diverse, but I didn't start out looking for an educational institution as that site. It could have been anything. I just stumbled into it because I had a friend who had a friend who is a teacher, and the school she taught at seemed perfect because it was 60 percent white and 40 percent Mexican American and within each population there were working and middle class students, which made that four way comparison possible. I didn't have a background in Chicano studies. I knew I wanted to compare white women with women of color, to do a cross racial analysis of class, and this site happened to be nearly half Chicana/o. This shows how often we don't really set out with clear intentions of what we are doing as researchers.

What made you choose this particular approach—that is, participant observation and interviews—and what do you see as its main strengths and limitations?

I've always only been interested in qualitative research rather than quantitative. For me, it's just much more telling and I see the social sciences really as interpretive endeavors like the humanities. I came of age immersed in postmodernism and poststructuralist feminist theory. To me, the strengths of a qualitative approach are that it acknowledges that what you are doing is an interpretation; it doesn't pretend to be objective or value-free. I find it to be a more honest approach, given that all knowledge is perspective and you can never really be outside of that. I also think the qualitative approach is the most interesting in terms of theory building; it provides us with concepts and theories that help us see the social world in ways that help shift power relations. Before I did this study, I was writing about race and class by analyzing the television show *Roseanne*. That was a textual kind of analysis, not ethnographic, and I kept thinking "I need to go out and talk to real people and get a sense of what is really going on out there, rather than just a textual representation of it." So in spite of my postmodern training, I went looking for the "real." But when I interviewed girls and spent time with them and started writing it up, it became apparent that, of course, it is *still* a representation—my own textual representation of what I heard from them. I try to tell my students that you have to be cautious about thinking that you somehow really know what is going on if you do ethnography. Because you were there, you think you can make this "I was there" knowledge claim, but it is still interpretive. Someone else doing that might well come up with a different interpretation. So both the strengths and limitations of this approach are sort of the same, coming from the fact that it is interpretive.

How did you deal with some of the challenges of getting access and gaining the trust of the students you studied?

As I mentioned already, I gained access through a teacher that a friend knew. She became my advocate, got me in, and introduced me to the principal whose permission I needed to do the study. After the initial access, of course, getting access was still ongoing—every teacher, each girl, trying to get people to talk to me. I met girls in different ways. With the middle class girls, I could go into a classroom, with permission from the teacher, and when I told them about the project and my need to interview them, they were likely to participate because they could identify with it. But it was harder to recruit the working class girls, because the classroom isn't always a comfortable place for them. This was especially true for the working class girls who were working class "performers" as opposed to those who were upwardly mobile. So I was more likely to meet them through some other trusted person, such as a school nurse. The main way I met girls was by getting to know one girl, who would then introduce me to her whole circle of friends—sort of a snowball sample. It was better to meet girls through other girls rather than through adults. I tried to distance myself from adults while I was there. That was a trust issue. I ended up interviewing teachers and other adult officials—administrators and such—but I did it at the end of the school year, and in a private setting so I wouldn't be seen by the students. I didn't want them to think that I was reporting back to them (the adults) on what I had found. Sometimes during the school year adults would ask questions about what I was finding, and I was clear about not violating the trust that I had with the girls. It was a bit harder to establish rapport with Mexican American girls than with the white girls, given who I was. What helped, though, was that the teacher who got me access to the school, who is also a white woman, is someone whom the Chicana students trust—so much so that when they were pushing for the school to start a Chicano studies class, the students were going to ask her to teach it. So I had an automatic legitimacy because of my association with her, which also made it easier for me to gain the trust of Mexican American students. That helped me a lot.

Qualitative research typically yields reams of data, which can be unmanageable. How did you deal with that?

I am somewhat embarrassed to admit that I made sense of it mainly with Post-it notes. I know there are elaborate software programs for dealing with qualitative data and if I were going to do this again, I would use one. However, when I did the research I was a graduate student and I didn't have money to buy the software or time to figure out how to use it (this was my dissertation research). So I took copious notes and came home and typed them up every day—field notes, in addition to tape recorded interviews and lots and lots of documents and data. I put everything into different binders. I had a binder that was all field notes, a binder that was all interviews, a binder that was all handouts and brochures from the school, and a binder that was what I called an "analysis journal"—my thinking about all these things as I went along throughout the year. Altogether I had hundreds and hundreds of pages of material. Then I went through and coded it all by hand, using Post-it notes of different colors to identify different themes. So, for example, I used pink Post-it notes to code the theme "family values" so when I wrote that section, I went through the binders and looked for every pink note. I wrote everything down, because with this kind of research, you cannot rely on your memory. This was my dissertation research, and it was years later that I wrote it up into a book. Even though in the moment it is easy to think you will remember what you are observing, years later you will not remember if you don't have it written up.

How did you keep notes in the field?

I tape recorded interviews, but when I took notes, I tended to go off to a private place—like I would go into the bathroom and hide behind the stall door or find another place where people wouldn't notice that I was taking notes. Then at the end of the day I would sit in my car with my laptop or go home and type them up.

Were there any unexpected events, problems, or developments that you faced? If so, how did you deal with them?

Much to my surprise, there really were few problems. One thing that was unexpected was how easy it was to establish rapport with the Chicana students. I had done lots of reading about insider/outsider issues and was really convinced that, as a white woman, I couldn't do this kind of research. But when I got there, I was surprised how warm and accepting they were of me and how much they wanted me to include them in what I was doing; they didn't want me to write only about white girls because of my whiteness. So that was really nice . . . a nice surprise.

What about your findings? Were they expected or unexpected?

There were expected and unexpected findings. I believe that we never go into a setting *tabula rasa*—that is, with no idea of what we will find—and I certainly went in to this one with ideas and expectations. But I don't think that biases a researcher, because even though you may have expectations, you go in also with the openness to being surprised, to finding something different from what you thought you might find. Here is an example of an unexpected finding: I expected to find that subcultural styles were politically vacuous styles performed by middle class youth who were victims of the mass cultural industry. Instead I found that these styles were much more important to how students understood both race and class differences than I would have anticipated—though not in ways that directly reflect what the cultural industry puts out there.

What contributions do your findings make to our understanding of the impact of race, class, and gender on mobility?

A key contribution is that although current cultural, feminist, and social theory generally suggests that race, gender, and class are key forces, they are not equal and parallel kinds of forces. That is, though they may be parallel in some ways, each of them has a specific effect in any historical moment. I argue that even though we live in a culture that is particularly inarticulate about class and even though class was often invisible in the discourse of the people I talked to, it is still, of course, a salient force. So a key finding was to reveal the invisibility of class and how it works in relationship to race and gender, and to show how essentialized notions of race and gender help keep the difference of class invisible. And, in the end, to recognize that women are, in fact, class subjects.

What are the implications of your research for policy?

I didn't set out intending to inform education policy, or even to study education per se, but by the end I did see a handful of policy implications in my research. One has to do with bicultural curricula—that schools could better promote mobility by offering students of color a bicultural identity that makes it possible to be middle class and maintain a racial/ethnic identity of color simultaneously, rather than conveying the idea that to be authentically of color, you must be working class. Another has to do with affirmative action, which I talk about briefly in the article. Affirmative action without class is of little help to the mass of working class students, regardless of color, as they are all tracked out of a college prep curriculum in middle and high school. Affirmative action based on race/ethnicity, class, and gender would help qualified students of color across class and upwardly mobile working class students across race. Along these lines, I also think we should include class difference, not instead of but along with race and gender as an integral variable in multicultural curricula. So much multicultural education gives attention to race/ethnicity and gender, but only as consequences of discrimination and prejudice—with "tolerance" as the remedy—rather than looking at how those things are institutionalized in class inequality as well as exist outside of and apart from class inequality. We also need curriculum content, such as labor history, that prepares students to be citizens by providing a discourse about class that helps them see themselves as class subjects; as workers in a global economy. In the end, although the kinds of inequality that I am studying are reproduced in educational sites, schools are neither the cause nor the cure for such social inequality. There is much that needs to be done quite apart from schools, such as creating inclusive unions that make class visible by constructing us all as politicized class subjects.

Did your research present any particular ethical challenges or issues? How did you deal with them?

As I said, I made an effort to protect the students' privacy by not providing information to administrators and other adults. Also, when I wrote up the results, I worked hard to obscure the girls' identities, partly because where I did the research is a pretty small town. I did this by changing certain facts about them, such as switching this girl's parents' occupations with that girl's parents' occupations when they are in the same socioeconomic class. I tried hard to do this without distorting it so much that it became inaccurate. The only other ethical issue, and one that is unavoidable in ethnography, is the issue of betrayal. Because I was narrating a story through the eyes of students, I end up somewhat "othering" teachers [not presenting from their perspective] at times, which made me feel as if I betrayed them in a certain way. I try to make clear, in my book, that they are people with good intentions who were working really hard at their jobs, and that the analysis is not meant to be critical of individuals, but of social systems, processes, and ideologies in our culture that recruit them as individuals and inform their actions. The same thing was true with regard to the girls. The middle class girls sometimes come off looking like the "villains" in the story in relation to working class girls. Again, the point is that I don't mean to be critical of them as individuals, but to look critically at the social circumstances and forces that are informing their lives. What feels like betrayal in some ways really isn't when you look at the larger picture. Although the research itself has no actual benefit for the girls that I study, in the larger picture it contributes to the larger project of understanding young women's lives, and that makes it worthwhile.

What was the most difficult or frustrating aspect of doing the research?

There were many. It was emotionally draining. Also, I found it difficult to feel always as if I had to hide myself. I didn't present myself as something that I wasn't, but I had to try to be neutral. That meant that my own personality and flair and style and who I am was constantly suppressed, and to have to do that every day was very difficult. This was especially hard given what I was writing about—race, class, girls, body image, and clothes. I felt that I couldn't dress how I would dress if I weren't doing this research, that I couldn't just be myself because I was busy trying to be neutral and not threatening. The other difficult thing was the fact that I don't speak Spanish. Often it didn't matter because I spent most of my time with second and third generation Mexican American girls, who were bilingual (most of them spoke English at school and Spanish at home). But I can't help but think that made a difference in terms of the insider knowledge that I might otherwise have had access to, even with second and third generation students, especially Spanish language popular culture. Also, had I spoken Spanish I could have included first generation immigrant students in the study and rounded it out in a way.

What was most satisfying about the research?

Getting to know these girls and coming to see them as amazingly creative cultural workers and performers. They were incredibly smart and strategic and creative in the way that they approach the world. Interestingly, they were too young to know how remarkable they were. They were accomplishing and overcoming so much, and they were so inspiring to me as I watched them navigate and negotiate life at this age, at this moment in time, in this particular cultural context. They were amazing, but they didn't know that yet. I liked them so much but couldn't express that fully. I would love it if they could read my book and see how amazing I thought they were.

If you were to do the research again, what would you do differently?

I would use software, rather than Post-it notes, to organize and analyze the data! I also think that, if I were again to do research with people who are "other" to me, that I would want a co-researcher to do it with me—in this case, someone who is Chicana and a Spanish speaker. It may or may not have changed the findings and content, but it certainly would have reduced my angst about it.

What important lesson, drawn from your experience, would you share with students?

That ethnographic research is really difficult, but it has a very high pay-off. Some other approaches are easier, but ethnography gives us a different order of "data" that is incredibly valuable. Another lesson is how messy research is. It is not a linear process, but you have to go for it anyway—just jump in and swim in the stream and see what happens. Also, try to resist the common hesitancy about studying people who are different from ourselves—"other" to us. Again, this is very difficult, but very much worth the effort because we learn so much from each other that it pushes us forward significantly toward achieving a just world.

Questions to Think About

1. What are all the different methods of data collection that Bettie uses? What does each contribute to her overall study?

2. Describe the process by which Bettie gained access to her site and to the girls that she ended up interviewing for this study. In what ways and for what reasons does she suggest that this sample might be somewhat biased?

3. Briefly summarize Bettie's main findings. Then restate one of her findings in the form of a testable hypothesis and explain in some detail how you would go about testing that hypothesis by using large-scale survey research.

4. Discuss the relevance of the concept of *the other* (*otherness, othering*) to Bettie's research.

5. What does Bettie see as the strengths and limitations of field research? What do you see as its strengths and limitations, particularly in regard to this study?

The Glass Phallus

Pub(lic) Masculinity and Drinking in Rural New Zealand

Hugh Campbell

In this article I report the findings of an ethnographic study of men's pub drinking in rural New Zealand. By using the idea of hegemonic masculinity and incorporating theoretical ideas of gender performativity, the analysis focuses on aspects of drinking performance that are central to the establishment of hegemony by a particular version of masculinity in this community. Two important characteristics of pub drinking performance are *conversational cockfighting* and the *disciplines of drinking*. These combine to ensure that a particular version of masculinity, here called *pub(lic) masculinity,* is able to reproduce itself. A further finding is that masculinity in this kind of performative situation develops a degree of invisibility. Using the metaphor of the "glass phallus," I engage with the difficulties of analyzing an invisible masculinity and argue that rendering masculinity visible is an important task for any sociological analysis of both public leisure sites in rural society and the embodied performance of alcohol consumption by men in public spaces.

Rarely has any social site been mythologized to the same extent as the rural pub. From the idyllic haven of the English rural pub, to the last-chance saloon of the American West, to the crocodile-wrestling mateship of a corrugated iron shed somewhere in the Australian outback, rural drinking sites have been ascribed by both the popular imagination and academic analysis with pronounced mythic qualities. Such lay mythologies place the rural pub squarely within what rural sociologists term the "rural idyll" (Mingay 1989). In the rural idyll, the characteristics of a nostalgic fic-

tion of yesteryear are attributed to nonurban communities: they are a retreat from the brutalities of urban living, where people live closer to nature in simpler and (by implication) happier lives.

There is no doubt that the idyllic vision of rurality has influenced all of what Jones (1995) calls lay, media, and academic discourses about rurality. The debate between Philo (1992) and Murdoch and Pratt (1993) establishes that academics have often been susceptible to their own form of mythologizing about what constitutes "rurality" and the "rural community." Clearly, academics are not alone: various film, TV, and advertising constructions of the rural pub have soundly endorsed the idyllic tradition. Often they represent pubs as a social world that reflects the idea of being both "closer to nature" and, by that fact, a more "natural" social world (Bell 1994).

Although a few scholars have attempted to demystify the rural pub (e.g., Hunt and Satterlee 1987; Whitehead 1976), the realm of pub studies has tended to use functionalist modes of analysis (Clark 1981). While Clark documents this as being true for pub studies in general, it is doubly true for studies of rural pubs, which are often accepted uncritically as part of the functioning structure of rural society.

One consequence of this academic acceptance of the idyllic rural pub is that the relationship between pubs and masculinity becomes obscured. Some New Zealand commentators have tried to describe the pub as a "last bastion" of male camaraderie, a museum exhibit recalling an admirable and less complicated world (McLauchlan 1994).

The ethnographic findings reported here, however, suggest otherwise (also see Campbell and

Phillips 1995; Fairweather and Campbell 1990). Male pub drinking practices have not persisted as a nostalgic memorial to a simpler life; they persist because they are a site of male power and legitimacy in rural community life. Further, rural pubs can actually operate as a key site where hegemonic forms of masculinity are constructed, reproduced, and successfully defended. Consequently, by seeking to move beyond the rural idyll, or functionalist analysis, we must reestablish the relevance of the rural pub to the wider concerns of rural sociology. We must examine the various ways in which pubs operate as a social site, where male power is constructed in rural communities, and also the way in which symbolic notions of rurality are integral to the construction of gendered power in rural space.

In the analysis presented in this article, I outline the characteristics of a hegemonic form of masculinity in one rural community in New Zealand, and examine how such hegemony might be achieved in the context of a public social site such as the pub. I present ethnographic data to demonstrate that through the public performance of masculinity, dominant understandings of legitimate masculine behavior are reinforced and defended. Further, when pub behavior is linked with the wider empowerment of men in one rural community, it becomes clear that rural pubs are far from idyllic and must undergo a revision within rural sociology. Although the ethnographic data presented here suffer the traditional limitations of any analysis that is conducted primarily in one setting, my intention is to delineate gender practices in these particular rural pubs as the first step in a broader qualitative analysis of the links between public leisure sites and gendered power in rural communities.

Hegemonic Masculinity, Public Space, and Drinking

The idea of a hegemonic masculinity has come to represent a number of theoretical developments in masculinity theory. In this article, rather than trying to engage with all of these developments, I draw on three aspects of the idea of hegemonic masculinity which are integral to the original formulation of Connell (1987, 1995). First, Connell poses questions about how a particular version of masculinity becomes powerful at a particular point in time and space. Second, men's legitimacy is not assumed to be achieved automatically. Connell leads us to ask "How does a particular version of masculinity become *hegemonic* in that it is secured through social practice and accepted as natural and normal by most participants in a social site?" Finally, what are the consequences of hegemonic power both for women and for other groups of men?

These basic characteristics of theories of hegemonic masculinity have tended to foster a particular style of research, which seeks to address the changing specificities of masculinity in space and time. Connell himself has moved between ethnographic engagement with groups of men and a more biographical life-history approach (see Connell 1995). In this article I report on a similar style of ethnographic fieldwork, in which I utilize an intensive analysis of a particular social site (the rural pub) while also engaging with the history of the community to clarify specifically how hegemony has emerged and has been reproduced in this community.

Although the analysis presented here is situated within the broad framework of hegemonic masculinity theory, the specific qualities of this particular social site—the rural pub—also demand examination.

First, how is hegemonic masculinity secure and reproduced in a specifically *public* social site? A wider body of social research has identified public space as a place where numerous groups of men have been able to mobilize and exert forms of control. Phillips (1987) also discussed the historical emergence of a particularly powerful construction of military masculinity in New Zealand, which was played out in the *public* life of soldiering (also see Woodward 1997). Connell (1995) examined the biographies of young men who had enacted their masculinity through motorbikes, cars, surfing, and other public forms of display. Similarly,

McElhinney (1994) identified the way in which female police recruits became masculinized in the public performance of policing in the United States.

Public space is only one social site in which gender power might be contested or secured; achieving hegemony in such a space requires specific strategies and dynamics, and raises questions about gender as "performance." In recent work, Butler (1993) and Savran (1998) use the notion of gender as constituted *performatively*, in that gender is not a static structure or set of ideas but something that is enacted continually. Performance is the process by which discursive constructions of gender are enacted in social practice while their historical roots are obscured: "[I]t is always a reiteration of a norm or set of norms, and to the extent that it acquires an act-like status in the present, it conceals or dissimulates the conventions of which it is a repetition" (Butler 1993:13).

These ideas of performance seem particularly apt for the kinds of *public* behavior enacted by the drinking men in this ethnography. This point, however, implies more than merely an understanding of Goffman's (1959) theorization of the social implications of theatricality in social interaction. Rather, the performance of masculinity in the pub repeatedly represents a historically embedded notion of masculinity, integrated both in the drinking men's personal biographies and in their sense of localness, while powerfully excluding competing notions of what constitutes legitimate gender behavior. As Butler (1993:13) puts it, "[Performative practice] is not primarily theatrical; indeed, its apparent theatricality is produced to the extent that its historicity remains dissimulated." Consequently, public (or theatrical) performance provides only one aspect of performative understandings of gender. The important point is to recognize public performance as a particular site of performative enactment, and not to conflate it with the wider notion of gender performativity.

In the following analysis, I examine a particular body of performative practice. I term this *pub(lic) masculinity* to recognize not only the specificities of this performance as it relates to pub drinking,

but also the way in which such practice is intrinsically display-oriented and is under constant public observation. The term *pub(lic) masculinity* also captures some sense of the way in which the *pub* performance of masculinity strongly influences the wider *public* power of masculinity in this community. The performative enactment of pub(lic) masculinity contains overtly theatrical elements, particularly what I call *conversational cockfighting*; this is the central public activity through which legitimacy and hierarchy are evaluated.

The notion of performance in pub(lic) masculinity leads to a second key issue: the relationship between masculinity and drinking. Many masculinity theorists have noted this relationship, but only a few studies have actually addressed it (see Campbell, Law, and Honeyfield 1999). The symbolic associations of masculinity with alcohol are important; the physiological effects of alcohol consumption are equally so. Connell (1995) argues that the agency of bodies in social practice has not been acknowledged adequately in past masculinity research. The theorization of gender performance clearly incorporates the notion that these are embodied performances, and that public drinking by men clearly involves the agency of their bodies. In this ethnography, the activity of beer drinking is embodied in the successful performance of pub(lic) masculinity through what I term the *disciplines of drinking*. Further, the successful defense of masculinity in this site is premised in part on these disciplines.

Both conversational cockfighting and the disciplines of drinking are incorporated into a performance of masculinity that is characterized by one baffling quality: the actual attributes and ideal composition of this version of masculinity are never directly mentioned or addressed by participants in this social site. No one inside the pub is prepared to state what real or authentic masculinity might be. Masculinity therefore is transparent—subject to endless scrutiny—and yet invisible. This is the quality that makes performativity such a useful way to understand structures of hegemony. The entire performance enacts a particular version of masculinity that is powerful and legitimate;

yet through the performance this masculinity is rendered invisible and, in an important sense, unchallengeable.

Finally, although the performance of pub(lic) masculinity obscures the specifically masculine attributes of the performance, other ideological notions are more visible. In particular, the degree to which men can establish a sense of "localness" or historical embeddedness is integral to a successful performance. In this overt construction of the idealized "local," notions of rurality become an important legitimizer of local masculine practice as a historically embedded or "natural" form of gender relations.

Delimiting Space and Time: Pub(lic) Masculinity and After-Work Drinking in a Rural Community

The data presented here are based on the findings of 18 months of participatory ethnographic fieldwork conducted in 1989 and 1990 at two pubs in a South Island village in the Canterbury region of New Zealand (Fairweather and Campbell 1990). I then returned to live in the community for another three years. During that time, the understandings generated by the original research were augmented by the response of various sections of the community to our initial findings,[1] by further fieldwork insights, and by the continual emergence of new theoretical ideas in relation to masculinity, particularly discussions about hegemonic masculinity, embodiment, and performativity.

In combination, these two periods of fieldwork provided more than 100 formal interviews, approximately 200 hours of participant observation in the pubs, and an even greater abundance of informal discussion and dialogue with members of the community. Pub drinking involved about 150 to 200 men in the community of 1,000 permanent residents. As the following description makes clear, the pub itself was not an appropriate forum for formal methods such as recorded interviews; I relied on field notes written in the car or at home after observing pub drinking.[2] Throughout the five years of residence in the community, however, I

came to know many of these men through a variety of social locales such as sports clubs, churches, and voluntary organizations, and in their workplaces. Consequently the following account is constructed both from ethnographic observation in the pub and from many years of informal conversation and dialogue, including some vigorous feedback on our initial research findings, with men (and women) in the community.

The village has existed since the 1870s, when it emerged as a pooling site for itinerant laborers seeking work on the burgeoning sheep and wheat farms of the surrounding area (and a place to "blow their pay" in brothels, billiard halls, and pubs). In the twentieth century, the size of farms decreased, thus requiring less labor, and the character of the village changed towards more permanent residence by blue-collar workers and an increasing number of small farm service businesses. The only contemporary remnants of "wilder" days are the two remaining pubs in the center of town; these are frequented by a faithful clientele, are deeply embedded in particular versions of local history, and are the main site for the performance of pub(lic) masculinity in the village. Since the mid-1970s, the development of a ski area near the village has resulted in a new wave of economic development. Yet despite the arrival of many new bars, cafes, and even a nightclub, the two historic hotels are the only public drinking sites frequented by long-term village residents.

I chose this community for the original fieldwork period because of its reputation as a "drinkers' town," and the data presented below are an account of pub life in which the defense of masculinity has been accentuated strongly by a clash between tourism and blue-collar conservatism. This accentuation is useful, however, in that it provides a forum in which the various strategies and tactics involved in defending hegemonic masculinity come into sharp focus.

Pub(lic) masculinity involved a core group of 150 to 200 men who worked in farm service industries, were farm workers, owned or managed small farm service firms, or (a minority) were bachelor farmers. Manual laborers on farms and in farm service industries constituted the majority, but men from the agricultural petite bourgeoisie also were represented consistently. Consequently, although the practices of pub(lic) masculinity strongly resemble accounts of working-class drinking in other settings, this particular group involved men from a range of class positions. The space in which pub(lic) masculinity was enacted was the public bar of the two historic hotels. (Women, children, and "outsiders" could drink in the lounge bar of each hotel.)[3] A hierarchy of locations within each public bar further divided this space: high-status men commanded the bar stools, while lesser drinking groups stood around small elevated tables.

Not all men in the community or the surrounding farming area could participate in pub(lic) masculinity because its most important performance was delimited in time and space. This performance was the after-work drinking session. The temporal parameters of after-work drinking strongly influenced which local men could join the pub(lic) performance of masculinity. The participants labored according to what Donaldson (1996) calls "industrial time" and lived in the village, thereby opening up the social space and time between work and home. Farming men worked according to "natural time" and engaged in leisure patterns in a completely different way. Although some farmers managed to attend daily after-work drinking sessions, only a few could attend regularly enough to manage a highly successful performance of pub(lic) masculinity.

At least farming men were eligible to attend if they so desired. Three other groups in the community were excluded. The first was the recently arrived group of ski-industry workers (some of whom became permanent residents) and tourists visiting the ski area. The second group was the small body of transient white-collar professionals in the town. The final excluded group—women—was the most numerically significant and symbolically the most important for the pub(lic) performance of masculinity. Local women were employed in numerous occupations in the town and finished work at the same time as their male counterparts. Yet the after-work drinking session was populated entirely by men; only a few women came to the pub later in the evening. If women were accompanying men home from work, they drank in the lounge bar or more often, according to one woman, "went shopping" or "sat in the car with the kids for a couple of hours."

The exclusion of these other groups leaves us with a specific group participating in pub(lic) masculinity during after-work drinking. They all designated themselves as "workers," but not all were working class. The significant feature of this group is that the men who gathered in the pubs also tended to be the most influential members of sports clubs, charities, the local council, and (non-tourist-related) business. The after-work drinking session was not an isolated enclave of male activity, but the center of a network of association among men in the community. This is not entirely surprising in a rural community given the small population, the density of local networks, and the tendency toward long-term (intergenerational) residence in the community by prominent families. Consequently, to understand wider men's power in this community, one must understand the performance of pub(lic) masculinity as it is enacted at the daily meeting point of the various networks in the community: the pub.

The Performance of Pub(lic) Masculinity

My first, quite intimidated impression of the after-work drinking session was of an aggressive, chaotic melee. This impression changed somewhat over time, and I came to realize that for the majority of men—particularly the regular drinkers—after-work drinking followed distinct patterns of consumption, conversation, and behavior.

The second assumption to dissolve in the face of fieldwork experience was the notion that drinking men adhere rigorously to the ideology of egalitarianism. The public performance of drinking actually involved intensely competitive interaction that resulted in distinct hierarchies among the men present. They were not an inclusive, egalitarian social gathering but an exclusive, hierarchical group of men. This was indicated in part by the near-absence of reciprocal "rounds buying," which is identified as a social leveler in many other pub studies.

In this hierarchical context, conversational cockfighting and the disciplines of drinking became important. The performative enactment of pub(lic) masculinity involved continual conversational cockfighting, during which other drinkers scrutinized men's performance. At these times, hierarchies of knowledge, historical embeddedness, and legitimacy were established. The entire performance was premised on a series of disciplines that required an individual to maintain control over both the social and the bodily aspects of pub(lic) masculinity.

The Disciplines of Drinking

My own encounters with the after-work drinking scene clearly revealed the difference between myself and the core drinkers who had learned the disciplines throughout their drinking life. The disciplines involved accumulated knowledge, practice, and bodily fitness, which could be gained only over a long period. Men who were well schooled in the disciplines of pub(lic) masculinity tended to be those who had participated in after-work drinking sessions for many years.

The first discipline was local knowledge, which involved both an intimate knowledge of local history and a sweeping grasp of the details of contemporary life in the community. This kind of knowledge was demonstrated clearly to me on my first visit to the pub, when one man asked me where I was living.

Hugh: In Cleary's farm cottage.

Ray: But it isn't Cleary's anymore, is it. [as a statement, not a question]

Peter: Young Cleary's only managing the place for someone in Christchurch.

Ray: Old man Cleary's doing something in town now, isn't he?

Mike: He's with Matson and Company.

The conversation then proceeded to a discussion of the undesirability of urban investment in farm property, as had occurred when the Clearys sold their third-generation family farm to an investor. In other research I had identified 400 to 500 farms that were served by this community; the farm on which we were living was at the very periphery of this group. The three men who took my statement as a cue (and who then ignored me) were local laborers who showed an intimate knowledge of dealings on a farm that lay at the very edge of the local community.

Knowledge of history was also important, especially if men could present a convincing biography about their own role and that [of] their family in local history. Yet the accounts of local history generated in the pub differed somewhat from the official accounts that tended to be written by retired farmers in the district. Hatch (1992) noted a similar dynamic in a nearby community, whereby farming families became the arbiters of respectability. This dynamic was manifested in part in the production of what I term *respectable history*. In contrast, pub men mobilized a different set of facts and measures to create *pub history*. This history involved intimate knowledge of families, kinship, marriages and divorces, and deaths; a social tollbooth of arrivals and departures from the district; and a litany of prodigious adventures, parties, and other performances by local men. Although the narrative of pub history was contested somewhat, the point at which history blended into contemporary knowledge was contested even more strongly. One key aspect of the successful performance of pub(lic) masculinity was the degree to which a local man could claim a legitimate understanding of important local activities such as business, farming, sport, politics, and other local interests. I was continually amazed by the depth of local knowledge possessed by some men and their ability to find historical precedent for a particular interpretation of contemporary events.

This combination of local knowledge and history was exemplified when a local racehorse (a trotter) won the New Zealand Cup. This was not entirely unusual because the local area had always been a major center for breeding trotters. For weeks the event had dominated pub discussion: men in the pub reached back as far as the 1960s to find precedents for successful training secrets (often closely guarded local and family matters), and situated their own families as participants in developing the successful local culture of trotting. During this process the older, high-status men sitting on the barstools reigned supreme; they were able to integrate personal history and detailed local knowledge in a compelling performance.

Learning the disciplines of local knowledge and history could be achieved only over time. The same quality was evident in another of the disciplines: bodily control over the effects of beer consumption. At the after-work drinking session, men consumed beer served in one-liter jugs. Mean beer consumption was about three jugs; some men drank eight jugs a day. Even more important for male drinkers was the discipline of consuming such large quantities of beer and yet maintaining the appearance of total sobriety and self-control. It was imperative for the successful performance of pub(lic) masculinity that this impression of self-control be maintained.

Here, what Connell (1995) calls *body reflexivity* comes into play. Consuming alcohol has unavoidable effects on the body, which can be more easily tolerated (and therefore disguised) as what I call *drinking fitness* increases. Control is centered especially on the ability to maintain alertness in thinking and conversation, control over fine motor coordination, and control over the diuretic effects of drinking. It is no coincidence that a socially accomplished performance involves a degree of physical tolerance to drinking that can be attained only with years of practice.[4] The ability to "hold your piss" (literally in terms of repressing the need to urinate, and figuratively with *piss* used as a common term for alcohol) was imperative for a successful performance. Those who become visibly inebriated were derided with "Can't hold your piss" or "piss-poor performance."

This point was exemplified on a recreational trip involving men in their early twenties. When the bus stopped beside a public toilet, the men who had been drinking most heavily refused to use the toilets. When I questioned their wisdom, I received the following advice: "Hugh, you don't *break the waters*. If you do, you're history, you can't hold it back." One of the other young men added, "The first piss is the easiest to repress." This interesting use of metaphor expressed masculine control over femininity through the allusion to childbirth, as well as an insight into controlling the physiological effects of alcohol consumption.

I have used the term *disciplines* to underscore the extent to which some of the key components of a successful performance can be learned only over time. This is one reason why farm men who could attend the after-work session only infrequently struggled to maintain the disciplines, especially the intricate details of local knowledge that circulated continually in the pub, and the bodily capacity for consuming alcohol. With a few notable exceptions, farmers often found themselves in the position of a novitiate on their rare visits to the pub. In other words, the disciplines involved in the performance of pub(lic) masculinity were achievable primarily by men who could attend the after-work drinking session very regularly over many years.

Conversational Cockfighting

Having identified the disciplines that lie at the heart of the performance of pub(lic) masculinity, I discerned an associated process through which the disciplines were mobilized in performance. This process was conversational cockfighting. Within the drinking groups of four to seven men that tended to form around upright "beer stands," men engaged in continual discussion of local events, people, work, politics, and sport.

As a bystander to these discussions (and sometimes a participant), I was mindful of previous ethnographic attempts to describe men's public drinking behavior. Clark (1981) identified a clearly functionalist tone to many pub studies, particularly those which claimed that pub life fulfilled the function of providing a "secure and sociable" environment for drinkers. Central to this idea was the practice of "conversational sociability," which apparently achieved a number of integrative functions for the drinking individual.

While I was watching the competitive argumentation and verbal "sledging" of drinkers that was intrinsic to pub(lic) masculinity, this functionalist explanation of pub behavior seemed quite inadequate for my own ethnographic location. Pub interaction was generally competitive, and seemed to exclude more people than it included. A more accurate ethnographic comparison could be found in Buckley's (1983) account of men in Irish pubs "one-upping" each other and enjoying "wrongfooting" outsiders. These terms recognize a particular tone and style of conversation which is both humorous and serious; at times it involves seemingly extreme verbal abuse, which was not intended to give offense but to test whether a man could "take it." Often wrongfooting involved physical intimidation or interference with another man's performance. Sometimes a leg trip was verbal, sometimes physical.

I found an even more powerful comparison, however, in Geertz's participants in the Balinese cockfight, which captured some sense of the degree to which masculinity and manhood were at stake (Geertz 1973). Geertz acknowledged that underneath the playful teasing and banter in the cockfight were the serious tasks of betting and fighting—and the potential for a shattering loss of face for cockfighting men. This was indeed "deep play," with much more at stake than is indicated by the term *conversational sociability*. For pub(lic) masculinity, conversational cockfighting involved intense knowledge of local events and people. The outcome of these often feisty struggles directly influenced status in the after-work drinking scene.

Although conversational cockfighting often involved discussions lasting more than an hour on any one topic, the following extracts from field notes indicate the style of these conversations. The first extract involves a discussion about a mysterious woman:

Garth: Saw some blond girl on Back Track yesterday.

Alan: Did you chat her up?

Garth: I was in my car.

Alan: Even better. [men laugh]

Garth: She was actually parking a truck.

Simon: That's Matthew's exchange student.

Alan: Where from?

Simon: Sweden.

[Men laugh because of their association of Sweden with the pornography industry]

Garth: Matthew's a worry with all those students.

Peter: At least he gets ones that can handle trucks.

Alan: Did you say "trucks"? [men laugh again]

This conversation was not particularly competitive by pub standards and was characterized by the skills of double entendre and repartee. Its most important feature, however, is the slow leakage of information as Garth and Simon established their local knowledge about a topic as obscure as the identity of one woman seen on a road some 10 miles from the pub. Each man established certain facts: Simon's statement about Sweden was delivered straight, and was not intended to be funny. Alan, who knew nothing of events on Back Track, played the role of joker, which gave him a standing in the conversation that otherwise might not have been available to him.

The second extract is more competitive. The topic under discussion was the arrest of a young man the previous night for a speeding violation. Adam raised the topic, and despite a spirited challenge from Steve, managed both to display his superior knowledge of events and to cast doubt on Steve's skills and capacities.

Adam: Young Philip won't be a happy chappy this morning.

Steve: Well it serves him right, he stuffed up badly.

Mike: What happened?

Adam: He went through a trap [police car with speed radar] and then tried to outrun the cops.

Mike: I'd back him, though, a Cordia Turbo versus a cop Commodore.

Adam: Oh, he thought he'd outrun him OK, but Gary [the local policeman] got close enough to have a guess who it was and then backed off. Then he went around to his house a few minutes later and checked the car motor, which was red hot. Gary isn't a total fucking idiot.

Steve: As I said, he stuffed up badly. All he had to do was hit 180 [km/h = 110 mph] and then turn his lights off. And then take the next turn, using the gears so the brakelight wouldn't flash.

Adam: [unimpressed] Oh, really?

Peter: [humorously] Which is why the manufacturers considerately give you that little dial on the dash, to turn down the dash lights and help your night vision come on as quickly as possible.

Steve: I've done it myself.

Adam: [dismissively] Piss off, I haven't heard of you crashing any cars lately.

Although this conversation continued for a while, Adam always had the better of it. He introduced the topic and had the best information, and when Steve suggested his somewhat dangerous plan for evasion, Adam used it to suggest that Steve's own driving performance wouldn't live up to his claims. (As an outsider, I have no idea whether Steve's suggested plan was serious.) While Peter and Mike made some contribution, the real contest here was between Steve and Adam.

No matter how skilled one's conversational abilities are, however, successful cockfighting, in Geertz's understanding, also depends on how well one's bird can actually fight. In the context of pub(lic) masculinity, mastery over the disciplines was critical in making sure you weren't suddenly left holding a dead rooster. Without a disciplined store of local knowledge, one quickly became a bystander in conversational cockfights. Likewise, by maintaining bodily control over the effects of

drinking, men could make the necessary subtle distinctions between verbal abuse, which is merely "winding you up" or seeing whether "you can take it," and seriously intended insult. In perhaps the worst form of "losing it," visibly drunk men took umbrage during the trading of humorous insults and reacted violently. Put simply, men who are disciplined, experienced, and in control know when something is humorous and when it isn't.

In one fieldwork incident, a drunk young local farmer, Rocko, tried to participate in the topic under discussion, namely the local rugby team. The rest of the men in his drinking group became increasingly abusive and taunting in their replies (while enjoying this among themselves). The increasingly inebriated Rocko eventually was reduced to replying several times "What the fuck would you know?" The fun for the local men ended when one finally announced "Hey Rocko, time to fuck off home now." This line was both an order of expulsion and a reference to home as the appropriate place for men who couldn't "hold their piss." Exit Rocko holding a dead rooster.

Another important characteristic of conversational cockfighting, exemplified in this incident, was that the most aggressive conversations took place on the boundaries of the after-work drinking group. Rocko was a marginal local who couldn't hold his piss, and the disciplined drinking men enjoyed this rather one-sided cockfight. The closer one moved towards the high-status drinkers, however, the more the drinking groups seemed to share an unstated body of opinion. Fewer attempts were made to trip others up (although they were not absent by any means).

Finally, it was clear to me, while I observed the melee of after-work drinking, that not all the men were on an equal footing. Men who had a "biography" that linked them to the area as "locals" were integrated into legitimate pub history; those who worked in a historically legitimate job were at a major advantage, even before the learned disciplines of pub(lic) masculinity and the skills of conversational cockfighting were considered. Yet although the performance of pub(lic) masculinity resulted in a high degree of differentiation between the men participating in the after-work drinking scene, all at least were participating in "the game": the performance of pub(lic) masculinity totally excluded others as potential participants in after-work drinking (and in wider masculine public networks). This exclusion was premised on the process of "feminization," which excluded not only women but also a range of "others."

The Glass Phallus: Masculine Invisibility, Feminization, and Negation

One of the first things I noticed in one pub was an erect glass phallus perched above the bar. This was undoubtedly a polysemic object for many bar participants, and so it became for this ethnographer. On one level it came to represent, for me, the *transparency* of masculine performance: men were scrutinized intensely, and their performance was dissected, during after-work drinking. But on another level, I came to see that the *invisibility* of the erect phallus was also significant. Never once in the entire fieldwork process did I hear one of the men describe someone as a "real man" or positively define attributes that might constitute legitimately masculine behavior. Yet their overall performance proclaimed the existence of a masculine ideal, which some men evidently had reached.

The defining process took place through a form of binary categorization between masculine and feminine, in which the masculine end of the binary was unmarked, invisible, anonymous, and unacknowledged: the *glass phallus* of pub(lic) masculinity. In other words, pub discourse constantly defined what masculinity *wasn't,* by continually constructing notions of femininity and using these to undermine and exclude the claims of all who fell outside the legitimate construction of pub(lic) masculinity. According to the ideas of literary theory, masculinity was an *unmarked* category, while femininity was *marked*. Therefore pub(lic) masculinity involved not so much a striving towards some defined ideal of masculinity as a desperate struggle to avoid and negate any accusation or appearance of femininity.

Consequently, highly disciplined and controlled men derided inept drinkers for "drinking like girls," and pub performances were policed for any signs of femininity ("Do you sit down to take a piss?"). Physical performance was gendered: spilling or slopping beer, leaving beer unconsumed in a glass, and an inability to "hold your piss" were characteristic of women and children. Such gendering involved both the embodied disciplines of drinking and a wider assessment of men's skills outside the pub. Occupations outside the acceptable range of manual laboring, agriculturally related activities were also feminized derisively. This constant process of defining by negation was the principal reason why nearly all women and feminized men didn't want to drink at the pub. As one local woman commented to me, "Why in the world would you want to subject yourself to that stuff?" The few women who ventured into the pub usually did not contest this process of negation while in the pub.[5]

As Butler (1993) argues, the notion of performance, especially in its more theatrical and public display, is actually a constant process of dissimulation and concealment of the historical constructions and norms that are reproduced in performance. The glass phallus of pub(lic) masculinity is exactly this kind of performance: it enables a very specific version of masculinity to merge into the background of social practice. It becomes part of the unquestioned fabric of social interaction, while the performers' gaze is constantly turned outwards in continual negation of any threat from without.

The second characteristic of hegemonic masculinity is that it can defend and secure legitimacy over time. As indicated clearly by the ethnographic data presented above, the performance of pub(lic) masculinity possesses several endogenous features that enable hegemony to be defended. The disciplines of pub(lic) masculinity necessarily advantage those men who can participate in after-work drinking over a long period. These disciplines make it difficult for any alternative version of masculine drinking behavior to subvert pub(lic) masculinity from within.

These ethnographic data are supported by other research in New Zealand. Phillips (1987) describes a particular embodied performance of masculinity that was characteristic of pub drinking during the era of six o'clock closing in New Zealand. Similarly, Hodges' (1984) ethnography of student drinking includes a description of the extraordinary act called "bonging."[6] Although the embodied disciplines of drinking were different in these two cases, they share the quality of being learnable only over time. This learned quality, rather than the specifics of the social and embodied disciplines in each social site, implicates the disciplines in the maintenance of hegemony.

The other predominant dynamic, conversational cockfighting, also secures hegemony. This process clearly enables any person who challenges the status quo of pub(lic) masculinity to be marginalized, while creating a hierarchy among men within pub(lic) masculinity. The ethnographic parallels between this dynamic and competitive masculinity in other locales have been reviewed already. Even so, recognizing the centrality of conversational cockfighting to pub(lic) masculinity (and possibly to many other public drinking sites) suggests that we must reject the functionalist notion, set forth in prior pub studies, of "conversational sociability," which provided the individual male with positive integrative functions; and that we must discredit the attendant assumption that most pubs are characterized by egalitarianism.

Further, the two key dynamics in the performance of pub(lic) masculinity may be relevant to the broader study of hegemonic masculinity as it is enacted in specifically rural sites. Although hegemony is always legitimized and secured in different ways in different places, the data presented here can form the basis of a wider comparison between rural sites.

The first relevant point is the degree to which "biography" links successful performance to residence in a particular locality. The locality studied here is overtly rural, dominated by agriculture and farm service businesses, and characterized by men's long-term residence stretching over generations. Consequently, successful performance and defense of hegemony are premised on a style of residence and male embeddedness in locality that is characteristic of rural and small-town society. This embeddedness will be examined in future work exploring the relationships between public drinking sites and male control of the local labor market in this community.

A second issue relevant to rural sociology is the importance of public leisure sites to gendered power in small rural communities. The small scale of this community and the high degree of networking between pubs, clubs, and other associations, combined with the high level of participation by men from across class groups, made the pub a daily site where knowledge was generated and legitimate meaning was negotiated. These pubs, far from being an isolated arena where a small group of men formed opinions carrying little weight or influence, were the key sites for maintaining the legitimacy of hegemonic masculinity in the wider community.

While these two points relate to the way in which the structure of rural community life influences the practice and outcomes of pub(lic) drinking, the above analysis also demonstrates the relationship between ideological notions of rurality and hegemonic masculinity. Rurality is not a concept used widely by male drinkers; Jones (1995) noted this point in his observation that rurality is often a conceptual term more familiar to academics than to the subjects of their research. The male drinkers' notion of locality, however, contains all the attributes of what might be regarded ideologically as rural. Locality, in their conception, is characterized by long-term residence and by farming or primary industry-related employment; is organized predominantly around kinship rather than class groups; is virtuous and morally superior to city life; and represents a more "natural" social order for human life. Therefore, the pub(lic) performance of hegemonic masculinity not only is mediated through the structural characteristics of a specifically rural community; it also mobilizes notions of locality/rurality that reinforce the embeddedness, and thus the "naturalness," of this particular version of masculinity.

This negation of femininity (and the rejection of any semblance of female control over men) came into sharpest focus every day in what Fairweather and Campbell (1990:117) termed the "dinner battle." A critical part of successful masculine performance was the ability to act as if one were symbolically unmarried, and had no domestic responsibilities. One barmaid put it succinctly when I asked her (away from the pub) how many of the men in the bar were married. She replied "There aren't any married men drinking in this pub—not that you could tell anyway." Hence a general denial of any need to go home and eat dinner was an established part of pub(lic) masculinity, and the ability to delay the moment of departure was integral to a successful performance.

Throughout the fieldwork period, when people found out that I was interested in the pub, they told me the story of Metty, whose wife turned up at the pub and laid his dinner on the bar in front of him. There were subtle variations in the account, however: local women ended at the point where Metty was confronted and embarrassed in front of his mates, while local men added that Metty had turned to his wife and demanded "Where is my pudding?" [dessert].

This story had a mythic quality in the community, which merely reinforced the extent to which the dinner battle was central to pub(lic) masculinity. The importance of the dinner battle was reinforced by research in a nearby community, in which women described the uncertainty and disempowerment that stemmed simply from not knowing when men would arrive home each night (Smith 1988).

Conclusion: Pub(lic) Masculinity, Hegemony, and the Rural

The evidence presented so far makes the case that pub(lic) masculinity is characterized by a strong degree of exclusiveness. But how should pub(lic) masculinity be understood as a form of hegemonic masculinity? The findings presented here deal directly with two aspects of hegemonic

masculinity. First, how is a particular version of masculinity rendered legitimate? Second, how is this legitimacy secured and reproduced over time?

In the above description I outlined the way in which pub(lic) masculinity establishes the legitimacy of its understanding of masculinity through a vigorous process of negation. Although no one actually names what masculinity should be, the whole dynamic of pub(lic) masculinity names what it *shouldn't* be. In this way, the glass phallus of pub(lic) masculinity operates as an unmarked category. This does not mean, however, that it has no legitimacy. Instead, by operating through constant negation of all those marked "others" in the community, pub(lic) masculinity is constructed performatively in a way that makes it very hard to challenge.

When the rural pub is seen in this light, rural sociologists must move quickly beyond viewing it as just another aspect of the rural idyll. We must grasp the significant implications of pub drinking for the operation of gendered power in rural communities, and as a site where rural masculinities are enacted and defended. As rural sociologists, we can choose either to render the glass phallus visible or, like the performers of pub(lic) masculinity, continue to allow rural masculinity to remain invisible in the backdrop of rural social life.

NOTES

1. This ranged from total acceptance to outright rejection, illuminating the fragmented nature of the "community." For further discussion on the difficulties of research reflexivity and accountability in this study, see Campbell (1993).

2. Some conversations were recorded in my car shortly after they took place in the pub. Some inaccuracy in reproduction was inevitable, but several local people read the transcripts of pub dialogue and felt that there was no inauthentic transcriptional or editorial influence on the text.

3. Pubs in New Zealand were legally required to have two drinking areas: the public bar and the lounge bar. Although the laws mandating these two separate spaces have been redundant for a long time, the spaces persist: local men still only frequent the public bar.

4. Riordan's (1998) study of a rural Australian community shows a similar dynamic in that all of the "legends" were men who had actually developed the bodily skills needed for playing certain sports (and for drinking).

5. Campbell and Phillips (1995) document the violent consequences of resistance for two women in these pubs.

6. In "bonging," a tube is inserted down into the stomach and jugs of beer are poured in until the stomach is full and the contents are regurgitated. The physical effect was described as unique.

REFERENCES

Bell, M. M. 1994. *Childerley: Nature and Morality in a Country Village*. Chicago: University of Chicago Press.

Buckley, A. D. 1983. "Playful Rebellion: Social Context and the Framing of Experience in an Ulster Community." *Man* 18:383–95.

Butler, J. 1993. *Bodies That Matter: On the Discursive Limits of "Sex."* New York: Routledge.

Campbell, H. 1993. "Conducting Ethnography 'at Home': Issues Arising From the Study of Male Drinking Groups in Methven." Pp. 89–93 in *Proceedings of a Workshop on Rural Community Studies,* edited by R. W. M. Johnson, Wellington: Ministry of Agriculture and Fisheries.

Campbell, H., R. Law, and J. Honeyfield. 1999. "What It Means to Be a Man: Hegemonic Masculinity and Beer in New Zealand." Pp. 166–86 in *Masculinities in Aotearoa/New Zealand*, edited by R. Law, H. Campbell, and J. Dolan. Palmerston North: Dunmore Press.

Campbell, H. and E. Phillips. 1995. "Masculine Hegemony in Rural Leisure Sites in Australia and New Zealand." Pp. 107–26 in *Communications and Culture in Rural Areas,* edited by P. Share. Wagga Wagga: Center for Rural Social Research.

Clark, W. B. 1981. "The Contemporary Tavern." *Research Advances in Alcohol and Drug Problems* 6: 425–70.

Connell, R. W. 1987. *Gender and Power: Society, the Person, and Sexual Politics*. Sydney: Allen and Unwin.

———. 1995. *Masculinities*. Sydney: Allen and Unwin.

Donaldson, M. 1996. *Taking Our Time: Remaking the Temporal Order*. Nedlands: University of Western Australia Press.

Fairweather, J. R. and H. Campbell. 1990. *Public Drinking and Social Organisation in Methven and Mt. Somers*. Research Report 207, Agribusiness and Research Unit. Lincoln University, Canterbury, NZ.

Geertz, C. 1973. *The Interpretation of Cultures*. New York: Basic Books.

Goffman, E. 1959. *The Presentation of Self in Everyday Life*. New York: Doubleday.

Hatch, E. 1992. *Respectable Lives: Social Standing in Rural New Zealand*. Berkeley: University of California Press.

Hodges, I. 1984. "Make Mine a Large One: An Anthropological Study of the Rules and Symbols of Drinking Rituals intended to Reconstruct Social Relations Between Men in Southern New Zealand." PhD dissertation, Department of Anthropology, University of Otago, Dunedin.

Hunt, G. and S. Satterlee. 1987. "Darts, Drink and the Pub: The Culture of Female Drinking." *Sociological Review* 35:575–601.

Jones, O. 1995. "Lay Discourses of the Rural: Developments and Implications for Rural Studies." *Journal of Rural Studies* 11:35–49.

McElhinny, B. 1994. "An Economy of Affect: Objectivity, Masculinity and the Gendering of Police Work." Pp. 159–71 in *Dislocating Masculinity: Comparative Ethnographies,* edited by A. Cornwall and N. Lindisfarne. London: Routledge.

McLauchlan, G. 1994. *The Story of Beer: Beer and Brewing—A New Zealand History*. Auckland: Viking.

Mingay, G. E. 1989. *The Rural Idyll*. London: Routledge.

Murdoch, J. and A. Pratt. 1993. "Rural Studies: Modernism, Postmodernism and the 'Post Rural.' " *Journal of Rural Studies* 9:411–27.

Phillips, J. 1987. *A Man's Country: The Image of the Pakena Male—A History*. Auckland: Penguin.

Philo, C. 1992. "Neglected Rural Geographies: A Review." *Journal of Rural Studies* 8:193–207.

Riordan, R. 1998. "Blokes and Legends: A Study of the Value of Performance Amongst Men in a Western Australian Rural Community." PhD dissertation, Department of Anthropology, University of Western Australia, Perth.

Savran, D. 1998. *Taking It Like a Man: White Masculinity, Masochism, and Contemporary American Culture*. Princeton: Princeton University Press.

Smith, R. 1988. The Place of Alcohol in the Lives of Some Rural Eastern-Southland Women. *Report 7,*

The Place of Alcohol in the Lives of New Zealand Women Project, Department of Anthropology, University of Auckland.

Whitehead, A. 1976. "Sexual Antagonism in Herefordshire." Pp. 169–203 in *Dependence and Exploitation in Work and Marriage,* edited by D. L. Barker and S. Allen. London: Longman.

Woodward, R. 1997. "It's a Man's Life!: Soldiers, Masculinity and the Countryside." *Gender, Place and Culture* 5:277–300.

Hugh Campbell is an associate professor in social anthropology at the University of Otago, New Zealand. His research specialties are the anthropology of rural society and the sociology of agriculture. His first job after graduating in anthropology was as a contract ethnographer studying drinking behavior in a small, rural community—a study that he has returned to and reflected on both in this article and elsewhere. Campbell completed his Ph.D. in rural sociology in 1994 at Charles Stuart University, Australia, defending a thesis studying the adjustment strategies of farm households and rural small businesses during a period of economic crisis. Since 1994, he has been employed by the Department of Anthropology at the University of Otago. In 2000, he coedited (with Mike Bell of the University of Wisconsin, Madison) a special issue of *Rural Sociology* on the topic of rural masculinities. He and Bell are currently coediting a book collection entitled, *Country Boys: Masculinity and Rural Life.*

An   interview   with . . .

Hugh Campbell

First, how is it that you became interested in the topic of masculinity and, more specifically, hegemonic masculinity as it is reproduced in public settings and its relationship to drinking?

I arrived in this field site by accident rather than design—as is often the case. My prior university work had nothing to do with masculinities, but in 1989 I took a job as a contract ethnographer on a project about alcohol use in rural areas of New Zealand. It was not until a few years later that I came across the masculinities literature and began to reinterpret and reconsider some of that ethnographic work in the light of new theories about masculinity. In particular, another academic who read our original ethnographic monograph on public drinking (I was working as the junior research partner with the project leader Dr. John Fairweather at Lincoln University, New Zealand) commented that my experience of strong exclusionary behavior in the pub, and my feelings of subordination and powerlessness, were the kinds of dynamic that Bob Connell had been writing about in his work on hegemonic masculinity. In particular, Connell's work argued that there were not only power divisions in society between men and women, but that there were also power divisions between different groups of men. Some men managed to achieve a hegemonic position in relation to others. This looked to me like exactly the kind of dynamic I had been observing in the pub. So I returned to my field notes and our original monograph and began to look again for evidence of the kinds of behavior that made some men legitimate, powerful, and thus hegemonic, while excluding both all women and a number of different groups of men. So, the article was really a reexamination of my original field data some years after the event. It shows, above all, that you should never burn your field notes!

What made you choose this site (this pub) and decide on this particular approach to your research question?

My original training was in social anthropology (or what would be termed cultural anthropology in the U.S.) and my department is well known for its emphasis on conducting fieldwork "at home": rather than continually sending ethnographic researchers into exotic locations to research other cultures, we tended to use anthropological methods to conduct ethnography within our own society. So, it was easy for me to decide that an ethnographic approach was the right way to approach this study. Choosing the village was more challenging. I originally conducted a survey of thirty-two pubs in the region sketching out the broad styles and types of pubs that were present. The members of the project team had to decide between choosing a "typical" pub according to our survey, or perhaps finding a community where things were a bit different. We chose the latter option, and the village I studied was a little unusual in that it had a reputation as a "drinker's town." It was the most predominantly blue collar community in an otherwise farming region. It had a long history of riotous public drinking as it was just over the "wet" side of the regional boundary that separated New Zealand into wet and dry zones during a long period of prohibition. The village was strongly focused on pub life. The village was also characterized by a high degree of gender conflict. So, why did we chose an atypical community? The answer is mainly because the original project was focused on policy issues and solutions to drinking problems in rural areas. The project team felt that if these policy solutions could work in one of the toughest drinking towns in New Zealand, they would work anywhere.

There are lots of distinctive challenges that social scientists face doing ethnographic research—issues of access, ethics, role of the researcher, taking field notes, and so on. What were the major challenges that you faced in doing this particular project? How did you deal with them?

This was a very challenging study. While the study took place prior to the establishment of ethics committees at New Zealand universities, I think that if this project were to be reviewed by an ethics committee today, they would ask some hard questions about not only the community, but also my personal safety as the ethnographic researcher. There were times when I was physically threatened, verbally abused, and challenged to undertake all sorts of activities that I didn't want to (like having to drink a lot more than I wanted to). This was a powerful male in-group, and I was in a vulnerable position as an out-sider male with no legitimate role in the town (conducting academic research didn't really make it as legitimate work to many of these men). That is not to say that all the men in this town were dangerous or unwelcoming. Many were great to work with and strongly assisted the research, but there were enough uncomfortable moments to make it a less than happy eighteen months of par-ticipant research.

I have often been asked about how we did the research and the question is a fair one. I have often observed that despite the penchant for new theories about masculinity, there are actually very few ethnographic-style studies that really engage with any potentially threatening masculine worlds (of course, with some notable exceptions). The first key methodological issue was actual access and engagement with the field site. This may not sound too difficult in what were essentially *public* bars, but it turned out to be harder than I had ex-pected. I set myself the target of going to pubs for 300 hours over the first twelve months of the project. It may not sound like a lot, but I found that going alone was difficult. I can quickly assure those readers asking the obvious question that I didn't have a research budget for alcohol. After a while, I found that going with my partner, and then in groups of friends (some from univer-sity, and some whom we made during the study) was by far the best way to study pub activities. After I had joined the golf club and spent some months at-tending club days, I found regular golf club members drinking at the pub whom I could drink with.

I did not try to take notes in the pub. That could have been at best counter-productive, and at worst, dangerous. I used to take breaks and go out to the car and write, or write up in the car on the way home (when accompa-nied by my partner who was acting as driver). I would review my notes the next morning and add in some more thoughts. When I went with friends we would often debrief about key conversations we had had. When publishing from this research, I have tried to stay away from using direct quotes, unless they were conversations we had directly participated in, and had a very good recall of.

My second most-asked question about this research is "did you drink"? The answer is yes. These pubs were sites where alcohol consumption was mandatory for actual participants in pub activity. For me to engage with groups of drinking men, I had to drink beer. Men who hang back and don't participate in drinking are singled out for a certain amount of harassment by the wider group. I sought to avoid this kind of negative attention, while trying to stay as sober as possible. It was an interested balancing act, and my writing about the embodied experiences of drinking for men in the pub is strongly in-formed by my own experience. As time went by, my capacity to drink and tol-erate alcohol increased significantly and this helped the research a great deal. One negative effect, however, is that I do instinctively now associate beer drinking with those rather stressful fieldwork situations and I've become only an occasional beer drinker—usually drinking beer to avoid embarrassing a host or friend. I now sympathize with teetotalers and vegetarians. Food and drink can become quite a coercive aspect of our daily lives once we start to notice it.

What findings were least surprising? Most surprising?

The reaction to my research had some very surprising aspects. In particular, a number of New Zealand academic women commented to me that they were fascinated to know what life was like inside a rural pub because they had never actually been in a rural pub. Why was this surprising? Because, pubs are literally public spaces. There is no legal barrier to women entering pubs (well, there was before 1967, but that is another story), so why had so many women never been participants in this kind of public space? Clearly, there are areas of life that are simply threatening to people (and with good reason). Women do not feel comfortable in these sites, and they are actively made to feel uncomfortable if they do try to participate in them. This was one of the features of the study that made me think a lot about public space and the idea of what is public. So, at one level, the pub seems to be operating as a threatening space for women, where many choose never to participate at all. However, at another level, the pub is characterized in popular culture as an idyllic site where happy mateship takes place, where "everybody knows your name," where cheeky barmaids joke with happy customers, almost a sacred space where people go to escape the troubles of life. The absolute dissonance between the rendering of the rural pub in popular culture and the reality of a threatening social space provided the greatest surprise to me. Did I have any idea what I was letting myself in for when I signed up for the job? Not even slightly!

What were the ethical challenges or issues involved in your research? How did you deal with them?

Ethical challenges in research are an important part of contemporary research. I've already mentioned that this study took place before ethical scrutiny became mandatory for university projects. However, you don't need ethics committees to tell you what most researchers will encounter on a common sense level in the field. First, I tried to disguise the name of the village—you'll note that I don't use it here—as well as disguising the identity of individuals. Second, we decided that as alcohol consumption was a potentially difficult area of study, we would only study public drinking. By being in a public place, people have already consented to public scrutiny in a way that would not be the case if I had inveigled myself into private households and recorded people's home life unawares. I had made myself known to people in the community, was open about the study taking place, and generally was accepted—until the results were published!

Then we discovered a problem. When I had talked to community leaders about studying drinking problems in the town, many townsfolk had interpreted this as being specifically to do with youths' drinking, and drunk driving. This was how townsfolk constructed the idea of "drinking problems." When I published research describing a problematic drinking culture in the daily behavior of a wide group in the town, some people were very upset. Not all. Some felt I hadn't been critical enough, and some felt that I should have said more, as a "hard drinking reputation" would be good for encouraging a certain kind of tourist trade!

It was a very revealing process for me as a researcher. When seeking to gain consent from the community, I had reified a particular group as representing the community and its ethical views. The final outcome was much more complex and revealed the fractured nature of power and divisions in community life—particularly serious divisions of gender. I could not have presented the results in any way without disadvantaging some segment of the community. If I had romanticized and softened the narrative—and allowed local men to censor my findings—those local women who were strongly disadvantaged by (and often the victims of) local drinking culture would have suffered a grave injustice. Likewise, if I had become even more critical (and certain narratives from the local Alcoholics Anonymous counselor would have made for juicy reading) I would have risked demonizing drinking men as the root of all evil in the town. It was a salutary lesson in research positioning, and in the end I decided to simply use the ethnographer's privilege and tell it like I saw it.

What was the most frustrating or difficult aspect of doing this research?

I've already touched on most of the key points here. It was surprisingly difficult gaining access to the men's drinking groups. But, in the end, that difficulty itself became a central process in understanding the exclusionary nature of men's drinking groups.

What was most satisfying about the experience?

Good ethnography tries to give voice to people who might not otherwise see the light of day. This study gave voice to two groups of people who were positioned in conflict with each other. First, it provided a public voice for drinking men and their activities inside pubs. I'm not sure that they enjoyed that kind of exposure, but I think it was important. The second group was women in the town who have been trying to resist men's drinking culture for decades. They found my publication very encouraging and maybe even empowering. So, I think that I had managed to give public visibility to what had previously been an invisible gender struggle in that town.

If you were to do this research again, what might you do differently?

After my difficulties in this study, I never aspired to undertake this kind of research again. It was with a degree of innocence and naivety that this research took shape, and it wasn't until I was deep in the field that I realized that this was a potentially very toxic research site. The final strategies we adopted as a research team needed to be in place from the outset—namely, that it was not safe for a lone man or women to try and study pub drinking. We needed to conduct research in groups, which would have assisted with safety, with note taking and recall of pub activities, and with making sure that there was a sober driver to get us home!

The second thing to note would be a potentially different approach to the community—not reifying certain "leaders" as the legitimate voice of the community. An action research process that recruited actual members of different parts of the community into the project would have helped, although given the nature of the gender conflict in the town, that might simply have added a highly destructive dynamic to the research team.

What important lesson drawn from this research experience would you share with students?

It is often a shock to students, when they first take on participant observation, to experience the absolute indifference, or even hostility, of everyday folk to being the objects of study. People often just don't like to be studied, and when they do like being studied, it is usually on pretty safe terrain that makes them look good. There is a moment of ontological crisis in these studies when you really wonder what right you have to be invading these people's lives. I experienced this, and many of my colleagues report the same—even from fieldwork sites less hostile than mine. My answer to this is that you really must have established for yourself that you do have the right. If possible, you need to have negotiated that right with the people you are studying. And you need a sense of the politics of your research site. If the political situation you are studying is difficult, you need to know whether your academic research will serve a useful purpose by revealing those politics to public scrutiny, and thus whether it is worth the risk to yourself and to others.

Finally, if you do decide to put yourself into a tricky fieldwork locale, you need to have a good exit strategy in place. My great mistake was to live in the community, very close to where I was drinking at the pub. This seemed a good idea at the time, but it really meant that I never felt I could escape should things get seriously out of control. In these kinds of potentially hostile sites, you need an exit strategy to protect yourself as researcher. A lot of the criticism of recent research is directed at the potential damage that researchers can do to the communities they are studying. While I agree with this concern, I also think that we need to be very conscious of the amount of damage communities can do to researchers.

Questions to Think About

1. If you were to study a topic similar to Campbell's—that is, masculinities in public spaces—how might you do so using an approach other than field research? Do

you think field research has particular advantages with regard to this sort of research topic? If so, why?

2. Draw up a list of six to ten dos and don'ts for doing field research that you learned from Campbell's article and interview.

3. Pretend you are the chair of the Institutional Review Board that was asked to review and approve Campbell's research plan. Would you? If not, what would be your suggestions to bring the research in line with ethical standards of research?

4. What symbolic meaning(s) does Campbell give to the glass phallus? How does his discussion about its meaning illustrate some of the central attributes of field research?

5. What are some ways that field researchers assess the validity of their data and constructs? How does Campbell do this?

6. Briefly explain each of the following concepts that Campbell uses to describe and analyze patterns of behavior in the pub: hegemonic masculinity, hierarchies of knowledge, conversational cockfighting, disciplines of drinking, definition by negation.

chapter 8

Historical and Comparative Research

Much research in the social sciences focuses on a single, contemporary society or on one small aspect of that society. However, historical and comparative researchers are interested in studying social life as it has evolved and changed over time and as it varies across nations and cultures. Historical and comparative research encompasses a variety of methods and uses both quantitative and qualitative analysis. It is grounded in the belief that focusing attention beyond recent events in a single country can yield valuable insights about social organization, social processes, and social change. Although historical and comparative research still represents a relatively small segment of all social scientific research, it has a distinguished history in sociology and seems to be gaining popularity—as indeed it should in an era of increasing globalization and the growing awareness of our responsibilities as citizens and scholars of the world.

Historical and comparative researchers typically draw on a wide variety of primary and secondary sources for their data: historical documents (everything from legal contracts to personal letters and diaries), official government sources (including census data), organizational records, media reports (such as newspaper articles), oral histories, websites, and many others. As with all research, the aim is to identify patterns in the data—in this case, as they reveal constancy or change in human behavior and social arrangements over time and across nations.

Although researchers can simultaneously adopt both historical and comparative foci, we have included two articles, each of which illustrates only one of these approaches. In the first, Barbara Perry traces the evolution of the hate movement in the United States over the last several decades, with the idea that understanding changes in its messages over time helps us better understand the current strategies that hate groups use to promote their interests. As is often the case with historical research, Perry relies on a variety of sources, including the groups' websites, written brochures and other materials produced by the groups, population surveys, social scientific research, and secondary sources written by historians. A significant challenge, and one that faces most historical sociologists, was assembling and organizing enough information to be able to analyze the groups' metamorphoses. Although she uses some quantitative data, hers is essentially a qualitative approach. She interprets and draws meaning from all her sources to present a holistic picture of recent changes in the hate movement.

Comparative researchers focus on some social phenomenon across two or more nations at a single point in time or, in some cases, over time. The example of comparative research that we include in this chapter is a study by Constance Flanagan and four colleagues, each from a country other than the United States (and from a range of different disciplines as well). The article nicely shows how social scientists from five different countries can collaborate on a project that uses data from all of their countries (plus two others) and how they work together to deal with the considerable challenge of obtaining data that are valid and consistent across nations.

Flanagan and her colleagues are interested in knowing what factors contribute to civic commitment in young people, an especially timely topic given the increased interest and number of programs in service learning and community service in schools across the United States and in other countries. By taking a comparative perspective, the researchers are able to determine the influence not only of individual level variables, but also social structural variables such as gender, social contextual variables such as family emphasis on social responsibility, and even macro-level variables such as the stability of the form of government (three of the countries are stable democracies, four are transitional democracies). The authors begin with a broad theoretical approach that includes how family and institutions beyond the family (e.g., schools) transmit values regarding young people's responsibility to the public interest and what it means to be part of a political community (the "social contract"). For those interested in understanding adolescents' involvement in community service and factors that shape their sense of civic commitment in the United States, this research offers a rich perspective and useful results that would not be available by examining U.S. data alone.

These two articles and the authors' interview comments also reveal much about the distinctive challenges of historical and comparative research. Some we have already alluded to, such as the difficulties of ensuring crosscultural measurement validity and identifying parallel and comparable samples in five different sites, challenges with which Flanagan and her colleagues dealt. Perry had to deal with the limitations of available data sources, a complication that is common in historical research. She notes that websites and even chat room communications of hate groups are "sanitized," so that she did not have access to the more inflammatory and extremist aspects of hate group language and ideology. Much has been written elsewhere about the difficulties of locating useful and usable primary and secondary historical sources, but none of this offsets the value of looking beyond a single time and place for answers about how the social world works.

"Button-Down Terror"

The Metamorphosis of the Hate Movement

Barbara Perry

This paper explores the extent to which the hate movement in the United States has taken on a new, modern face. The strength of the contemporary hate movement is grounded in its ability to repackage its message in ways that make it more palatable, and in its ability to exploit the points of intersection between itself and prevailing ideological canons. In short, the hate movement is attempting to move itself into the mainstream of the United States culture and politics. I conclude by arguing that antiracist and antiviolence organizations must continue to confront hate groups through legal challenges, monitoring, and education.

The contemporary reconstruction of the hate movement is grounded in a profound sense of dislocation motivated by the perceived "crisis of identity" spawned by the civil rights movement. Since the 1960s, diverse social movements have voiced their claims to group autonomy, political inclusion, and freedom from discrimination. What these movements shared was a commitment to the equal valuation and treatment of all social groups—an approach that directly challenged long-standing and deeply embedded ideologies and practices which consciously sought to devalue "Otherness": Jim Crow laws, job segregation, and sodomy legislation, for example. In contemporary terms, it is precisely this form of inclusive and egalitarian politics that hate groups would seek to overturn. As the People's Resistance Movement sees it, "political moves and social changes are now taking place which . . . are rapidly weakening our institutions and threaten to end in chaos and anarchy." Jared Taylor, founder of the virulently racist *American Renaissance* magazine, is similarly explicit about the source of his hostility.

Traditional arrangements in racial and gender relations, he argues, "served the country well, so long as . . . the two traditional minorities—Blacks and Indians—did not have voices. All this changed, beginning in the 1960s. The civil rights movement gave voices to Blacks and Indians, and changes in immigration law brought a massive influx of non-whites. It was the end of a certain kind of America" (cited in Anti-Defamation League [ADL] 1996a, p. 178). The "American" is no longer (as if it ever was) an uncontested vision. Instead, the very meaning of American identity, and especially the meaning of "Whiteness," has been seriously thrown into question. As they have in the past, contemporary hate groups have mobilized in an effort to reassert a narrow, exclusive understanding of the national identity. This is not an unexpected or surprising development, since hegemony and the practices of insurgency are inherently dynamic and unstable. It is the case that "the insurgent process is one whereby subordinate group members introduce a particular tactic, [and] the dominant group, over time, adjusts, counteracts, and often neutralizes that particular subordinate group strategy. . . . The end result of the struggle is often a reshaping of the existing stratification structure" (Roscigno 1994, p. 112). While I would argue that there is no ultimate "end result" of this ongoing process, Roscigno's point is well taken: counter-hegemonic threats to the established racial and gendered order are consistently met with counter-mobilization on the part of the traditionally dominant groups(s). Extremist hate groups are explicitly organized to neutralize the threats posed by minority groups such as people of color, women, and gay men and women. Many, like the Church of Jesus Christ in Israel, are fully prepared for a Racial Holy War (RAHOWA) which would "return power to the white race"

(Charles Scott, cited in "Merchants of Hate," online). Similar sentiments are to be found among adherents of the Montana Freemen who insist that "We are not to allow women or foreigners, colored people, jews, and/or citizens of the United States to rule over us" (cited in ADL, "The Freemen Network," online). Thus, these hate groups take it upon themselves to mobilize a movement against what they perceive to be invalid usurpers.

However, the legacy of the civil rights movement means that the historically effective means of responding to the threat of Otherness—lynching, genocidal practices, and legal exclusion—have less resonance today. They are as likely to be condemned as applauded within hate groups. To a certain extent, this is a "kinder, gentler nation" than it was at the beginning of the twentieth century. Consider the public outcry and condemnation of the murderers of James Byrd and Matthew Shepard. The savvy, organized hatemongers of today are not ignorant of this limitation, and so are forced to alter their tone and tactics. If they are to recruit, if they are to establish public credibility, they must distance themselves from the likes of John William King—as the Klan did when it, too, denounced the lynching of Byrd in Jasper, Texas. This does not mean that racial or religious or gender violence is no longer a part of their arsenal. Rather, it means that such violence is increasingly contextualized within a more contemporary, sanitized "look" and "feel," intended to render the appearance of moderation. Consequently, the hate movement is in the midst of a metamorphosis that brings it into the mainstream. Contemporary changes in the presentation, membership, and technologies of hate have enabled the extremists of the 21st century to repackage the movement in ways that find resonance and legitimacy among the general public.

This paper is an exploration of the renewal of the hate movement in the United States. In dramatic ways, hate groups threaten to extend their impact beyond the immediate membership. Their mantra of intolerance is gaining considerable legitimacy in light of the changing messengers and media that carry their message. In this paper, I address the significance of contemporary hate groups, in terms of their connections to generalized attitudes about race and gender, to the political mainstream, and to the growing militia movement. I also explore the implications of their strategic and recruitment use of modern communication. Together, these patterns facilitate hate groups' abilities to make some claim to legitimacy, and therefore, acceptance. Before I begin to trace these alignments, however, I present a brief descriptive overview of the current nature of and activities associated with the hate movement.

Scope and Activities

The existing supremacist groups are a diverse lot, ranging from the contemporary incarnations of the traditional Ku Klux Klan (KKK), to the loosely organized skinheads. While these myriad groups are characterized by differences in age, class, and gender structures, as well as in ideologies, practices, and national visibility, what they share is a commitment to clean up the "cultural pollution"—however defined—which has apparently sullied the United States (Perry 1999). The most prevalent manifestations of the pollution, from this perspective, are racial and ethnic minority groups. Thus, most hate groups are oriented around white supremacist and anti-Semitic platforms. Nonetheless, women, homosexuals, atheists, and other minority groups may also be on the "hit lists" of these groups. Increasingly, the liberal welfare state is becoming the focus of wrath: the state is to blame for the rising "impertinence" of minority groups. While antigovernment militias are most commonly associated with the latter, Dees (1996), Ridgeway (1995), and the ADL (1996a, 1996b) make it clear that the boundaries between hate-motivated extremists and anti-state extremists are becoming more and more blurred. In his role as director of the Southern Poverty Law Center, Dees (1996) has marshaled substantial evidence supporting the notion that adherents of white supremacist organizations—such as Louis Beam of the Aryan Nations—are infiltrating militia groups.

Excluding militia groups, Kleg (1993) suggests that it is possible to identify five distinct categories of hate groups operative in the 1990s: Identity Church adherents; neo-Nazis; skinheads; Ku Klux Klansmen/women; and Posse Comitatus. It is important to bear in mind, however, that the distinctions between these groups are becoming increasingly blurred—membership is fluid, with people moving in and out of groups and maintaining memberships in several at once. Moreover, there is considerable interaction and cooperation between groups in terms of rallies, information sharing, and links on hate lines, for instance.

The first of the groups, the Identity Church movement, incorporates some of the most active and violent organizations of the 1990s, including Aryan Nations, The Order (now defunct), the Covenant, Sword and Arm of the Lord, and Rev. Pete Peters's Church of Christ. Groups in this class ground their anti-Semitic and racist virulence in a scriptural reading that posits white Christians as God's "chosen" people, and Jews, especially, as the children of Satan. Neo-Nazis turn not to the Bible, but to tracts of Germany's Third Reich to inform their "Americanism, Nazi-style—send the blacks to Africa and the Jews to the ovens" (cited in Kleg 1993, p. 201).

The "White Power" rhetoric of neo-Nazi groups such as the National Socialist White Peoples' Party (NSWPP) or the National Alliance is shared in a somewhat less orderly and consistent manner by the rising numbers of skinheads. Skinheads tend to be more loosely organized but also more violent than many other hate groups. Bullard (1991) claims that the skinheads of the 1990s were every bit as violent as was the KKK of the 1920s and 1950s.

The KKK—currently in a state of fragmentation—addresses contemporary problems like AIDS, crime, welfare, or immigration "solely through the prism of race and offers not solutions but a licence to hate" (ADL 1991, p. 2). In part, the resurgence in KKK membership can be explained by its change in tactics, toward mainstreaming, best exemplified by David Duke's smooth professional persona. Finally, the Posse

Comitatus shares the anti-Semitism of other hate groups, alongside the anti-statism of the militia groups. Indeed, the two targets of opprobrium are inherently linked in the belief in the Zionist Occupied Government (ZOG). From this perspective, the only legitimate form of government exists at the local level, since the federal government is orchestrated by Jewish financial interests.

The membership represented by hate groups in the United States is difficult to ascertain; estimates of the number of active group members vary widely. Starr (1997; online) offers a conservative estimate of 25,000 actively involved in hate groups, but also notes that an additional 150,000 Americans may be "armchair racists" who receive literature and possibly attend rallies without necessarily taking any other action. Feagin and Vera (1995) provide similar numbers for the early 1990s, suggesting 20,000 to 30,000 active white supremacists, representing 300 groups, and 150,000 "armchair" supremacists. Ridgeway's (1995) extensive review of the history of white supremacist groups in the United States identifies 25 major hate groups, with extensive offshoots of each. This appears to be a conservative estimate, in that Kleg (1993) and Bullard (1991) number Identity Churches alone at 40 and 150 respectively. Bullard's (1991) estimate of the total number of hate groups—350—is closer to that of Feagin and Vera (1995). The Southern Poverty Law Center's (SPLC) Klanwatch project suggested that in 1996, 240 hate groups were active in approximately 40 states (Klanwatch 1997). By the time the organization published its 1998 report, the number had jumped an astonishing 20 percent, up to 474 active groups nationwide (Klanwatch 1998).

In terms of specific groups' membership, Klanwatch (1998) reports a dramatic increase in the number of Klan chapters nationwide by the end of the 1990s, when 127 chapters were identified. Bullard (1991) asserts that in 1990 the KKK counted its numbers at only 5,000, the century's nadir. This corresponds with the ADL's estimate of 4,000–5,000 for 1995, as compared to a high of five million in 1925. In fact, by 1990, Identity

Church membership had surpassed that of the KKK, with somewhere between five and ten thousand participants (Bullard 1991); by 1998, Identity Churches could boast 81 chapters across the country (Klanwatch 1998). Skinheads, too, probably outnumber the Kluxers, although these are even more difficult to count due to their lack of organizational structure. The ADL consistently puts their numbers at 3,500 in the 1990s (ADL 1993, 1996a, 1996b), while Kleg's (1993) estimate ranges from five to ten thousand. The SPLC (Klanwatch 1997) tracks an alarming growth in the number of skinhead groups, from 30 in 1995 to 37 in 1996, and 42 in 1998 (Klanwatch 1998).

With the possible exception of skinhead groups, the statistics cited above—which are undoubtably conservative—represent a decline in numbers of both groups and group membership between the 1980s and mid-1990s. For example, a Klanwatch *Intelligence Report* of 1997 shows a reduction in hate groups from 300 in 1992, to 240 in 1996. Consider also Bullard's (1991) evidence that, although the KKK enjoyed a growth in numbers over the late 1970s and early 1980s (from 9,000 in 1978 to 11,000 in 1981), by 1990 the various splinter groups included only about 5,000 members. This is also supported by the ADL (1996) figures of approximately 10,000 in 1981, 9,000 in 1982, 6,000 in 1984, 5,000 in 1988, and 4,000 in 1991. A Klanwatch (1997) analysis suggests several reasons for these declining numbers, including low unemployment (leading to lessened "scapegoating"), competition from Patriot and militia groups which may or may not have racist undertones, and changes in strategies from visible actions to more clandestine activities. The latter is related to the increased "mainstreaming" of hate groups and hate figures, as exemplified by the likes of David Duke. It might also be attributed to the success of federal and state actions taken against such groups (Klanwatch 1996, 1997). For example, the squashing of The Order—one of the most violent offshoots of Aryan Nations—was accomplished largely through the prosecution of its leaders.

However, the celebration must unfortunately be tempered with later evidence that, as the decade and the century drew to a close, there seemed to be a resurgence of hate group activity and membership. Brian Levin is quoted by Klanwatch (1998, p. 6) as saying that "there are a growing number of apocalyptic thinkers . . . and the problem is that they're creating their own apocalypse. Some are committing suicide, and others are blowing up federal buildings or trying to initiate a race war that will lead to apocalypse." Consequently, it is hardly the time to declare hate group violence dead. On the contrary, the earlier decline and the more recent regrowth in numbers seems to have been accompanied by corollary increases in the level of violence perpetrated by these groups (ADL 1993). Here I refer to both the elevated brutality and scope of impact. This is most evident among skinhead groups, who by 1990 accounted for over one half of violent racial assaults (Bullard 1991). Klanwatch (1997) documented a dramatic jump in skinhead crimes from 29 in 1995 to 51 in 1996. Moreover, skinheads were responsible for 22 bias motivated homicides between 1990 and 1993, compared to only 6 between 1987 and 1990 (ADL 1996). In all, between 1988 and 1998, skinheads alone were responsible for 49 homicides (Klanwatch 1998). One must look beyond the numbers to get a real sense of the impact of hate group violence. Consider once again skinhead activities. The violence perpetrated by these predominantly young haters often consists of multiple skinheads besetting one or a few targets, armed with a range of lethal weapons. Their brutality is legend, as illustrated by the following incident which occurred near Boston in 1996: "Amid shouts of 'you're gonna' die,' over a dozen members of the group invaded the party, wielding knives, chains, pipes, an ax handle and a broomstick . . . The Skinheads directed most of their rage at 22 year old Jason Linsky . . . The leader of the group . . . straddled the victim's beaten body and stabbed him nine times" (Klanwatch 1997, p. 1). Such extreme violence is not restricted to skinheads. A recent ADL (1998) report, *Explosion of Hate: The Growing Danger of the National Alliance,* argues that the National Alliance might be considered the "most dangerous organized hate group in America today." Many factors combine to lead the ADL to this conclusion: its sophistication and success in recruiting; its exploitation of communication technologies; its relationships to politicians and to other organized hate groups; and the extensive record of violence and robbery. However, other supremacists also represent dramatic threats to minority communities, as the next example from Jackson, Mississippi, reveals:

> A black man, D. Q. Holyfield, 49, was shot to death when a gunman opened fire at a restaurant in a predominantly black neighborhood. Ten others were injured during the shooting spree allegedly aimed at blacks. Larry Wayne Shoemaker, 55, a reported white supremacist, committed suicide after setting the restaurant ablaze. During a search of his residence, police found two AK-47 assault rifles, 3 empty 30-round clips, a MAC-11 assault weapon, a 12-guage shotgun, an AK-15 assualt rifle, two handguns, white supremacist literature, and Nazi flags. (Klanwatch 1994, p. 33)

The latter example also illustrates an important element of the contemporary violence perpetrated by hate groups: they are heavily armed. They are fully prepared for the much awaited "race war" in which they will defend the white race. A 1993 ad in the anti-Semitic Liberty Lobby's *Spotlight* newsletter offered for sale (under an alias often used by Timothy McVeigh) such items as an anti-tank weapon and ammunition. Hate group members have been found in possession of night vision equipment, automatic weapons, and explosives. They are training to use them in pseudo-military encampments, like Butler's Aryan Nations retreat at Hayden Lake. And they are utilizing their weapons and their lessons. Alleged Los Angeles gunman Buford O'Neal Furrow Jr. and Chicago gunman Benjamin Smith (and very likely the Sacramento arsonists) very clearly had ties to neo-Nazi organizations (ADL 1999). At least six adherents of the Christian Identity group called the Phineas Priesthood are suspected of being responsible for a violent crime spree in Spokane, Washington. Three members have been charged with armed robbery of

a bank, bombing of a newspaper office, and bombing of an abortion clinic. According to a Klanwatch (1996a, p. 1) report, the Priests are motivated by an extreme religious credo: "Interracial marriage, the banking system, homosexuality and abortion are contrary to 'God's law.' . . . Murder, armed robbery, bombing and counterfeiting are justified in the fight against these 'evils.' "

Such violence is considered both acceptable and necessary to cleanse the white race of the impurities introduced by minorities and "sexual deviates." Alarmingly, the Priests are not alone in their use of explosives in order to further their mission. Antiracist activists and law enforcement authorities agree that this particular form of domestic terrorism is on the upswing.

What emerges from this cursory overview of the scope and nature of hate group activity is that a relatively small number of people are engaging in a small number of violent acts perpetrated against minority groups and against the state. It is likely that organized hate groups are responsible for little more than 10 to 15 percent of all hate crime (Levin and McDevitt 1993). This is not to downplay the seriousness of their actions, especially in light of the foregoing discussion of the nature of hate group violence. Nonetheless, it is clear that hate groups are not the primary perpetrators of bias-motivated crime. The vast majority of such crime is committed—singly or in groups—by people who are not directly connected to any organized form of hate.

Cultivating Hate on Fertile Ground

This raises the question of why it is important to examine hate groups. The answer is aptly summed up by Langer (1990, p. 85), who states that "At the least, there appears to be a kind of multiplier effect whereby one thing leads to another and the mere existence of the movement acts as an enabling force for the open expression of racism." And, as the ADL (1999, p. 1) has recently observed, "The shootings in Los Angeles and Chicago and the synagogue burnings in Sacramento did not begin with a gun or a firebomb.

They began with ugly, hateful words and ideas from racist, anti-Semitic groups, and from the extremist manifestos of white-supremacist hate-mongers." Hate groups are an extreme expression of the widespread racism, sexism, and homophobia that pervade United States culture. These groups lend voice, and perhaps some legitimation, to sentiments held by those unaffiliated with the Klan or skinheads, for example. The ideologies they endorse provide a framework within which others can also articulate and legitimate their own antipathies to potential minority victims. Antonio Gramsci, the noted Italian Marxist, asserted that, in the ongoing struggle for hegemonic supremacy, the appeal of any rhetorical formation depends upon "previously germinated ideologies . . . [which] come into confrontation and conflict, until only one of them, or at least a single combination of them, tends to prevail" (Gramsci 1971, pp. 181–182). This applies to the ability of hate groups to extend their ideologies of hate and intolerance to the broader public. In other words, in order to have an impact on the actions of others, hate groups must strike a chord in the broader community. The message of hate disseminated by hate groups speaks to existing popular concerns—this is at the heart of the legitimacy of their rhetoric. The vitriol of the hate groups is not so much an aberration as a reaffirmation of racialist and gendered views that permeate society. One observer of hate groups in Canada contends that the hate groups "expand societal tolerance for hatred, discrimination and prejudice. In fact, one of the dangers of hate groups is that they normalize extreme hatred and violence by justifying it as protection for the 'white race' against 'cultural invasion' " ("Merchants of Hate," online).

The rhetoric of hate does not fall on deaf ears. Degradation of the other is on fertile ground in a culture with a history of—indeed origins in—a world view which saw non-whites as heathen savages, for example. The United States is itself a legacy of centuries of persecution of minorities, whether they be Natives, immigrants, women, or "sexual deviants." Such a history normalizes mistreatment of those who do not appropriately con-form to the preconceived hierarchies. That leaves us with a culture reflected in bitter letters to the editor, and opinion polls that seem to tap deep divisions and resentment—fodder for the hate movement. Hate groups are adept at exploiting existing fears and discontent.

Feagin and Vera (1995) present ample survey data to support the contention that individual Americans subscribe to a range of intolerant and bigoted attitudes and stereotypes that might make them at least sympathetic to the positions of hate groups. Whatever the questions tapped—beliefs about criminal activity, industriousness, welfare dependency, interracial marriages—white respondents tended to characterize ethnic and racial minorities in negative terms. For example, an NORC survey in 1990 found that a majority of white respondents evaluated Blacks at the high end of the scale with respect to tendencies toward both violence and welfare dependency. A succession of Gallup polls further confirm broad antipathy and hostility to African Americans (Gallup 1993a), gay men and lesbians (Gallup 1992, 1993b), and immigrants (Gallup 1993a, 1993c).

Negative perceptions and suspicions of the Other provide fruitful ground for the rhetoric of hate groups. They enable these groups to play on public sentiment, exploiting fears and stereotypes that permeate white culture (Feagin and Vera 1995; Omi and Winant 1994). The egalitarian changes wrought by the civil rights initiatives of the 1960s and 1970s were perceived by a large bloc—not just white supremacists—as a dramatic threat to their social and economic well-being. Already in the 1970s, racial subtexts were informing discourse around the economic woes of the nation, as Asian imports and Hispanic immigrants took the blame for job and profit loss in the United States, as well as for the dilution of the United States' cultural hegemony. The national identity, "who 'we' were as a nation—seemed to be moving under their feet, and the tremors called into question not just the authority of traditional values, but the identities bound up with those values" (Karst 1993, p. 8).

This uncertainty leaves the most fearful and most alienated elements of society vulnerable to the recruitment efforts of the hate movement, which provides "easy answers" to America's woes. They share with white supremacist organizations one of the elements McAdam (1982) insists is crucial to the development and cohesiveness of any social movement: a shared consciousness or perception of unjust conditions. Dobratz and Shanks-Meile (1997), for example, found the "white man's struggle" and "fear of falling" to be important bases for white supremacists' decisions to become part of the movement. Significantly, an increasing proportion of the hate movement's membership seems to be characterized by nontraditional demographics, as more middle-income, white-collar workers become drawn to the message of salvation (Klanwatch 1998; Dobratz and Shanks-Meile 1997; Ferber 1998). The hate movement represents a beacon since

> . . . it is diverse in its expression, which can provide a haven for those seeking an explanation of the social conditions of white disenfranchisement along with a call to action. The "new rural ghetto" consists of formerly middle-class people who had achieved "American cultural goals" and lost it. Often forgotten, they are filled with rage as they "watch in hunger" as others eat at tables that not long ago were their own. (Dobratz and Shanks-Meile 1997, p. 279)

Moreover, slight modifications in the presentation of intolerance have made the contemporary hate movement more palatable, more acceptable to a public sensitized by a generation of discourse of equality, multiculturalism, and diversity. In a word, hate is increasingly "mainstream," and thus increasingly legitimate. In part, this has been accomplished by toning down the rhetoric, and engaging in symbolic racism. This "new racism" couches the old hostilities in abstract, ideological terms or "code words" that appear to have rational rather than emotive connotations. Grand Wizard Thomas Robb, for example, asserted that Klan leaders would be "taught to avoid statements that

sound hateful and turn people off" (cited in Kleg 1993, p. 216). He and others of like mind speak of love of the white race, rather than hatred of others. ZOG becomes "government interference"; White Christian becomes "average citizen"; cross-burnings become "illuminations"; African Americans became "welfare cheaters." Don Black, for example, eschews the pejorative connotations of "racist" in favor of the term "White Nationalist." Revisionist historians focusing on holocaust denial are perhaps the most gifted at couching their anti-Semitism in euphemisms. Rather than speaking of the "holohoax" or Jewish conspiracies, they artfully phrase their appeals in terms of scientific evidence, such as aerial photography, or DNA evidence. Whatever the rhetoric, the message remains the same: the "other" is not to be trusted; the "other" threatens the white Christian heterosexual hegemony.

Moreover, the paraphernalia long associated with the Klan are also—at least temporarily—a thing of the past. Nazi symbols have been eliminated, and "the white sheets and hoods are being replaced by the security uniform, consisting of a white shirt, black tie, Klan emblem (a cross with a drop of blood in the center), black trousers and black boots" (Kleg 1993, p. 216). In spite of his persistence in using racist and homophobic rhetoric, Metzger is largely in agreement with this more professional presentation. He urges his colleagues and followers to opt for suit and tie, rather than army fatigues. Moreover, it is not surprising that hate groups have used the media to disseminate this new image, appearing well dressed and articulate on television interviews, for example. More important in the contemporary era, however, is the ability to exploit the Internet.

Cyberhate

Consistent with the shifting demographics (i.e., middle class) and sophistication of the hate movement is an increasing willingness to take advantage of the Internet as a tool both for recruitment and unification. Traditionally, the primary means by which hate groups recruited members or spread their message of intolerance have been by word of mouth or by pamphleteering. However, several current factors have combined to change this. On the one hand, cheaper, faster, and more accessible means of transmission and communication have emerged—telephone messaging and computer messaging, to name just two. On the other hand, hate group leaders have become much more sophisticated to the extent that they are in a position to take advantage of these developing technologies. Tom Metzger, founder and continued leader of White Aryan Resistance (WAR), has a particular genius for exploiting new, hi-tech communication options. He and his counterparts in other hate groups have been blessed with a novel marketing gift in the form of the Internet. This particular form of communication is superior to all others as a means of widely and quickly disseminating hate propaganda. Computers are increasingly affordable. At the very least, they can be easily accessed through work, local schools, universities, and colleges. Web sites are easily and cheaply maintained. They allow coordination of collective endeavors that cross state, national, and global boundaries, thereby facilitating the strategies of "leaderless resistance" favored by the likes of Louis Beam. Best of all, from the perspective of hate groups, the 'Net remains unregulated. In short, readiness and ability to exploit the Internet ensures effective communication between current and potential movement membership, which, according to McAdam (1982) is also vital to movement solidarity.

The origins of "Cyberhate" are generally traced to white supremacist Donald Black. Black became proficient at using the computer while serving time for conspiracy to overthrow the government of Dominica. Upon release, he put his new skills to work in 1995 by creating a web page, *Stormfront,* which remains a predominant site to this day. Black's initiatives have been followed by the construction of hate-oriented and "White Power" sites at such a rate that it is virtually impossible to estimate the number of such web sites. The online Hate Directory professes to identify and monitor all existing hate pages. Yet their estimate of approximately 120 (as of May 1997) ap-

pears conservative in light of the fact that one Aryan Nations site (Plunder and Pillage) provides 128 "White Pride" links, each of which leads to dozens more not noted by either the Hate Directory or Aryan Nations. Klanwatch (1998) counted 163 cyberhate sites, connected with 81 groups. It is probably not an exaggeration to say that there are thousands of domestic and international web sites marketing various brands of hatred and intolerance. For many who may encounter these web pages, the ideas and images are antithetical to their understanding of American ideals of democracy and equality. As such, they are quickly dismissed. Yet for others, they reinforce or implant tolerance and hostility. Thus, those with embedded biases may find affirmation on the 'Net. Others—uncertain about "American" identity, or feeling dislocated by economic or cultural change—may find a pre-packaged answer to their questions.

Young people are especially vulnerable to the lure of the Internet. It is largely high school and college students, along with young professionals, who take advantage of the 'Net. ADL National Director Abraham Foxman notes that "high tech haters are all the more pernicious because they are targeting the television-reared, multi-media, computer literate generation: our youth" (ADL 1996a). Consider this example. A ninth grader researching weather systems on the 'Net enters "Stormfront" as her keyword for searching. While she will probably find some information on how weather systems develop, she is likely to happen upon Black's "Stormfront." This has one of the most extensive sets of cyberhate links available on the Internet. Its letters link, as well as many of the essay links contain virulent racist, sexist, and homophobic messages and images. One such link is Resistance Records, which may have particular appeal to a young person. His curiosity piqued, the student might link to the *American Renaissance* web page (of course, someone studying the Renaissance might also inadvertently find this page). There he could read an article that professes the following: "If massive non-white immigration continues, and welfare keeps encouraging high birth rates among Blacks and Hispanics, Whites will soon become a minority in the United States" (*American Renaissance,* online).

These are powerful messages which could be discovered quite accidentally. The impact would be heightened should the youths seek them out explicitly. Ideas gleaned from the Web solidify, if not mold, the perceptions of identity, difference, and culture which the individuals may or may not already bring to the site.

Additionally, there are many sites that would seem to be a especially alluring to the MTV generation—those sites that feature music. Resistance Records, mentioned above, is North America's largest distributor of White Power music. Their web site offers audio excerpts of dozens of such CDs. Moreover, it includes downloadable album covers, and online ordering. Operation Ghetto Storm goes one step further. In addition to all of the above, this White Power band site provides written lyrics of its music.

Veiled as it is often is in the sexiness of hi-tech and rock music, cyberhate is at once an insidious and powerful recruitment tool. Given the reification of technology in this culture, those who access computer based sites often take the data and arguments for literal truth. We have encouraged our youth to use this resource, to become 'Net-literate, without necessarily reminding them that what appears online is not all fair, accurate, or favorable. This is not at all unsatisfying to the hate groups:

> This is the hope of the haters: use the media to create an alternative channel to spread the word, to reach the impressionable, reinforce the beliefs of the converted, and create a community of the like-minded. On the Web, they preach on an easy-to-use, powerful and far-reaching platform that confers special legitimacy and filters out opponents. (ADL 1996b, p. 34)

It is this conferring of legitimacy that makes the use of the 'Net by hate groups particularly troubling. It places the rhetoric of these groups on an equal footing with all other forms of discourse.

Moreover, as the above quote suggests, the use of the Internet enhances communication between the "converted," that is, within the movement itself. This is vitally important in light of the earlier discussion of the diversity within the hate movement. While there are obvious points of convergence across the various Klan groups, or Identity Churches, or skinhead organizations, the hate movement has historically been varied and, in fact, fractured. Internet communication facilitates the creation of the collective identity that is so important to movement cohesiveness (McAdam 1982). As a recent Klanwatch (1998, p. 25) report observes, increasing reliance on email, web pages and electronic chat rooms "give[s] racists an empowering sense of community. Even lone racists, with no co-religionists nearby, feel they are part of a movement."

Internet communication helps to close the social and spatial distance that might otherwise thwart efforts to maintain a collective identity. Given the geographical dispersal of hate groups across the country, the medium of cyberspace allows members in Maine, Mississippi, and Idaho to engage in real-time conversations, to share the ritual and imagery that bind the individuals to the collective without having to travel great distances or incur great costs. Virtual conversations and ready access to Web pages aggressively asserting the shortcomings of the Other strengthen the resolve of individual members by creating the framework for a shared sense of both peril and purpose.

Moreover, Internet communication knows no national boundaries. Consequently, it allows the hate movement to extend its collective identity internationally, thereby facilitating a potential "global racist subculture" (Back, Keith, and Solomos 1998). There is no reason to expect that processes of globalization affecting commerce, politics, and demographics will not also affect the realm of identity politics played out by the hate movement (Weinberg 1998). Weinberg (1998, p. 79) argues that the Internet will in fact provide the vehicle for the construction of a "common racial identity reaching across the Atlantic."

Regardless of national affiliation, Internet communication allows white people across the globe to share in the celebration of a common race. Thus, for example, cyberhate sites are increasingly multilingual. They tend to exploit (White) multicultural symbols drawn from Nordic, Celtic, or Nazi mythology. And such sites facilitate the importation of outlawed documents and rhetoric so that all can share in the discourses of hate. For example, while Germany and many other European nations have criminalized the publication and dissemination of racist propaganda, these nations have yet to establish an effective means of regulating the virtual border crossing of cyberhate. In short, the potential of the Internet for creating an enhanced sense of unity among the computer mediated community of haters is vast, and in fact, global.

"The Militia Project"

In addition to enhanced internal affiliations, hate groups have also begun to make overtures to the militia movement. Given the broader appeal, audience, and membership of the militia movement, it is alarming that hate activists are beginning to infiltrate these organisations, where they can add their racial and sexist animosities to the militia's distrust of the state.

Recognizing a golden opportunity to extend their rhetoric of hate beyond traditional hate group membership, some leading hate activists have quickly joined ranks with the growing militia movement. Dees (1996) provides a rough estimate that there are over 440 active militia groups and over 360 Patriot groups nationwide, with cells in every state. The CDR (nd) suggests that by 1995, the militia movement boasted at least 100,000 members. Ironically, events like the Waco and Ruby Ridge sieges and the Oklahoma City bombing seem to have stimulated membership. However, much of the recent growth can also be attributed to the movement of supremacists from traditional hate groups into the militia. The CDR (1995, p. 4) claims that, while militias are not exclusively made up of supremacists, "the line be-

comes blurred as one out of five active white supremacists have not only become involved but have become national leaders" in the movement. Increasingly, the distinctions between the two types of organizations are becoming muted in terms of membership and ideology. Louis Beam, a long-time Klansman and virulent racist, is the architect of the militia movement's strategy of "leaderless resistance." Beam learned from his experiences with the Klan the danger of traditional lines of leadership and communication. "Leaderless resistance" advocates phantom cells and individual action as a means of defeating state tyranny. Ongoing dissemination of information through newsletters, computer online services, and leaflets would keep members informed and allow them to design viable strategies for attack. Beam also hosts an annual Aryan World Congress, where he takes the opportunity to encourage the formation of militias, and to encourage Aryan Nation members to join these antigovernment organizations.

As a guide to action for the militia, Beam's leaderless resistance is second only to William Pierce's *Turner Diaries*. Pierce, too, has assumed a leadership role within the militia movement. The role of his Diaries as a blueprint for action is most tragically illustrated by the Oklahoma City bombing. It followed to the letter the fictional account of the bombing of a federal building found in the Diaries. More recently, Pierce has launched a "Militia Project," the goal of which is to forge strong alliances with the militia movements. Specifically, Pierce argues that the militias "are being badly misled in the ideological realm and are in need of some Alliance input" (cited in Dees 1996, p. 204).

Pierce is concerned that the focus of the militia movement is too narrow. He seeks to extend the "ideological realm" beyond anti-statism, to incorporate his own brand of racism and anti-Semitism. Already it is apparent that the militia movement has embraced traditional supremacist ideologies. However, in order to ensure their welcome within the movement, supremacist ideologues had first to seek common ground. In this context, the glue that first bound the two movements together was anti-statism: the belief that the state was excessively interventionist, and illegitimate. This was the hook upon which Beam and Pierce, for example, were able to hang their racism. One means by which this is accomplished is by exploiting the strict constitutionalism of many of the militia groups. The militia movement had long rejected the legitimacy of the 13th through 15th Amendments. Their claim is that the Constitution guarantees rights only to the white "founding" race of the United States. Thus, only white Americans are considered "true" citizens—all others are relegated to the status of "14th amendment citizens" with "alienable" rights. Robert Wangrud of an Oregon Christian Patriot group claims that "There is only one race that founded this country and that is the White Race. The Constitution recognizes this and clearly states that only white people can be citizens of this country. The 14th Amendment changed all that, but we feel it became law illegally and as such is not binding" (Clackamus County Review, May 28, 1993). From here, it is no great stretch to condemn non-white races as inferior, or justify their relegation to second-class status. For example, Aryan Nations leader Richard Butler, in league with Militia of Montana founder John Trochmann, forged a code of conduct that reflects this ideology. It reads in part:

Article I: Only Aryans (White Race) are allowed citizenship of the nation and only citizens can:
  1) vote and own property within the nation's borders.
  2) conduct business, possess (keep) and bear arms.
  3) hold office in government, industry or society.
  4) comprise military or law enforcement personnel . . .

Article II: Non-citizens can live in the Republic but only under the custodianship of a citizen.

Article III: All hybrids called Jews are to be repatriated from the Republic's territory, all their wealth redistributed to restore our people . . .

Such policies suit the hate movement's goals of excluding and disempowering the minorities which they claim threaten the survival of the white race. Yet it also corresponds to the militia movement's attention to the original Constitution.

Because racism within the militias is often presented in sanitized form—as patriotism or constitutionalism—it has the face of legitimacy. The violence and intolerance are downplayed and hidden behind questions of "rights" and "rights violations." This is what accounts for the broader appeal of the militia movement. It provides an apparently benign arena for dissatisfied citizens. Anyone from tax protesters, to racists, to bankrupt farmers, to unemployed workers can voice their hostility without necessarily being labeled as sexist, or homophobic, or racist. By crossing the line into the militia movement, hate groups are able to open themselves up to people who would otherwise resist joining a neo-Nazi or KKK organization. As Klanwatch director Joe Roy observes, "militias, common law courts and other Patriot organizations allow members to vent their anger in a manner that is more acceptable to mainstream America" (Klanwatch 1997, p. 17).

Beyond the dangers of increased numbers and the broader appeal of the militia movement lies the danger that inheres in mixing open-ended hostility and para-military activity. More so than the traditional hate groups, militias are heavily armed and trained to use the arms—as is their right according to the Second Amendment. In a letter of warning to Attorney General Janet Reno, Dees (1996, p. 107) clearly stated his fears in this context: "We have substantial evidence that white supremacists are infiltrating the leadership of these organizations. In our view, this mixture of armed groups and those who hate is a recipe for disaster." Similarly, Dees's associate Danny Welch concluded in a report on the militia movement that "it is a movement fuelled by religious fanaticism and racism, fully armed and willing to kill. Its members are capable of becoming Americanized versions of the kind of extremists you read about in other countries, a full-scale terrorist underground" (cited in Dees 1996, p. 105).

This potential is explicit in Beam's strategy of "leaderless resistance." He is very much in favor of a nationwide network of invisible cells armed and ready to engage in an all-out assault against the "menacing horde" of minorities and against the state. And it is explicit in the rhetoric of militia adherents across the country. All are ready to "take back" their country and disarm the federal state.

Even this cursory examination of the links between the militia and hate movements—and the implications thereof—suggests that the danger posed by supremacist ideologies and actions is growing. It has expanded into a dangerously armed and trained set of organizations that tend to have a broader public appeal. Ultimately, both the audience and potential harm derived from intolerance are extended by this intersection. But the message of hate is also increasingly inserted into the center by exploiting available political opportunities. Ironically, the anti-statism of the hate movement has not excluded its membership from attempting to forge links with the political mainstream.

Mr. Duke Goes to Washington (and Hate Goes Mainstream)

Omi and Winant (1994, p. 81) characterize the bulk of the United States' history of racial relations as a "war of manoeuvre" in which subordinate groups have been forced into a defensive role, oriented around self-preservation—against the threat of lynching, for example. Moreover, the state has been deeply embedded in this "war" since it is in fact a racial state, structured by and constitutive of racial politics. To continue the Gramscian analysis, they argue that "the racial order is equilibrated by the state—encoded in law, organized through policy making, and enforced by a repressive apparatus" (Omi and Winant 1994, p. 84). In other words, the state is embedded in the processes of legitimating and defining difference, and of constructing a racialized and gendered hegemonic formation.

Events of recent years, however, have upset the equilibrium of racialized as well as gendered politics.

Contemporary social movements—representative of a transition to the "war of position"—have placed both the state and the "warring factions" in qualitatively new roles. In the face of challenges from women, people of color, and gays, to name but a few, the state has been placed in a position of having to resolve a cultural "crisis of legitimacy" every bit as painful as the corresponding fiscal crisis. It in ironic that "by challenging the racial verities of the past and revamping the old political terrain, the racial [and gender] minority movements set the stage for the racial reaction" of the closing decades of the twentieth century (Omi and Winant 1994, p. 117). To maintain legitimacy, and to restore any semblance of equilibrium, the state is faced with the task of absorbing the reactionary challenge, just as it had previously absorbed the egalitarian challenges of an earlier era. Some elements of the contemporary hate movement have been quick to act on the recognition that "co-optation of civic and state structures by social movements, when successful, can greatly facilitate collective mobilizations" (McCarthy and Wolfson 1992, p. 274).

At the same time that some extremists are attempting to tone down their image, space is opening up in political forums, allowing the diffusion of the rhetoric of hate throughout the cultural and political landscape. These contemporary links between the racist right and mainstream politicians are consistent with the United States' history of right-wing populism, which consists of "strong themes of social injustice, exclusion and resentment . . . directed at . . . racial minorities, the blacks, the 'yellow peril,' and so on" (Omi and Winant 1994, p. 34). According to Omi and Winant (1994), the current era of "authoritarian populism" found its origins in George Wallace's rearticulation of racial politics in the 1960s. Wallace's appeals to law and order and other racial codes resurrected the historical link between general electorate fears and the agendas of diverse hate groups (Dobratz and Shanks-Meile 1997). Wider windows of opportunity were later created first by the Reagan administration, and then the Bush administration. Republican policies and rhetoric in the 1980s and 1990s have signaled a concerted effort—at the federal and state levels—to rearticulate the racial and gender balance which many felt had swung too far to the left (Omi and Winant 1994). Weinberg (1998, p. 20) explicitly argues that

> . . . the GOP has become a "big tent" under which a variety of ERGs (extreme right-wing groups) and individual right-wing racists have come to feel at home. The tie-in seems related to at least three themes central to the party's outlook: ardent anti-communism, opposition to the welfare state, and defense of "traditional" values.

The intersection of the ideological positions of right-wing extremists and the Republican party has proven fortuitous for both. Senator Trent Lott of Mississippi and Congressman Mel Hancock rode this crest to office, either in spite of or because of their association with the far right organization, Council of Conservative Citizens. Pat Buchanan also brings his own brand of racial and gender politics to the national arena. The ADL (online) reports the involvement of political leaders in Jubilee Celebrations which are sponsored by *Jubilee* magazine, the voice of Identity Churches, neo-Nazis and skinheads. In so doing, "mainstream political forces have, knowingly or unknowingly, lent their legitimacy to this force of bigotry. . . . 'Jubilation 1994' caused a furor because two of the scheduled speakers were Republican state Senators."

As part of the official political apparatus, such extremists have the appearance of legitimate actors with valid interpretations of the state of economic and cultural relations throughout the country. They are the visible and audible presence of right-wing extremism and intolerance within the machinery of the state.

Nowhere is the link between the hate movement and the political process more evident than in the political success enjoyed by David Duke—former Louisiana KKK Grand Wizard. Duke's recognition that legitimacy could come only with moderation and respectability is apparent in his

exhortation for Kluxers to "get out of the cow pasture and into hotel meeting rooms" (ADL 1996a, p. 36). So smooth was his presentation of self that Duke's often imitated style became known to journalists as "rhinestone racism" or "button-down terror." Rejecting the in-your-face aggression of traditional white supremacists, Duke instead adopted what Ridgeway (1995, p. 166) refers to as "the persona of the boyishly good-looking white rights activist." Who could be threatened by this benevolent and compassionate seeker of justice?

To further solidify his new identity, Duke publicly disavowed his Klan membership in 1980, only to re-emerge as the founder of the National Association for the Advancement of White People (NAAWP). Through this "White rights" organization, Duke continued to promote racial segregation. His efforts to mainstream his racist visions are apparent in his exhortations—similar to Robb's—to "never refer to racial superiority or inferiority; only talk about racial differences, carefully avoiding value judgements" (cited in Ridgeway 1995, p. 38). Duke reformed his own rhetoric along these lines once he turned to legitimate politics. While leader of the Populist Party in 1989, Duke made the following argument: "I wouldn't say Hitler was right on race, but I do believe that there are genetic differences between races and that they profoundly affect culture. . . . I think that, for instance, there's differences in physical ability, there's differences in musical abilities, there's differences in IQ" (cited in Ridgeway 1995, p. 172). Notice how Duke carefully avoids evaluating racial diversity, focusing instead on "difference" as though that were a neutral term. But in light of the cultural tendencies to evaluate difference in negative terms, and in light of the stereotypes implied by the references to physical, musical and intellectual disparities the connotations are indeed negative.

Following the trajectory established two decades earlier by Wallace, Duke's political campaigns, whether as a Populist or Republican, exploited the toned-down racial messages in his handling of such bread-and-butter issues as welfare, immigration, affirmative action, and crime. Consistently, these were used as code words to denigrate racial minorities without using the terms "Black" or "Hispanic," for example. Early on, at least, he struck a chord among voters. In March 1988, his run for president garnered him one-twentieth of the votes cast. In January 1989, he narrowly won a Louisiana state legislature seat. In 1990, he barely lost a bid for a United States Senate seat, but received 60 percent of the White vote. And, in 1991, Duke lost a bid for the Louisiana governor's position, while nonetheless managing to win 700,000 votes. Duke's political fortunes have continued to decline since 1991, yet he continues to pursue this line. The fact that he has been able to gain victory and later a significant number of votes speaks volumes to the effectiveness of his methods of delivery. As such, Duke lends legitimacy to an albeit muted ideology of intolerance that continues to lay the blame for cultural, moral, and economic decay squarely at the feet of minorities.

No less disturbing than Duke's involvement in politics are the links forged between legitimate politicians and hate activists by Larry Pratt. On the one hand, Pratt is a former Virginia state legislator, head of a PAC with ties to the Republican party, and a former co-chair of Pat Buchanan's presidential campaign. On the other hand, he is also director of Gun Owners of America and the Committee to Protect the Family Foundation (an anti-abortion organization), founder of English First, and a frequent speaker at white supremacist and militia gatherings. He has successfully blended his political career with his right-wing activism. Dees (1996, pp. 54–55) remarks that

> Pratt is equally at home with individuals who prefer combat boots to Gucci's, camouflage uniforms to three-piece, tailored suits, and the practice of guerrilla warfare tactics to the playing of politics. As a result, he frequently serves as a bridge between the two groups—the mainstream politicians, at both the federal and state levels, and far-right elements—by bringing them together at fund-raisers, dinners and other social events.

That Pratt sympathizes with the hate movement is evident in his relationship with extremist Pete Peters, and in his speaking engagements with white supremacist groups. The most infamous of these was his appearance at Estes Park, Colorado, at a gathering held in response to the shooting of Randy Weaver's wife and son at Ruby Ridge. However, it is also evident in his political stance on gun ownership and the formation of militias, both of which he interprets as legitimate constitutional rights. The goal of these militias would be to reverse the ills facing the United States: they could be used in the war on drugs, or against illegal immigrants, for example. Here we see the connection to the hate movement. Both of these illustrative themes are heavily endowed with racial undertones. The conclusion: militias are necessary to victory in the inevitable race war.

Conclusion: Unpacking Hate

The hate movement has taken on a new, modern face. It is no longer the preserve of uneducated bigots from the backwoods—if indeed it ever was. On the contrary, as the foregoing analysis suggests, it is now increasingly crossing into the mainstream. Consequently, its impact on public sentiments and—more ominously—public policy has grown. As Ezekiel (1995, p. 323) concludes on the basis of his interviews with hate group members,

> . . . the white racist movement is stronger . . . when respected leaders pander to racism (the Willie Horton ads in the Bush campaign) or encourage the white population to conceive of people of color as welfare cheats and criminals. The white racist movement is part of America, not an alien presence; it grows and wanes as general American racism grows and wanes.

The strength of the contemporary hate movement is grounded in its ability to repackage its messages in ways that make them more palatable, and in its ability to exploit the points of intersection between itself and the prevailing ideological canons.

Because the hate movement has shifted its place to the mainstream, it is there that it must be challenged. First and foremost, politicians must assume a leadership role in condemning rather than embracing organized hate groups. Omi and Winant (1994) argue for a politics of *left-wing populism* as an antidote to the spread of the hate movement's right-wing populism. Such an initiative would call for an ethical commitment to social justice grounded in justice rather than injustice, inclusion rather than exclusion, respect for rather than resentment of difference. Just as the hate movement has piggy-backed on the reactionary politics of the Republican party, so too might a progressive movement exploit the windows opening up within the Democratic party: Reagan has his counterpart in Clinton, David Duke in Jesse Jackson.

Beyond the long-term political agenda, however, the most effective means of confronting these groups is through the maintenance and support of antiviolence projects which do battle against them—in the courts, in the media, in public fora. Organizations like the Southern Poverty Law Center (SPLC), the Anti-Defamation League (ADL), and the Prejudice Institute perform an invaluable service for the public in their roles as monitors, litigators and educators. For example, since 1979, the SPLC Klanwatch project has closely monitored hate groups and hate crime nationwide. Consequently, they have unearthed evidence that has proven useful in the prosecution of civil rights suits against white supremacist groups. More significant is the role they have played in detecting and thus thwarting violent conspiracies against antiviolence organizations as well as state entities. The ADL (established in 1913) has effectively monitored and responded to anti-Semitic activity. In recent years, it has extended its scope to encompass hate and bias crime more generally. Like Klanwatch, the ADL publishes and distributes the data it collects.

These organizations must continue to play a critical educational role as well. Many regularly publish and distribute newsletters to members, police departments, and educational institutions. Whether monthly, quarterly, or yearly, these re-sources highlight the threats posed by hate group activities, and what can be done to dilute the threats. These regularly scheduled publications are supplemented by more specialized documents, such as the ADL's *Hate Crimes: Policies and Procedures for Law Enforcement Agencies*, Klanwatch's *Ten Ways to Fight Hate*, or the Prejudice Institute's *The Traumatic Effects of Ethnoviolence*.

The most compelling program in this area is the SPLC Teaching Tolerance project. This preventative initiative assists educators in designing curricula that encourage students to recognize, understand, and value difference. It is to be hoped that such interventions break the connections between difference and intolerance, so that subsequent generations will be less vulnerable to the messages of hate propagated by the hate movement. To the extent that educational activities—in the schools and in the community—are able to deconstruct the ideologies and activities of the hate groups, they will continue to be effective mechanisms by which to counteract extremist groups. While not all educators or students will be receptive to the alternative messages of tolerance, "for every school child and young adult that we can and do reach, we shall be influencing a world beyond our own" (Kleg 1993, p. 260).

REFERENCES

Anti-Defamation League (ADL). N.d. *Hate Crimes: Policies and Procedures for Law Enforcement Agencies*. New York: ADL.

———. 1991. *The KKK Today: A 1991 Status Report*. New York: ADL.

———. 1993. *Young Nazi Killers: The Rising Skinhead Danger*. New York: ADL.

———. 1996a. *Hate Groups in America*. New York: ADL.

———. 1996b. *Danger: Extremism*. New York: ADL.

———. 1996c. *Web of Hate: Extremists Exploit the Internet*. New York: ADL.

———. 1998. *Explosion of Hate: The Growing Danger of the National Alliance*. New York: ADL.

———. 1999. *Frontline*. New York NY: ADL.

Back, Les, Michael Keith, and John Solomos. 1998. "Racism on the Internet: Mapping Neo-Fascist

Subcultures in Space." Pp. 73–101 in *Nation and Race,* edited by Jeffrey Kaplan and Tore Bjørgo. Boston: Northeastern University Press.

Bullard, Sara. 1991. *The Ku Klux Klan: A History of Violence and Racism.* Montgomery, AL: Southern Poverty Law Institute.

Center for Democratic Renewal. N.d. *Militias: Exploding Into the Mainstream.* Atlanta: CDR.

———. 1995. *1994: A Year of Intolerance.* Atlanta: CDR.

Dees, Morris. 1996. *Gathering Storm: America's Militia Threat.* New York: Harper Perennial.

Dobratz, Betty and Stephanie Shanks-Meile. 1997. *"White Power, White Pride!" The White Supremacist Movement in the United States.* New York: Twayne Publishers.

Ezekiel, Raphael. 1995. *The Racist Mind.* New York: Penguin.

Feagin, Joe and Hernán Vera. 1995. *White Racism.* New York: Routledge.

Ferber, Abby. 1998. *White Man Falling: Race, Gender and White Supremacy.* Lanham, MD: Rowman and Littlefield.

Gallup. 1992. "Public Opinion Divided on Gay Rights." *Gallup Poll Monthly* (June): 2–6.

———. 1993a. "Racial Overtones Evident in Americans' Attitudes About Crime." *Gallup Poll Monthly* (Dec.): 37–42.

———. 1993b. "Public Polarized on Gay Issues." *Gallup Poll Monthly* (April): 30–34.

———. 1993c. "Americans Feel Threatened by New Immigrants." *Gallup Poll Monthly* (July): 2–96.

Gramaci, Antonio. 1971. *Selections from the Prison Notebooks.* New York: International Publishers.

Karst, Kenneth. 1993. *Law's Promise, Law's Expression.* New Haven, CT: Yale University Press.

Kerchis, Cheryl and Iris Marion Young. 1995. "Social Movements and the Politics of Difference." Pp. 1–28 in *Multiculturalism from the Margins,* edited by Dean Harris. Westport, CT: Bergin and Garvey.

Klanwatch. 1994. *Ten Ways to Fight Hate.* Montgomery, AL: Southern Poverty Law Center.

———. 1996a. *Intelligence Report.* Montgomery, AL: Southern Poverty Law Center.

———. 1996b. *False Patriots: The Threat of Anti-government Extremists.* Montgomery, AL: Southern Poverty Law Center.

———. 1997. *Intelligence Report.* Montgomery, AL: Southern Poverty Law Cenkar.

———. 1998. *Intelligence Report.* Montgomery, AL Southern Poverty Law Center.

Kleg, Milton. 1993. *Hate Prejudice and Racism.* Albany: SUNY Press.

Langer, Elinor. 1990. "The American Neo-Nazi Movement Today." *The Nation,* July 16/23:81–107.

Levin, Jack and Jack McDevitt. 1993. *Hate Crimes.* New York: Plenum.

McAdam, Doug. 1982. *Political Process and the Development of Black Insurgency, 1930–1970.* Chicago: University of Chicago Press.

McCarthy, John and Mark Wolfson. 1992. "Consensus Movements, Conflict Movements, and the Cooptation of Civic and State Infrastructures." Pp. 273–297 in *Frontiers in Social Movement Theory,* edited by Aldon Morris and Carol McClurg Mueller. New Haven, CT: Yale University Press.

Omi, Michael and Howard Winant. 1994. *Racial Formation in the United States,* 2nd ed. New York: Routledge.

Perry, Barbara. 1999. "Defenders of the Faith: Hate Groups and Ideologies of Power." *Patterns of Prejudice* 32(3):32–54.

Prejudice Institute. 1994. *The Traumatic Effects of Ethnoviolence.* Towson, MD: Center for the Applied Study of Ethnoviolence.

Ridgeway, James. 1995. *Blood in the Face,* 2nd ed. New York: Thunders Mouth Press.

Roscigno, Vincent. 1994. "Social Movement Struggle and Race, Gender and Class Inequality." *Race, Sex and Class* 2(1):109–126.

Southern Poverty Law Center. 1997. *SPLC Report.* Montgomery, AL: SPLC.

Weinberg, Leonard. 1998. "An Overview of Right-Wing Extremism in the Western World: A Study of Convergence, Linkage and Identity." Pp. 3–33 in *Nation and Race,* edited by Jeffrey Kaplan and Tore Bjørgo. Boston: Northeastern University Press.

INTERNET SITES

Adelaide Institute: www.adam.com.au

ALPHA: www.alpha.org/whyalpha

American Renaissance: www.amren.com

Anti-Defamation League: www.adl.org

Aryan Nations: www.stormfront.org/an.html

Hate Directory: www.dpscs.state.md.us.80/hatedir.htm

Hate Watch: www.hatewatch.org

Institute for Historical Review: www.kaiwan.com/~ihrgreg

National Socialist White People's Party: www.capecod.net/~ndemonti

Operation Ghetto Storm: www.whitepower.com/ghettostorm

People's Resistance Movement—The Christian Alternative: www.powertech.no/aolsen/txt/forside.html

Plunder and Pillage: wwwexcaliber.com/thor

Resistance Records: www.resistance.com

Starr, Erin: www.darkwing.uoregon.edu/~bfmalle

Stormfront: www.stormfront.org

Strom (Kevin Alfred): www.com/FREESP

White Nationalist: www.nationalist.org

Yggdrasil: www.netcom.com/pub/yg/ygg

Barbara Perry is an associate professor of criminal justice at Northern Arizona University. Her work emphasizes issues of inequality and (in)justice. She has published in the areas of hate crime, ethnoviolence, and hate groups in journals such as *Sociological Focus; American Behavioral Scientist;* and *Sociology of Crime, Law and Deviance.* Her book, *In the Name of Hate: Understanding Hate Crimes* (Routledge), is a theoretical exploration of hate crimes as a mechanism for constructing difference. In her recently published reader, *Hate Crime: A Reader,* Perry brings together essential literature in the field. Perry is also the coeditor of *Investigating Difference: Human and Cultural Relations in Criminal Justice* (with Marianne Nielsen).

An interview with . . .

Barbara Perry

What got you interested in this subject?

This was the second or third paper I did looking at the hate movement. It came out of my broader interest in hate crime and the role of hate groups in creating an environment or providing a venue for some of the racist and homophobic views that might be more broadly held. So I was really interested in how the hate movement played into that. For the first paper, I really tried to identify a series of ideologies held by the hate groups and that got me into this paper, looking at the contemporary shift in the hate movement. So I guess it's sort of a logical progression, coming from my interest in hate crimes generally.

How did your interest in hate crimes develop?

I always laugh when people ask me this. It was very serendipitous. The man who is now my husband had gone back to school at a relatively late date, and he was doing a research project on police reporting of hate crimes. He managed to get copies of police reports of hate crimes in Portland, Maine, where we were living at the time. I was reading along with him, and I became absolutely fascinated, and that's how it all began—a research project that my husband did. Also, I had just come to the United States from Canada and I was trying to find myself as a research scholar in the U.S., and this topic is really not too far removed because my work in Canada was around the charter rights and legal and human rights issues in that country. So this is not that far away from what I had been doing; it is a different manifestation of human rights issues.

How do you see this research contributing to an understanding of the hate movement?

I think probably the most important thing is the changing nature of the movement. I mention in the paper this move from the white cloaks and the white hoods, the brown shirts to the three-piece suit. I almost think that that makes the hate movement more dangerous because it is much more subtle. If you look at the websites, for example, they are very slick, very smooth, and very professional; they appear to be very scientific and sometimes even to be very scholarly. So I think the important lesson is to realize that the hate movement is no longer, even in the public mind, such a backwoods voice looking to stir up trouble in local communities. It is a global movement now, and part of the contemporary scene as well. So I think that is probably the most important thing: to understand that the hate movement is now a very different, very slick movement and also a very global movement thanks in large part to the Internet.

What were the strengths and limitations of using historical research to examine the hate movement?

In this case, obviously, I was interested in the transition from what we used to think of as the hate movement—the KKK image of hoods—to this new, very contemporary, almost mainstream movement. So I wanted to look at that transition. But what is most important to me is to put the analysis of any phenomenon in historical context, whether it is a piece of legislation or whatever the case may be, so that we can really understand why such changes or phenomena have emerged out of this particular historical juncture—in this case, what other conditions in the social or political or economic environment facilitate the emergence of this mainstream, "button-down" hate movement. That, I think, is the most important thing: placing a phenomenon in a historical context relative to other changes that are taking place in the environment. Another strength of this approach—especially using the websites of the hate groups—is that it really does allow the objects of the research their own voice without engaging in direct interviews. So although I take it out of context, obviously, it is the words of the hate movement that I use throughout the research. So the most important two are context and using the words of the movement.

There are at least two main weaknesses in this particular approach. You do get the tenor of the transition to this new movement, this new face, if you will, but just relying on the Internet sources and not using earlier documents shortens the timeline a little. But more than that is the idea that the statements that are made by the hate movement on their websites, and in some newsletters I used as well, are public statements. So in some sense these statements are more sanitized than what you might see if you went to a rally, for example, or if you were able to eavesdrop on e-mail communication. Even the chat rooms are watered down very often. So you really are only seeing the tip of the iceberg and not the more extremist groups that have been involved in arson and bombings and bank robberies. Obviously, we are not going to see on the website the plans for that kind of activity. So, I guess that is the strongest weakness here—that I was able to get only a rather sanitized version of the hate movement.

How did you decide what materials to study? Did you have any difficulty getting access to these materials? What was the process of organizing and analyzing your materials like?

As I said, this article emerged out of "broader" work that I was doing, trying to identify key threads and key ideologies that ran through the white suprema- cist discourse. So I started with a couple of web pages and thehatedirectory. com, which at that time was a fairly up-to-date site, with links to extremist organizations—hate groups' websites that were available at the time. I started with that set of websites and then also used the essential hate movement web- sites, and I quickly followed through the links of each of the websites. The or- ganization really fell out on its own. As I was working on ideas for these other articles, things that were niggling at me, I would take little notes on things that did not fit into the first paper I was working on. So, I had a series of Post-it notes all over my office: "Remember to come back to this." So, I allowed the themes to emerge naturally on their own.

What was most challenging about doing this research? What unexpected events or developments (if any) occurred during the course of this research?

The biggest challenge for me was maintaining my distance and being objective, because the rhetoric on these pages is so frustrating and it made me so angry. When I was writing about the hate movement, I tried to maintain some of that emotional distance, not to be too judgmental, not to evaluate the language as I was describing the organizations and the rhetoric. But beyond that (I remem- ber this quite distinctly, an unexpected event if you will), at one point I had to step away from working in this area. I was online several hours a day for sev- eral weeks, and I started to have nightmares about guys in cloaks, sort of frightening nightmares and dreams about members of the movement coming after me and raping me and burning crosses and all those images that are asso- ciated with the hate movement. So, I had to put it aside for several weeks at one point, because it was just tearing me up. Really interfering with my sleep, with my appetite, and my ability to work. That was the biggest thing; I didn't see that coming. It's only words on the website, it is not something directed at me, but it really did have a traumatic effect on me.

Could you describe any specific ethical issues that you confronted in this research?

Maintaining objectivity was the main ethical issue that I faced. The other one was—maybe even more with the first paper than with this one—I was always a little anxious about whether I was providing a platform for the movement by publicizing their rhetoric. And the whole issue of taking their words and phrases out of context was also a concern. But the most important thing was whether I was giving too much voice to the organizations. That was probably the key ethical issue for me.

If you were to do this research again, is there anything that you would do differently? If so, what?

If I could find the courage, I would love to do interviews with movement members, especially leadership, because that's really who is the public face and sets the public tone. As the paper suggests, it has been leaders like Tom Metzger and David Duke, of course, who have really pushed for and made the call for a much more professional look, a more sanitized presentation of the hate groups. So I would really love to be able to talk to them about how they perceive the contemporary hate movement and to see what sorts of language they would use off-the-cuff rather than well prepared, as it is on the public website. So, that is probably the key thing that I would like to do: supplement the history with the interviews.

What was most frustrating to you in doing this research? What was most satisfying?

The most frustrating was reading that rhetoric and trying to keep my own emotions under control, in the interest of the work itself. That was probably the most frustrating, reading the homophobic and racist and sexist language again and again. The most satisfying was just watching the themes emerge. It was almost tidy the way that things fell together. It's like a giant jigsaw puzzle, with everything making sense as the threads were emerging as I was reading the hate movement literature. So, that was probably most satisfying—tying all of these threads together and being able to identify what was new in the hate movement as opposed to what was traditional or what new spin they put on traditional rhetoric. Instead of talking about race specifically, they use code words like "welfare" and "immigration" and that sort of thing. So, being able to make those things come to light, if you will, was very exciting for me.

Could you talk about how your own research has evolved through these projects?

As I say, I started just being very intrigued. A lot of "ideals" came out of the hate movement, and I wanted to look a little more deeply into the literature to see how broad and how narrow it was. In the end I identified eleven themes that emerged consistently through the websites and some of the newsletters. So that was really the foundation for my work in this area, and for my work on hate crime as well—to look at cultural "permission" to hate, if you will; and some of these ideologies came through in the mainstream as well, not just in the hate movement. They inform my broader work on hate crime. And as I worked on each paper, other themes came to my attention. The next paper I wrote was for a book that will be coming out later this year. It looks at what

I call the politics of reproduction, and how the hate movement attempts to promote, through its ideology and rhetoric, white racial purity and intraracial relationships. This comes through in its rhetoric against abortion for whites but in favor of abortion for people of color, oddly enough. So I come back to some of those themes that I identified, and I keep examining them in different contexts, and developing different areas or themes, too.

Before I started the tape, you mentioned some of your research now on hate crimes against Native Americans. Could you elaborate on that?

I am on sort of the third leg now of a series of interviews, here in the Southwest. Most of the people I interviewed were Navajo, and some were Hopi, and some Apache. In the fall of 2002, I did some interviews in Wisconsin and Minnesota mostly with the Ojibway, and this summer I will go to Montana and interview members of the Blackfeet and Crow reservations. What I am looking at is primarily the experience of victimization. There is absolutely no literature in this area, although if you look at the Uniform Crime Report data, every year you see incidents of the victimization of Native Americans and, on a given day, I could ask any number of my Native American students in class and they would be able to identify more than that. So it was really conversations with my students that got me interested in exploring this in more detail—especially trying to understand victimization in the context of Native American rights, which came through very clearly in Wisconsin and Minnesota around the area of traditional spearfishing of walleye. I am looking at the extent to which these issues reenergize the anti-Indian movement, which is fairly strong in the Midwest and the Pacific northwest and the Northern Plains—a real identifiable movement there. So I am trying to understand victimization in its broader context, looking at the conditions in a particular region that give rise to anti-Indian activity—whether it is the perpetuation of stereotypes in the area, the use of Native American mascots for high school sporting teams, that kind of thing, as well as the way that those forms of violence fit into broader patterns of oppression—the marginalization and exploitation that Native Americans have experienced.

What important lesson or illustration of doing good research can you share with students from your experiences in this research project?

I can think of a couple. One is that if you are examining a particular movement or some broader process, I think it is important to study the actors—in particular, to use the actors' voices to illustrate the themes. In this case, it was direct use of voices—not through interviews (which is more traditional), but using what were very public documents online to introduce that voice into the work. I think that is really important—the use of the actors' own terms and words. The other has to do with the way that the Internet can be used. I often actually discourage my students from using the Internet as the sole means of doing research, which so many students want to do now because it is so easy.

You don't have to trek to the library. You don't have to pick up a book. You know, it is all right there at your fingertips. However, none of us is very astute yet at identifying what are truly legitimate websites as opposed to something that anyone can post online. But this research is one case in which the Internet becomes a very useful tool. The Internet is not really the mechanism of the research, it is not a vehicle for doing the research, but is in some ways the actual subject of the research—that is, we are looking at the use of the Net by the movement as a means of understanding the transition to more professionalism and the more contemporary shape of the movement. So in this case, I am using the Internet not for secondary research but for primary research as public documents, public statements, by the movement. And in general terms, the Net can be really helpful for understanding anything about a social movement, especially virtual communities. As I've said, the hate movement is becoming a global and virtual community. Where previously it was very difficult to maintain very strong connections between the U.S. movement and, say, the German movement, now it is very easy to maintain connections and very easy to reinforce the validity of their claims and observations to one another, living in different nations. I think that is important—that the Net can be used not just as a vehicle but as the platform for the research itself.

Questions to Think About

1. What are the primary and secondary sources that Barbara Perry uses for her research? What are some of the strengths and limitations of each? In particular, what does her research suggest about the advantages and limitations of using websites as a source of data?

2. In what ways is Perry's research similar to and different from other qualitative research that you have read in this book (and perhaps elsewhere) in terms of things such as nature of the data, modes of analysis, challenges, and so on?

3. Do you think that Perry's topic is an important one? Why or why not? What are some implications of her findings?

4. What are two or three testable hypotheses that are suggested by Perry's findings? How might you go about studying them both in the United States and perhaps comparatively?

Correlates of Adolescents' Civic Commitments in Seven Countries

Constance A. Flanagan, Jennifer M. Bowes,
Britta Jonsson, Beno Csapo, and Elena Sheblanova

The relationship of voluntary work, school climates, and family values to public interest as a life goal of adolescents is presented for a sample of 5,579 12–18 year olds in three stable and four transitional democracies. In five of the seven countries, females were more likely than males to be engaged in voluntary work, and in all seven countries girls were more likely than boys to report that their families encouraged an ethic of social responsibility. Regardless of gender or country, adolescents were more likely to consider public interest an important life goal when their families emphasised an ethic of social responsibility. In addition, engagement in volunteer work and a sense of student solidarity at school were formative components of public interest as a life goal for youth in some but not all countries.

A citizen is, most simply, a member of a political community, entitled to whatever prerogatives and encumbered with whatever responsibilities are attached to membership. The word comes to us from the Latin civis; the Greek equivalent is polites, member of the polis, from which comes our political.

—(Walzer, 1989, p. 211)

In this article we employ Walzer's definition to advance two theses about the developmental processes that undergird citizenship: first, that family values inform children's developing concepts of a political community and of their responsibilities to the public interest; second, that experiences of membership in institutions beyond the family are necessary for the social integration of young people into a political community and for their identification with a common good. We pay particular attention to the role of volunteer work and the institution of the school in this regard. Because the work focuses on young people, our framing of citizenship goes beyond state-sanctioned adult rights and obligations (such as voting and military service). Instead, we are interested in the developmental processes whereby concepts of self, a political community, and the ties that bind them evolve.

Adolescents' Interpretations of the "Social Contract"

The empirical basis for our work is drawn from a large survey of adolescents conducted in 1995 in middle and secondary schools in seven countries. The choice of countries for this study was based on two criteria: the length of their experience as democracies and the role of the state in the provision of social welfare. The former criterion is more germane to this article. Four countries in the study (Russia, Bulgaria, the Czech Republic, and Hungary) could be considered fledgling democracies. Because these nations have had only a short period when democratic institutions or infrastructure could develop, we have labeled them _transitional democracies_. In contrast, the other three countries in the study (Australia, Sweden, and the United States) have enjoyed longer histories as democratic polities. In these societies practices in schools, families, and youth organizations have evolved over time with the goal of developing democratic dispositions in young people. Children, especially those from middle-class backgrounds, are encouraged to form their own opinions and to voice them, even if that means disagreeing with adult authorities. Underlying such practices is the belief that the foundation of a democratic system is a citizenry that can think independently and disagree in a civil fashion.

We refer to this project as "Adolescents' Interpretations of the Social Contract," by which we mean their views of the bargain that binds members of a polity together. We contend that political ideologies and understandings, like other aspects of social cognition, are rooted in social relations. In other work we have employed this metaphor to show that, in countries with a strong social welfare contract, adolescents are more likely to hold the state accountable for the welfare of citizens (Flanagan, Macek et at., 1998). We have also applied the social contract metaphor at a more proximal level to look at ways in which practices in developmental settings communicate the ethos of the social order. For example, the form and function of such mundane activities as household chores appear to vary in ways that are consistent with the principles of the social order. Although children in all seven countries in the study are expected to do chores at home, according to the adolescents, these jobs are more likely to be linked to wages in the capitalist nations, with payment of an allowance considered normative. Self-reliance is considered the primary lesson learned in such work. In contrast, in nations with a strong social welfare contract, adolescents are more likely to oppose payment for the chores they perform and responsibility to the group is considered the primary lesson children learn from engaging in such work (Bowes, Chalmers, & Flanagan, 1997; Bowes, Flanagan, & Taylor, 1998).

Youths' Civic Commitment

In the present article, we apply the "social contract" metaphor to and examination of factors related to the development of civic commitment in adolescents. By civic commitment we refer to the importance adolescents attach to public interest as a personal life goal (i.e., when considering their life and future, how important it is that they do something to help their country and to improve their society).

We regard this as a political issue in adolescent development for several reasons. First, identity is focal during adolescence (Erikson, 1968). Thus, future goals that adolescents consider important are core aspects of their evolving sense of self. In this study, future goals are indicators of the extent to which the adolescent identifies with the public interest or common good. Democratic systems depend on a citizenry that invests in the common good. As national studies of Americans point out, contributing to the common good is overwhelmingly the reason why citizens become active in civic and political affairs (Verba, Schlozman, & Brady, 1995).

Second, concerns have been raised that self-interest has eclipsed the public interest in the goals of young people. From the early 1970s through 1986, trend studies of high school seniors (Bachman, Johnson, & O'Malley, 1986) and first-year college students (Astin, Green, & Korn, 1987) in the United States point to a decline in commitment to the welfare of the broader community and an increase in materialist aspirations. During that period young people retreated from politics and civic concerns and chose occupations for financial remuneration rather than public service or self-fulfillment (Easterlin & Crimmins, 1991).

Finally, a vibrant and strong civil society can stabilize political regimes by instilling in their members a sense of belonging and of identification with the public interest. Although youth have been neglected in most discussions of civil society, it is the very properties of a strong civil society (trust, reciprocity, a dense network of community institutions, and caring adults) that keep young people out of trouble and promote their integration into the broader polity (Blyth & Leffert, 1995; Sampson, 1992). Thus, understanding the correlates of youths' identification with public interest goals should shed light both on political development as an aspect of human development and on the role of developmental environments in promoting a strong civil society as well.

In summary, to return to Walzer's definition, we focus on the responsibilities of citizenship and ask,

What factors may be related to the development of a civic ethic? Why would youth identify with a common good? What developmental experiences might serve as ties that bind youth to the broader polity? We examine voluntary work in the community as well as the culture of schools and the values espoused by families as possible formative influences. Although we present comparisons among countries, we also adopt what Kohn (1989) has referred to as a "nation as context" approach and look for similar patterns in the correlates of youths' civic commitments across different national settings.

Eastern/Central Europe

The question of how a civic ethic develops is of particular consequence to the fledgling democracies of Eastern/Central Europe. The stability of democratic regimes rests on broad support in the population for the principles of those regimes. Globalization presents threats to the traditional mechanisms by which diffuse support for polities develops. Thus, it is especially important to identify the "ties that bind" members of these new and evolving democracies together. Not only have the social contracts of these nations undergone radical change, but the institutions and settings of youth development such as schools or youth organizations have had little time to evolve.

The development of democratic dispositions was not high on the agendas of the old regimes in Central and Eastern Europe. During the Communist period, one of the major tasks of schools, media, and youth organizations was to achieve political homogenization by minimizing differences between individuals (Karpati, 1996; Pastuovic, 1993). Thus, the current generation of young people grew up with relatively few opportunities to practice open public debate (Csepeli, German, Keri, & Stumpf, 1994; Karpati). At the same time there were strong norms of patriotism and civic involvement. For young people this meant that membership in groups such as the Young Pioneer and Comsomol Organizations was the norm (Csapo, 1994). Although these groups provided opportunities for the social integration

of young people and for their identification with the nation, they did not seek to inculcate democratic values.

However, there were differences between these nations in the exercise of political autonomy. Hungary led all others in its market and cultural experiments, whereas the Czech Republic had the longest history of democratic institutions. Even now there are differences in the more "Western" religious and cultural customs of the Czech Republic and Hungary compared to the Eastern Orthodox traditions of Bulgaria and Russia. In the latter nations the relationship between citizens and state is more paternalistic, which should be reflected in a greater allegiance of youth to their country. In summary, the Eastern/Central European nations in our study provide an ideal opportunity to investigate the developmental correlates of youths' civic commitments in nations that are themselves charting new democratic futures.

Youth Engagement in Volunteer Work

Youth engagement in voluntary work has been promoted as an antidote to the decline in public interest goals reported in Western societies over the past two decades. Youth groups from the Scouts to 4-H to the Young Pioneers include public service as a core activity, considering it a mark of a good citizen. In fact, such organizations often provide the only opportunity for young people to engage in civic activities.

The question of whether the work is voluntary or mandated is not the concern of our study. Nor do we consider the source of the young person's motivation. Volunteerism may serve very different functions for individuals and self-oriented motivations rather than altruistic ones may be related to a longer length of service (Omoto & Snyder, 1995). Although the motivation for volunteering is an important question, we are interested in volunteer work because it is one of the rare occasions when young people can link with other citizens they would normally not meet, understand the concept of public work, and conceive of themselves as civic actors. For these reasons engaging in such activity should be positively related to the adolescent's identification with public goals. In other work we have found that environmental projects are typical of the kind of work in which youth in Eastern/Central Europe engage and that environmental goals are at the top of their list of civic commitments (Flanagan, Jonsson et al., 1998). In summary, not only does the voluntary sector provide the social integuments of civil society, it provides an outlet for adolescents to identify with public goals.

Family Values and Youths' Civic Commitments

Values are core beliefs about how one ought to behave (Rokeach, 1972) as well as a basis for political views (Jennings, 1991; Kinder & Sears, 1985) and civic action (Verba et al., 1995). Erikson (1968) considered values or ideological guides "a psychological necessity" (p. 133) for adolescents, enabling them to purse what could be a confusing world into meaningful choices. In this study our interest was in family values, conceived as the principles that parents instruct their children to live by. In other work we have argued that parents interpret the world and the relationship with others in the world in the values they emphasize with their children and have found that family values are related to adolescents' political views on poverty, unemployment, and homelessness (Flanagan & Tucker, 1998). Likewise, in this study we expected that family values would be related to adolescents' identification with public interest as an important life goal.

Other work has shown that children develop empathy and altruism when compassion and social responsibility are emphasized as core values in their families (Clary & Miller, 1986; Eisenberg & Mussen, 1989; Hart & Fegley, 1995; Rosenhan, 1970). In addition, retrospective studies of adults who were active in political movements or in acts of political resistance suggest that values of compassion, empathy, and social responsibility learned in their families were instrumental in their decisions to act (Dunham & Bengston, 1992; Franz & McClelland, 1994; Oliner & Oliner, 1988; Rosen-

han; Wood & Ng, 1980). Hoffman (1989) has theorized that empathy felt for disenfranchised groups may provide a motive base for prosocial activism as well as the foundations for a political ideology. A logical extension of this thesis is tested in the present study, that is, that a family ethic emphasizing social responsibility would be positively related to adolescents' endorsement of public interest as a life goal.

Role of Schools as Institutions in Democracies

As the earliest formal public institutions children encounter, schools are like mini polities where children can explore what it means to be a member of a community beyond their families, where they learn that they are the equal of other citizens, and where they can learn how to negotiate their differences in a civil fashion. In contrast to the religious and voluntary organizations with which youth might choose to affiliate, the school is an institution they are obliged to attend. In these public settings, students can disagree with or even dislike one another, yet they have to learn to work together.

For these reasons schools are settings where children develop ideas about the rights and obligations of citizenship. By the kind of public space they provide, schools are a place where children can develop an understanding of what it means to live in a civil society and how members of such a society treat one another. The role of schools as preparatory institutions in democracies is especially salient in fledgling democracies. Prior to 1989 in the nations of Central and Eastern Europe pedagogical practices typically discouraged debate. Teachers themselves had relatively little autonomy in instructional decisions (Jordanova, 1994; Long, 1990; Rust, Knost, & Wichmann, 1994). Despite these ideological constraints, local schools were one of the institutions of civil society where citizens could exercise some level of autonomy and decision making. Since 1990 building democratic institutions has become a high priority of these nations (Csepeli et al., 1994), with changes in curricular content and instructional styles in schools recommended as a primary means for achieving that goal (Rust et al.).

In this study we focus on two dimensions of school climates: students' right to an autonomous opinion and their sense of membership in and identification with the institution of the school. The first concerns how authority is negotiated in the classroom, an aspect of school climates that has received some attention in the literature. The evidence suggests that in classrooms where students are free to dissent and are also expected to listen to different perspectives, they are more aware of and able to think critically about civic issues (Newmann, 1990), know more about international affairs (Torney-Purta & Lansdale, 1986), tolerate conflicting views and are aware and critical of simplistic appeals to patriotism as a motivator of action (Torney-Purta, 1991). However, students' interest in political participation may be responsive to other aspects of classroom practice. In a study of 10 democratic nations, Torney, Oppenheim, and Farnen (1975) found that an emphasis on patriotism, ritual, and rote learning at school was related to less support among students for democratic values but to high interest in political participation.

The second aspect of school climates has received less attention in the literature. This dimension, alluded to in Walzer's definition of a citizen, taps students' sense of membership, pride, and identification with the institution of the school. Political goals are typically achieved through collective action. But a sense of solidarity with others and identification with group goals are prerequisites for collective action. Thus, the second question about school climates addressed in this article is, If students perceive their schools as settings where identification with the institution and a commitment to the common good are widely shared, do such school climates generalize to the young person's commitments to the broader polity?

Gender

The literature provides little basis for positing gender differences in adolescents' civic commit-

ment as we have defined it in this article. However, there is evidence for gender differences in the factors that we posit may play a role in the development of civic commitment. For example, studies of community service in the United States suggest that females are more likely than males to participate (Hart, Atkins, & Ford, this issue; Independent Sector, 1996). Likewise, the salience of social responsibility as an ethic in families may vary for male and female adolescents. Studies of altruism (Berndt, 1981; Fabes, Eisenberg, & Miller, 1990) and empathy (Eisenberg, 1985; Radke-Yarrow, Zahn-Waxler, Richardson, Susman, & Martinez, 1994; Zahn-Waxler, Radke-Yarrow, Wagner, & Chapman, 1992) have shown that girls are more likely than boys to exhibit these characteristics and to feel guilty when they have not been compassionate (Williams & Bybee, 1994). National surveys of American high school students from the mid-1970s through the early 1990s revealed that females were more likely than males to feel compassion or concern for the well-being of others. And this gender difference held regardless of social class or how religious the youth were (Beutel & Marini, 1995).

With few exceptions (Carlo, Koller, Eisenberg, DaSilva, & Frohlich, 1996) these studies have been conducted in the United States. It remains an open question to what extent gender differences in volunteering and social responsibility might be consistent across countries. Helping others can be consonant with the social roles of both men and women, and gender differences in helping others may depend on factors such as the definition of *helping* and *other* and the duration of the act (Eagly & Crowley, 1986). Although political interest inventories typically find that women are less interested in politics than men, this gender gap may well be a function of the narrow ways in which the issues have been framed. For example, Anderson and Johnston (1993) discovered interesting gender differences in the knowledge retained by American high school students who watched the current events broadcast by Channel One in their schools. Whereas girls were more likely to remember health-related issues including information about AIDS, boys tended to remember stories covering state or international affairs. In a similar vein, gender differences in political attitudes may reflect the responsibilities and the socialization pressures of males and females. For example, in other analyses of the data set that is the basis of this article we found that girls were more likely than boys to feel that the state should provide social welfare benefits for needy individuals and families (Flanagan, Macek et al., 1998).

The concern of the present study was with the correlates of youths' civic commitment, which was operationalized as the importance they attached to helping their country and to doing something to improve their society. We did not expect to find gender differences in this outcome nor in its correlates. However, as outlined below, we did expect that levels of those correlates would differ for males and females.

Hypotheses

The following hypotheses were tested in this study. With respect to country level analyses, we had no predictions regarding differences in youths' civic commitments, family values, or the sense of membership they felt at school. However, we did expect that youth in the transitional societies would report lower mean levels of democratic climates in their schools. This was expected to be especially marked in Bulgaria and Russia, where there is a stronger cultural ethos of respect for authority. In terms of gender differences, we expected that females would be more likely than their male compatriots to report that their families emphasized an ethic of social responsibility in their upbringing. In addition, consistent with trends reported in other studies, we expected to find a consistent gender difference in youth volunteering, with girls more likely than boys to be engaged in such work. In terms of models predicting youths' civic commitment, we expected that family values and a sense of membership at school would play a strong role for males and females in all countries.

Methods

Participants

Data were gathered via surveys administered in schools in a large urban area of each country between March and May 1995. An effort was made to recruit youth from high- and low-status backgrounds based on parental education and the school type (e.g., vocational, gymnasium) that the youth attended. A minimum of 500 adolescents from each country, ranging in age from 12 to 18, with a mean age of 15.5, participated.

Procedures and Measures

During a designated class period, research assistants described the project as a study of young people's opinions about issues in society. It was made clear both verbally and in written form that there were no right or wrong answers and that the information was being collected anonymously. Although the survey tapped a wide range of topics, we focus in this article on those described in the following sections.

Dependent Measure: Civic Commitment

Adolescents' civic commitment was based on the personal importance they attached to two indicators similar to those used to measure public interest in studies of youth in the United States (Astin et al., 1987, Bachman, Johnston, & O'Malley, 1987). Students were asked, "When you think about your life and your future, how important is it to you personally to (a) contribute to your country and (b) do something to improve your society?" Respondents rated the importance of these public interest goals on a Likert-type scale (1 = not at all important to 5 = very important). The mean of these two goals was used as the measure of *civic commitment*, and alphas were above .68 in all countries.

Independent Measures

Voluntary work.   As part of the survey, adolescents were asked, "Do you ever do volunteer work in the community?" This dichotomous (yes/no) item was used to measure an adolescent's engagement in voluntary work.

Family ethic of social responsibility.

Our measure of family values was based on adolescents' reports of how much emphasis their parents placed on a set of four items that tapped the need to be attentive to others, especially to less fortunate members of society. Items were adapted from Katz and Hass's (1988) Humanitarianism-Egalitarianism scale. We have labeled this construct a *family ethic of social responsibility*. Cronbach's alpha was .74 in the stable and .70 in the transitional democracies.

School climates.

Adolescents' perceptions of two dimensions of school climate were assessed. The first, *democratic climates at school*, concerns the extent to which the teacher involves students in shared governance and the attitude toward authority that the teacher conveys. Items, adapted from Maehr & Midgley (1990), assess the degree to which students are encouraged to assume leadership in the school and are invited by the teacher to express their opinions, even if they might disagree with the teacher. Responses to all items were based on a Likert-type (1 = strongly disagree to 5 = strongly agree) format. Cronbach's alpha was .65 and .72 for this three-item measure in the transitional and stable democracies, respectively.

A second dimension of the school's culture is alluded to in Walzer's definition. *A sense of membership at school* taps a student's perceptions of their fellow students and of the collective properties of the student body. The three items measure the extent to which students in general are proud to identify with the institution of the school, feel like members who count, and move beyond the boundaries of individual friendships out of concern for the well-being of all members of the student body. Again responses to all items were based on a Likert-type (1 = strongly disagree to 5 = strongly agree) format. Cronbach's alphas were .59 and .61 for this measure in the transitional and stable democracies, respectively.

Analyses

We conducted a series of analyses to assess the correlates of youths' civic commitment across countries. First, chi-square tests of independence were run to determine whether there were gender differences in the likelihood of adolescents' being involved in voluntary work in the community. Next, analyses of variance (ANOVAs) were conducted to test for country (7) and gender (2) differences in the importance of public interest goals, in adolescents' perceptions of their school climates, and in the extent to which social responsibility was a value they felt was emphasized in their families. Finally, separate multiple regressions were performed for girls and boys in each country. Youths' civic commitment was the dependent variable, and volunteer work, the two school climate measures, and the family's emphasis on social responsibility were the independent variables.

Results

Bivariate Analyses

Table 1 summarizes the results of the chi-square tests of independence. The results indicate that, in five of the seven nations, females were more likely than males to report that they had engaged in volunteer work in their communities. In the Czech Republic and Sweden, there were no gender differences on this variable. The results also point to the normative nature of youth volunteering across countries. In Hungary, the United States, the Czech Republic, and Bulgaria between 40 and 50% of the adolescents reported that they had done voluntary work. In contrast, the practice appears to be less normative in Australia, Sweden, and Russia, where approximately 20–25% of the youth reported that they had done such work.

Table 2 provides a summary of the means and standard deviations on the key constructs for adolescents in each country. There was a main effect of country, $F(6, 5416) = 23.88$, $p < .001$, on the importance that adolescents attached to doing something to help their society and country. Post

TABLE 1   *Percentages of Male and Female Adolescents in Each Country Who Are Engaged in Volunteer Work*

	AUSTRALIA % (N)	UNITED STATES % (N)	SWEDEN % (N)	HUNGARY % (N)	CZECH REPUBLIC % (N)	BULGARIA % (N)	RUSSIA % (N)
Males	23% (62)	46% (147)	19% (73)	54% (250)	44% (253)	37% (146)	16% (42)
Females	34% (87)	56% (217)	22% (78)	68% (329)	49% (262)	45% (238)	30% (101)
Total N in sample	530	708	754	951	1,112	913	611
Chi-square	7.22**	6.22**	1.08	20.08***	3.33	5.97*	16.27***

Note: $*p < .05$ $**p < .01$. $***p < .001$.

hoc Scheffé tests indicated that Bulgarian youth were more likely than all others to endorse this goal whereas Swedish and Hungarian youth were less likely than others to consider this an important life goal.

Multivariate Analyses

The results of the multiple regressions predicting boys' and girls' civic commitments in each of the seven countries are presented in Tables 3 and 4, respectively. The most robust finding is the consistent and significant effect that a family ethic of social responsibility has on adolescents' civic commitment. In every country and for both girls and boys, those who heard this ethic emphasized in their families were more likely than their compa-

triots to consider helping their country and doing something to improve their society an important life goal. Next in importance was the adolescents' report that a sense of membership and caring characterized the student body at their school. This aspect of the school climate was significantly related to the civic commitments of boys in Australia, Hungary, and Russia and marginally in Bulgaria and of girls in the United States, Sweden, Hungary, and Russia and marginally in Australia. In contrast, democratic climates at school (i.e., the extent to which adolescents felt that their teachers encouraged student autonomy) predicted boys' and girls' civic commitments in the Czech Republic and was marginally related for boys in the United States. Finally, adolescents' engagement in volun-

TABLE 2   *Comparisons of Adolescents' Reports of Civic Commitment, School Climates, and Family Values Across Countries*

PREDICTOR	AUSTRALIA M (SD)	UNITED STATES M (SD)	SWEDEN M (SD)	HUNGARY M (SD)	CZECH REPUBLIC M (SD)	BULGARIA M (SD)	RUSSIA M (SD)
Civic commitment	3.47 (.81)	3.52 (.89)	3.27 (.81)	3.34 (.81)	3.57 (.70)	3.68 (.80)	3.56 (1.0)
Democratic school practices	3.13 (.83)	2.97 (.85)	2.92 (.78)	2.88 (.79)	2.60 (.73)	2.63 (.88)	2.32 (.98)
Sense of membership at school	2.93 (.74)	2.74 (.78)	2.56 (.66)	2.74 (.73)	2.55 (.63)	2.76 (.81)	2.31 (.90)
Family ethics of social responsibility	3.80 (.65)	3.90 (.69)	3.65 (.68)	3.54 (.62)	3.56 (.58)	3.60 (.67)	3.78 (.71)

TABLE 3 *Comparisons of Male and Female Adolescents in Each Country*

		CIVIC COMMITMENT		FAMILY ETHIC OF SOCIAL RESPONSIBILITY		DEMOCRATIC SCHOOL PRACTICES		SENSE OF MEMBERSHIP AT SCHOOL	
		M	*SD*	*M*	*SD*	*M*	*SD*	*M*	*SD*
Australia	Male	3.43	(.86)	3.71	(.60)***	3.13	(.73)	2.88	(.78)
	Female	3.53	(.75)	3.90	(.69)	3.13	(.68)	2.98	(.69)
United States	Male	3.50	(.93)	3.74	(.72)***	2.96	(.75)	2.65	(.77)*
	Female	3.54	(.86)	3.98	(.64)	2.98	(.71)	2.81	(.78)
Sweden	Male	3.32	(.84)+	3.53	(.68)***	2.82	(.74)***	2.51	(.66)*
	Female	3.22	(.78)	3.76	(.64)	3.02	(.61)	2.61	(.65)
Hungary	Male	3.43	(.85)**	3.50	(.62)+	2.90	(.70)	2.74	(.79)
	Female	3.26	(.76)	3.58	(.61)	2.87	(.66)	2.72	(.68)
Bulgaria	Male	3.73	(.85)	3.52	(.70)***	2.76	(.72)***	2.87	(.80)*
	Female	3.64	(.76)	3.67	(.64)	2.56	(.74)	2.73	(.80)
Czech Republic	Male	3.57	(.74)+	3.49	(.60)***	2.59	(.70)	2.52	(.67)*
	Female	3.56	(.65)	3.61	(.54)	2.61	(.62)	2.60	(.60)
Russia	Male	3.55	(1.08)	3.68	(.73)**	2.22	(.83)**	2.30	(.93)
	Female	3.57	(.95)	3.85	(.68)	2.40	(.77)	2.31	(.88)

Note: + = $p < .10$.　* = $p < .05$　** = $p < .01$.　***$p < .001$.

TABLE 4 *Predictors of Boys' Civic Commitments*

PREDICTOR	AUSTRALIA	UNITED STATES	SWEDEN	HUNGARY	CZECH REPUBLIC	BULGARIA	RUSSIA
Engagement in volunteer work	.08	.17**	.15**	.02	.12**	.03	.08
Democratic school practices	.03	.13*	.03	.08	.14**	.08	.06
Sense of membership at school	.23***	.03	.08	.21***	.05	.12*	.17**
Family ethics of social responsibility	.25***	.26***	.21***	.35***	.26***	.34***	.36***
R^2	.17	.15	.09	.23	.14	.17	.23

Note: *$p<.05$.　**$p<.01$.　***$p<.001$.

teer work was significantly related to boys' civic commitment in the United States, Sweden, and the Czech Republic and to girls' civic commitment in the Czech Republic, Bulgaria, and Russia.

A comparison of adolescents' perceptions of democratic climates in their schools also revealed significant main effects of country $F(6, 5437) = 72.35$, $p < .001$, and a gender by country interaction,

Method of Analysis

Multiple Regression

Multiple regression is a statistical test to help researchers measure the simultaneous influence of two or more independent variables on a dependent variable. The dependent variable in this research is an attitude—civic commitment. The researchers asked respondents about two aspects of this variable: (1) their personal sense of importance of contributing to the country and (2) their personal commitment to doing something to improve society. Scores were received on a scale of one to five, and the average score on these two items is the measure of civic commitment. The researchers test for the possible influence of four independent variables: participation in voluntary work, family ethic of social responsibility, extent of democratic climate at school, and sense of membership at school. Thus, multiple regression is used to tell us the extent of influence that these four variables together have on civic commitment (and the influence of each variable individually). Tables 1 through 3 present average scores for the students surveyed in the seven countries. The results of the multiple regression are in Tables 4 (boys) and 5 (girls). The four independent variables are listed in the far left column. We can learn several things about civic commitment from these tables, but we will concentrate on three points of interpretation. First, although it is not indicated in the tables, the numbers in the tables are called "beta weights". These numbers tell us how much influence each of the variables individually has on civic commitment. A minus sign means the variables are inversely related (that is, as one goes up, the other goes down). The highest number in

this column identifies the independent variable that has the largest influence on civic commitment. For boys, family ethic of social responsibility has the largest influence on civic commitment in all seven countries, and for girls, it is the largest influence in five of the seven countries. The .26 coefficient for boys in the United States means that for every one-unit increase in family ethic (remember it is measured on a scale of one to five), civic commitment increases by .26.

Second, the presence of one, two, or three asterisks after the coefficients tells us how sure we are that variable really influences civic commitment. One asterisk means that we are more than 95 percent sure that factor influences civic commitment (with only a 5 percent chance that results are due to chance). Two asterisks mean we are more than 99 percent sure, and three asterisks means that we are more than 99.9 percent sure. You can see which variables influence civic commitment with the greatest likelihood. Finally, R^2 (located under family ethic in both tables) tells us how much influence all of these variables together have on civic commitment. The possible range of R^2 is 0 to 1.0 (with zero meaning no influence, and one meaning that we have fully identified influences). In this case, the value ranges from .09 to .23 in the seven countries for boys and from .09 to .19 for girls, which means that these variables explain something less than 25 percent of the variation for boys and less than 20 percent for girls. These coefficients would be interpreted as telling us that these variables are very important in explaining civic commitment, but also that there are additional variables not studied in this research that are important influences.

$F(6, 5437) = 5.32$, $p < .001$. As expected, more students in the stable democracies, especially Australia and the United States, were more likely than their peers in the transitional democracies to report that their teachers encouraged them to voice their opinions, even if this entailed a challenge to the teacher's view. What was not expected was that Hungarian youth were as likely as their peers in Sweden and the United Slates to report this democratic climate in their schools. In contrast, students in Bulgaria, Russia, and the Czech Republic were less likely to feel that such democratic climates characterized their schools. (All gender by country interactions are presented in Table 5 and are discussed below.)

There was a main effect of country, $F(6, 5430) = 47.24$, $p < .001$, and a gender by country interaction, $F(1, 5430) = 3.50$, $p < .001$, on students' sense of membership in and identification with the institution of the school. Whereas Russian youth

TABLE 5 *Predictors of Girls' Civic Commitments*

PREDICTOR	AUSTRALIA	UNITED STATES	SWEDEN	HUNGARY	CZECH REPUBLIC	BULGARIA	RUSSIA
Engagement in volunteer work	.02	.05	.07	.02	.18***	.13**	.16**
Democratic school practices	–.04	–.06	.03	.03	.16***	.03	.03
Sense of membership at school	.13*	.22***	.22	.23***	.13**	.08	.17**
Family ethics of social responsibility	.27***	.23***	.18***	.29***	.17***	.29***	.29***
R^2	.09	.12	.12	.19	.15	.14	.18

Note: *$p<.05$.   **$p<.01$.   ***$p<.001$.

were less likely than their peers in any other country to hold this view, Australians were more likely than all others to endorse this dimension of their schools. Swedish and Czech youth were more likely than their Russian peers but less likely than all others to report that their schools were characterized by a general sense of pride and membership. Finally, there were main effects of country, $F(6, 5491) = 31.82$, $p < .001$, and gender, $F(1, 5491) = 91.42$, $p < .001$, on adolescents' reports that social responsibility was a value strongly endorsed in their families. Post hoc Scheffé tests revealed that adolescents from the United Slates, Australia, and Russia were more likely than those in Hungary, the Czech Republic, Bulgaria, and Sweden to report that this value was emphasized in their families. The significant main effect of gender reflected the fact that in all countries, girls were more likely than boys to say that an ethic of social responsibility was a value that their families emphasized in their upbringing.

Table 5 provides a summary across countries of male and female perceptions of each of the constructs in the study. There was only one gender difference in adolescents' civic commitments, with Hungarian males more likely than their female peers to consider the public interest an important life goal. In contrast, in every country, females

were more likely than males to report that an ethic of social responsibility was a value emphasized in their families. This result was significant at $p < .01$ in every country except Hungary, where the difference was marginal, $p < .10$. There were no consistent differences in either dimension of classroom climate. Whereas girls in Sweden and Russia reported more democratic classroom practices when compared to their male compatriots, boys in Bulgaria were more likely than their female peers to report that teachers encouraged democracy in the classroom. In terms of students' sense of membership at school, girls in three countries (Sweden, the United States, and the Czech Republic) reported higher levels than boys. However, as in the perceptions of democratic classroom climates, Bulgarian boys perceived a stronger sense of inclusion in their classrooms when compared to their female peers.

Discussion

Interest in questions of citizenship and its developmental antecedents tends to increase during periods of social change. It is then that we wonder, What happens as children are growing up that engenders a sense of loyalty to the polity and identification with a common good? Globalization presents threats to the traditional mechanisms by which diffuse support for polities develops. Global economic reorganization is already redefining the political communities to which people will have allegiances. In fact, there are concerns that those who are marginalized by this reorganization will be ignored as members of political communities (Rifkin, 1995; Wolfe, 1989). Such outcomes are not inevitable, however. But if we are to avoid them it will be important for future generations to appreciate that their fate is linked with others who are not like them. And in a global context it will be increasingly important to understand how the choices we make reverberate in the lives of people we may never meet.

Toward that end we have argued that young people need opportunities to identify with individuals, groups, and institutions beyond the borders of their families and friends. In this regard the results of our study provide at least marginal support for the idea that engagement in voluntary work and student solidarity at school are factors related to an adolescent's identification with the public interest. A number of years ago Erikson (1968) observed that the formation of social cliques was a natural outcome of the adolescent's search for identity and a social niche. However, he also warned that cliques pose dangers for democracy if youth have no opportunities to link to the broader polity. Without meaningful institutional affiliations and connections to the community, adolescents may experience what he termed "identity-vacua," a lack of direction and purpose and disaffection from the polity.

Teaching practices that encouraged student participation in shared governance were not as strongly related to the importance youth attached to public interest goals. These results should not be taken to mean that such teaching practices have no bearing on other civic competencies, such as the development of democratic dispositions in young people. However, our results do point to an understudied aspect of the school as an institution where young people develop their ideas about the prerogatives and obligations of citizenship. They suggest that a sense of membership and solidarity among peers that cuts across cliques in a school

can be a factor in adolescents' identification with a common good.

Globalization can also cause us to reflect on the future we envision for our children and the values we want them to live by. The results of this study point to the powerful role that a family ethic of social responsibility might have in this process. In all seven nations and for both girls and boys this ethic was significantly related to the importance that adolescents attached to improving their society and helping their country. It was an ethic that girls in all countries were more likely to hear. This gender difference deserves more attention in future research if, as Hoffman (1989) has suggested, such empathic concerns may form the basis of political ideologies. Elsewhere, Vaclev Havel (1992) has observed that values are an essential foundation for democratic states:

> I am convinced that we will never build a democratic state based on the rule of law if we do not at the same time build a state that is—regardless of how unscientific this may sound to the ears of a political scientist—humane, moral, intellectual and spiritual, and cultural. The best laws and the best-conceived democratic mechanisms will not in themselves guarantee legality or freedom or human rights—anything, in short, for which they were intended—if they are not underpinned by certain human and social values. (Havel, 1992, p. 7)

We have adopted the metaphor of a social contract or covenant to emphasize the idea of reciprocity in the concept of citizenship. We contend that young people will endorse this covenant to the extent that they feel a sense of membership in the broader political community. Developmental opportunities for identifying with the *we* and not just the *I* include the sense of solidarity that the student culture of a school may provide. Likewise, voluntary work in the community can link young people to other citizens who are unlike them and can provide the grounds for identifying with public concerns. The social contract metaphor also implies that, in the course of growing up, children come to understand the principles that make their society work. A democratic polity works when people are committed to public, not merely self-interest goals. In this regard, the results of this study point to the fundamental role that families play across societies in emphasizing social responsibility as a norm of citizenship.

REFERENCES

Anderman, E. M., & Johnston, J. (1993, March). *Adolescents' motivational goal orientations and knowledge about AIDS and current events.* Paper presented at the meeting of the Society for Research in Child Development, New Orleans, LA.

Astin, A. W., Green, K. S., & Korn, W. S. (1987). *The American freshman: Twenty year trends, 1966–1985.* Los Angeles: University of California, Los Angeles, Higher Education Research Program.

Bachman, J. G., Johnston, L. D., & O'Malley, P. M. (1986). Recent findings from "Monitoring the future: A continuing study of the lifestyles and values of youth." in F. M. Andrews (Ed.), *Research on the quality of life* (pp. 215–234). Ann Arbor: University of Michigan, Institute of Social Research.

Bachman, J. G., Johnston. L. D., & O'Malley, P. M. (1987). *Monitoring the future: Questionnaire responses from the nation's high school seniors.* Ann Arbor, MI: Survey Research Center, Institute for Social Research.

Berndt, T. J. (1981). Effects of friendship on prosocial intentions and behavior. *Child Development, 52,* 636–643.

Beutel, A. M., & Marini, M. M. (1995). Gender and values. *American Sociological Review, 60,* 436–448.

Blyth, D., & Leffert, N. (1995). Communities as contexts for adolescent research. *Journal of Adolescent Research, 10,* 64–87.

Bowes, J. M., Chalmers, D., & Flanagan, C. (1997). Children's involvement in household work: Views of adolescents in six countries. *Family Matters: Australian Journal of Family Studies, 46,* 26–30.

Bowes, J. M., Flanagan, C., & Taylor. A. J. (1998). *Adolescents' ideas about individual and social responsibility in relation to children's household work: Some international comparisons.* Manuscript submitted for publication.

Carlo, G., Koller, S. H., Eisenberd, N., DaSilva, M. S., & Frohlich, C. B. (1996). A cross-national study on

the relations among prosocial moral reasoning, gender role orientations, and prosocial behaviors. *Developmental Psychology, 32,* 231–240.

Clary, E. G., & Miller, J. (1986). Socialization and situational influences on sustained altruism. *Child Development, 57,* 1358–1369.

Csapo, B. (1994). Adolescents in Hungary. In K. Hurrelmann (Ed.), *International Handbook of Adolescence* (Pp. 77–91). Westport, CT: Greenwood.

Csepeli, G., German, D., Keri, L., & Stumpf, I. (Eds.), (1994). *From subject to citizen: Hungarian studies on political socialization and political education* (Vol. 3). Budapest, Hungary: Hungarian Center for Political Education.

Dunham, C., & Bengston, V. (1992). The long-term effects of political activism on intergenerational relations. *Youth and Society, 24,* 31–51.

Eagly, A. H., & Crowley, M. (1986). Gender and helping behavior. A meta-analytic review of the social psychological literature. *Psychological Bulletin, 100,* 283–308.

Easterlin, R. A., & Crimmins, E. M. (1991). Private materialism, personal self-fulfillment, family life, and public interest. *Public Opinion Quarterly, 55,* 499–533.

Eisenberg, N. (Ed.). (1985). *Altruistic emotions, cognition, and behavior.* Hillsdale, NJ: Lawrence Erlbaum.

Eisenberg, N., & Mussen, P. H. (1989). *The roots of prosocial behavior in children.* New York: Cambridge University Press.

Erikson, E. (1968). *Identity: Youth and crisis.* New York: W. W. Norton.

Fabes, R. A., Eisenberg, N., & Miller, P. (1990). Maternal correlates of children's emotional responsiveness. *Developmental Psychology, 26,* 639–648.

Flanagan, C. Jonsson, B., Botcheva, L., Csapo, B., Bowes, J., Macek, P., Averina, I., & Sheblanova, E. (1998). Adolescents and the "social contract": Developmental roots of citizenship in seven countries. In M. Yates & J. Youniss (Eds.), *Community service and civic engagement in youth: International Perspectives* (pp. 135–155). New York: Cambridge University Press.

Flanagan, C., Macek, P., Botcheva, L., Csapo, B., Averina, I., Sheblanova, E., Jonsson, B., & Bowes, J. (1998, February). Adolescents' perceptions of the "New Deal" in Central Europe: An impetus for reframing theories of youth political development. In Hans Oswald (Chair), *Political socialization in former Communist countries.* Symposium conducted at the biennial meetings of the Society for Research on Adolescence, San Diego, CA.

Flanagan, C., & Tucker, C. J. (1998). *Adolescents' explanations for political issues: Concordance with their views of self and society.* Manuscript submitted for publication.

Franz, C. E., & McClelland, D. C. (1994). Lives of women and men active in the social protests of the 1960s: A longitudinal study. *Journal of Personality and Social Psychology, 66,* 196–205.

Hart, D., & Fegley, S. (1995). Prosocial behavior and caring in adolescence: Relations to self-understanding and social judgment, *Child Development, 66,* 1347–1359.

Havel, V. (1992). Politics, morality, and civility. In V. Havel, *Summer Meditations* (P. Wilson, trans., p. 7). New York: Knopf.

Hoffman, M. L. (1989). Empathic emotions and justice in society. *Social Justice Research, 3,* 283–311.

Independent Sector. (1996). *Giving and volunteering in the United States.* Washington, DC: Independent Sector.

Jennings, M. K. (1991). Thinking about social injustice. *Political Psychology, 12,* 187–204.

Jordanova, R. (1994). The Bulgarian teacher and perceptions of educational values. In V. D. Rust, P. Knost, & J. Wichmann (Eds.), *Education and the value crisis in Central and Eastern Europe* (pp. 253–266). Frankfurt am Main: Peter Lang.

Karpati, A. (1996). Hungarian adolescents of the 1990s: Ideals, beliefs and expectations. In D. Brenner & D. Lenzen (Eds.), *Education for the new Europe* (pp. 29–42). Providence, RI: Berghan Books.

Katz, I., & Hass, R. G. (1998). Racial ambivalence and American value conflict: Correlational and priming studies of dual cognitive structures. *Journal of Personality and Social Psychology, 55,* 895–905.

Kinder, D. R., & Sears, D. O. (1985). Public opinion and political action. In G. Lindzey & E. Aronson (Eds.), *Handbook of social psychology* (3rd ed.). Reading, MA: Addison-Wesley.

Kohn, M. (1989). Cross-national research as an analytic strategy. In M. Kohn (Ed.), *Cross-national research in sociology* (pp. 77–103). Newbury Park, CA: Sage.

Long, D. H. (1990). Continuity and change in Soviet education under Gorbachev. *American Educational Research Journal, 27,* 403–423.

Maehr, M., & Midgley, C. (1990). *Home and school cooperation in social and motivational development:*

Replication. Washington. DC: U.S. Department of Education, Office of Special Education Research.

Newmann, F. M. (1990). A test of higher-order thinking in social studies: Persuasive writing on constitutional issues using the NAEP approach. *Social Education,* 369–373.

Oliner, S., & Oliner, P. (1998). *The altruistic personality.* New York: Free Press.

Omoto, A. M., & Snyder, M. (1995). Sustained helping without obligation: Motivation, longevity of service, and perceived attitude change among AIDS volunteer. *Journal of Personality and Social Psychology. 68,* 671–686.

Pastuovic, N. (1993). Problems of reforming education systems in post-communist countries. *International Review of Education, 39,* 405–418

Radke-Yarrow, M., Zahn-Waxler, C., Richardson, A., Susman, A., & Martinez, P. (1994). Caring behavior in children of clinically depressed and well mothers. *Child Development, 65,* 1405–1414.

Rifkin, J. (1995) *The end of work: The decline of the global labor force and the dawn of the post-market era.* New York: G.B. Putnam's Sons.

Rokeach, M. (1972). *Beliefs, attitudes, and values.* San Francisco: Jossey-Bass.

Rosenhan, D. L. (1970). The natural socialization of altruistic autonomy. In J. Macauley and L. Berkowitz (Eds.), *Altruism and helping behaviors* (pp. 251–268). Orlando, FL: Academic Press.

Rust, V. D., Knost, P., & Wichmann, J. (1994). Education and youth in Central and Eastern Europe: A comparative assessment. In V. D. Rust, P. Knost, & J. Wichmann (Eds.), *Education and the value crisis in Central and Eastern Europe* (pp. 281–308). Frankfurt am Main: Peter Lang.

Sampson, R. J. (1992). Family management and child development: Insights from social disorganization theory. In J. McCord (Ed.), *Advances in Criminological Theory. Vol. 3. Facts, frameworks, and forecasts* (pp. 63–93). New Brunswick, NJ: Transaction Publishers.

Torney, J., Oppenheim, A., & Farnen, R. (1975). *Civic education in ten countries.* New York: John Wiley and Sons.

Torney-Purta, J. (1991). Recent psychological research relating to children's social cognition and its implications for social and political education. In I. Morrisset & A. M. Williams (Eds.), *Social/political education in three countries* (pp. 91–111). Boulder, CO: Social Sciences Education Consortium.

Torney-Purta, J., & Lansdale, D. (1986). Classroom climate and process in international studies: Data from the American Schools and the World Project. Paper presented at meeting of the American Educational Research Association, San Francisco.

Verba, S., Schlozman, K. L., & Brady, H. E. (1995). *Voice and equality: Civic voluntarism and American politics.* Cambridge, MA: Harvard University Press.

Walzer, M. (1989). *Citizenship.* New York: Cambridge University Press.

Williams, C., & Bybec, J. (1994). What do children feel guilty about? Developmental and gender differences. *Developmental Psychology, 30,* 617–623.

Wolfe, A. (1989). *Whose keeper? Social science and moral obligation.* Berkeley and Los Angeles: University of California Press.

Wood, J. L., & Ng, W. C. (1980). Socialization and student activism: Examination of a relationship. In L. Kriesberg (Ed.), *Research in the social movements, conflicts, and change* (Vol. 3, pp. 21–44). Greenwich, CT: JAI Press.

Zahn-Waxler, C., Radke-Yarrow, M., Wagner, E., & Chapman, M. (1992). Development of concern for others. *Developmental Psychology, 28,* 126–136.

Constance A. Flanagan is a professor of youth civic development in the Department of Agricultural and Extension Education at Penn State University. She also has appointments (by courtesy) in the departments of Comparative and International Education, Human Development and Family Studies, and Women's Studies. Her program of work, "Adolescents and the 'Social Contract,' " concerns the factors in families, schools, and communities that promote civic values and competencies in young people. Two new projects include a longitudinal study of peer loyalty and social responsibility as they relate to teens' views about health as a public or private issue and to their inclinations to intervene to prevent harm to one another, and a study of the developmental correlates of social trust. Flanagan is a William T. Grant Scholar and a member of the MacArthur Foundation's Network on the Transition to Adulthood and Public Policy. She is on the advisory board of the Center for Information and Research on Civic Learning and Engagement (CIRCLE) and the editorial boards of four journals.

Jennifer Bowes is an associate professor and head of the Institute of Early Childhood at Macquarie University in Sydney, Australia. Her work includes research on child care and child development, work–family issues and child health, and parenting in relation to early childhood services.

Britta Jonsson is a senior lecturer and associate professor of sociology at the Stockholm Institute of Education. Her current program of work includes a multidisciplinary project on issues about basic values in a changing world and ethical and moral dilemmas in the new teacher education in Sweden.

Beno Csapo is a professor of education at the University of Szeged, Hungary, and the head of the Research Group on Development of Competencies, Hungarian Academy of Sciences. His work includes studies of cognitive development, problem solving, the application of knowledge, and cognitive aspects of democratic thinking.

Elena Scheblanova is a chair of the Laboratory of Psychological Diagnostics Methods at the Moscow Psychological-Pedagogical University and a leading researcher in the Laboratory of Giftedness Psychology at the Psychological Institute of the Russian Academy of Education. She won the 1998 Russian President Award and is currently involved in longitudinal projects on giftedness in school-age children.

Two other scholars have contributed substantially to this project, although they are not coauthors of this article. **Luba B. Botcheva** is a developmental psychologist and Program Director of the Children's Health Council's Outcomes Research Consulting Service in Palo Alto, California, and former Director of the Youth and Social Change Program at the Center for Interdisciplinary Studies in Sofia, Bulgaria. **Petr Macek** is a professor of social psychology in the School of Social Studies at Masaryk University in Brno, Czech Republic, where he directs the Department of Psychology.

An interview with . . .

Constance A. Flanagan

What got you interested in this subject?

I really love developmental psychology, and I have always loved politics in its broadest sense, and it just seemed in the developmental psychology world that we were ignoring the kinds of formative influences on people's political beliefs. I had some great opportunities to meet people from some of the emerging democracies in Eastern Europe, and I asked them if they would be interested in investigating what young people thought about the state and its citizens and issues. It is always easier to study topics such as this during a period of social change, especially dramatic social change, when people's political beliefs are in the forefront of their mind[s]. So, it is a confluence between my own interests in pursuing civic and political development, and the formative aspects of it in development, and then meeting these scholars whose worlds were sort of turning upside down politically. There was great interest in doing the collaboration, and that is how we got started.

How do you see this research contributing to an understanding of civic commitment?

In cross-comparative work, it is common to find divergent ways of thinking. For example, in Eastern Europe and in Sweden, people expect the state to do more for the population, whereas in Australia and the United States, we are not as accustomed to thinking that way. But, the relationship among variables may be the same within all of the countries, that is, there are certain consistent features across countries. On average, you might find school climates to be different in some parts of the world than in others because of the role of the school within the society, but it may still be the case that the role of democratic and inclusive climates at school produce a certain feeling of membership about your participation in the wider society. So, even though the mean level might differ across societies, you get a correlation for the outcomes. You know if civic commitment is the outcome of interest, there may be similar influences in different parts of the world. So what we try to do in this article is to acknowledge differences in setting but identify similar practices producing civic commitment.

What were the advantages and disadvantages of using surveys in this research?

I think you can actually learn more about political theories by going in depth, which is ultimately through interviews or through focus groups. Typically, surveys do not allow the same amount of depth as more qualitative techniques. However, they have the advantage of being less expensive. In this study the researchers used e-mail to discuss the concepts in the study, how they could be operationalized, and how survey items could be standardized across settings. That is a lot harder to do through qualitative work. Also, you can get better measures as long as the researchers take a lot of advance time to thoroughly discuss the concepts. Some survey researchers do work with items that were developed in one place but use them in another. In this project, we tried not to do that. We tried to develop our own ways of conceiving of these things, so we could get crosscultural validity. And, we were able to translate into various settings the very same concepts, and we collected data from a large sample of kids. So, surveys also have the advantage of allowing a broader representation of the population being studied.

What were the special challenges of using a comparative approach in this research?

I would say the biggest challenge was developing constructs that made sense to people in different countries, and I don't mean just with regard to the wording. In the United States, we use terms such as "sense of community" and "neighborhood." We may think that these concepts have universal meaning, but they do not. We worked with the concept, "democratic climate in school," but in some places that was not a common concept. So, I would say the biggest challenge was coming up with constructs that were fair to all the countries and would allow all of the kids to weigh in. A second challenge was getting a comparable sample in all of the sites. We did not have the money to do nationally representative samples across countries, so some of the challenge was determining what would make sense to a kid growing up in a particular setting in each country. We decided that we would use a large metropolitan area in each country but not necessarily the capital, because sometimes people flooding into the capital are not representative of the population. So, comparability of the samples was a challenge to discuss. Finally, e-mail makes comparative work much easier than it was prior to electronic communication. However, it can also be problematic. Sometimes it was not working in all of our sites. At one point, people in Bulgaria lost electricity, and they lost everything. We already had the data stored in a central spot in Hungary, but one of our colleagues was writing a paper, and she lost everything.

What unexpected events or developments (if any) occurred during the course of this research?

An interesting unexpected event occurred in Bulgaria. In Bulgaria, one of the teachers had a connection to a local radio station, and somebody got hold of the questionnaire and found it pretty interesting. So, he read it on talk radio. I don't think it ever affected anything we were doing, but it was interesting that somebody decided they would make that a general conversation.

Could you describe any specific ethical issues that you confronted in this research?

Whenever you do cross-national research in schools, there are ethical considerations in how consent for student participation is obtained. In most places, we first went through the principal or headmaster to talk about the study, because we wanted to be sure that we were wanted in the schools. We didn't have any problem with people rejecting us, but we did have to go through the ethics of how you do research within particular countries. The data were collected anonymously, so we used regular permission procedures for the kids to sign, and we never connected their names to any data. So in that sense it wasn't problematic. One interesting thing that relates to an ethical matter was a sensitivity on the part of our colleagues in the central and eastern European countries, having lost their national autonomy when they were part of the Soviet bloc, to being referred to as post-Soviet countries. Two of the colleagues stated emphatically that that was not the right way to talk about them anymore. So we searched for a term by which they could be grouped, and we started using "transitional societies," "fledgling democracies," and "societies in democratic transition" but not in terms of post-Soviet anything.

If you were to do this research again, is there anything that you would do differently? If so, what?

I would definitely not collect the data anonymously, because I think it would be very interesting to follow up the samples, particularly in places where social change was happening so rapidly. This was the generation in eastern Europe that was really caught in the changes. They went to school under one set of rules, and they were going into adulthood under a new set of political and economic rules. And it would be really interesting to go back to them ten years later and find out what direction their lives had gone and what they think now after the changes. But we can't do that since we never linked names to data.

What was most frustrating to you in doing this research? What was most satisfying?

I was the one who invited other people, and I was not bold enough in trying to raise more money. I did get money that was able to support the data collection, but we really did it on a shoestring. It was not that anybody did not cooperate as a result, but I think that people really put in a lot of time when we did not actually have a lot of compensation. So we were all really working on a shoestring, and it was people's dedication that made them persist. So I think having more funds to have met more frequently and to have supported people in each country in their research would have been helpful.

The high level of interest among my colleagues was very satisfying. And I have been delighted in how much people have been interested in the results. It has helped generate much more interest in the developmental foundations of civic and political commitment. I'm glad this study contributed in some way to that.

What important lesson or illustration of doing good research can you share with students from your experiences in this research project?

Two things. The first is not to assume that the way we conduct research in the United States, the way we assume that people are supposed to act or governments are supposed to act, is the norm. Immersing yourself as an undergraduate in another culture just to put your own culture into perspective is a huge thing for your future whether you go into research or not. The second thing I would say for people who really do want to go into research pertains to the way that we often test for the validity and reliability of our measures by testing them on very narrow populations. There is too little concern with the real meaning of a construct. One thing we really learned in this project is not to focus attention to the measures that are already out there but to actually think about the concepts and what you want to test and then to find existing measures or develop your own. That is really what validity means—the true value of something is the way that it plays out in the real world, not its internal consistency properties, not on how some set of undergraduate students answered this set of items.

Questions to Think About

1. List all the independent and dependent variables that were included in this study. For each, explain how it is measured, what the authors report about its validity and reliability, and what particular difficulties come with measuring such a variable in different cultural settings.

2. What is the particular value of studying young people's volunteer work and civic commitment in both stable and transitional democracies? What do the authors find with regard to differences in the two different kinds of societies, and what might be the implications of their findings?

3. How do the researchers select their samples? What are some things they must take into account as they attempt to select equivalent samples in seven different countries? What might be some sources of bias in their samples?

4. Think of two or three studies that you have read in this book that lend themselves to a comparative approach. For each one, explain what other countries you might include in your analysis, what sort of method you would use, and what results you might expect to find.

Credits

Thomas P. O'Connor, Dean R. Hoge, and Estrelda Alexander, "The Relative Influence of Youth and Adult Experiences on Personal Spirituality and Church Involvement," from the *Journal for the Scientific Study of Religion, 41*(4), pp. 723–732. Reprinted with permission of Blackwell Publishing.

Carl Mazza, "Young Dads: The Effects of a Parenting Program on Urban African-American Adolescent Fathers," from *Adolescence, 37*(148). Reprinted with permission of Libra Publishers, Inc.

Marjorie MacDonald and Nancy C. Wright, "Cigarette Smoking and the Disenfranchisement of Adolescent Girls: A Discourse of Resistance?" from *Healthcare for Women International, 23*(3). Copyright © 2002. Reproduced by permission of Taylor & Francis, Inc., www.routledge-ny.com.

Penny Tinkler, "Rebellion, Modernity, and Romance: Smoking as a Gendered Practice in Popular Young Women's Magazines, Britain 1918–1939," from *Women's Studies International Forum, 24*(1), pp. 111–122. Copyright © 2001. Reprinted with permission of Elsevier.

John Zipp, "The Impact of Social Structure on Mate Selection: An Empirical Evaluation of an Active Learning Exercise," from *Teaching Sociology, 30* (April 2002). Reprinted with permission of the American Sociological Association.

Richard Scribner and Deborah Cohen, "The Effect of Enforcement on Merchant Compliance with the Minimum Legal Drinking Age Law," from the *Journal of Drug Issues, 31*(4), pp. 857–866. Reprinted with permission of Florida State University.

Wendy Walsh, "Spankers and Nonspankers: Where They Get Information on Spanking," from *Family Relations, 51*(1), pp. 81–88. Copyright © 2002. Reproduced by permission of the National Council on Family Relations via Copyright Clearance Center.

David C. May and R. Gregory Dunaway, "Predictors of Fear of Criminal Victimization at School Among Adolescents," from *Sociological Spectrum, 20*, pp. 149–168. Copyright © 2000. Reproduced by permission of Taylor & Francis, Inc., www.routledge-ny.com.

Melvin E. Thomas and Linda A. Treiber, "Race, Gender, and Status: A Content Analysis of Print Advertisements in Four Popular Magazines," from *Sociological*